Jesus, Teach Me How to Pray

A Year in The Lord's Prayer and other Bible Basics

A Children's Church, Sunday School or

Mid-Week Children's Curriculum

For Kids ages 4-10

Lynne Modranski

Other Books By Lynne Modranski

Children's Ministry

Heroes, Heroines, Champs, and Chumps (A fifty-two week curriculum)
The Fruit of the Spirit Is . . . (A nine lesson curriculum)
Into the Promised Land (Eight lessons from the life of Joshua)
Journey to Greatness (Eleven lessons from the life of Joseph
Children of the King (Thirteen Lessons from the life of David)

Fiction

Adira: Journey to Freedom

Devotions

Devotions for Church Leaders and Small Groups
Devotions Inspired by Life
Quiet Times for Busy Moms
A Reflection of the Beauty of God
First Steps for New Christians
I'm Pretty Sure I Messed This Up

Bible Studies

Embracing Your Priscilla
Dive In to A Life of Freedom
Marks on the Wall

Visit LynneModranski.com to see the full collection
including free resources

Jesus, Teach Me How to Pray

A Year in The Lord's Prayer and other Bible Basics

A Children's Church, Sunday School or

Mid-Week Children's Curriculum

For Kids ages 4-10

LYNNE MODRANSKI

JESUS, TEACH ME HOW TO PRAY
© 2010 , 2024 by Lynne Modranski
www.LynneModranski.com

All rights reserved. No part of this publication may be reproduced, distributed, or transmitted in any form or by any means, including photocopying, recording, or other electronic or mechanical methods, without the prior written permission of the publisher, except in the case of brief quotations embodied in critical reviews, copies that meet the criteria below, and certain other noncommercial uses permitted by copyright law.

Published by Mansion Hill Press
Steubenville, Ohio
www.MansionHillPress.com

ISBN:

Scripture quotations marked (NIV) are from THE HOLY BIBLE, NEW INTERNATIONAL VERSION®, NIV® Copyright © 1973, 1978, 1984, 2011 by Biblica, Inc.® Used by permission. All rights reserved worldwide.

Scripture quotations marked HCSB are taken from the Holman Christian Standard Bible®, Copyright © 1999, 2000, 2002, 2003, 2009 by Holman Bible Publishers. Used by permission. Holman Christian Standard Bible®, Holman CSB®, and HCSB® are federally registered trademarks of Holman Bible Publishers.

Scripture quotations marked NCV are taken from the New Century Version®. Copyright © 2005 by Thomas Nelson. Used by permission. All rights reserved.

Scripture quotations marked NLT are taken from the Holy Bible, New Living Translation, copyright © 1996, 2004, 2015 by Tyndale House Foundation. Used by permission of Tyndale House Publishers, Inc., Carol Stream, Illinois 60188. All rights reserved.

"Scripture taken from the NEW AMERICAN STANDARD BIBLE®, (NASB) Copyright © 1960,1962,1963,1968,1971,1972,1973,1975,1977,1995 by The Lockman Foundation. Used by permission."

King James Version (KJV) – Public Domain

Special thanks to Sycamore Tree Church
for using this curriculum in it's un-proofed form!

Permission to photocopy this curriculum is granted for use in the program of the original purchaser for the use of multiple teachers. Additional permission to make multiple copies of student pages is also granted.

Should you purchase a print copy that has all graphics in black and white,
please contact Lynne@LynneModranski.com to acquire a color PDF of all graphics and photos

Visit www.lynnemodranski.com/CCprayer/resources.pdf to find links to all online
resources mentioned or recommended in this curriculum.

Jesus, Teach Me How to Pray

A Year in The Lord's Prayer and other Bible Basics

TABLE OF CONTENTS

UNIT #	UNIT NAME	LESSON	PAGE
Unit 1	Our Father in Heaven	A Father Who Wants to Talk to Us	11
	Our Father in Heaven	A Father Who Loves Us	17
	Our Father in Heaven	A Father Who Forgives us	21
Unit 2	Hallowed be thy Name	God's Name is Special	29
	Hallowed be thy Name	God's Name is Holy & Powerful	35
	Hallowed be thy Name	God's Name: He Has Lots of Them	39
Unit 3	Thy Kingdom Come	The Kingdom of God: It's Inside You	49
	Thy Kingdom Come	The Kingdom of God: What is it Like?	55
	Thy Kingdom Come	The Kingdom of God: It IS for Kids!	61
Unit 4	Thy Will be done	Abraham Did God's Will	67
	Thy Will be done	Jesus Did God's Will	73
	Thy Will be done	Josiah Did God's Will	79
Unit 5	On Earth as it is in Heaven	Worship On Earth Like in Heaven	87
	On Earth as it is in Heaven	Joy on earth Like in Heaven	93
	On Earth as it is in Heaven	Beauty on Earth Like in Heaven	97
Unit 6	Give us this day	God Gave us Bread from Heaven	103
	Give us this day	Jesus is the Bread of Life	107
	Give us this day	Jesus Provides Bread For Our Lives	113
Unit 7	Forgive us our debts	Forgive Because God Forgave Us	117
	Forgive us our debts	Forgive Because Jesus Asks	125
	Forgive us our debts	Forgive Because We Are Forgiven	131
Unit 8	Lead us not into temptation	The Very First Temptation	135
	Lead us not into temptation	Tempted to Be Like Everyone Else	141
	Lead us not into temptation	Never More Than We Can Handle	147
Unit 9	Deliver Us from Evil	God Delivered Noah from an Evil World	153
	Deliver Us from Evil	Thankful That God Delivers us from Evil	159
	Deliver Us from Evil	God Wants to Deliver Us From Evil	165
Unit 10	For Thine is the Kingdom, Power & Glory	The Power of God	171
	For Thine is the Kingdom, Power & Glory	The Glory of God	181
	For Thine is the Kingdom, Power & Glory	Why Do We Say "Amen" at the end?	185

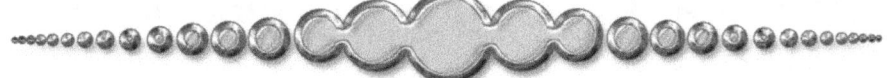

UNIT #	UNIT NAME	LESSON	PAGE
Unit 11	Psalm 23	I Have Everything I Need	191
	Psalm 23	I Have No Fear	199
	Psalm 23	I Have No Worries	207
Unit 12	The 2 Greatest Commandments	Love God and Love Your Neighbor	213
	Commandment 1 & 2	No gods But the True God	221
	Commandment 3 & 4	Don't Misuse God's Name or God's Day	229
	Commandment 5	Honor Your Father & Mother	237
	Commandment 6 & 7	Don't Murder & Be True to Your Marriage	245
	Commandment 8	No Stealing	253
	Commandment 9	No Lying	259
	Commandment 10	You Can't Want Your Neighbor's Things	265
Unit 13	World Communion Sunday	Communion	271
	Thanksgiving	Thanksgiving	283
	Advent 1	What is Advent	289
	Advent 2	A Time for Surprises	295
	Advent 3	A Time to Prepare to Love & Serve God	303
	Christmas	Jesus is Born	307
	New Year & The Magi	Jesus was an Important Baby	311
	Palm Sunday	Christ's Triumphal Entry	315
	Easter	He is Risen	319
	Pentecost	Happy Birthday Church	325
	Back to School Party	God Wants to Give you A Great Future	329

Jesus, Teach Me How to Pray

A Year in The Lord's Prayer and other Bible Basics

Introduction

In these fifty-two lessons, children will learn the basics of The Lord's Prayer, Ten Commandments, 23rd Psalm, and a highlights of the Christian year. The focus of the lessons will be the Lord's Prayer, and one of the goals each week will be to conclude your time with the children with this age old prayer. Hopefully, by the time the children repeat this prayer fifty-two times, they'll know it by heart, and it will become a model for their daily prayers.

This was designed to be led by a rotating group, so you'll see some things repeated each week. Additionally, I designed the "bonus" lessons to slide in during special seasons. Simply use units one through in order inserting the holiday lessons when appropriate and units eleven and twelve as needed. .

Each week features a variety of activities to help you reinforce the lesson. You'll find songs, skits, video clips, games, illustrations, crafts, and more. Choose activities that best fit your skills, personality and time frame. And don't forget to have fun!

52 Weeks of Lessons for Kids age 4-10

Unit 1: Our Father in Who Art Heaven
- Week 1: A Father Who Wants to Talk To us
- Week 2: A Father Who Loves Us
- Week 3: A Father Who Forgives Us

Unit 2: Hallowed be thy Name
- Week 1: God's Name is not Art or Howard
- Week 2: God's Name is Holy & Powerful
- Week 3: God's Name is Worthy of our Praise

Unit 3: Thy Kingdom Come
- Week 1: The Kingdom of God: It's Within You!
- Week 2: The Kingdom of God: What Is It?
- Week 3: The Kingdom of God: It IS for Kids!

Unit 4: Thy Will be done
- Week 1: Abraham was obedient
- Week 2: Jesus was obedient
- Week 3: King Josiah was obedient

Unit 5: On Earth as it is in Heaven
- Week 1: Worshipping on Earth Like in Heaven
- Week 2: As much Joy on Earth as in Heaven
- Week 3: Earth as Beautiful as it is in Heaven

Unit 6: Give us this day our Daily Bread (Option for Lent)
- Week 1: God is our Provider
- Week 2: Jesus is All the Bread We Need
- Week 3: Jesus Gives Us All We Need

Unit 7: Forgive our debts as we Forgive Our Debtors
- Week 1: We Forgive so We Can Be Forgiven
- Week 2: We Forgive because God Asks Us To
- Week 3: We Forgive Because We were Forgiven

Unit 8: Lead us not into temptation
- Week 1: The Very First Temptation
- Week 2: Tempted to be Like Everyone Else
- Week 3: Never Tempted More Than We Can Handle

Unit 9: Deliver Us from Evil
- Week 1: God Delivered Noah From an Evil World
- Week 2: I'm Thankful God Delivers Us from Evil
- Week 3: God wants to Deliver us from Evil

Unit 10: For Thine is Kingdom, Power & Glory Forever
- Week 1: The Power of God
- Week 2: The Glory of God
- Week 3: Why Do We say Amen at the end?

Unit 11: Psalm 23
- Week 1: Psalm 23:1-3 No needs
- Week 2: Psalm 23:4 No Fear
- Week 3: Psalm 23:5-6 No Worries

Unit 12: Commandments
- Week 1: The 2 Greatest Commandments
- Week 2: Commandment 1 & 2
- Week 3: Commandment 3 & 4
- Week 4: Commandment 5
- Week 5: Commandments 6 & 7
- Week 6: Commandment 8
- Week 7: Commandment 9
- Week 8: Commandment 10

Unit 13: Holidays of the Church
- Communion (Option For World Communion)
- Thanksgiving
- Advent: Be Prepared
- Advent: A Time to Prepare for God's Surprises
- Advent: A Time to Prepare to Love & Serve God
- Christmas: A Savior is Born
- Christmas 2: Jesus was an Important Baby
- Palm Sunday
- Easter
- Pentecost
- Back to School Party Time

Sample Lesson Sequence

with the Bonus lessons "plugged in" at appropriate places.

52 Week Overview
beginning with Thanksgiving or January 1

This sample schedule begins in late November or Advent. To begin on January 1, simply skip the first Bonus Unit and start with Unit 1.

Easter and Pentecost may need adjusted depending on when they fall

Unit 13 : Holidays of the Church
  6 Lessons
  Thanksgiving through the boyhood of Jesus

Unit 1: Our Father in Who Art Heaven

Unit 2: Hallowed be thy Name

Unit 3: Thy Kingdom Come

Unit 4: Thy Will be done

Unit 13 : Holidays of the Church
  Palm Sunday and Easter

Unit 5: On Earth as it is in Heaven

Unit 6: Give Us This Day our Daily Bread

Unit 13 : Holidays of the Church
  Pentecost

Unit 7: Forgive our Debts as we Forgive Our Debtors

Unit 8: Lead Us Not Into Temptation

Unit 9: Deliver Us from Evil

Unit 13 : Holidays of the Church
  Back to School Party Time

Unit 10: The Kingdom, Power & Glory Forever

Unit 11: Psalm 23

Unit 12: Commandments

Bonus Unit: Holiday
  World Communion Sunday (for the first Sunday in October)

52 Week Overview
for a program beginning in September (after Labor Day)

If you begin before Labor Day, you may want to move the last lesson (Back to School) to make it the first lesson of the curriculum.

Easter and Pentecost may need adjusted depending on when they fall

Unit 1: Our Father Who Art in Heaven

Unit 13 : Holidays of the Church
  World Communion (The First Sunday in October)

Unit 2: Hallowed be thy Name

Unit 3: Thy Kingdom Come

Unit 13 : Holidays of the Church
  6 Lessons
  Thanksgiving through the boyhood of Jesus

Unit 4: Thy Will be done

Unit 5: On Earth as it is in Heaven

Unit 6: Give Us This Day our Daily Bread

Unit 13 : Holidays of the Church
  Palm Sunday & Easter

Unit 7: Forgive our Debts as we Forgive Our Debtors

Unit 8: Lead Us Not Into Temptation

Unit 13: Holidays of the Church
  Pentecost

Unit 9: Deliver Us from Evil

Unit 10: The Kingdom, Power & Glory Forever

Unit 11: Psalm 23

Unit 12: Commandments

Unit 13 : Holidays of the Church
  Back to School Party Time

Preparing for The Lesson

As you prepare these lessons, I encourage you to look over the material at least seven to ten days before you present it. Put a check mark beside each part of the lesson that you'd be most comfortable using and make a list of supplies you need. If your Children's Ministry Coordinator gets supplies, be sure to contact him or her as early as possible. If your church secretary makes copies, you'll want to give that person advance notice also.

The first page of each lesson will give you an overview of what you can expect to find in the following pages. I suggest you take the scripture listed on that page and read it at least every other day the week before the lesson so you're very familiar with what the Bible says about what you will present. In the lesson itself you'll find a "child-sized" synopsis of the Bible Lesson you can read word-for-word or inflect your own personality into. You may even want to read it right from the scripture or a Children's Bible. If you do any reading be sure to make your voice as interesting as possible to keep the kid's attention.

The crafts, games, and illustrations you'll find with each lesson were designed to reinforce the Key Phrase. If you change any of these elements, be sure you tie them in with the lesson. If you need help tying something in or would like more suggestions, ask other children's leaders or your Children's Ministries Coordinator.

Statistics show that most people who don't accept Christ before they graduate from High School never will. This ministry is vital to the eternal future of these kids' lives. Don't dismiss it as a babysitting hour or a story telling time. We are working together to make true disciples for Jesus Christ so that as they make their way into adulthood, they'll have Christ to help them through the truly tough times.

Leading a Child To Christ

If a child comes to you and asks how to be a Christian or how to make Jesus his or her Savior, here are a few simple steps:

1. Make sure the child understands that God created him, and he is special to God. (Genesis 1:26-27 & Psalm 139:14)

2. Help him see that no matter how hard we try to be good, we can't be good enough all by ourselves. (Romans 3:23)

3. Be sure the child understands that Christ was perfect, and only a perfect sacrifice can make us good enough to live with God forever. (Romans 5:8)

4. Explain that if we believe in Christ's death on the cross for our sins, if we believe that He died and rose again, and if we ask God to forgive our sins, we can be saved. (1 John 1:9 & Romans 10:9)

5. Lead them in a prayer that includes something like this: "I believe that you died for my sins. Forgive me for . . .. Please be my Savior." There are no special words or magic formula, just a sincere heart.

6. It's very important we share our new faith with someone. Encourage the child to make sure they tell the pastor, their parents or grandparents, or their friends.

This page and others like it are left blank intentionally.

*This prevents any lesson being back to back with another,
allowing you to dismantle the printed book and pass it out as needed
or print two sided from a digital copy with ease.
You are welcome to duplicate pages to be used in the church who made the original purchase.*

Jesus, Teach Me How to Pray
A Year in The Lord's Prayer and other Bible Basics

Unit 1: Our Father Who Art in Heaven
Week 1: A Father Who Wants to Talk To Us

Lesson Overview

Today we'll begin learning the Lord's Prayer. You will have this opportunity to introduce the prayer to the group, and for the first time have them repeat it line by line after you, so they can begin to memorize it.

In this first unit the children will learn about their Father in heaven. It's our job as adult leaders to help them understand that we are not just "repeating words," we are talking to our Dad. The Lord's Prayer is a conversation between God and us. Whenever you have an opportunity, reiterate the key phrase, so that every child will go home repeating, "God wants to talk to me, and He wants me to talk to Him."

KEY PHRASE: God Wants to Talk To Us, and He Wants Us to Talk to Him

SETTING UP THE LESSON   5-10 Minutes

Introduction: It's hard to communicate without words
(You can also use the Illustration, Video, Song, Skit, etc. for the set up)

PRESENTING THE LESSON   10-15 Minutes

Scripture Basis: Luke 11:1-4 (also found in Matthew 6:9-13)

MAKING IT REAL TO KIDS TODAY   *(Choose as many as you have time for)*

Game: Charades or Win, Lose or Draw   5-10 Minutes
Supplies: Slips of paper with common sports, activities, movies, or actions (at least one for each child). *Examples: Baseball bat—School Bus—Mickey Mouse—Happy Meal—Bedtime—Tooth Fairy—Hot Dogs—Cat—Dance*

Craft: Prayer Boxes   10-15 Minutes
Supplies: Small boxes (jewelry style gift boxes), slips of paper (about 2.5"x4"), markers, jewels, sequins, ribbons, foam shapes, scissors, glue

Video: Finding Nemo Clip   8-10 Minutes
Supplies: Video clips or DVD from *Finding Nemo*

Song: New verse to "Jesus Loves Me"   3-5 Minutes

WRAPPING IT UP—SENDING IT HOME   5-7 Minutes

Clean Up & Prayer Time

KEY PHRASE: God Wants to Talk To Us, and He Wants Us To Talk to Him

SETTING IT UP   5-10 Minutes

Introduction: It's hard to communicate without words

As you begin today, don't use any words. Get the kids attention by waving or banging on the table. Make them figure out what you are saying. You might make signs to indicate we aren't going to talk right now. Try getting the children to follow you around in a "Follow the Leader" type game without talking. Gently drag one child out behind you and indicate they should follow, but no talking. After you walk around a time or two with that child add another until all or most have figured it out. If you have another adult helper, ask him or her to be prepared to act like they have figured it out so they can follow too and demonstrate what to do.

After a time or two around the room (or into a hall if there's one nearby that won't bother anyone) with all the children following, motion for everyone to stop and sit back down. Say "Whew, we made it! Now we can talk (if they all begin to talk at once you might say, "OH Wait a minute, I meant I could talk").

Ask the kids:

How difficult was it for you to understand me when I was only motioning?

Do you like being quiet and not talking?

What does it make you feel like if someone won't talk to you, even by accident?

Someone will probably relate to being ignored by a friend or even a parent. It makes us feel terrible. Say: Yes, we feel bad when our friends or family ignore us or are mad at us. How do you think God feels when we go a whole day without even saying a word to Him?

(Allow for discussion). God wants to communicate with us so badly that He sent Jesus to get to know us, and then Jesus told us the best way to talk to His Father. That's what we're going to talk about not only this week, but most of the next year. Your Father up in heaven (God) wants to talk to you.

PRESENTING THE STORY   10-15 Minutes

Scripture Basis: Luke 11:1-13 (also found in Matthew 6:9-13)

You do not have to read this directly from the Bible—use the story form below or reword it to fit your personality

One day when Jesus and the twelve guys He hung out with all the time were by themselves . . . Wait a minute, do you know what we call those twelve guys? (Wait for responses) Yes, Jesus hung out with the twelve apostles (or disciples). One day when Jesus and His twelve disciples were hanging out by themselves, Jesus was praying. When He got done, His twelve friends asked Him to teach them how to pray. So Jesus taught them a simple prayer they could use to remind them of the things that were important to talk to God about when they pray.

Here's the prayer He taught them. Why don't you repeat each line after me? Let's bow our heads and fold our hands. (Pause at each * so the kids can repeat. If you have a helper, let him or her lead in the "repeat")

Our Father which art in Heaven * Hallowed be Thy Name * Thy Kingdom Come * Thy will be done *

On earth as it is in Heaven * Give us this day our daily bread *

And forgive us our debts * As we forgive our debtors *

Lead us not into temptation * But Deliver us from evil *

For Thine is the Kingdom the power and the glory forever * Amen

That was great! That is the prayer Jesus taught His disciples. He wanted them to know how important it is to talk to God, because just like God is Jesus' Father, God was the disciples' Father. And you know what? He's our Father, too.

God is our Father and He wants us to talk to Him every day.

How would you feel if you went to school and your friend didn't talk to you? (Allow for response) It makes God just as sad when we don't talk to Him everyday.

KEY PHRASE: God Wants to Talk To Us, and He Wants Us To Talk to Him

Ask some questions about talking to God—use these as starters or come up with some of your own:

- How often do you talk to God?
- When do you talk to God?
- What are some things you say to God when you talk to him?
- Why should we pray? *(Because God is our Father and He wants us to talk to Him)*

MAKING IT REAL TO KIDS TODAY

Game: Charades or Win, Lose & Draw   10-15 Minutes
Supplies: Slips of paper with common sports, activities, movies, or actions (at least one for each child).
Examples: *Baseball bat—School Bus—Mickey Mouse—Happy Meal—Bedtime—Tooth Fairy—Hot Dogs—Cat—Dance*

Prior to your meeting prepare slips of paper with phrases or words that the kids will be familiar with. This can be anything, because the point of the game is to discover how difficult it is to communicate without talking. Be sure to have at least one slip for each child. Gather the children into a circle or semi-circle. Allow each to have a turn acting out or drawing clues to get the group to guess the phrase or thing that they draw. The child who guesses can be the next artist/actor—if that child has already had a turn allow them to choose the next artist/actor. Be sure to emphasize they aren't allowed to talk or make noises.

The Teaching Moment: After everyone has had a turn (or you need to quit because of time) talk to the kids about how hard it was to figure things out or make others understand without talking. Remind them that God is our Father and He wants us to talk to Him because He loves us and wants to know what we're doing.

Video: *Finding Nemo* "First Day of School"   8-10 Minutes
Supplies: Video clips or DVD from *Finding Nemo*

This clip is from the beginning of the Movie. If you don't have a copy, you might borrow it from someone at your church, rent it at a video store or borrow it from the local library. At the main menu pick "Scene Selections," choose "First Day of School" Nemo is excited about school and doesn't want to take time to listen to his dad. He's in a hurry to have fun. The clip ends just as Nemo gets taken by the diver. To shorten it a bit, or if you don't have access to the DVD, you could play two clips back to back:
Nemo's First Day at School: https://vimeo.com/271168976
Nemo Gets Taken By the Diver: https://www.youtube.com/watch?v=eTHXFzB4mU8

The Teaching Moment: Ask the kids: Do you sometimes get in a hurry and forget to listen to your parents? What happens when you do that? *(Allow for answers.)* A lot of times we get in trouble, or we might even miss out on fun things. When we learn to pray, we'll find out that God wants to talk to us too. And the same thing happens when we don't listen to our heavenly Father. Even adults get in trouble when they forget to listen. What can we do to make sure that we take time to pray everyday and listen to God in case He has something important to tell us? *(Allow for answers.)*

KEY PHRASE: God Wants to Talk To Us, and He Wants Us To Talk to Him

Craft: Prayer Boxes   10-15 Minutes

Supplies: Small boxes (jewelry style gift boxes), slips of paper (about 2.5"x4"), markers, jewels, sequins, ribbons, foam shapes, scissors, glue

You may want to put a hole in the top of the box prior to meeting with the children.

Give each child a small box and decorating elements. On the top of the box have all the children write "<his/her name>'s Prayer Box." Allow them to decorate the box any way they'd like.

The Teaching Moment: As they decorate, ask them what kind of things they say to God when they talk to Him. Help them write these things on the slips of paper and let them put them in the box. Ask each child to have at least one slip that is a praise to God and another that has the name of someone in this group. Remind them when we talk to God, we need to praise Him and thank Him for our friends as well as pray for them. Encourage them to take their boxes home and use them each day as they pray. Tell them they can take out the slips. If they see one that God has answered, say a prayer of thanks. If God hasn't answered yet, pray for it again. They can add slips to it each day. Remind them to add words of praise to the box also.

Song: "Jesus Loves Me"   3-5 Minutes

Use the tune of "Jesus Loves Me" with these words—sing it through a few times so they'll get the words.
Use the signs to help them remember.

- Jesus Loves Me when I pray
  (SIGNS— **Jesus:** Point to the center of each hand, **Loves:** Cross arms over chest, **Me:** point to self, **Pray:** fold hands like praying)

- He wants to hear me every day
  (SIGNS—**He:** point heavenward, **Hear:** hand near ear, **Me:** Point to self, **Everyday:** Put right elbow in left hand with arm straight up then move right hand down into left elbow like the sun is setting)

- Morning, noon and nighttime, too
  (SIGNS—**Morning:** Put left hand inside right elbow with arm straight out then lift arm toward body, **Noon:** Keep right elbow in left hand and hold right arm straight up on top of left hand, **Nighttime:** Keep right elbow in left hand and drop right hand in front of left elbow)

- Every moment all day through.
  (SIGNS- **Every Moment:** Wave both hands from center out, **All day through:** Start like "noon" above and then put right hand down into left elbow like the sun is setting)

- Yes, Jesus Loves Me (3x)
  (SIGNS- **Yes:** make fist with right hand and then hold it up and nod it up and down (like nodding your head yes), **Jesus:** Touch the center of your left then right palm, **Loves:** Cross arms over chest, **Me:** Point to chest)

- The Bible Tells me So
  (SIGNS- **The Bible:** Touch center of palms like you did for "Jesus" then make your hands into a book (Jesus' Book), **Tells:** index finger—or three fingers- start at chin and move away **Me:** Point to chest, **So:** Make a big sweeping motion with index finger from forehead pointing forward then toward floor)

KEY PHRASE: God Wants to Talk To Us, and He Wants Us To Talk to Him

WRAPPING IT UP—SENDING IT HOME   5-10 Minutes

Cleaning Up

We want the children to learn to be responsible, so be sure they help with the clean up, but remind them not to go anywhere, the group is going to talk to their Father together one more time.

Closing Worship and Prayer

Either gather the children in a circle holding hands or allow them to sit down to pray. If you choose to join hands, remember that it's OK if some children prefer not to join the circle. Explain they should be respectful of others as they pray and not make any noise. You can help them get quiet by singing the new verse to "Jesus Loves Me" found earlier in the lesson (even if you used it before).

As you close, ask the children if there's anything that they would like you to pray about for them. No prayer is too small, however, children will tend to keep going and be "inspired" by other prayer requests, so feel free to stop taking requests and tell them they can say anything that didn't get said out loud quietly to God themselves while you're praying. You may close with your own prayer or use the one below for help. End with "we pray as Jesus taught us to pray" and the Lord's prayer. For these first few weeks allow the kids to repeat after you. If you have a helper, encourage them to pray with the kids.

If you need some guidance for your prayer, you can use this:

Father in Heaven *(you may want to allow kids to repeat after each phrase)*. I'm so glad you want me to talk to you. Help me to remember to talk to you everyday. Please bless all of these things the kids have asked prayer for today *(or you can mention them individually)* as we pray the way you taught your disciples to pray: *(end with the Lord's Prayer one line at a time)*.

Our Father who art in heaven, hallowed be thy Name. Thy kingdom come; thy will be done on earth as it is in heaven.
Give us this day our daily bread, and forgive us our debts as we forgive our debtors.
Lead us not into temptation but deliver us from evil. For Thine is the Kingdom and the power, and the glory forever, Amen.

Jesus, Teach Me How to Pray   Unit 1: Our Father Who Art in Heaven —15

Page intentionally left blank for printing and copying purposes

Jesus, Teach Me How to Pray
A Year in The Lord's Prayer and other Bible Basics

Unit 1: Our Father Who Art in Heaven
Week 2: A Father Who Loves Us

Lesson Overview

Today, we're going to focus again on the fact that God is a good parent. The prodigal son will be the main character in our lesson today. Jesus told this parable to help us understand that God loves us unconditionally. He is our Father, and we can't do anything bad enough to make him stop loving us. Likewise, we can't earn God's love. Don't forget to repeat today's key phrase as often as possible: God is our Father and He loves us.

KEY PHRASE: God is Our Father He Loves Us

SETTING UP THE LESSON   1-5 Minutes

VIDEO CLIP: Marlin Risks Danger to Find His Son
Supplies: *Finding Nemo* DVD or https://www.youtube.com/watch?v=Ycmp6K1KPLo

PRESENTING THE LESSON   10-15 Minutes

Scripture Basis: Luke 15:11-24
Optional Supplies: Play money, a bucket of food scraps a few days old, a beautiful robe or gown, a big ring and more!

MAKING IT REAL TO KIDS TODAY   *(Choose as many as you have time for)*

Game: Going Home   5-10 Minutes
Supplies: Masking tape

Craft: Jesus Loves Me Foam Door Hanger   10-15 Minutes
Supplies: Pre-cut foam door hangers or cut them out of card stock or foam using the pattern at the end of this lesson, foam Letters "God Loves Me" one set per child (pattern at end of lesson or they can write God Loves Me), other foam decorations or jewels, glue, markers (optional)

Song: New verse to "Jesus Loves Me"   3-5 Minutes

WRAPPING IT UP—SENDING IT HOME   5-7 Minutes

Clean Up & Prayer Time

KEY PHRASE: God is Our Father He Loves Us
SETTING IT UP   5-10 Minutes

Video Clip: Marlin Risks Danger to Find His Son

Supplies: *Finding Nemo* DVD or https://www.youtube.com/watch?v=Ycmp6K1KPLo

If you don't have this DVD, borrow it from someone at your church, rent it at a video store or borrow it from the local library. Marlin faced grave danger in order to find Nemo. This clip is Marlin with the sea turtles. In "Scene Selections" choose "Marlin Tells His Story" He tells the baby turtles his story, and they pass it along. Scene ends when the pelican tells Nemo his dad is looking for him.

The Teaching Moment: Ask the kids: What dangers did Marlin face during his sea adventure? *(Allow for answers.)* Why did Marlin face this danger? *(Allow for answers.)* (Answer: because he loved his son so much) I know it's hard to imagine, but God loves us just like Marlin loves Nemo. Today we're going to hear a story that Jesus told his disciples so they would understand how much God loves them.

PRESENTING THE STORY   10-15 Minutes

Scripture Basis: Luke 15:11-24

You do not have to read this directly from the Bible— use the story form below or reword it to fit your personality

You can have a lot of fun with this parable. Here are a few props you might want to use: Play money, a bucket of food scraps a few days old, a beautiful robe or gown, a big ring and more!

Once upon a time there was a man with two sons. One day the younger son came to his dad and said, "Dad, I want half of all your money. Give it to me today so I can go away from this place, I'm tired of living here." This made the boy's dad very sad. But he loved his son very much. He gave his son everything he asked for, and the next day the son left home. *(If you have a helper, he or she could look very sad here and hand you the play money.)* His dad missed him so much!

The younger son took the money that his dad gave him and went far away. He started spending the money on all kinds of things he didn't need. It was like he was throwing it away. *(Toss the money left and right very carefree.)* Pretty soon he didn't have any money left. This was a problem He couldn't buy food and had no place to live. So he had to get a job. But no one wanted to hire him. Finally he found a job feeding pigs. *(Pick up your bucket with scraps.)* What a nasty job. The pigs were dirty, and he had to feed them this stinking slop. But even with his job, he didn't have enough money for food. He was really hungry. One day he was so hungry he thought about eating the pig food. Here, you want to try some? *(Kids should go "oooo" or something here.)*

Finally he came to his senses. He figured out that even the guys who work for his dad live better than he did. So, he decided to go home, tell his dad he was sorry, and see if he could get a job there. He knew he wouldn't get his old room back and wouldn't get any of the cool things he had when he lived with his dad. No Nintendo or radio, no TV or DVD's, but at least he'd get some good food.

But when he got there, his dad was standing in the driveway waiting for him. The dad loved his son so much that he stood there every day for a while. He was so excited when his son returned home! As soon as he saw him coming, he ran down the road to meet him. *(Run a bit.)* Then he took him in his house, and put his favorite robe and a great big ring on the son. *(The helper could now put the robe and ring on the leader.)* And if that wasn't enough, the dad threw a huge party to welcome the son home!

That's how much God loves us. Even when we don't do the things we should, he still loves us. He sent Jesus to die for us. That's how much he cares. And all God wants is for us to love him back.

Even when you're having a day when you feel like no one else loves you, never forget that God and Jesus love you very much!

KEY PHRASE: God is Our Father He Loves Us

MAKING IT REAL TO KIDS TODAY

Game: Going Home 5-10 Minutes
Supplies: Masking tape

Have kids stand on one end of the area *(Use a long section of the room)* Stand as far away from them as possible with a strip of masking tape in front of you to create a line that you'll call "Home."

Say. The youngest son really wanted to get back home after he realized how good he'd had it. Today we're going to play a game called "Going Home" I'll give you instructions and you can try to follow them to get from there to here.

First I'll say a sentence, then you'll follow the directions in the sentence to get "Home" *(across this line)*. If I say "baby step" you'll walk in tiny steps. If I say "walking steps" - just walk normally. If I say "giant steps" make the steps as big as you can. *(Demonstrate steps)* Keep walking slowly until I turn around. If you are still moving when I turn around you're out. I will be watching to see if you are moving when I turn around. The winner is the last one still in the game.

Have all children line up on one end of the room. You stand at the other with your back to the group and one at a time read the phrases above. Wait a moment and turn around. Anyone still moving is out. Keep playing and repeating until everyone is out or one person gets home..

Use these or create similar statements :

- The younger son wanted to leave home. Take walking steps toward the finish line—as soon as I turn around, you must stop.

- The younger son asked his dad for $1000 of dollars worth of stuff. - take baby steps backward to remind you that the son walked away from his father.

- The father gave the son everything he asked for-Take giant steps forward to remind us how big the Father's love is for us!

- The younger son took his dad's money and left—take baby steps backwards to remind us how selfish the younger son was.

- The younger son quickly spent all his money—take baby steps backward and pretend to throw away money to remind us he was walking away from his father.

- The younger son had to slop the hogs every day—take baby steps forward as you pretend to feed the hogs.

- Finally, the younger son realized that what His dad had was much better—take small steps forward.

- When his father saw him coming, he ran to meet his son—Take giant steps forward to remind us how big the Father's love is.

- The younger son told his dad he was sorry and asked him to forgive—Take baby steps forward.

- The father allowed his son to come back home—Take giant steps forward, to remind us that God wants us to come to him.

- God loves us so much! Take giant steps toward "home."

The Teaching Moment: Did you noticed what part of the story we remembered each time we took giant steps? *(Allow for answers.)* Every time we took giant steps we remembered God's love and how big it is. We should always walk toward God's love because He loves us so much..

KEY PHRASE: God is Our Father He Loves Us

Craft: Foam God Loves Me Door Hanger   10-15 Minutes
Supplies: Pre-cut foam door hangers or card stock/foam cutouts using the pattern at the end of this lesson, foam Letters "God Loves Me" one set per child *(pattern at end of lesson)*, other foam decorations or jewels, glue, markers *(optional)*

Write "God Loves Me" on a chalk/white board or poster board. Children could use all the letters, write God Loves ‹their names›, or God ‹cut out heart› ‹names›. They could optionally write God Loves Me on the door hanger. After the words are on the door hangers, allow them to decorate them any way they wish.

The Teaching Moment: Encourage children to hang this on their bedroom doorknob to remind them often that God is our Father and He loves us.

Song: "Jesus Loves Me"   3-5 Minutes

Use the tune of "Jesus Loves Me" with these words - Sing it through a few times so they get the words.

- Jesus Loves Me when I'm good
  (SIGNS— ***Jesus:*** *Point to the center of each hand,* ***Loves:*** *Cross arms over chest,* ***Me:*** *point to self,* ***Good:*** *Put four fingers on chin and pull hand down and away palm up*)

- And I do the things I should
  (SIGNS— ***I:*** *point to self,* ***Things:*** *hold right palm face up in front of you, lift it slightly and put it back down just right of where it was* ***I:*** *Point to self,* ***Should:*** *Hold index finger slightly curved and point downward a few times*)

- Jesus loves me when I'm bad
  (SIGNS— ***Jesus:*** *Point to the center of each hand,* ***Loves:*** *Cross arms over chest,* ***Me:*** *point to self,* ***Bad:*** *Put four fingers on chin and turn it over as you push downward*)

- Though it makes him very sad
  (SIGNS– ***Makes Him:*** *Point Up,* ***Sad:*** *Open all fingers wide and draw them down in front of your face—like tears*)

- Yes, Jesus Loves Me (3x)
  (SIGNS– ***Yes:*** *make fist with right hand and then hold it up and nod it up and down (like shaking your head yes),* ***Jesus:*** *Touch the center of your left then right palm,* ***Loves:*** *Cross arms over chest,* ***Me:*** *Point to chest*)

- The Bible Tells me So
  (SIGNS– ***The Bible:*** *Touch center of palms as you did for "Jesus" then make your hands into a book,* ***Tells:*** *index finger—or three fingers– start at chin and move away* ***Me:*** *Point to chest,* ***So:*** *Make a big sweeping motion with index finger from forehead pointing forward then toward floor*)

(*See Week 1 of this Unit to find words and signs for verse from last week.*)

The Teaching Moment: This song has a lot of important truth. Understanding that Jesus always loves you and all those around you is vital. It's important to remember that God is our Father and loves us like a the best Father ever.

KEY PHRASE: God is Our Father He Loves Us

WRAPPING IT UP—SENDING IT HOME
5 Minutes

Cleaning Up

We want the children to learn to be responsible, so be sure they help with the clean up, but remind them not to go anywhere, the group is going to talk to God together one more time.

Closing Worship and Prayer

Either gather the children in a circle holding hands or allow them to sit down to pray. If you choose to join hands, remember it's OK if some children prefer not to join the circle. Ask them to be respectful of others as they pray and not make any noise. You can help them get quiet by singing the new verse to "Jesus Loves Me" found earlier in the lesson (even if you used it before).

As you close, ask the children if there's anything that they would like you to include in the prayer. Though no prayer is too small, children will tend to keep going and be "inspired" by other prayer requests, so feel free to stop them and tell them they can quietly say anything that didn't get said out loud to God themselves while you're praying. You may close with your own prayer or use the one below for help. End with "we pray as Jesus taught us to pray" and the Lord's prayer. For these first few weeks, have the kids to repeat after you. Encourage your helper (if you have one) to pray with the kids.

If you need some guidance for your prayer, you can use this:

Father in Heaven *(Allow kids to repeat after each phrase)*. I'm so glad that you love me so much. Thank you for never giving up on me. Please bless all of these things the kids have asked prayer for today *(or you can mention them individually)* as we pray the way you taught your disciples to pray: *(end with the Lord's Prayer one line at a time)*.

Our Father who art in heaven, hallowed be thy Name.
Thy Kingdom come, thy will be done on earth as it is in heaven.
Give us this day our daily bread and forgive us our debts as we forgive our debtors.
Lead us not into temptation and deliver us from evil. For thine is the kingdom and the power and the glory forever, Amen.

Remind the kids to take their craft home (if you made one).

Jesus, Teach Me How to Pray
A Year in The Lord's Prayer and other Bible Basics

Unit 1: Our Father Who Art in Heaven
Week 3: A Father Who Forgives Us

Lesson Overview

Today our objective is to help the kids get a better understanding of God's forgiveness. Ahab was one of the most evil kings in the Bible, but when he repented, God forgave Him.

KEY PHRASE: God is Our Father. He Forgives Us

SETTING UP THE LESSON   10 Minutes

Introduction: The Changing Picture Step One
Supplies: Cardstock (half or quarter sheet for each child), crayons, hair dryer, wood skewers or something similar and black matte tempra paint with a squirt of dish soap in it. (This goes with the craft-you can alternately use scratch off paper available at Oriental Trading or Amazon)

PRESENTING THE LESSON

Scripture: 1 Kings 21   5-10 Minutes

MAKING IT REAL TO KIDS TODAY   *(Choose as many as you have time for)*

Game: The Father Says   5-10 Minutes

Video: Finding Nemo—Marlin forgives   3-5 Minutes
Supplies: Finding Nemo DVD or YouTube clip https://www.youtube.com/watch?v=CrcU8g47S14

Song: "Jesus Loves Me" (another new verse)   3-5 Minutes

Craft: The Changing Picture Step Two   10-15 Minutes

WRAPPING IT UP—SENDING IT HOME   6-8 Minutes

Clean Up & Prayer Time

KEY PHRASE: God is Our Father. He Forgives Us.

SETTING UP THE LESSON 5-10 minutes

Introduction: Today's introduction goes with the craft, so if you use this section you'll need to ALSO USE THE CRAFT in order for this to be effective.
Supplies: cardstock (half or quarter sheet for each child), crayons, hair dryer, wood skewers or another dull pointed instrument and thick black matte tempra paint with a squirt of dish soap in it.

Spread newspaper on the tables. Give each child a piece card stock. Have them color the entire paper with crayons. Every inch must be covered. They can scribble, use one color, or every color in the box. (Discourage black, brown or dark blue.) As they color, tell them this represents our life. Full of color. God created us and he made our life exciting and vibrant. As kids finish their full color art, quickly brush a thin layer of black tempra over the crayon so no color remains visible. This black paint represents what sin does to our world. It causes the beauty God made to be black and covers up all the beauty. Next have your helper speed the drying process with the blow dryer while you move on to the story for today.

PRESENTING THE LESSON 5-10 Minutes

Scripture Basis: 1 Kings 21
You do not have to read this directly from the Bible— use the story form below or reword it to fit your personality
Props you might use: - Large stack of play money - Burlap Bag

Once upon a time Israel had a famous king named Ahab. King Ahab had a neighbor named Naboth, and the King wanted Naboth's vineyard. Do you know what a vineyard is? (*Leave a moment for answers.*) A vineyard is a place where grapes grow on vines.

Well, the King wanted Naboth's vineyard, so he tried to buy it, but Naboth didn't want to sell it. The King offered him a LOT of money. How much money do you think he offered Naboth? (*Leave a moment for answers and accept all answers. We don't know how much, but you can prompt them with statements like "More than that" or "at least that much."*) Naboth's dad and granddad and great granddad had all picked the grapes off of those vines, so Naboth didn't want to sell it.

But King Ahab and his wife weren't very nice. King Ahab's wife found two scoundrels to lie about Naboth. Do you know what scoundrels are? (*Allow for answers.*) Scoundrels are people who lie and cheat and act mean to people all the time. So, the scoundrels lied about him, and Naboth was killed because of those lies.

After Naboth died, Ahab went over and just TOOK Naboth's vineyard. Yep, he stole it! The next thing Ahab knew, God's prophet, Elijah, came to talk with him. Do you know what a prophet is? (*Allow for answers.*) A prophet is a man or a woman who does things the way God asks. God tells prophets the things he wants to say and sends them to say it. So Elijah the prophet came to Ahab and said, "How can you steal Naboth's property? Because you did this, you're going to have to die."

Ahab had always done the wrong thing. But after he heard Elijah's message, Ahab felt bad for the first time in his life. Have you ever felt bad for doing the wrong thing? (*Allow for answers.*) How did you feel about being bad? (*Allow for answers.*) Ahab felt so bad that he ripped his fancy King clothes and put on sackcloth. Do you know what sackcloth is? (*Allow for answers.*) Sackcloth is rough material that they put animal food in. (*Pass around burlap if you have some.*) King Ahab was so sorry that he didn't eat for a few days and didn't even yell at people. He acted very sorry for days. He turned away from his bad ways and began to try to do things that would make God happy.

When God saw how sorry he was and that he was trying to do right, God told Elijah that he would forgive Ahab, and Ahab wouldn't have to die. Because Ahab repented and decided to live for God from then on, God forgave him. Do you know what it means when God forgives? (*Allow for answers.*) It means that God doesn't hold anything against us anymore. It's like when your friend does something mean and then says "I'm sorry" and you decide to still be his friend.

When we realize we are doing things that are bad and quit doing them, God forgives us too. He wants to be our friend. We just have to turn away from doing the wrong thing and decide to do what's right and God will forgive any bad we've done.

KEY PHRASE: God is Our Father. He Forgives Us

MAKING IT REAL TO KIDS TODAY

Game: The Father Says — 5 Minutes

This game is like Simon says. except when you want the kids to do what you're telling them to do, you say, "The Father Says." When you DON'T say "The Father Says," they should do the EXACT OPPOSITE of what you say. For example if you say "hop on your left foot" they could hop on the right one. You can either take one child out every time he or she messes up or just keep it going and create a point scale to give points to the ones who mess up—the one with the lowest points would win.

The Teaching Moment: When we accept God's forgiveness, we do "what the Father says." And most of the time we should do just the opposite of what the world around us would like us to do.

Video: Finding Nemo—Marlin Forgives — 5 Minutes

Supplies: Finding Nemo DVD or YouTube clip https://www.youtube.com/watch?v=CrcU8g47S14

This is a very short clip at the end of the movie. If you choose to use the DVD/Video rather than the YouTube clip, you'll find the snip here: At the Main Menu select "Scene Selections" then "Reunion." Nemo has just rescued Dorie and the tuna. He is laying injured on the ocean floor. He tells his dad he's sorry for saying he hated him and Marlin forgives him.

The Teaching Moment: Remind the kids that God wants to forgive us just like Marlin forgave Nemo. Just like Marlin is a loving father trying to find and forgive Nemo, God is the same (only better).

SONG—"Jesus Loves Me" — 3-5 Minutes

Use the tune of "Jesus Loves Me" with these words - Sing it through a few times so they get the words.

- Jesus Loves Me He who died
  (SIGNS— **Jesus:** *Point to the center of each hand,* **Loves:** *Cross arms over chest,* **Me:** *point to self,* **He:** *point upward* **died:** *Stretch out arms like on a cross*)

- Heaven's Gates to open wide
  (SIGNS—*Keep left arm stretched out, bring right hand to left hand then make a large sweeping arc with right hand*)

- He will wash away my sin
  (SIGNS— *pretend to wash hands*)

- Let his little child come in
  (SIGNS- **Let his little child:** *both hands up* **Come in:** *both hands down*)

- Yes, Jesus Loves Me (3x)
  (SIGNS- **Yes:** *make fist with right hand and then hold it up and nod it up and down (like shaking your head yes),* **Jesus:** *Touch the center of your left then right palm,* **Loves:** *Cross arms over chest,* **Me:** *Point to chest*)

- The Bible Tells me So
  (SIGNS- **The Bible:** *Touch center of palms like you did for "Jesus" then make your hands into a book,* **Tells:** *index finger—or three fingers– start at chin and move away* **Me:** *Point to chest,* **So:** *Make a big sweeping motion with index finger from forehead pointing forward then toward floor*)

(Last Week's Verse)

- Jesus Loves Me when I'm good
  (SIGNS— **Jesus:** *Point to the center of each hand,* **Loves:** *Cross arms over chest,* **Me:** *point to self,* **Good:** *Put four fingers on chin and pull it downward*)

- And I do the things I should
  (SIGNS— **I:** *point to self,* **Things:** *hold right palm face up in front of you, lift it slightly and put it back down just right of where it was* **I:** *Point to self,* **Should:** *Hold index finger slightly curved and point downward a few times*)

- Jesus loves me when I'm bad
  (SIGNS— **Jesus:** *Point to the center of each hand,* **Loves:** *Cross arms over chest,* **Me:** *point to self,* **Bad:** *Put four fingers on chin and turn it over as you push downward*)

KEY PHRASE: God is Our Father. He Forgives Us

- Though it makes him very sad
  (SIGNS– **Makes Him:** *Point Up,* **Sad:** *Open all fingers wide and draw them down in front of your face—like tears*)

(Week 1 Verse)

- Jesus Loves Me when I pray
  (SIGNS— *Jesus: Point to the center of each hand, Loves: Cross arms over chest, Me: point to self, Pray: fold hands like praying*)

- He wants to hear me everyday
  (SIGNS—*He: point heavenward, Hear: hand near ear, Me: Point to self, Everyday: Put right elbow in left hand with arm straight up then put right hand down into left elbow like the sun is setting*)

- Morning, noon and nighttime, too
  (SIGNS—*Morning: Put left hand inside right elbow with arm straight out then lift arm toward body, Noon: Hold right arm straight up on top of left hand, Nighttime: Keep right elbow in left hand and Cup right hand and drop it in front of right wrist*)

- Every moment all day through.
  (SIGNS- *Every Moment: Wave both hand from center out, All day through: Start like "noon" above and then put right hand down into left elbow like the sun is setting*)

Craft: The Changing Picture   10 Minutes

You'll need to do this last so the paint has time to dry. If you don't think it will dry in time, you can purchase "magic color scratch paper" (available at Oriental Trading and Amazon) and let them take their painted creations home next week. You could also have a blow dryer prepared to help speed the drying.

If you use the pictures the kids made in the inro, the kids will now use the skewers (or some other stiff utensil—a fork or butter knife could also work). Help the kids scratch "ME" in the paint. Make the letters wide so that a lot of crayon shows.

The Teaching Moment: Tell the kids that when we turn from sin, God forgives us and begins to wipe away the things in our lives that make them dark. Just like our scraping reveals the beauty of our picture, God's forgiveness reveals the beauty in our lives.

WRAPPING IT UP—SENDING IT HOME

Cleaning Up

We want the children to learn to be responsible, so be sure they help with the clean up, but remind them not to go anywhere, the group is going to talk to God together one more time.

Closing Worship and Prayer

Either gather the children in a circle holding hands or allow them to sit down to pray. If you choose to join hands, remember that it's OK if some children prefer not to join the circle. Ask them to be respectful of others as they pray and not make any noise. You can help them get quiet by singing the new verse to "Jesus Loves Me" found earlier in the lesson (even if you used it before)

As you close, ask the children if there's anything that they would like you to pray about for them. Remember that no prayer is ever too small, however, children will tend to keep going and be "inspired" by other prayer requests, so feel free to stop taking requests and tell them they can say anything that didn't get said out loud quietly to God themselves while you're praying. You may close with your own prayer or use the one below for help. End with "we pray as Jesus taught us to pray" and the Lord's prayer—for these first few weeks allow the kids to repeat after you. Encourage the helper to pray with the kids.

KEY PHRASE: God is Our Father. He Forgives Us

If you need some guidance for your prayer, you can use this:

Father in Heaven *(Allow kids to repeat after each phrase)*. I'm sorry that I do things everyday that make you sad. Forgive me when I don't listen to my parents or I'm mean to my friends. Thank you for loving me enough to send Jesus to die in my place. Thanks for loving me enough to forgive me. Please bless all of these things the kids have asked prayer for today *(or you can mention them individually)* as we pray the way you taught your disciples to pray: *(end with the Lord's Prayer one line at a time)*.

Our Father who art in heaven, hallowed be thy Name. Thy Kingdom come, thy will be done on earth as it is in heaven.
Give us this day our daily bread and forgive us our debts as we forgive our debtors.
Lead us not into temptation and deliver us from evil. For thine is the kingdom and the power and the glory forever, Amen.

Notes

Jesus, Teach Me How to Pray
A Year in The Lord's Prayer and other Bible Basics

Unit 2: Hallowed Be Thy Name
Week 1: God's Name is Special

Lesson Overview

Because the Lord's Prayer has words we don't use anymore, many kids think that the beginning of the prayer sounds like God's name might be Art or Howard.

Today we're going to look at a familiar story—Moses and the Burning Bush. However, we're going to focus on the part of the story where Moses asks God what His name is, and God answers, "I am who I am." We will look at the fact that God's name means that he has always been who He is, he has no beginning. We'll look at a few other names of God while we're at it.

KEY PHRASE: God's Name is Special. He is the LORD

SETTING UP THE LESSON   5-7 Minutes

Introduction: What Do the Words ART and HALLOWED Mean?

PRESENTING THE LESSON

Scripture: Exodus 3:1-15   10-15 Minutes

MAKING IT REAL TO KIDS TODAY   *(Choose as many as you have time for)*

Game: What's in a name?   10-15 Minutes

Craft: Tetragrammaton   10-15 Minutes
Supplies: Poster Board or Chalk Board, Big Fat Marker or Sidewalk Chalk,   One 1/2 sheet of paper for each child—You could use pieces of a brown grocery bag, Crayons or Markers or Sidewalk Chalk, Ribbon (Optional)

Song: "Jehovah Jireh" or "Lord, I Lift Your Name on High"   5 Minutes

WRAPPING IT UP—SENDING IT HOME   5-10 Minutes

Clean Up & Prayer Time

KEY PHRASE: God's Name is Special. He is the LORD.

SETTING UP THE LESSON   5-7 Minutes

Introduction: What do the words ART and HALLOWED mean?

The kids have been saying the Lord's Prayer for four weeks now, so let's see if they remember the first two lines.

Say: *Who remembers the first two lines of the Lord's Prayer?* Give them a moment to answer—hopefully, they won't need a clue, but if they do, try saying *"Our Father"* then pause. After they get through the first two lines, stop them. Ask them *"do you know what it means when you say, "Our Father who art in heaven."* Pause Then ask: *what does "art" mean?* Hopefully they'll know "art" means "is." Then say, *"Yes, it's like saying, our Father who IS in heaven."*

Next ask them, *"What does 'Hallowed be thy name' mean?"* This will probably be tougher for them. Some may think that you said "Howard" If they do, affirm that it DOES SOUND like Howard, but that's not it. If no one answers, explain that "Hallowed" means "holy" or perfect and clean. So God's name is perfect. When we pray and say "Hallowed be Thy Name," we're telling God that we think His name is special.

PRESENTING THE LESSON   10 Minutes

Scripture Basis: Exodus 3:1-15
You do not have to read this directly from the Bible— use the story form below or reword it to fit your personality
Even when you read from here, keep your Bible open so the children know where the story comes from.

Many of the kids will have heard the story of Moses and the Burning Bush.

Allow them to begin to tell you the story. Stop them where needed to interject corrections.

Moses was living in Midian as a shepherd. One day when he was out with the sheep, he noticed that a bush was on fire, but it wasn't burning up. It seemed very strange to him, so he walked over to it. When he did, he heard God call his name from the bush. "Moses!" God called from the bush. "Stop," God said. "Don't come closer. Take off your sandals. This is holy ground"

Then God told Moses it was his job to lead all the Israelites out of Egypt. But Moses was scared. There were a lot of Israelites. What if they didn't believe God really sent him? So, Moses asked God, "What if they ask what your name is?" God told Moses, "Tell them, "I AM WHO I AM. If they ask who sent you, tell them I AM sent me." Then God said, "Tell them, 'The LORD, the God of your fathers has sent me. This is my name forever."

The kids probably won't know anything from the second paragraph. After you tell the story (or finish the story, use these questions to have a bit of review).

- What was Moses' job in Midian? . . . Shepherd
- How did Moses feel when God put him in charge of leading the Israelites? . . . Afraid
- What did Moses want to know about God? . . . His name
- What did God say His name is? . . . I AM WHO I AM *or* Yahweh

God told the people His name—I AM WHO I AM. God told Moses that He always was and always will be. He doesn't have to prove himself and doesn't have just one name like we do. He is who he is. He is God and will always be God.

God also said that His name is LORD. Lord is the word that we say. The Israelites probably said it Yahweh (Yah—way) or Jehovah. The reason we don't know for sure is because they thought God's name was so special they didn't say it or write it completely. They didn't want to ever be disrespectful when they said God's name.

Moses and the Israelites loved God and knew how special His name is.

KEY PHRASE: God's Name is Special. He is the LORD.

MAKING IT REAL TO KIDS TODAY

Craft: Tetragrammaton
Supplies: Poster Board or Chalk Board, big fat marker or sidewalk chalk, one 1/2 sheet of paper for each child—You could use pieces of a brown grocery bag, crayons or markers or sidewalk chalk, ribbon (Opt)

Pass out the paper and **SAY:** Today we're going to make something that will remind us of God's name and how special it is.

First we're going to do something to remind us that God's name is very old. It was more than 3000 years ago when God told Moses his name. So take your piece of paper and tear just a little bit from each of the edges (Show them how to tear about 1/4" from each edge to make it very ragged) Now we're going to crumble it all up very tight. After you get it all crumpled, straighten it out again. Use your hands to make it as flat as you can. (Option: you can let the kids rub a little sidewalk chalk on their hands and then flatten the paper out to make it look a little more aged. - Might want to have a rag or wipes handy to wipe off hands afterwards if you do.)

Remember that the Israelites thought that God's name was so special they didn't want to accidentally be disrespectful when they said it. They were very careful when they wrote it too.

The way they wrote it looks like this:

יהוה

That's written in Hebrew. Hebrew goes from RIGHT TO LEFT—NOT left to right like we write. The

is the first letter. Write the characters from right to left so the kids can copy them.

SAY: The letters we use for these four letters are YHWH. And the Israelites did something we might think is funny. They wrote from the right to the left instead of left to right the way we do.

י = Y

ה = H

ו = W

ה = H

The Teaching Moment: This was Moses' special name for God. Every time Moses saw this word, He thought of God and how special His name is. So, every time you look at this, you can be reminded how special God's name is.

If you have extra time and would like to, you can use the ribbon to tie the paper into a scroll.

KEY PHRASE: God's Name is Special—He is the LORD.

Song: "Jehovah Jireh" or "Lord, I Lift Your Name on High"   5 minutes

Tell the Children: God is so big that He has a lot of names to help us understand who He is. One of those names is Jehovah Jireh (JIE—rah). *(Invite the Children to say Jehovah Jireh.)* Jehovah is another way to say Yahweh. So Jehovah Jireh means God who provides. Do you know what provides means? *(Allow time for answers)* "Provides" means gives me what I need.

If you're using Jehovah Jireh, say: Here's a song that helps us remember this name of God. (You'll find music on the last page of this lesson)

If you use "Lord, I Lift Your Name on High," you may want to use the Go Fish Guys Music Video (https://www.youtube.com/watch?v=Lg6TInxDfIE) Then move to the teaching moment..

The Teaching Moment: "Lord, I Lift Your Name on High" - Remind the kids that God's name is special and Holy so we praise His name and that's what "lifting it on high" means.

"Jehovah Jireh" - Remind the children that God has many names. One name is God, my provider. Jehovah Jireh is the Hebrew phrase that says that.

Game: What's in a Name?   10-15 minutes
Supplies: Something very soft for "it" to tap with.

Have each child come up with a nickname they'd like to be called. Go around twice and have everyone share with the group their nickname.

Select one child to be "it." Have all the kids stand in a circle with "it" in the center. Give "it" the soft supply (small pillow, stuffed animal, very short pool noodle). You begin by calling out one nickname. The person with that nickname must say his or her nickname and then shout the nickname of someone else. That person then says their nickname followed by another persons' nickname. "It" will try to tag the one who is speaking BEFORE they mention the second name. If "it" gets to the person before they mention the second name the person they tag is now "it." Play continues for as long as you have time.

The Teaching Moment: We had a lot of fun having different names. Was it hard to remember everyone's extra name? God has many different names, and each one of them is special and helps us to know who God is a little better.

WRAPPING IT UP—SENDING IT HOME   5-10 Minutes

Cleaning Up

We want the children to learn to be responsible, so be sure they help with the clean up, but remind them not to go anywhere, the group is going to talk to God together one more time.

Closing Worship and Prayer

You can either gather the children in a circle holding hands or allow them to sit down to pray. If you choose to join hands, remember that it's OK if some children prefer not to join the circle. Just ask them to be respectful of others as they pray and not make any noise. You can always begin your prayer time with a quiet song if you like.

As you close, and if there is time, ask the children if there's anything that they would like you to pray about for them. Remember that no prayer is ever too small, however, children will tend to keep going and be "inspired" by other prayer requests, so feel free to stop taking requests and tell them they can say anything that didn't get said out loud quietly to God themselves while you're praying. You may close with your own prayer or use the one below. End with "we pray as Jesus taught us to pray" and the Lord's prayer—for these first few weeks allow the kids to repeat after you. Encourage the helper to pray with the kids.

If you need some guidance for your prayer, you can use this:

Father in Heaven *(you might allow kids to repeat after each phrase)*. Your name is so special and you are so wonderful. Thank you for telling Moses your name. Thank you for being everything that I need. Thank you for loving us. Please bless all of these things the kids have asked prayer for today *(or you can mention them individually)* as we pray the way you taught your disciples to pray: *(end with the Lord's Prayer one line at a time)*

Our Father who art in heaven, hallowed be thy Name. Thy Kingdom come, thy will be done on earth as it is in heaven. Give us this day our daily bread and forgive us our debts as we forgive our debtors.

Lead us not into temptation and deliver us from evil. For thine is the kingdom and the power and the glory forever, Amen.

Jehovah Jireh

Public Domain

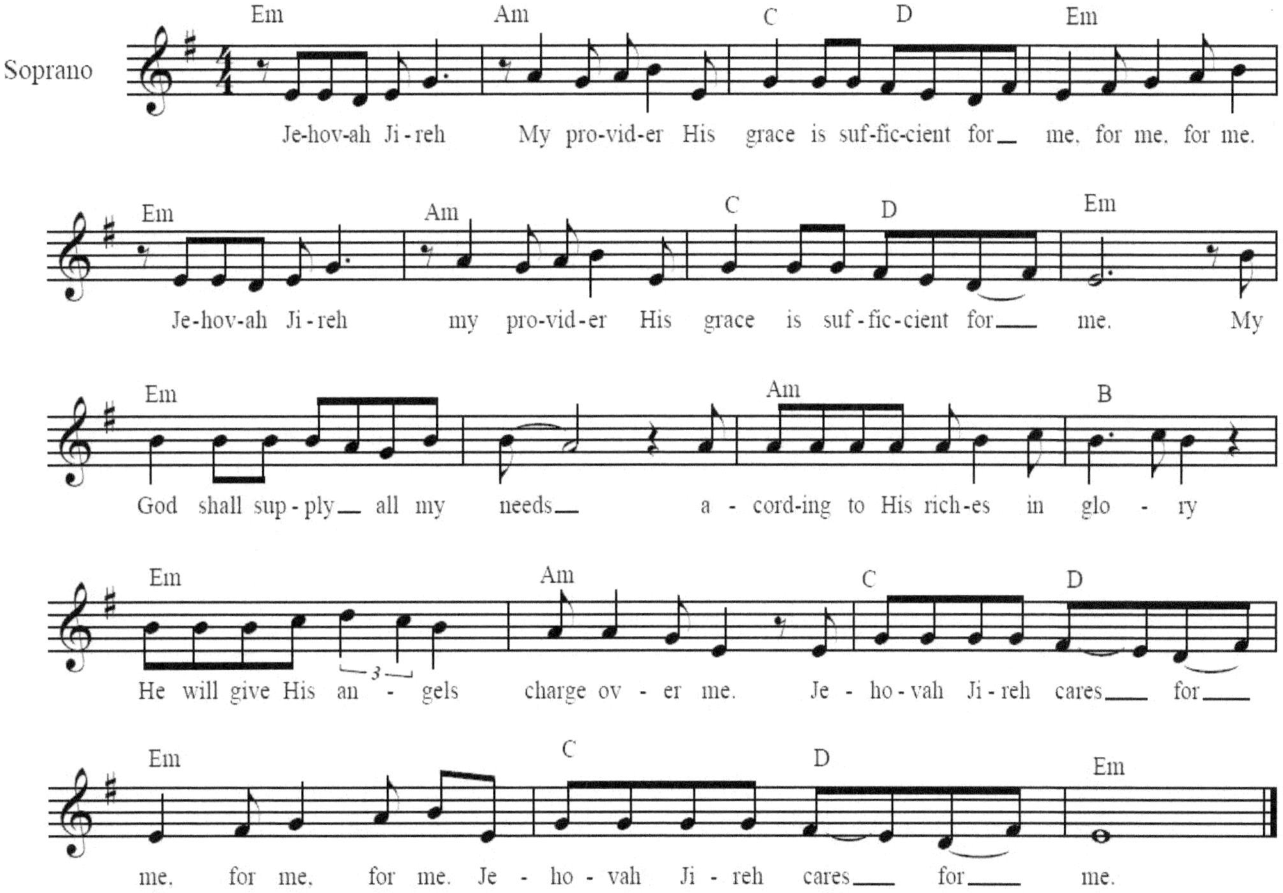

(Soprano)

Je-hov-ah Ji-reh My pro-vid-er His grace is suf-fic-ient for me, for me, for me.

Je-hov-ah Ji-reh my pro-vid-er His grace is suf-fic-ient for me. My

God shall sup-ply all my needs a-cord-ing to His rich-es in glo-ry

He will give His an-gels charge ov-er me. Je-ho-vah Ji-reh cares for

me, for me, for me. Je-ho-vah Ji-reh cares for me.

Notes

Jesus, Teach Me How to Pray
A Year in The Lord's Prayer and other Bible Basics

Unit 2: Hallowed Be Thy Name
Week 2: God's Name is Holy & Powerful

Lesson Overview

God said over and over again that we are supposed to be holy because He is holy. The scripture for this lesson is just one of those occasions. Today we'll attempt to help the children understand that God's name is Holy, special and should be revered. The story for this week is David fighting Goliath. The kids will probably know the story, but today we're going to focus on David's statement that he came in the name of the Holy God.

KEY PHRASE: God's Name is Special (Holy) and Powerful

SETTING UP THE LESSON 5-7 Minutes

Introduction: What Does Your Name Mean?
Supplies: An online name dictionary, paper and pencils and crayons

PRESENTING THE LESSON 10-15 Minutes

Scripture: Leviticus 11:44-45 & 1 Samuel 17:1-54
Optional Supplies: Video Clip from David and the Giant Pickle 3 Minutes

MAKING IT REAL TO KIDS TODAY (Choose as many as you have time for)

Game: The Name Game (Action Syllables) 10-15 Minutes

Craft: Names of God Bracelet or Key Chain 10-15 Minutes
Supplies: Pony beads, letter beads, string and/or elastic string, key chain ends

Song: "Lord, I Lift Your Name on High" 5 Minutes

WRAPPING IT UP—SENDING IT HOME 5-10 Minutes

Clean Up & Prayer Time

KEY PHRASE: God's Name is Special (Holy) and Powerful

SETTING UP THE LESSON 5-7 Minutes

Introduction: What does your name mean?
Supplies: An online name dictionary, paper and pencils and crayons

Today we're going to help children discover how special their names are. Give each child a piece of paper and a pencil. Have them each write their name in large letters on the paper, then ask them to be very quiet so that you can help each one find out what his or her name means. You may want to look up as many of the names as possible before your meeting so you'll be able to move quickly. Go around the room and tell each child what his or her name means. Help them write the meaning on the page with their name. As they are waiting for you to get to them or after you've helped them, let them spend the time decorating the paper. They can add a frame of butterflies, hearts, flowers or squiggles to go around their name. Talk about how special their name is, that it was chosen for them especially by their parents. Then remind them that when we say "Hallowed be Thy Name," we're telling God we believe His name is special.

PRESENTING THE LESSON 10-15 Minutes

Scripture Basis: Leviticus 11:44-45 1 Samuel 17:1-54

You do not have to read this directly from the Bible— use the story form below or reword it to fit your personality

(If you plan to use the Veggie Tales, "David and the Giant Pickle" video clip to tell the end of the story, be sure to have it cued to the black screen just before David gets to the stream to find the stones
About 15:35 in this video clip: https://www.youtube.com/watch?v=6A0ipXpaacQ)

Who knows the story of David and Goliath? (*Let kids share.*) David was the youngest in his family. His dad sent him to take lunch to his brothers and check on them because they were soldiers in the king's army. They were fighting against the Philistines—can you say Philistines? (*Encourage children to repeat*) The Philistines were really tough. They had one guy on their side who was especially big. Some folks thought he was a giant because he was nine feet tall. (*Show the kids something that is nine feet tall—the ceiling perhaps. You might tell them, "He was even taller than..." then name the tallest guy in your church.*) His name was Goliath. Everyone in the Israelite army was afraid of Goliath, so no one would go and fight him, but someone had to! If they didn't fight Goliath and win, the Philistines were going to take over their city.

Then David showed up. Do you remember what I told you he was supposed to do? (*Allow for answers.*) He was only supposed to take some lunch to his brothers and see how they were doing. But when David got there, Goliath was making fun of the Israelites, the people of God, and that made David angry. David loved God, and he believed that God would help him win the battle against Goliath. So he went to the king and volunteered to fight.

The king tried to give David his big fancy sword and armor. Do you know what armor is? (*Let kids answer*) Armor is a heavy suit that protects against arrows and swords. But the King's armor and sword were too big and heavy for David, so he told the King he was going to fight without it.

Then David went out to the battle field, and this is what happened.

Show the video clip here - end it after Goliath falls down or if you have time play to the end. Then skip this paragraph and move to the final one.

Alternately, you can just tell the rest of the story:

David got five stones and put them in his pouch. Then he walked right up to that giant and said, "You have a sword, but I'm fighting with the name of God, the God of the Israelites." Then he took his sling and put one of the stones in it. He flung it around and around (*swing your hand over your head like a lasso*) until it was going really fast and then he let it go. (*act like you are throwing the stone*) Who knows what happened? (*Allow for answers.*) David's stone hit the giant right in the head, and he fell over dead. David was the hero! The Philistines ran back to their homes, and everyone thought David was a hero.

KEY PHRASE: God's Name is Special (Holy) and Powerful

Skip to this paragraph after the video or keep going if you're telling the story—So tell me, what was David's secret in fighting Goliath?—(*Allow for answers, but try to wait until one of them says, "He fought in the name of God."*) David told Goliath he came in the name of the Living God. David knew how powerful and holy God's name is. He knew that God's name was special, and if He fought in God's name, He could win even though he was very small and not a soldier at all.

MAKING IT REAL TO KIDS TODAY

Game: Action Syllables   10-15 Minutes

With the group standing in a circle by age (youngest to oldest), have the participants each choose an action for each syllable of their name. For example: Johnny might choose a hip shake when he says "John" and a snap when he says "ny" (for smaller kids you might just have one action for their name).

Have the youngest person say their name and do the motion they chose. Then the whole group repeats. The second person then says their name with the actions they've chosen, the group repeats and then repeats the first again. Continue until they go all around the circle. You may choose to not allow the kids to repeat any action that someone else has used. It will make it a bit tougher for the older kids who are last.

The Teaching Moment: *Tell the Children:* Today you gave your name a special twist. Even if you share a name with someone, your name was especially chosen for you to set you apart from everyone else. Just like our moves, claps, and snaps were different for each person, your name is unique and special. But no matter how special our names are, God's name is even more special. His name is holy and perfect and powerful. We need to always respect God's name because it is so special.

Craft: Names of God Bracelet or Key Chain   10-15 Minutes
Supplies: Pony beads, letter beads, string and/or elastic string, key chain ends

Tell the children: It's important that we always remember that God's name is Holy. God said that because he is Holy, He wants us to be holy. To help us remember God's holiness we're going to make bracelets (or key chains.) We're going to put one of the names of God on it, so we'll remember. You can chose from Holy, Perfect, Jireh (that means provider), God, Jesus, or some other special name of God with less than 9 letters.

Let the children pick the beads they want to use along with the appropriate string for their project or key chain end. If they are using elastic string, have them tie it on to the first bead and then continue. They can make any pattern they like as long as the one of the names of God is in their project. Don't forget to make rounds and check everyone's progress.

The Teaching Moment: *Tell the children:* Every time you see their bracelet or key chain, they need to remember how wonderful and powerful God's name is.

Song: Lord, I Lift Your Name on High   5 Minutes

The "Go Fish Guys" music video would be a great addition to this lesson. Encourage the children to sing along. *https://www.youtube.com/watch?v=Lg6TInxDflE*

The Teaching Moment: *Tell the Children:* God's name is Special and Holy and Powerful, so we "lift His name on high." Which means we praise His name.

KEY PHRASE: God's name is Special Holy and Powerful

WRAPPING IT UP—SENDING IT HOME 5-10 Minutes

Cleaning Up

We want the children to learn to be responsible, so be sure they help with the clean up, but remind them not to go anywhere, the group is going to talk to God together one more time.

Closing Worship and Prayer

You can either gather the children in a circle holding hands or allow them to sit down to pray. If you choose to join hands, remember that it's OK if some children prefer not to join the circle. Just ask them to be respectful of others as they pray and not make any noise. You can always begin your prayer time with a quiet song if you like.

As you close, and if there is time, ask the children if there's anything that they would like you to pray about for them. Remember that no prayer is ever too small, however, children will tend to keep going and be "inspired" by other prayer requests, so feel free to stop taking requests and tell them they can say anything that didn't get said out loud quietly to God themselves while you're praying. You may close with your own prayer or use the one below for help. End with "we pray as Jesus taught us to pray" and the Lord's prayer. For these first few weeks, allow the kids to repeat after you. Encourage the helper to pray with the kids.

If you need some guidance for your prayer, you can use this:

Father in Heaven, *(Allow kids to repeat after each phrase)* Your name is so special and powerful. Thank you for helping David be strong when he fought Goliath in your name. Thank you helping me be strong when I follow your name. Please bless all of these things the kids have asked prayer for today *(or you can mention them individually)* as we pray the way you taught your disciples to pray: *(end with the Lord's Prayer one line at a time so the kids can repeat after you).*

Our Father who art in heaven, hallowed be thy Name.
Thy Kingdom come, thy will be done on earth as it is in heaven.
Give us this day our daily bread and forgive us our debts as we forgive our debtors.
Lead us not into temptation and deliver us from evil. For thine is the kingdom and the power and the glory forever, Amen.

Jesus, Teach Me How to Pray
A Year in The Lord's Prayer and other Bible Basics

Unit 2: Hallowed Be Thy Name
Week 3: God's Name - He Has a Lot of Them

Lesson Overview

When we're learning to praise God's name it's good to remember that God is bigger than just "our Father" and "holy." As Christians, we often put God in a box and limit Him. He has many names, and there are countless adjectives that describe Him because His power and potential are limitless. Today we'll look at several scriptures that tell us about God's name.

KEY PHRASE: The Bible Has a Lot of Names for God

SETTING UP THE LESSON   5-7 Minutes

Introduction: Word Search
Supplies: Copies of the word search at the end of the lesson—pencils

PRESENTING THE LESSON   10-15 Minutes

Scripture: Isaiah 9:6, John 10:11, John 8:12

MAKING IT REAL TO KIDS TODAY   *(Choose as many as you have time for)*

Game: Musical Names   10-15 Minutes
Supplies: One squeaky toy, CD player and a CD of one or two worship songs that features the names of God (ie: "Jesus, Messiah" by Chris Tomlin or "I Really Want to Worship You, Lord" by Lynne Modranski)

Game: Names of God Game   10-15 Minutes
Supplies: Make two copies and cut apart the "Names of God" sheet from the last page of this lesson, blank paper and crayons or pencils

Craft: Names of God Coloring Sheet   5-7 Minutes
Supplies: Copies of the coloring sheet at the end of this lesson and crayons

Song: "Jehovah Jireh" or "Lord, I Lift Your Name"   5 Minutes
Optional Supplies: The Go Fish Guys DVD of "Lord, I Lift Your Name"

WRAPPING IT UP—SENDING IT HOME   5-10 Minutes

Clean Up & Prayer Time

KEY PHRASE: The Bible Has a Lot of Names for God

SETTING UP THE LESSON   5-7 Minutes

Introduction: Word Search
Supplies: Make copies of the word searches at the end of this lesson. There is a harder one for older kids and an easier one for the younger.

Pass out the word searches. Let the kids work for about five minutes, then tell them that the words they are looking for are some of the names of God. If they aren't able to get finished, allow them to finish at the end or take it home.

PRESENTING THE LESSON   10-15 Minutes

Scripture: Isaiah 9:6, John 10:11, John 8:12

Today we will be reading the actual scriptures—invite older kids to read the short passages. Then after each one, we'll talk about it with the kids. Today's concepts might be more difficult for the younger kids to understand because they are a bit abstract. Don't worry too much if the younger ones don't completely get it. Plant the ideas within them. Someday they'll understand even better.

READ: Isaiah 9:6

Ask the students: What does Isaiah call God? *(Allow for answers.)* Isaiah calls God Wonderful Counselor, Mighty God, Everlasting Father, and Prince of Peace. Let's talk about what those mean. What's a Counselor? *(Allow for answers. Some kids may have visited a counselor, and that may be what they think about. Help them see that a counselor can be more.)* A counselor gives advice and helps you make decisions. You might have a good friend who is a counselor.

How is God a Wonderful Counselor? *God wants to guide us. He really wants to help us always go the right way. When we pray and then listen to Him, He'll give us good advice and help us make decisions*

The next part says Everlasting Father. How will God be an everlasting Father? *Everlasting means just that, lasting forever. God always was and always will be.*

When Isaiah said Prince of Peace, he was talking about Jesus. How is Jesus the Prince of Peace? *Jesus is a prince - help them see that princes are rulers or leaders, and if we allow Christ to be our leader, He will bring peace to our lives. You could talk for a minute about what it means to have peace. To a child it means no fighting and not worrying about grades and friends. Older children may even worry about the world, but peace is discovering we don't have to worry. Christ is in control and He will take care of everything.*

READ: John 10:11

What did Jesus call Himself in this verse? *(Allow for answers.)* Jesus called Himself "the Good Shepherd."

What does a shepherd do? *(Allow for answers.)* Shepherds take care of the sheep, feed them, water them, and protect them from the wolves and bears.

If Jesus is the shepherd who are the sheep? *(Allow for answers.)* Jesus followers are his sheep.

How is Jesus our shepherd? *(Allow for answers.)* Jesus wants to take care of us and protect us. He feeds us with His Word.

READ: John 8:12

What did Jesus call Himself in this verse? *(Allow for answers.)* Jesus said, "I am the Light of the World."

Tell me about lights. Why do we need lights? *(Allow for answers.)* Lights help us see in the dark. They keep us from tripping over things and help us find things.

How is Jesus the Light of the World? *(Allow for answers.)* Jesus helps us see clearly. If we follow Him, we can see where we should go much more clearly.

Do you know any other names of God? *(Allow for answers.)* The Bible has a lot of names for God, more than we can count, and all are holy and special.

KEY PHRASE: The Bible Has a Lot of Names for God

MAKING IT REAL TO KIDS TODAY

Game: Musical Names   5-10 Minutes

Supplies: One squeaky toy, CD player and a CD of one or two worship songs that features the names of God (ie: "Jesus, Messiah" by Chris Tomlin or "I Really Want to Worship You, Lord" by Lynne Modranski)

Have the kids sit in a circle on the floor and give one the squeaky toy. When the music begins, have them pass the toy to the left around the circle. When the music stops whoever is holding the toy should squeeze it and say one of the names of God they've learned during the last three weeks or another that they know. If they can say a name they get a point. After the first five kids say new names, tell them the point system will now change. If they say a name that hasn't been mentioned before they now get two points. If they repeat a name they get one point. The one with the most points at the end wins. You can optionally give the winner a prize if you like.

The Teaching Moment: God is bigger than one name can describe. It takes all of these names to truly know God. What is your favorite name for God? *(Allow for answers.)* All of God's names are holy, but each one helps us know Him better.

Game: Names of God Game   10-15 minutes

Supplies: Make two or three copies of the "Names of God" sheet from the last page of this lesson and cut them apart, blank paper and crayons or pencils

If you have an even number of students, put one pair of names in a basket for every pair of children. (If you have six students, put in three pair of names.) If you have an odd number either you can either include yourself in the group or if it's a multiple of three, use three copies of names, divide the number of students by three, and put that many sets of names in a basket or bowl.

Let every child draw one name of God. Then tell them to walk around, and as fast as they can, find the other person(s) in the room with the same name as they have. After they find their match, have them take a piece of blank paper and work together to draw a picture so that everyone else will know what word they have. Give them about six minutes minutes to do this. When time is up, encourage each set of kids to present their drawing and see if the others can guess it. If you have time, talk about what each name of God means.

ALTERNATELY: You could copy the names of God on heavy cardstock and make this into a memory style game. This would be especially useful for a smaller group.

The Teaching Moment: God's name is very special. He is greater than we can imagine, so he has many names that help people get to know Him better.

Craft: Names of God Coloring Sheet   5-7 Minutes

Supplies: Copies of the coloring sheet at the end of this lesson and crayons

Encourage the children to color in the names on the sheet. Have them read them as they color them and talk about what each one means as they color.

The Teaching Moment: God has many names in the Bible and each one is special and holy. You can use each of these names as you pray because they can help us remember that God is holy and mighty.

Song: "Jehovah Jireh" or "Lord, I Lift Your Name on High"   5 Minutes

Lead the children in singing one or two songs. If you use "Lord, I Lift Your Name," try to get a copy of "The Go Fish Guys" Video. See link in last lesson. You'll find the music for "Jehovah Jireh" on the last page of this lesson. You could also teach the kids "I Really Want to Worship You" by Lynne Modranski. This song includes many of the names of God.

KEY PHRASE: The Bible Has a Lot of Names for God

The Teaching Moment: All the names of God are special and holy. When we say Hallowed be Thy Name, we are remembering the holiness and power of God's name. And when we sing praise, we tell God how much we appreciate His name.

WRAPPING IT UP—SENDING IT HOME   5-10 Minutes

Cleaning Up

We want the children to learn to be responsible, so be sure they help with the clean up, but remind them not to go anywhere, the group is going to talk to God together one more time.

Closing Worship and Prayer

Either gather the children in a circle holding hands or allow them to sit down to pray. If you choose to join hands, remember that it's OK if some children prefer not to join the circle. Just ask them to be respectful of others as they pray and not make any noise. You can always begin your prayer time with a quiet song if you like.

As you close, and if there is time, ask the children for prayer requests. Though no prayer is ever too small, children will tend to keep going and be "inspired" by other prayer requests, so feel free to stop taking requests and tell them they can say anything that didn't get said out loud quietly to God themselves while you pray. You may close with your own prayer or use the one below for help. End with "we pray as Jesus taught us to pray" and the Lord's prayer. For these first few weeks allow the kids to repeat after you. Encourage the helper to pray with the kids.

If you need some guidance for your prayer, you can use this:

Father in Heaven *(Allow kids to repeat after each phrase)*, Mighty God, Wonderful Counselor, Light of the World, Promised Messiah, my Savior and King. You are as wonderful as all of your awesome names. We just want to praise you today for being so tremendous. Please bless all of these things the kids have asked prayer for today *(or you can mention them individually)* as we pray the way you taught your disciples to pray: *(end with the Lord's Prayer one line at a time so the kids can repeat after you)*

Our Father who art in heaven, hallowed be thy Name. Thy Kingdom come, thy will be done on earth as it is in heaven. Give us this day our daily bread and forgive us our debts as we forgive our debtors.
Lead us not into temptation and deliver us from evil. For thine is the kingdom and the power and the glory forever, Amen.

Names of God

Word Search for Younger Kids

I	I	T	T	H	N	M	M	K	O	E	J	E	T
R	E	H	T	A	F	I	Y	I	T	N	C	N	E
E	T	S	I	A	M	I	N	N	A	E	O	I	O
I	K	F	O	N	M	L	N	G	J	S	L	P	N
L	I	T	R	L	H	V	L	E	A	H	T	F	J
E	E	K	I	I	R	V	S	R	H	F	H	L	E
Y	L	O	H	G	E	U	I	E	P	S	G	O	H
L	G	E	G	J	S	N	F	N	C	K	I	L	L
S	S	P	I	R	I	T	D	O	E	N	L	I	V
O	N	R	I	T	G	E	L	E	L	O	I	L	S
I	S	I	G	S	I	O	R	H	O	R	I	R	R
N	L	I	U	E	C	I	D	E	R	I	N	J	P
I	I	R	L	E	O	T	A	E	D	R	R	P	L
I	L	E	E	R	E	P	I	T	I	F	L	I	R

Prince
Lord
Holy
Vine
Father
Friend
I Am
God
Light
Spirit
King
Jesus

Names of God for Older Kids

T	M	M	E	U	R	E	D	N	E	I	R	F	L
C	L	H	E	V	R	S	S	P	I	R	I	T	O
O	E	C	E	S	E	E	A	F	A	T	H	E	R
U	A	N	A	I	S	R	D	H	E	A	L	E	R
N	E	A	O	V	L	I	L	E	L	I	G	H	T
S	H	R	O	D	M	A	A	A	E	O	E	R	C
E	S	B	I	A	M	P	P	H	S	M	I	A	R
L	A	D	O	G	F	O	N	O	S	T	E	U	N
O	V	Y	O	S	E	H	S	S	E	D	I	R	D
R	I	R	A	P	R	O	V	I	D	E	R	N	A
L	O	G	G	H	E	L	E	T	E	A	G	D	G
O	R	N	S	N	W	Y	N	P	R	I	N	C	E
R	S	I	I	H	C	E	J	E	S	U	S	T	T
D	S	K	T	N	M	S	H	R	V	I	N	E	R

Vine   Jesus   King   Provider

Branch   Savior   Prince   Healer

Son of God   Messiah   Everlasting   Friend

Son of Man   Holy   Lord   Redeemer

Jehovah   Counselor   Spirit   Wonderful

Light   Father   I Am

Rock	Creator	Father
Light of the World	Shepherd	Ruler
Friend	Lamb of God	Holy
Wonderful Counselor	Bread of Life	Morning Star
King	Healer	Prince of Peace
Teacher	Vine	Door

Prince of Peace
Holy One
Jesus
I Am
Bread of Life
Wonderful Counselor
Yahweh
God
Commander of Angel Armies
Light of the World
Everlasting Father
Spirit
Lord of Lords
Jehovah Jireh
King of kings
Indescribable Gift
Ancient of Days

Jehovah Jireh

Public Domain

Notes

Page intentionally left blank for printing and copying purposes

Jesus, Teach Me How to Pray
A Year in The Lord's Prayer and other Bible Basics

Unit 3: Thy Kingdom Come
Week 1: The Kingdom of God: It's Inside of You!

Lesson Overview

During the time Jesus walked on the earth, everyone was waiting for the Kingdom of God to come. They were looking for it everywhere and had some definite expectations for God's Kingdom. Jesus' message was foreign to the people of His day, and it's a little difficult for us to understand even yet today. Because it's such an abstract concept, it may be hard for your group, especially the younger kids, to truly grasp what it means when Jesus says, "the Kingdom of God is within you." And when we pray "Thy Kingdom Come," we are really asking for God to put His Kingdom within us. Don't panic if the kids don't completely understand this concept. Just present it as simply as possible and pray as you prepare that God will allow their young hearts to accept it.

KEY PHRASE: The Kingdom of God Can't Be Seen, it's Inside of You.

SETTING UP THE LESSON   5 Minutes
   Introduction: What is a kingdom anyway?

PRESENTING THE LESSON   5 Minutes
   Scripture: Luke 19:11 & Luke 17:20-37

MAKING IT REAL TO KIDS TODAY   (Choose as many as you have time for)

   Video: The Lion King   5 Minutes
   Supplies: Find the video here: https://www.youtube.com/watch?v=GibiNy4d4gc

   Game: King for a day   10-15 Minutes

   Illustration: The Incredible Egg   5 Minutes

   Craft: Heart Pocket   15 Minutes
   Supplies: Craft foam, string or laces, hole punch, pattern on last page

WRAPPING IT UP—SENDING IT HOME   5-7 Minutes
   Clean Up & Prayer Time

KEY PHRASE: The Kingdom of God Can't Be Seen, it's Inside of You

SETTING UP THE LESSON   5 Minutes

Introduction: What is a Kingdom anyway?

To really understand what the Kingdom of God is, the kids will need to understand what a Kingdom of any kind is. If you have a world map, consider using it.

Today we're going to start talking about the next line in the Lord's prayer. Let's review. Who can tell me what the first line is? (*Allow for an answer*) That's right it starts "Our Father who art in heaven" What's next? (*Allow for an answer*) "Hallowed be Thy Name." What does that mean? (*Allow for an answer*) It means God's name is Holy and special.

Today we're going to start talking about the third line. Does anyone know what that is? (*Allow for answers.*) "Thy Kingdom Come" But, tell me, what is a kingdom, not God's Kingdom, but any kingdom? (*Let them share their ideas of a Kingdom.*) A Kingdom is any place and every place the King rules. For instance, the country of Denmark is a kingdom. They have a queen. And anyplace a king or queen rule is a kingdom.

Where are you the king or queen right now? Where do you rule? What is your kingdom? (*Allow for answers. Suggest their swing set, bedroom, king over their pets, etc.*) Yep, everything you get to be in charge of is your kingdom. So the Kingdom of God is everywhere God is the ruler.

PRESENTING THE LESSON   5 Minutes

Scripture: Luke 19:11 & Luke 17:20-37
Older children could read directly from the Bible.
For younger children, have the Bible open in front of you
and use the story form below or reword it to fit your personality

When Jesus lived on the earth a lot of people thought the Kingdom of God would appear at any moment. The people who lived in Israel were really tired of being part of the Roman kingdom. The Roman king treated them pretty bad, so they wanted God's kingdom to come soon. They expected God's Kingdom to be an earthly kingdom. They expected a God's army to start a huge battle and defeat all the other nations, so they wouldn't have to listen to the mean Roman king anymore.

One time the Pharisees asked Jesus when the kingdom of God would come. Do you remember what a kingdom is? (*Allow for answers.*) A kingdom is a place where the king rules. They wanted to know when God would come take over and rule the earth again like He did in the Garden of Eden. There were looking for a human looking kingdom.

But Jesus told them that they shouldn't look for God's kingdom here on earth. He told them, "Don't say the kingdom of God is 'here' or 'there.' And don't believe it when someone tries to trick you into believing they found the Kingdom." He told them that they wouldn't be able to see the Kingdom of God the way they saw earthly kings. He said the Kingdom of God would be inside of them.

And that's how the Kingdom of God comes today. But how do you think the Kingdom of God gets inside us? (*Allow for answers..*) When we pray the Lord's prayer, we ask God for His Kingdom to come. If we really mean that, we have to ask Jesus to be our Savior. We have to understand that we sin. Everyone does things and thinks things that separate them from God, and the only thing that can make sin right with God is a sacrifice. So, Jesus' became our sacrifice when He died on the cross. If we recognize our sin and believe that Jesus' blood will cover it, we can ask Jesus to be our Savior. Then, His kingdom lives inside of us. When we invite Jesus to live in our heart, He becomes the king of our life, and His Kingdom lives inside of us.

KEY PHRASE: The Kingdom of God Can't Be Seen, it's Inside of You

MAKING IT REAL TO KIDS TODAY

Video: The Lion King — 5 Minutes
Supplies: Find the video here: https://www.youtube.com/watch?v=GibiNy4d4gc

You could start this clip at one minute or two minutes and play to the end depending on how much time you have. You'll want to make sure the kids get to see the animals bow.

The Teaching Moment: Who is the king in this movie? *(Allow for answers.)* Mufasa is the king, and Rafiki is introducing Simba because he will be the next king. Did you see what all the animals did when Rafiki held up the new king? *(Allow for answers.)* They got excited then they all bowed down because they knew that Mufasa and his son were the leaders of the kingdom. Wherever Mufasa ruled was his kingdom, and all those animals lived in his kingdom.

God's kingdom is wherever God is the King. We should bow down before God like the animals bowed in front of Mufasa. That's how we acknowledge a king. God wants to be the King of our lives and our hearts, and when He is, then His Kingdom is within us.

Game: King for a Day — 10 Minutes
Supplies: Masking tape and wadded up pieces of paper (newspaper, construction paper, paper bags, etc) enough for each child to have at least 4 balls

Be sure to have a lot of room for this game. In the middle of the space, mark off an area about 3 feet wide (your neutral area) using the masking tape. The area behind each piece of tape is a "Kingdom." Divide the kids into two groups. Try to have an equal amount of older and younger kids on each team. Place one chair in each "Kingdom." Next assign one team to each "kingdom" and have each team select one person to be "King." Their goal is to protect their King and not allow papers to accumulate in their kingdom. Give each team 1/2 of the wadded paper (you can even let them wad it up if you like)

```
  ○
Kingdom 2
-----------
Neutral area
-----------
Kingdom 1
  ○
```

When you say "GO," the teams begin throwing the wadded paper. The King can duck, but can't move from his "throne" or throw any paper wads. The team must protect the king from being hit. The teams keep throwing until one king gets hit by a piece of paper. Then you say "STOP." Count the wads of paper on each side. The team that hit the other's king gets one point and the team that has the least amount of wads on their side gets a point (so one team could get 2 points). Now have the teams select a new king (you may want to do this on a youngest to oldest rotation to make it easy) and then begin again.

Play continues until all kids have had a chance to be king or you run out of time. The team with the most points at the end of play wins.

The Teaching Moment: We had a lot of fun pretending to protect our "Kings" and "Kingdoms." Fortunately, God doesn't need us to protect Him; however, He does need us to protect the Kingdom that He allows to grow within us. It's up to us to make sure we keep the bad movies, curse words, and songs with inappropriate lyrics out of God's Kingdom. To protect God's Kingdom in us, we should be sure to only read good books and choose good friends. We have to put Godly stuff into our lives so our Kingdom will be protected from the wads of stuff that will ruin it.

Illustration: The Incredible Egg — 5 Minutes
Supplies: At least two eggs—one hardboiled, the other raw—you could make one brown and the other white if you have a brown egg available, or you can mark one so you can remember which is boiled - a clear bowl.

KEY PHRASE: The Kingdom of God Can't Be Seen, it's Inside of You

God gave us a lot of things that help us understand his message a bit more clearly. One of those things is a simple egg. Do you see these two eggs? How are they the same? *(Allow for answers)* How are they different? *(Answers - they probably won't guess that one is hard-boiled, because there's really no way to tell.)* You are right, but there's one more thing you didn't guess. This egg is raw *(break the egg into the clear glass bowl.)* It needs cooked before we eat it. We like the egg, but if something isn't done soon, it will start to smell VERY bad.

The second egg is a little different. It had a life changing experience. That might sound funny about an egg, but look what happens when I break it. *(Crack the egg over the same bowl.)* What happened? *(Allow for answers.)* Wait. Look, I can peel away the cracked pieces. What do you think is in here? *(Allow for answers.)* This egg has been cooked inside it's shell. It's been changed, and it can't ever be a raw egg again.

That's a lot like what happens when the Kingdom of God comes inside of us. When we ask Jesus to be our Savior, He changes us. God's Kingdom makes us different and better.

Craft: Heart Pockets   10 Minutes
Supplies: Craft foam, string or lacing, one color page for each student (see last page) hole punch

Use the pattern at the end of this lesson to cut two hearts per student out of the craft foam or allow older students to cut out their own.

Use the hole punch to make holes down both sides of the hearts. Have the children take the string or lacing and sew together the two hearts leaving the top open. You can optionally put a handle or strap between the top two holes if you like. Give each student a color page and allow them to color the words on the color page and cut them out. Discuss what each word means, then put each one inside the heart pocket.

The Teaching Moment: We put a lot of good things inside these cut out hearts. This is to remind us that if God's Kingdom is within us, we need to constantly put good things inside of us. *If you have time, ask the children how they can put these things into their lives:* Love, Faith, Truth, Bible, Jesus and Light. These things will bring us closer to God and help God's Kingdom within us to grow to become the best Kingdom it can be.

WRAPPING IT UP—SENDING IT HOME   5-10 Minutes

Cleaning Up

We want the children to learn to be responsible, so be sure they help with the clean up, but remind them not to go anywhere, the group is going to talk to God together one more time.

Closing Worship and Prayer

Either gather the children in a circle holding hands or allow them to sit down to pray. It's fine if some children prefer not to join the circle. Just ask them to be respectful of others as they pray and not make any noise. You can always begin your prayer time with a quiet song if you like.

As you close, and if there is time, ask the children for their prayer requests. Though no prayer is ever too small, children will tend to keep going and be "inspired" by other prayer requests, so feel free to stop taking requests and tell them they can say anything that didn't get said out loud quietly to God themselves while you're praying.

This week we talked about salvation. So, as we pray, we'll invite the children to accept Jesus as their Savior. You may close with your own prayer or use the one below for help. End with "we pray as Jesus taught us to pray" and the Lord's prayer. The children may be able to pray with you or they can repeat.

If you need some guidance for your prayer, you can use this:

Father in Heaven *(Allow kids to repeat after each phrase. Pause at **.)* You are the King. I am grateful** because Your Kingdom can live inside of me.** I believe that Jesus came to earth ** and died for my sins. ** I believe that He rose from the dead after three days, ** and I believe that because He died and rose, ** your Kingdom can live in my heart. ** Forgive me for my sins. ** Help me to live everyday ** like your kingdom lives in me ** and be my Savior. ** Please bless all of these things the kids have asked prayer for today *(or you can mention them individually)* as we pray the way you taught your disciples to pray: *(End with the Lord's Prayer. You can pray one line at a time so the kids can repeat or let them pray with you.)*

Our Father who art in heaven, hallowed be thy Name. Thy Kingdom come, thy will be done on earth as it is in heaven.
Give us this day our daily bread and forgive us our debts as we forgive our debtors.
Lead us not into temptation and deliver us from evil. For thine is the kingdom and the power and the glory forever, Amen.

Jesus, Teach Me How to Pray
A Year in The Lord's Prayer and other Bible Basics

Unit 3: Thy Kingdom Come
Week 2: The Kingdom of God: What's it Like?

Lesson Overview

Today's Scripture is one of Jesus' explanation of what the Kingdom of God is like. In this passage He tells His disciples that the Kingdom of God is like a mustard seed and yeast. Both of these things are small and very inconsequential. However, they have the power and the potential to become sometime much more. When the Kingdom of God is within us, it starts out small, but if we work it (like yeast) and it's nurtured, (like a mustard tree) it can become big and beautiful.

KEY PHRASE: The Kingdom of God Might Start out Small, But it Grows!

SETTING UP THE LESSON   5 Minutes

Introduction: Little to Big
Supplies: Uninflated balloons, popcorn kernels and microwave popcorn packets, any thing else you can think of that starts out small, but ends up big.

PRESENTING THE LESSON   5-10 Minutes

Scripture: Luke 13:18-21

MAKING IT REAL TO KIDS TODAY   (Choose as many as you have time for)

Craft: Yeast/Sand Art and Mustard Tree   15-20 Minutes
Supplies: Mustard seeds, dry yeast, and very fine bread crumbs (optional), heavy (cardstock or heavier) copies of the tree and bread from the last page of this lesson, crayons or markers, paint brushes & glue

Game: Balloon Frantic   10-15 Minutes
Supplies: One to three balloons inflated for each child

Illustration: Pride Rock   5 Minutes
Supplies: Either *The Lion King Video* or two illustrations of Pride Rock—one from Mufasa's Kingdom and a second from Scar's kingdom

WRAPPING IT UP—SENDING IT HOME   5 Minutes

Clean Up & Prayer Time

KEY PHRASE: The Kingdom of God Might Start Out Small, But it Grows!

SETTING UP THE LESSON   5 Minutes

Introduction: Little to Big
Supplies: Uninflated balloons, popcorn kernels and microwave popcorn, napkins, anything else you can think of that starts our small, but ends up big.

1. *Show the kids the small balloons. If you like, you could have one for each child. Tell them:* Look at this balloon. How big is it? *(Allow for answers.)* How big do you think we can make it? *(Allow for Answers—the kids may know this because they've probably blown up balloons before. If you have enough for everyone, allow them each to blow up their balloon and see how big they can get it without breaking. Do not allow them to go to far. Popped balloons can be dangerous.)* How does something so small get so large? *(Allow for answers - If they start to play too much with the balloons, suggest that if they listen carefully there might be time for a balloon game later.)*

2. *Measure out about 1/4 cup of popcorn kernels and have enough Microwave popcorn popped for each child to have a small handful, but have the popped popcorn hidden from view. Show the kids the 1/4 cup of un-popped popcorn (or 1/4 cup for each bag you popped). Beware of food allergies. Ask the students:* Does anyone know what this is? *(Allow for answers.)* How many people do you think this handful of popcorn will feed? *(Allow for answers.)* What if I told you that every one of us could have a small handful of popped popcorn with just this little bit? *Pass out napkins, bring out the big bowl of popcorn and give each a child sized handful of the popcorn.* You see, just this little bit of popcorn makes a big full bowl, enough for each of us to have some. Today we're going to hear a lesson from the Bible where Jesus talked about little things that became big.

PRESENTING THE LESSON   5-10 Minutes

Scripture Basis: Luke 13:18-21
You may read this directly from the Bible, use the story form below, or reword it to fit your personality

Supplies: a mustard seed (opt.) and a packet of yeast — tortillas and a loaf of bread– Pla-doh (opt.)

Jesus wanted his disciples to understand what the Kingdom of God was like. To help them, He compared it to things they knew a lot about. I showed you a balloon and popcorn because you know all about them. Jesus compared the Kingdom of God to a mustard seed. The people Jesus talked to knew a lot about mustard seeds because they planted them all the time. We don't plant mustard seeds too often around here, we just go to the store and buy our mustard. Do you know what a mustard seed is? *(Allow for answers. If possible, have a mustard seed to show them.)* A mustard seed is a very small seed that becomes a pretty big bush, big enough for birds to land in. Jesus told the disciples, "The Kingdom of God is like a mustard seed that grows and becomes the biggest plant in the garden."

How does such a little seed become a bush taller than some of you? *(Allow for responses and lead them through these steps. Ask things like "What do you have to do first?" If they miss a step ask, "Is that really what you do next?")*

1. Plant the seed
2. Water the seed
3. Fertilize the seed
4. Keep the weeds away
5. Make sure it gets a lot of sun

How fast will the seed grow? *(Allow for answers.)* It takes all summer for the mustard seed to become big enough to turn into mustard. Do you think the seed grow if it doesn't get water, fertilizer, and sun? *(Help the kids understand that the seed won't grow without a lot of work and nurturing.)* Growing any kind of garden takes a lot of energy.

Jesus told His disciples that the Kingdom of God was like one more thing. He said it was like yeast. Do you know what we use yeast for? *(Allow for answers.)* Yeast is what the baker puts in bread to make it get really fluffy. Without yeast it stays flat like a tortilla or taco shell. *(Show the tortilla if you have one.)* But when she adds yeast the bread looks soft and fluffy.

KEY PHRASE: The Kingdom of God Might Start Out Small, But it Grows!

The baker takes the yeast *(You might open a packet of dry yeast and dump it in a small bowl to let the children see what it looks like)* and puts it in warm water. The warm water and the yeast work together and it begins to grow. Then the baker adds it to the flour and water and butter, and mixes it. *(If you have a can of play-doh, you might bring it out and pretend to knead dough.)* They don't just stir the dough, they knead it. Can you say, "knead the dough"? *(Allow them to repeat.)* That's what the baker does. He squashes it and turns it and squashes it and turns it. He keeps squashing and turning the dough until the yeast is mixed in every part. Then he lets the dough sit in a warm place for a while and kneads it again before he puts it in a bread pan and into the oven. After it's baked, it looks like a real loaf of bread. *(Show bread if you have one.)*

Do you remember last week's lesson? Where did we say the Kingdom of God is? *(Allow for responses).* The Kingdom of God is inside of us, in our heart. When we pray to ask God to put His Kingdom in our heart, it starts out small, like the mustard seed or the little tiny pieces of yeast.

When we pray the Lord's prayer and say, "Thy Kingdom Come," we're asking God to put His Kingdom in our hearts. But like the mustard tree, when God plants the Kingdom of God in our heart, we have to take care of it. We need to water it by praying and putting good things in it like Sunday School, Children's Church and reading our Bibles. We have to keep the weeds out. How do you think we'd keep the weeds out of our lives? *(Allow for answers.)* We have to choose friends who help us do the right things and make sure our video games, music, and TV shows don't have bad words or bad ideas.

What about the yeast? How do we put the Kingdom of God in our hearts like yeast? *(Allow for answers.)* Just like the yeast has to be worked through the flour and shortening, the Kingdom of God needs worked through our heart. We need to study the Bible and pray and work at being Jesus' friend so the Kingdom of God will grow in us.

And just like the bush grows tall and the yeast that makes the bread rise up, the Kingdom of God will grow big inside of us if we take care of it and work it. How big do you think the Kingdom of God can get in your life? Let's stand up and make yourself look like a big bush. Show me how big you can get. *(Stand with the kids and show them how to make themselves great big like a tree.)*

MAKING IT REAL TO KIDS TODAY

Craft: Mustard Seed Trees or Yeast Art loaves of Bread   15-20 Minutes
Supplies: Mustard seeds, dried green peas or lentils, dry yeast and fine dry bread crumbs (optional), heavy (cardstock or heavier) copies of the tree and bread on the last page of this lesson, crayons or markers, paint brushes & glue—You could have the children do one or the other or both depending on your time or supply availability.

MUSTARD SEED TREE: Use a paint brush to cover the yellow flowers with glue, then cover them with mustard seeds.

YEAST ART BREAD: If you have time, let the children color the towel under the bread. Then, much like sand art, paint the loaf of bread with glue, then take the yeast and sprinkle it all over, pour off the excess. If you're using bread crumbs also, make sure they are very fine. Optionally, you could have the children glue only the top or bottom of the bread and sprinkle with the bread crumbs. Then paint the other half with glue and sprinkle it with yeast.

The Teaching Moment: *As the kids are decorating their trees and bread (or after), review the lesson.* What did Jesus the the disciples the Kingdom of God was like? *(Hopefully someone will answer "a mustard seed and yeast.")* Why did Jesus compare the Kingdom of God with a mustard seed and yeast? *(Allow for answers.)* The Kingdom of God may start out small inside of you, but it can grow big like a mustard seed bush and a loaf of bread. Let you picture remind you that the Kingdom of God starts small inside of you, but it has the potential to grow big and be something beautiful like a big tree and wonderful like a fresh loaf of bread.

KEY PHRASE: The Kingdom of God Might Start Out Small, But it Grows!

Game: Balloon Frantic　　　　　　　　　　　　　　　　　　　　　　　10-15 Minutes
Supplies: One to three inflated balloons per person and a stopwatch.

Give each student one balloon, with the rest in a nearby pile. Start a stopwatch, and everyone begins bouncing their balloons in the air. Every five seconds, another balloon is added. See how long the group can keep the balloons in the air before receiving six penalties. A penalty is announced loudly (to create stress) by the leader when a balloon hits the floor, or if you prefer, if is not back into play within five seconds. The leader will shout the penalty number often to create more stress. When the leader gets to "six", time is stopped. After some discussion, the group can try to better the time with another attempt.

The Teaching Moment: Do you think you could have kept all those balloons in the air on your own? *(Allow for answers.)* How did working together make it easier? *(Allow for answers.)* As the number of balloons grew, you needed help to keep them up. The Kingdom of God needs the same kind of work. It is easier to keep growing when you hang out with others who love Jesus and want to help you grow.

Illustration: Pride Rock　　　　　　　　　　　　　　　　　　　　　　　5 Minutes
Supplies: If you have *The Lion King* you could show two different shots of Pride Rock, one when Mufasa was king and a second when scar was king. You'll also find photos here that you could show:
MUFASA'S KINGDOM: https://disney.fandom.com/wiki/Pride_Rock?file=Roca_del_Rey.png
SCAR'S KINGDOM: https://lionking.fandom.com/wiki/Famine?file=Lion-king-disneyscreencaps.com-8497.png

We're going to discuss the difference between the two kingdoms. Ask the children:

What do you notice about these two pictures of pride rock? *(Allow for answers.)* Nothing would grow while Scar was king. Have any of you seen the movie? *(Allow for answers. Assuming someone says yes, ask the next question. Otherwise skip past the question.)* How did it get so ugly while Scar was king? *(Allow for answers.)* Scar didn't know how to take care of a kingdom. He didn't know how to make it grow. Scar was selfish, so the kingdom couldn't grow and become big and beautiful with him in charge.

The Teaching Moment: When we don't allow God to be king in our lives, they get ugly like Scar's kingdom. Fortunately, we don't have to have a lot of God's Kingdom. We just need a small bit of it and if we take care of it by coming to Sunday School and learning more about God, it will grow into something big and beautiful.

WRAPPING IT UP—SENDING IT HOME　　　　　　　　　　　　　　　　5 Minutes

Cleaning Up and Closing Prayer

Gather the children in a circle holding hands or allow them to sit as you pray.

Consider asking for prayer requests as in past weeks, then close with your own prayer or use the one below for help. End with the Lord's prayer. Encourage the children to pray with you.

If you need some guidance for your prayer, you can use this:

Father in Heaven, thank you for telling us about your Kingdom in the Bible. We want your kingdom to grow in us like a mustard seed. Help us to put good things in our lives so your Kingdom will grow into something big and beautiful. Please bless all of these things the kids have asked prayer for today as we pray the way you taught your disciples to pray:

Our Father who art in heaven, hallowed be thy Name. Thy Kingdom come, thy will be done on earth as it is in heaven.
Give us this day our daily bread and forgive us our debts as we forgive our debtors.
Lead us not into temptation and deliver us from evil. For thine is the kingdom and the power and the glory forever, Amen.

The Kingdom of God is like a Mustard Seed

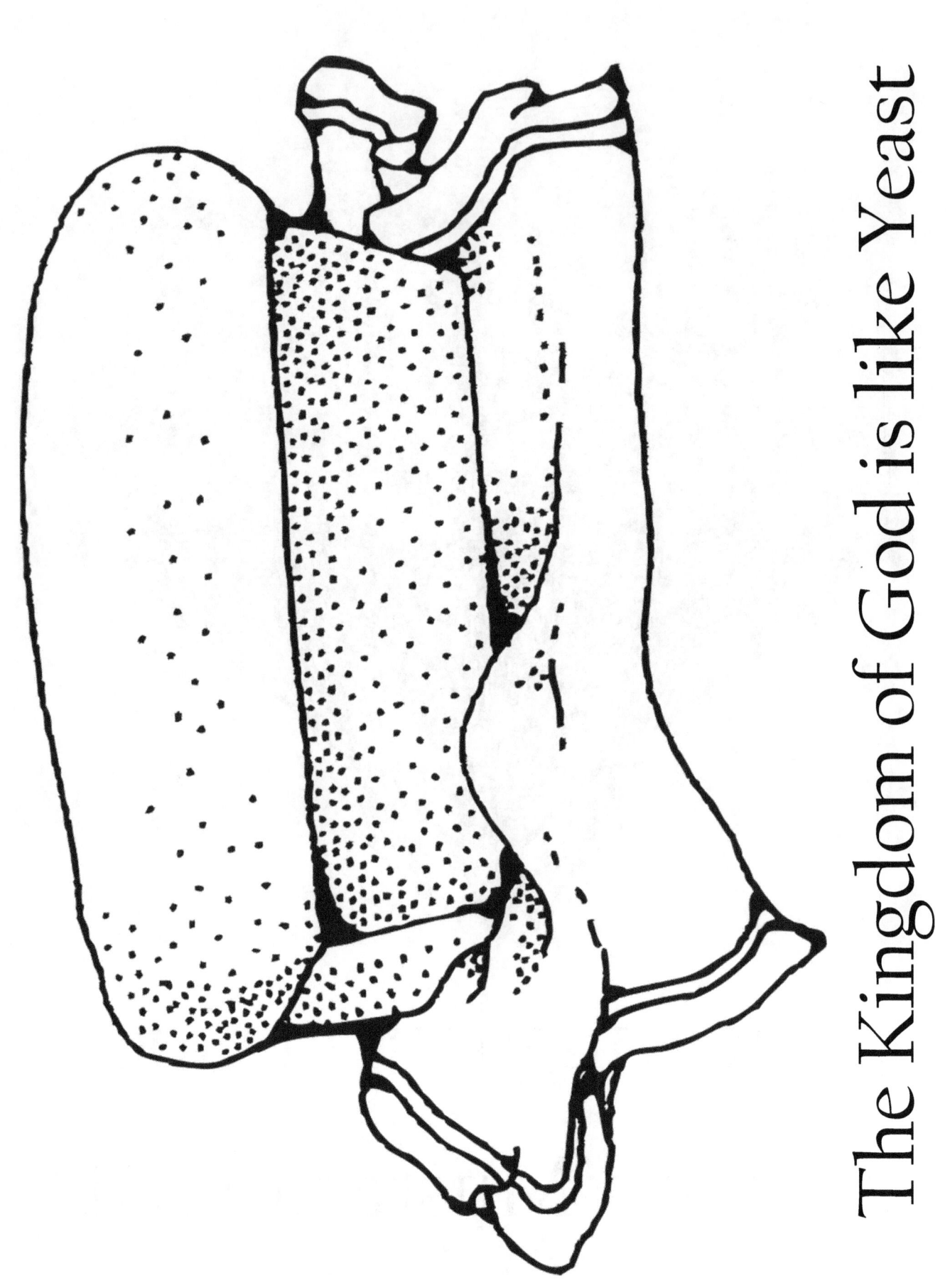

The Kingdom of God is like Yeast

Jesus, Teach Me How to Pray

A Year in The Lord's Prayer and other Bible Basics

Unit 3: Thy Kingdom Come
Week 3: The Kingdom of God: It IS for Kids!

Lesson Overview

These kids are probably all in a hurry to grow up. It's just a fact. Until we're twenty-something we want to get older, But today's lesson reminds us that Jesus said our attitude has to be childlike in order to inherit the Kingdom of God.

KEY PHRASE: The Kingdom of God Belongs to the Kids!

SETTING UP THE LESSON   5-7 Minutes

Introduction: The things kids can't do!
Supplies: Car keys, BIG knife, other items that kids would not be old enough to use (no liquor, cigarettes or adult movies, please).

PRESENTING THE LESSON   5-7 Minutes

Scripture: Luke 18:15-17

MAKING IT REAL TO KIDS TODAY   *(Choose as many as you have time for)*

Game: The Can Do Game—There are lots of things kids CAN do!   5-10 Minutes
Supplies: Bean bags (corn hole bags would work), 2 bowls, 12-20 cans or boxes (all the same size), 12 wiffle balls, 2 buckets, masking tape

Illustration: The "Can Do" Chart—More things kids CAN do!   7-10 Minutes

Video: The Lion King: I Just Can't Wait to Be King   5 Minutes

WRAPPING IT UP—SENDING IT HOME   5-7 Minutes

Clean Up Time & Prayer Time

KEY PHRASE: The Kingdom of God Belongs to the Kids!

SETTING UP THE LESSON 5-7 Minutes

Introduction: The things kids can't do!
Supplies: Car keys, BIG knife, matches, other items that kids would not be old enough to use (no liquor, cigarettes or adult movies, please).

Pull out the car keys, show them to the kids, pretend you don't know whose they are. Ask one student if they belong to them. Then another. When several say no, ask who they might belong to. Ask, "Don't they belong to one of you?" Then "Why Not?" and allow for answers.

Continue with similar questions for the knife and/or anything else you might have that would be best if kids didn't have access. Remember not to use anything that they probably should avoid even as adults.

When you've shown them everything, ask "Can't you do anything?" Hopefully, they'll get a little indignant and tell you all the things they can do. If they don't, get them started . . . "You probably can't even turn on the TV or clean your room."

Close the introduction by sharing this: "Jesus' disciples didn't think kids could do much. In fact, they didn't think kids should even come around Jesus, but listen to what Jesus said"

PRESENTING THE LESSON 5-10 Minutes

Scripture: *Luke 18:15-30*
You do not have to read this directly from the Bible— use the story form below or reword it to fit your personality

Once when Jesus was teaching the people about God, a lot of moms and dads brought their babies and kids your age so Jesus could touch them. These moms and dads knew that Jesus was God's Son, and they wanted Him to put a special blessing on their kids. But the disciples thought Jesus was too busy and important for the kids. The disciples knew Jesus was the Son of God, too. But they thought that meant He was too busy for kids. The disciples started to send the parents away, but Jesus stopped them. He told them to bring ALL the children to him because the "Kingdom of God" belongs to people who were like children.

What do you think Jesus meant when He said that the Kingdom of God belonged to people like kids? *(Allow for answers.)* Do you think he meant people who throw fits or fight with their brothers and sisters? *(Allow for answers.)* Jesus meant that He wanted people who didn't think they were too grown up to have fun and trust God. Sometimes grown-ups get so worried about what other people think they forget to have fun. And how many of you always want to "do it yourself"? *(Raise your hand to show them they should raise their hands.)* That's one of the first symptoms of being a grown up. Think about the two-year-olds you know. They don't mind getting help. But grownups get so big they quit asking for help. When we quit asking God for help, we can't have the Kingdom of God.

Do you know that besides being your mom & dad's kid you are also God's kid? Did you know that even *I* am God's kid? God wants us to never forget we are His kids. And sometimes when we try to be too grownup we forget that we are God's kid.

When Jesus was talking to the kids, a rich man came up and asked him how humans could live with God forever. Jesus told Him to give away everything He had. Jesus wanted him to trust God instead of his things. Could you give away everything you have? *(Allow for answers.)* That's hard to do, and the more grownup you get, the harder it is==maybe because you have less stuff when you're still a kid! Jesus said it's hard for people with a lot of stuff to get into the Kingdom of God.

There might be a lot of things you can't do because you're a kid, but don't worry, you'll grow up and be able to do all kinds of amazing things. In fact, God has a wonderful plan for you as you grow. But there are some ways you need to stay like a kid even when you grow up. In fact grownups need to always remember to ask God for help, listen to Him the same way you should listen to your parents, and never worry about what other people think. God wants us to never stop having fun or become afraid to tell people about Jesus. Remember that Jesus said the Kingdom of God belongs to people who know they are God's kids.

KEY PHRASE: The Kingdom of God Belongs to the Kids!

MAKING IT REAL TO KIDS TODAY

Game: The Can Do Relay 5-10 Minutes
Supplies: Bean bags (corn hole bags would work), 2 bowls, 12-20 cans or boxes (all the same size), 12 wiffle balls, 2 buckets, masking tape

Before the game, set up the relay—Use a long section of your room to make 2 playing fields (pictured below)—place a piece of masking tape on the floor with 6 waffle balls. About 2 feet from the tape place the bucket, about 2 feet from the bucket place 6-10 cans/boxes (not stacked)—about 2-3 feet from the cans/boxes place another piece of masking tape and then the bean bags and bowl. You should have two rows that look something like this:

When it's time to play the game, line the children up from youngest to oldest. Ask them to count off 1-2, 1-2, 1-2— All the 1's will be on a team and all the 2's will be on a team. This system should help you to spread out the younger kids with the older. This is a relay, begin with the older kids so the younger ones will see what they are supposed to do a few times. The first player on each team should stand by the first piece of masking tape with a wiffle ball in his hand. When you say go, they should try to throw the six balls in the bucket. They need to keep trying until they get them all in. Once all the balls are in, they move on to the cans/boxes and stack them as pictured above. (be sure to demonstrate how they should stand and then take the stack down). After all the cans are stacked, they should move on to the bean bag game and toss at least three bean bags into holes. They'll need to keep trying until all bean bags go into the hole. As soon as they get the bean bags in the hole, they can go back and take the cans apart (remind them to do it neatly so the next person will have an easy time collecting them to make the stack again) and then take the whiffle balls and put them back at the masking tape. Finally, they run back and tag the next person in the line. If one team has one less player instruct the first person to go last to even things out. The team who gets all the kids through the line quickest is the winner.

If you have a very small group, use 1/2 the supplies to set up one relay line and time each student. The fastest one wins. If you have a large gap in ages, take one second off the time of the younger players for every year he or she is younger than the oldest student. For instance a four-year-old would get eight seconds off his time if you have a twelve-year-old.

The Teaching Moment: *(You may want to share this before you play the game)* Even though you are young and there is a lot you can't do, these are four stages that you can complete. By doing your best, you will help your team win *(or be the fastest)*, plus you'll have fun! Grownups sometimes begin to say "I can't" or "I don't want to." Jesus said the Kingdom belongs to kids because He knew kids will keep trying and trying until they can get it right. Kids don't give up or get mad when they mess up because they know it takes time to learn to do something as good as an adult. As part of the Kingdom of God, we need to keep trying and keep trusting in God.

Video: *The Lion King* - Near the beginning, Simba sings, "I just can't wait to be King." 5 Minutes
If you don't own the video, borrow it from someone at your church, rent it at a video store or borrow it from the local library. This clip is also available on YouTube.

The Teaching Moment: Why would Simba think he would get to be King? *(Because His dad was king.)* Simba was just a kid. He liked having fun. But he knew that he was the King's son, so He acted like it. When God's Kingdom is within us, then we are sons and daughters of God (the King). We should make sure that God's Kingdom is real in our hearts and then act like we are children of the King. Who is the King? *(Allow for answers.)* Yes, God is our King. What do you think it means to "act" like a child of God? *(Allow for answers.)* A child of God tells the truth and tries his best to be kind to people. A child of God follows God and worships Christ.

KEY PHRASE: The Kingdom of God belongs to the kids!

Illustration: The "Can Do" Chart 7-10 Minutes
Supplies: Pens or Pencils—Copies of the chart at the end of this lesson

We already talked about the things that you CAN'T do because your still a bit young. So now we're going to talk about some things you CAN do.

Give each child a copy of the "Can Do" chart. Help them think of things they can do and write the list in the first column. Suggest things like read my Bible (or have someone read my Bible to me), pray, pick up my toys, make my bed, fold socks, dry dishes, tell someone about Jesus, etc. Accept anything worthwhile the kids come up with. Allow younger children to draw pictures of what they'll do. Then encourage the kids to take their chart home, hang it in their room or on the fridge and then make a check mark each day they complete the task. If you're likely to remember, you could offer a mini candy bar or something next week to every child who brings their chart back to you with at least 20 squares checked (or any standard you set).

The Teaching Moment: Help the children understand that although they are too young to do some things, they are still big enough to do a lot of things including worship Christ and follow God. On this chart are just a few of the things they can do to help them honor Christ. This would be a good opportunity to explain how to be saved (*see intro in the front of the book*). Be sure they know they are not too young to ask forgiveness for the things they do that don't honor Christ, accept Jesus' sacrifice on the Cross to pay for those things they do wrong and ask Jesus to be their Savior.

WRAPPING IT UP—SENDING IT HOME 5—7 Minutes

Cleaning Up

We want the children to learn to be responsible, so be sure they help with the clean up, but remind them not to go anywhere, the group is going to talk to God together one more time.

Closing Worship and Prayer

Either gather the children in a circle holding hands or allow them to sit down to pray. It's OK if some children prefer not to join the circle. Ask them to be respectful of others as they pray and not make any noise. You can always begin your prayer time with a quiet song if you like.

As you close, and if there is time, ask the children if they have any prayer requests. You may close with your own prayer or use the one below for help. End with "we pray as Jesus taught us to pray" and the Lord's prayer—for these first few weeks allow the kids to repeat after you. Encourage the helper to pray with the kids.

If you need some guidance for your prayer, you can use this:

Father in Heaven (*You might allow kids to repeat after each phrase*), thank you for telling us about your Kingdom in the Bible. We want to be a part of your Kingdom. We get in a hurry to grow up sometimes, but help us to always remember that we are your children, and we'll never be too big to ask for your help or follow you. Please bless all of these things the kids have asked prayer for today (*or you can mention them individually*) as we pray the way you taught your disciples to pray:

Our Father who art in heaven, hallowed be thy Name. Thy Kingdom come, thy will be done on earth as it is in heaven.
Give us this day our daily bread and forgive us our debts as we forgive our debtors.
Lead us not into temptation and deliver us from evil. For thine is the kingdom and the power and the glory forever, Amen.

MY "CAN DO" CHART

DAY THINGS I CAN DO	Sunday	Monday	Tuesday	Wednesday	Thursday	Friday	Saturday

Page intentionally left blank for printing and copying purposes

Jesus, Teach Me How to Pray
A Year in The Lord's Prayer and other Bible Basics

Unit 4: Thy Will Be Done
Week 1: Abraham Did God's Will

Lesson Overview

Today we're going to begin to help the children understand "Thy Will be Done." This can be a difficult phrase for even adults to comprehend. Abraham is a very good example of someone who does God's will. We'll look at several examples of how Abraham obeyed God, and God credited to it to him as being righteous. In fact, in the New Testament, James tells us that Abraham was called God's friend because he did God's will.

KEY PHRASE: Abraham Did What God Said and God Called Him Friend

SETTING UP THE LESSON   5-7 Minutes

Game: Simon Says

PRESENTING THE LESSON   5-10 Minutes

Scripture: Genesis 12:1-5; 15:1-6; 17:9-27; 22:1-18; Hebrews 11:8-19; James 2:23

MAKING IT REAL TO KIDS TODAY   *(Choose as many as you have time for)*

Memory Verse: James 2:23   3-5 Minutes
Supplies: Paper (half or quarter sheet for each student) and Pencils

Craft: Create a Covenant   5-10 Minutes
Supplies: Copies of the Covenant on the last page of this lesson

Illustration: What is a friend?   5 Minutes
Supplies: Half sheets of paper and pencils

Song: "I am a Friend of God" by Michael Gungor & Israel Houghton   5-10 Minutes

WRAPPING IT UP—SENDING IT HOME   5-7 Minutes

Clean Up Time & Prayer Time

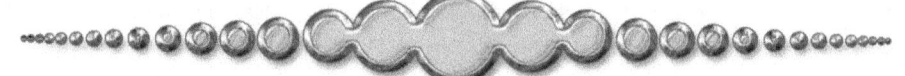

KEY PHRASE: Abraham Did What God Said and God Called Him Friend

SETTING UP THE LESSON   5-7 Minutes

Game: Simon Says

To set up today's lesson, play a traditional game of Simon Says.

In case you've forgotten how to play the game: Have one of the leaders or an older helper be "Simon." Instruct the kids that when the leader says: "Simon Says" they should do what the leader says. When the leader gives a command without saying, "Simon Says" they should continue to do the previous action. When a child messes up they sit out. Play until only one child is left or time is up. The beauty of "Simon Says" is that if you have a very small class area, you can do it sitting at a table or on the floor. Use commands like clap your hands or stick out your tongue.

The Teaching Moment: *Ask the kids:* What parts of the Lord's Prayer have we covered so far. *(Allow for answers)* For the last few weeks we've talked the first few lines, "Our Father, which art in heaven, hallowed be Thy name, and Thy Kingdom come." Do you remember what the next line is? *(Allow for answers)* The next line is "Thy Will Be Done on Earth as it is in Heaven." When we did the things that "Simon" said, we were doing Simon's "will." When we say "Thy Will be Done on Earth as it is in Heaven," we're telling God we want everything on Earth to be done just like God says. Today we're going to hear about a follower of God who did what God said better than most people.

PRESENTING THE LESSON   5-10 Minutes

Scripture: Genesis 12:1-5; 15:1-6; 17:9-27; 22:1-18; Hebrews 11:8-19; James 2:23
You do not have to read this directly from the Bible— use the story form below or reword it to fit your personality

The Bible tells us about a man who really lived named Abraham. Abraham followed God very well. He did whatever God told him to. One time God told him to pack up everything and move. Abraham didn't ask where he should go or why he was moving, he just packed up his family and his servants and started going the direction God told him. He didn't know where God wanted him to move, but he headed out. Abraham and his family went exactly where God told them to go and ended up in a place called Canaan.

Abraham and his wife, Sarah, didn't have any children. They prayed and prayed to have a baby, but it never happened. Finally, when Abraham was more than eighty years old, God told him that his wife Sarah was going to have a baby. Do you know anyone who is more than eighty years old? *(Allow for answers—encourage them to think of people in your church or great grandparents who might be older.)* Do you think they would believe it if God told them they were going to have a baby? *(Allow for answers.)* Most people that old don't have babies. But Abraham believed God. He believed that God was able to make him a daddy. The Bible said that God called Abraham his friend because he believed God when God told him something that seemed impossible was going to happen.

Then when Abraham was ninety-nine years old, God, said He wanted to make a covenant with Abraham. Do you know what a covenant is? *(Allow for answers.)* A covenant is a promise or an agreement. It's like a contract between two people. Today people sign contracts when one person promises to pay money and the other promises to do a special job for the money. They write down everything they promise to do, and then both people sign it. In the Bible when two people made a covenant, they did something to show they were serious about their promise. Sometimes when they made an agreement to sell a house or a piece of land, the person buying the land gave the other person his sandal in front of their friends to show his promise. God asked Abraham to promise to always follow Him and teach his children to always be the people of God. Abraham did what God asked. To show that he intended to keep his promise, he did exactly what God asked so everyone would know he made the promise. *(Because Abraham entered into this covenant by circumcising all the males in his company, it would be wise to not allow too much time for discussion here. This can be a difficult topic to discuss and probably should be left to parents.)*

Finally, when Abraham was more than 100 years old, God asked Abraham to give his only son Isaac to him forever. This meant that Abraham would never see his son ever again. Would you be sad if you never got to

KEY PHRASE: Abraham Did What God Said and God Called Him Friend

see your mom or dad again? *(Allow for answers.)* Abraham was very sad, but he told God he would do it. God asked him to bring Isaac up on a mountain and give Isaac to God. So Abraham took Isaac up on Mt. Moriah. There he was ready to give his son to God forever. That was going to be the hardest thing that Abraham had ever done. But when Abraham and Isaac got to the mountain, God sent an angel to tell Abraham that now God knew Abraham loved him more than anything since he was willing to give his only son to God. The angel told Abraham since he was willing to do exactly what God said, he didn't have to give God his son, he could take his son home.

Abraham really was a true follower of God. He knew what it meant to say to God, "Thy Will Be Done." Do you remember what the Bible said God called Abraham because he listened to God. *(Allow for answers.)* James 2:23 tells us that because Abraham believed God, God called Abraham his friend.

MAKING IT REAL TO KIDS TODAY *(Choose as many as you have time for)*

Memory Verse: James 2:23 3-5 Minutes
Supplies: Paper (half or quarter sheet for each student) and Pencils

Abraham believed God, *** and it was credited to him as righteousness," ***
and he was called God's friend.
James 2:23

Have the children repeat this verse several times. Pause at the *** so they can easily repeat after you. Encourage kids to write the verse on the paper. Invite younger students to draw a picture of themselves with God as their friend.

The Teaching Moment: *Ask the kids:* What does it mean to be righteous? *(Allow for answers. Help kids understand that righteousness means doing God's will.)* How did Abraham show that he believed God? *(Allow for answers.)* Abraham put his faith into action. He did whatever God asked him to. That proves our belief in God more than anything else. And what does God call the people who believe Him and do His will? *(Allow for answers)* God calls people who do His will His friends.

Craft: Create a Covenant 5-10 Minutes
Supplies: Copies of the Covenant on the last page of this lesson (*You can put them on parchment if you'd like it to be very special, but plain paper will be fine also.*)

Abraham made a covenant with God. He promised to always obey God and teach his children to be God's special people, and God promised to bless Abraham's children in a special way as long as they kept their promise to be his special people. Today we're going to look at some of the things in the Bible that God has asked us to do, and we're going to sign a covenant with God—a promise to do what He asks. *Pass out the covenants*

You'll read Deuteronomy 5:16, Malachi 3:10, John 15:7, and Hebrews 13:5

Take a few moments to talk about each of the four verses mentioned.

- *Read Deuteronomy 5:16:* Honor your father and your mother, as the LORD your God has commanded you, so that you may live long and that it may go well with you in the land the LORD your God is giving you. *Ask the children what it means to honor parents.*

- *Read Malachi 3:10:* Bring the whole tithe into the storehouse, that there may be food in my house. Test me in this," says the LORD Almighty, "and see if I will not throw open the floodgates of heaven and pour out so much blessing that there will not be room enough to store it. *Ask the children if they know what a "tithe" is? (10% or one dime from every dollar) Help them see that they can "tithe" their birthday money and extra money they get from grandparents, etc.*

KEY PHRASE: Abraham Did What God Said and God Called Him Friend

- *Read John 15:7:* f you remain in me and my words remain in you, ask whatever you wish, and it will be done for you. Talk to the children about what it means to remain in God and really trust God. When we remain in God, we stay close to Him by reading His Word and going to church often so we can learn more about Him.

- *Read Hebrews 13:5:* Be content with what you have, because God has said, "Never will I leave you; never will I forsake you. Discuss briefly what it means to be happy with what we have. Remind them when we always want more, it doesn't honor God..

Help the children pick at least one verse and put a check mark by it. They can choose more than one. Encourage them to take their covenant home and talk about it with their parents, then have their parents witness it. Explain that every contract and covenant had at least one person who watched the person promise to keep the covenant. Tell them it would be good to have their parents "witness" the contract/covenant.

Illustration: What is a Friend?   5 Minutes
Supplies: Half sheets of paper and pencils

Give each of the kids a half sheet of paper and ask them to write the names of three of their friends. Tell them it doesn't have to be spelled correctly, and the littler ones can just write the first letter of their friends' names if they can't spell yet. After just a minute or two, ask them why each of those people are their friends. After you've heard some of their reasons, ask how it makes them feel that God wants to be their friend. Remind them that God loves them and wants to hear them talk to Him, just like their school friends. Ask them if they talk to God as often as they talk to those friends. Help them see that when they "do God's will," God will call them His friend.

Song: "Friend of God" by Michael Gungor and Israel Houghton   5-10 Minutes

Get a recording of this song and play it while the kids do their covenant or just let them listen to it after you talk about what a friend is. You could also have them sing the chorus (or perhaps the whole song—it's pretty easy) with the recording if you have extra time.

VERSE: Who am I , you are mindful of me, that you hear me when I call?
   Is it true, you are thinking of me? How you love me. It's a amazing . . .

CHORUS: *I am a friend of God, I am a friend of God, I am a friend of God, He calls me friend*

The Teaching Moment: *In James 2:23, it says: "Abraham believed God . . . And God called him friend." Have children repeat it with you once again. Singing this song can remind us that God wants to be our good friend.*

WRAPPING IT UP—SENDING IT HOME   5-7 Minutes

Cleaning Up

We want the children to learn to be responsible, so be sure they help with the clean up, but remind them not to go anywhere, the group is going to talk to God together one more time.

Closing Worship and Prayer

As you close, and if there is time, you may take prayer requests. Close with your own prayer or use the one below for help. Encourage them to pray "The Lord's Prayer" with you.
Father in Heaven. Your name is so wonderful. We want your will to be done in our lives. Help us to know what you want us to do and then give us the courage to do what you ask, like Abraham. We want to be your friend just like Abraham. Lord, bless all of the things these kids have mentioned as prayer requests today (*if there's time, you can mention some of their requests*). We pray all of these things in Jesus' name, who taught us to pray: *(See the Lord's Prayer in the margin.)*

Our Father who art in heaven, hallowed be thy Name. Thy Kingdom come, thy will be done on earth as it is in heaven. Give us this day our daily bread and forgive us our debts as we forgive our debtors. Lead us not into temptation and deliver us from evil. For thine is the kingdom and the power and the glory forever, Amen.

MY COVENANT WITH GOD

Abraham made a covenant with God

A promise to always serve God and to teach his sons and daughters to be the people of God.

Abraham believed God . . . God called Him "friend" - James 2:23

Name _____

Promises to always try to do God's will (do what God says) in this verse:

Please check the verse or verses that you'd like to promise God you will try very hard to keep

☐ **My Promise**: Honor My Father and My Mother
   God's Promise: It will go well with me   Deuteronomy 5:16

☐ **My Promise**: To Give God a full tithe (10%) of everything I get
   God's Promise: To pour out His blessing on me   Malachi 3:10

☐ **My Promise**: To "remain" in God (trust Him, read His word and pray)
   God's Promise: He'll give me what I ask   John 15:7

☐ **My Promise**: Don't love money, be happy with what God gives me.
   God's Promise: Never to leave me alone   Hebrews 13:5

SIGNED: _____

Your signature here

DATE: _____

WITNESSED: _____

Parent signs here

WITNESSED: _____

Parent signs here

Page intentionally left blank for printing and copying purposes

Jesus, Teach Me How to Pray
A Year in The Lord's Prayer and other Bible Basics

Unit 4: Thy Will Be Done
Week 2: Jesus Did God's Will

Lesson Overview

Today's scripture focuses on Jesus' baptism. Traditionally, the church celebrates Jesus' baptism on the second Sunday of January. If you have a program that begins in September, this lesson could easily fall on or around that Sunday. If so, you may want to mention this to the children.

Jesus' baptism is the beginning of his earthly ministry. Today we're going to focus on the "why" of Jesus' baptism. He obviously didn't need John's "baptism of repentance," He didn't need to be baptized into the faith. But Jesus said He needed to do it to "fulfill all righteousness." In other words, Jesus needed to be baptized to do God's will and do what His Father says. In today's lesson, in addition to talking about Jesus doing God's will, we'll also briefly discuss baptism.

KEY PHRASE: Jesus Did What God Said and God Said He Was Pleased

SETTING UP THE LESSON   5-7 Minutes

I Am Pleased
Supplies: List of good things the kids have done in the past couple weeks. See next page for full description.

PRESENTING THE LESSON   10 Minutes

Scripture: Matthew 3

MAKING IT REAL TO KIDS TODAY   *(Choose as many as you have time for)*

Game: Twister   7-10 Minutes
Supplies: One Twister game for every 6-10 kids (ask around your church, you'll probably have several folks who will loan you one for the day) If you have a small space you could buy or create a mini Twister game to use on the table top.

Craft: Paper Dove   10-15 Minutes
Supplies: White Paper Doilies or a 7-9" white circle for each child

Video: Baptism video from YouTube or your church   5 Minutes

WRAPPING IT UP—SENDING IT HOME   5-7 Minutes

Clean Up Time & Prayer Time

KEY PHRASE: Jesus Did What God Said and God said He Was Pleased

SETTING UP THE LESSON
5-7 Minutes

Illustration: I Am Pleased
Supplies: If you have time, call each student's parents or guardians and ask them to tell one thing their child has done in the past seven days that "pleased" them. This would preferably be a time when the child did something the adult asked him or her to do or acted in a way they knew their parent would approve. For children whose parents you can't get in touch with or whose parents won't participate, you could ask a grandparent or teacher. Otherwise, you can write something for each student. Either way, create one piece of paper for each student with the answer to that question— "What has the student done to "please" a respected adult?" Then fold and seal the paper so they can't read it until you tell them to. If you have guests, try to remember to ask the adult they come with before church begins.

As you begin your lesson time, pass out the pieces of paper. Have each child read their notes. Ask them if they remembered doing the thing written on the paper. After each child has had a chance to read their paper, talk about how it feels when you are able to please someone. Allow kids to share what it feels like when they are pleased. Then move on to the story.

PRESENTING THE LESSON
5-10 Minutes

Scripture: Matthew 3

You do not have to read this directly from the Bible— use the story form below or reword it to fit your personality

When Jesus was about 30 years old, He knew it was time to begin to tell everyone about His Heavenly Father. Before He started this important job, there was one thing He had to do. Jesus knew He had to go down to the river and see His cousin, John.

John was different than most people. He wore clothes made out of camel hair. Do you know what camel hair is? *(Allow for answers.)* It's the hair off of a camel. Do you think it would be soft or itchy? *(Allow for answers.)* The Bible says John only ate locusts and wild honey. What are locusts? *(Allow for answers—There is a picture of a locust on the last page of this lesson)* Locusts are big hard shelled bugs. Do you think you'd like to eat locusts? *(Allow for answers.)* John was very different.

When Jesus went to see John, John was telling everyone that the Kingdom of God was near. Do you remember what the Kingdom of God is? *(Allow for answers.)* Maybe you remember that the Kingdom of God is wherever God and Jesus rule. John told people they had to repent. To repent means to change and be completely different. John said everyone needed to repent because God's Kingdom was near. He told them they needed to be baptized to show everyone they really had changed. People who had changed and decided to follow God came to John to be baptized. John took them into the river and dipped their heads under the water or poured water over their heads to show everyone they were new and different.

That's what John was doing when Jesus came to be baptized. John knew Jesus. They were cousins. But he also knew that Jesus was God's Son. What had Jesus done wrong that he needed to repent and be baptized? *(Allow for answers.)* Jesus had never done anything wrong, and John knew Jesus was perfect. He didn't need to repent or change. That means Jesus didn't have to be baptized.

But Jesus knew God wanted all of His followers to be baptized to show their dedication to Him. God expects everyone who loves Him to be baptized. And Jesus wanted to always do God's will. So, to follow God and do God's will, Jesus came to John to be baptized.

At first John said, "I can't baptize you, you should baptize me." But Jesus told him, "This is what we have to do to fulfill God's plan." So John baptized Jesus.

John and Jesus walked into the water, and John covered Jesus with water for a moment. As soon as Jesus came up out of the water, a dove came and sat on Jesus. Do you know what a dove is? *(Allow for answers—there is a picture of a dove on the last page of this lesson)* A dove is a quiet white bird. But this dove was the Holy Spirit. God's Spirit came and sat on Jesus, and God spoke in a voice from heaven. "This is my Son. I love Him and I'm pleased with Him." Jesus did God's will, and it pleased God. When we do God's will, God will be pleased with us, too.

KEY PHRASE: Jesus Did What God Said and God said He Was Pleased

MAKING IT REAL TO KIDS TODAY *(Choose as many as you have time for)*

Game: Twister   7-10 Minutes
Supplies: One Twister game for every 6-10 children

Place 2-3 children on each side of each Twister game, go around and alternately name each child either A or B. Using one spinner call out the first spin for kids who you named "A." Spin again for the "B" kids. Keep alternating between the two sets of kids. Remind the children that they are out if they put the wrong hand or foot down or if they fall. They may share a circle with another player. Play for as long as you have time. If you use mini Twister, sharing isn't allowed, and they are out if they can't reach two up to five circles with one hand.

The Teaching Moment: When you do what the "caller" says, you are doing his/her will. We had fun following directions, but in life, it's not always this much fun to do God's will. But just like Jesus when He was baptized, it's important to always do God's will. Do you remember how much fun it is when we play the game and get it right? That's what it feels like to be pleased. When we do what God says, He is pleased.

Craft: Paper Dove   10-15 minutes
Supplies: White paper doilies—one for each child (A white 7"-9" circle would also work)
Found here: http://www.origami-instructions.com/origami-dove.html
(good pictures here if you'd like to see the finished product)

1. Fold the doily or circle in half
2. Fold it in half again, give it a good crease, and unfold it
3. Fold both sides to meet the crease you made
4. Fold it in half on the crease you made in step 2
5. Beginning on the curved side (at the arrow on the illustration), cut a 1.5 to 2" line parallel and about 1" from the open side (not the side where you made the heavy crease) on the dotted line in the illustration.
6. Fold the blackened portion in the illustration up on both sides. Fold along light solid line in the illustration so that the bottom edge meets the heavy line in the illustration
7. Press the front tip in and down to make the head

The Teaching Moment: When Jesus came out of the water after He was baptized, the Holy Spirit came down from heaven in the shape of a dove. This dove can remind you that Jesus was baptized to do God's will, and God said He was pleased.

Video: Baptism Video   5 minutes
Supplies: Check out YouTube for videos of people being baptized or use a video from your church's baptism service. I really liked this one: http://www.youtube.com/watch?v=w9FSzYXMTP0

You could also talk to the kids to see if they've ever seen anyone baptized. Let them share their memories.

The Teaching Moment: Baptism is a person's public announcement that they are a follower of Jesus Christ. When each of the people in the video *(or that the kids have seen)* were baptized, they were asked if they believed that Jesus died on the cross to pay for their sins and that He came alive again three days later. Then they were asked if they were ready to do God's will for the rest of their life. Because they said yes to all of those questions, they could be baptized.

KEY PHRASE: Jesus Did What God Said and God said He was Pleased

WRAPPING IT UP—SENDING IT HOME 5-7 Minutes

Cleaning Up

Even the youngest child is able to help with the clean up. Responsibility is great for a child's self-esteem.

Closing Worship and Prayer

Gather children in a circle holding hands or allow them to sit to pray. If you choose to join hands, remember that it's OK if some children prefer not to join the circle. Remind them to be respectful of others as they pray and not make any noise.

If there is time, ask the children for prayer requests. Remember that no prayer is ever too small, however, children will tend to keep going and be "inspired" by other prayer requests, so feel free to stop taking requests and tell them they can say anything that didn't get said out loud quietly to God themselves while you're praying. You may close with your own prayer or use the one below for help. They should now be able to pray "The Lord's Prayer" with you instead of repeating after you.

If you need some guidance for your prayer, you can use this:

Father in Heaven. We praise Your holy Name. We want Your will to be done in our lives. Help us to do what You want us to do so we can please You. Lord, bless all of the things these kids have mentioned as prayer requests today (*if there's time, you can mention some of their requests*). And Lord, we pray all of these things in Jesus' name, who taught us to pray:

Our Father who art in heaven, hallowed be thy Name. Thy Kingdom come, thy will be done on earth as it is in heaven.
Give us this day our daily bread and forgive us our debts as we forgive our debtors.
Lead us not into temptation and deliver us from evil. For thine is the kingdom and the power and the glory forever, Amen.

Locust

Dove

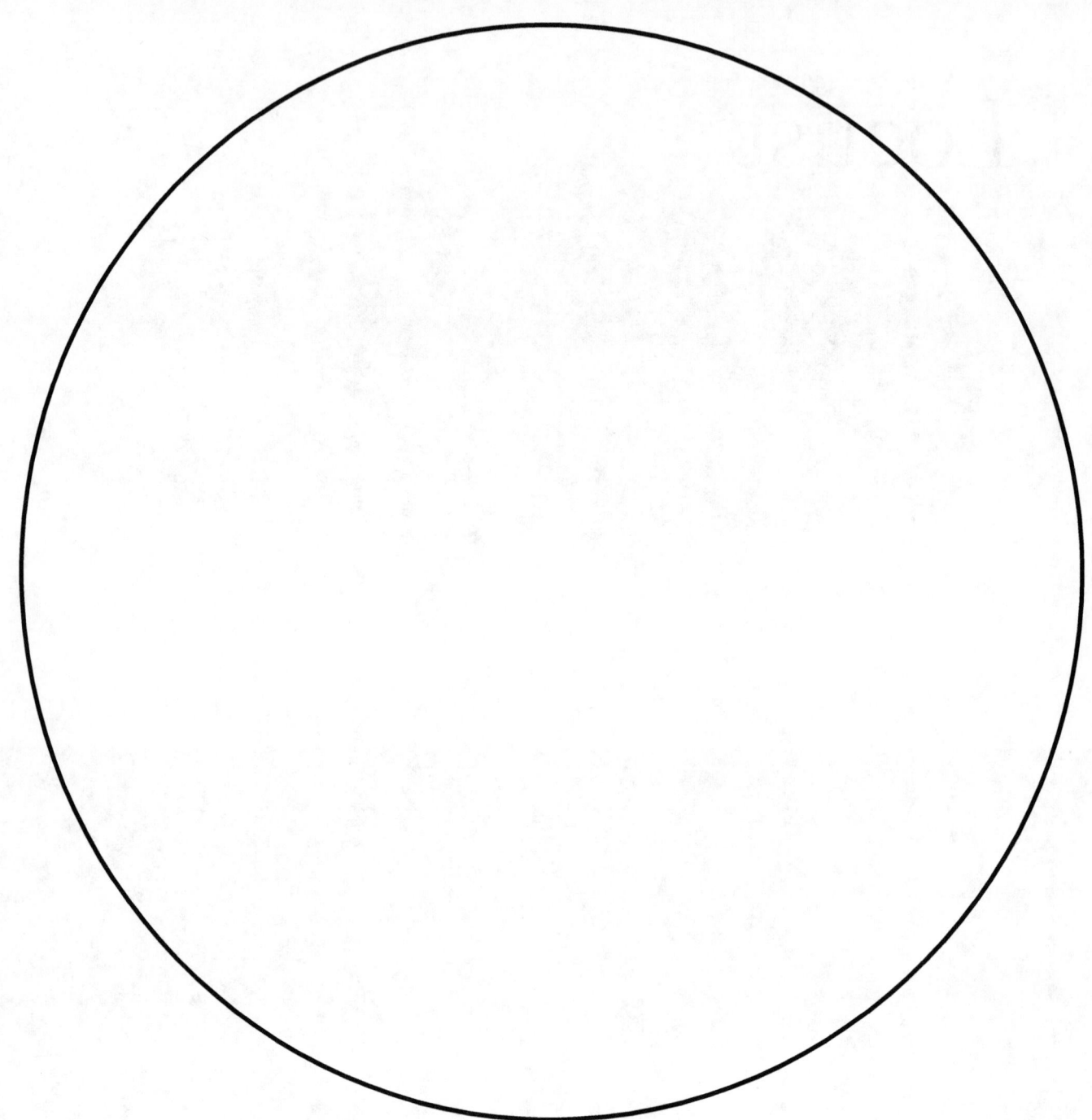

You can use this to make the dove

Jesus, Teach Me How to Pray
A Year in The Lord's Prayer and other Bible Basics

Unit 4: Thy Will Be Done
Week 3: Josiah Did God's Will

Lesson Overview

If you ask folks about the kings of the Old Testament, most will mention David and Solomon. A few more will know about Saul, but few can tell you the names of the men who ruled after Solomon. Following Solomon's rule, the nation of Israel split into two kingdoms. The northern kingdom kept the name Israel, and the southern kingdom took its name from the largest tribe in the area, Judah. Between the reign of Solomon and the time both nations were exiled to Babylon, Israel had only ungodly kings. Judah had fewer ungodly kings than their northern brothers, but they had their share. By the time Josiah became king of Judah at the age of eight, Judah was in pretty bad shape. God had already allowed the Assyrians to take the people of the northern kingdom into captivity, and Josiah's grandfather, Manasseh, was the most evil king Judah had seen. He lured the people into terrible sins. He invited them to worship other gods and brought these gods into the temple of the Living God. Josiah's father was just a bit less evil than Manasseh, but Josiah was nothing like either of them. He was a godly king. When he was twenty-six, he ordered that the temple be cleaned and repaired. When the workers found the books of Moses and Josiah learned just how bad his ancestors had been, he became repentant. He went to extreme measures to be sure the nation of Judah properly worshipped God. Because of his obedience, God promised to bless him and allow the country to live in peace during his time as King.

KEY PHRASE: Josiah Did What God Said and God Blessed Him

SETTING UP THE LESSON   5-7 Minutes

What is a Blessing?
Supplies: Scrap paper, Tootsie Rolls or other small candy (be aware of any food allergies kids may have)

PRESENTING THE LESSON   5-10 Minutes

Scripture: 2 Kings 22:1– 23:25

MAKING IT REAL TO KIDS TODAY   *(Choose as many as you have time for)*

Game: Count Your Many Blessings   5-10 Minutes
Supplies: Newsprint (or large sheets of paper), markers

Craft: The Blessing Book   10-15 Minutes
Supplies: Construction paper, stickers, markers and copies of the pages at the end of this lesson enough for 1 copy for each child.

WRAPPING IT UP—SENDING IT HOME   5-7 Minutes

Clean Up Time & Prayer Time

KEY PHRASE: Josiah Did What God Said and God Blessed Him

SETTING UP THE LESSON   5-7 Minutes

What is a Blessing?
Supplies: Scrap paper, Tootsie Rolls or other small candy (be aware of any food allergies kids may have)

Before the lesson begins, take scraps of paper and ball them up. Scatter it all over the floor of your classroom, creating a mess. As you begin today, ask the kids to do you a favor. Have them help you clean up. Ask them to each pick up at least one piece of the crumpled paper. When they are finished, have them take their seats and thank them for blessing you by helping you clean up. Ask them if they know what a blessing is. *(Allow for answers.)* Help them to see that a blessing is anything that helps make you happy or makes your work easier. Then tell them that because they did what you asked them to do, you want to give them a blessing. Pass out the tootsie rolls or other small candy. Then tell them we're going to talk today about a young boy who did what God said and God blessed him.

PRESENTING THE LESSON   5-10 Minutes

Scripture: 2 Kings 22:1– 23:25
You do not have to read this directly from the Bible— use the story form below or reword it to fit your personality

Many years ago kings ruled in Israel and Judah. Unfortunately, a lot of the kings didn't follow God. They worshipped fake gods and caused everyone in their country to sin against the One True God. One of worst kings in Judah had a grandson named Josiah. Josiah was eight years old when he became King of Judah. How many of you are almost that age? *(Allow for answers.)* Do you think you could be king when you are eight years old? *(Allow for answers.)* Would it be easier if you were nine or ten? *(Allow for answers.)* I don't think so.

The Bible says that Josiah was eight years old when he became king. And then it says that Josiah did what was right in the eyes of the Lord. Josiah had been the first king in a long time to do God's will. Do you remember what it means to do God's will? *(Allow for answers.)* Josiah was the first king in a long time who obeyed God or cared what God wanted. This means the temple hadn't been used, and it needed cleaned and repaired very badly.. Do you know what the temple is? *(Allow for answers.)* The temple was the place where people went to worship the One True God. It was like our church. But other kings before Josiah had taken their fake gods into the temple. They didn't care if the temple stayed nice for the One True God. So when Josiah turned twenty-six, he told the people in charge of the temple it was time to clean it up and make it beautiful for God again.

While the workers were cleaning and repairing the temple, they found some old books. No one had read the books for a long time. They were the first books of the Bible, and in them were all the words God had spoken to Moses many years before. The books had all the instructions God's people need so they can do His will. In fact, they are the first five books of our Bible. Does anyone know the name of those first five books? *(Allow for answers—should be Genesis, Exodus, Leviticus, Numbers & Deuteronomy.)* These books contain the 10 Commandments and other laws God gave His people hundreds of years before Josiah was born. But the people hadn't been following those laws.

When King Josiah heard all the words in those books, he was very sad. What do you do when you're very sad? *(Allow for answers.)* King Josiah was so sad he tore his clothes and wept. Do you know what it means to weep? *(Allow for answers.)* It means he cried hard because he was sorry for how bad Judah had become. King Josiah told the workers and all the people of the kingdom that they had to follow every word they found in those books. Josiah wanted to honor God and do everything he said. The people who were taking care of the temple took out all of the fake gods, and they made sure all the people who didn't worship the One True God were sent away. The Bible says that Josiah followed God with all his heart and all his soul and all his strength.

Because Josiah worked so hard to do God's will, God sent a woman name Huldah to give Josiah a special message. Can you say Huldah? *(Allow the kids to repeat.)* Huldah was a prophetess, a woman who shared God's truth with the people. Huldah told Josiah that God was pleased that Josiah wanted to lead Judah to follow Him the right way. Huldah told Josiah that God promised to bless him with peace while he was king of Judah because he was working to make Judah a holy and right country.

KEY PHRASE: Josiah Did What God Said and God Blessed Him

MAKING IT REAL TO KIDS TODAY
(Choose as many as you have time for)

Game: Count your Many Blessings 5-10 Minutes
Supplies: Newsprint (or large sheets of paper), markers

Divide the kids into two teams balancing older kids with younger kids on each team. Assign the oldest on each team to be the writer for the team. Give each team a sheet of newsprint or another large sheet of paper and a marker. Set a timer for five minutes (or less if you have less time) tell the kids they have until the timer rings to work together to write as many blessings as they can think of. Tell them to be sure to talk quietly so the other team doesn't hear their ideas. To get them started give them two examples: "parents," "allowed to go to school everyday."

When the timer rings, have each team read their blessings out loud one at a time back and forth. Have them cross out any blessing the other team has. The team that has the most <u>not</u> crossed out wins.

The Teaching Moment: It's important that we recognize the blessings of God. It's a good idea to write down our blessings at least once a week so we will appreciate the goodness of God. And when we do "God's will," (what God says), God gives us even more blessings!

Craft: Blessing Book 10-15 Minutes
Supplies: Construction paper, stickers, markers and copies of the pages at the end of this lesson enough for one copy for each child.

1. Give each child one-half sheet of construction paper. Help them fold it in half and decorate the right side (the side that will naturally be the front when folded).
2. Give each child one copy of each of the two sheets at the end of this lesson. Have the kids cut the sheets on the dotted line and then fold them on the solid line.
3. Nest the pages one inside another with the page that says "The Blessing Book" as the first page.
4. Put the piece of construction paper around the outside
5. If you have a long stapler, use it to "saddle-stitch" the booklet (put a staple right in the fold) if not, staple very close to the folded edge, or use a needle and thread to sew the pages together along the fold..

The Teaching Moment: God blessed Josiah because he did God's will. As Christians we can be a blessing to others, and others may want to bless us. Take this book home and ask the adults in your life to write words of blessing for you. You can ask adults in the church to write a blessing for you too. God wants to bless us and use others to bless us, especially when we are living out "Thy Will be Done."

Activity Sheet: God Blesses Those Who Do His Will 3-5 Minutes
Supplies: Activity Sheet on the last page of this lesson and pencils or crayons

Give each child a copy of the activity sheet and explain the instructions at the top of the page. When they've all had an opportunity to complete the activity, if you have extra time, ask the children about each picture. Why does that picture show doing (or not doing) God's Will? Ask them, "Do you think God blesses us when we act like that?"

The Teaching Moment: We know what we should and shouldn't do. When we do what pleases God, it makes Him happy, and He wants to bless us. When we pray God's Will be done, we say we want to please God however we can.

KEY PHRASE: Josiah Did What God Said and God Blessed Him

WRAPPING IT UP—SENDING IT HOME   5-7 Minutes

Cleaning Up

Remind the children helping with the clean up is doing God's Will.

Closing Worship and Prayer

Gather the children in a circle holding hands or allow them to sit down to pray. If you choose to join hands, remember that it's OK if some children prefer not to join the circle. Ask them to be respectful of others as they pray and not make any noise.

If there is time, you could ask for prayer requests. You may close with your own prayer or use the one below for help. They should now be able to pray "The Lord's Prayer" with you instead of repeating after you.

If you need some guidance for your prayer, you can use this:

Father in Heaven. You are a mighty and holy God. Thank you for all your blessings. Help us to do your will in everything we do. We want to be worthy of all you give to us. Lord, bless all of the kids prayer requests. *(If there's time, you can mention some of their requests).* We pray all of these things in Jesus' name, who taught us to pray: (now lead them in the Lord's Prayer)

Our Father who art in heaven, hallowed be thy Name. Thy Kingdom come, thy will be done on earth as it is in heaven. Give us this day our daily bread and forgive us our debts as we forgive our debtors.
Lead us not into temptation and deliver us from evil. For thine is the kingdom and the power and the glory forever, Amen.

The Blessing Book

God loves to bless those who do His will. In addition, Christians have the ability to bless others with our words and prayers. This book is for our Children's Ministry kids to receive blessings from the adults in their lives. If you're reading this, then the child who owns this book would like to receive a blessing from you. Use one of the pages in this book to write a blessing for the child. It can be as simple as "May God bless you" or as elaborate as "I wish you peace and beauty in your life as well as success." Simply give the child kind words and wishes for his or her life.

God Blesses Those Who Do His Will

Put an X across the pictures that show kids NOT doing God's Will
Circle the ones that will please God and bring a blessing.

Page intentionally left blank for printing and copying purposes

Jesus, Teach Me How to Pray
A Year in The Lord's Prayer and other Bible Basics

Unit 5: On Earth as it is in Heaven
Week 1: Worship on Earth Like They Worship in Heaven

Lesson Overview

Humans were created to worship God. It doesn't matter our age, race, occupation or ability. This assignment puts everyone on an even plane. We were created for worship. The two passages of scripture we're reading today describe worship in heaven. Both Isaiah and John had similar visions of heaven. Isaiah wrote his vision almost 800 years before Christ came to earth, while John recorded his vision within the first 100 years after Jesus died. Both saw the "One who sits on the throne" with angels crying out non-stop "holy, holy, holy." We'll use today's lesson to encourage the kids to worship God here on Earth like they do in Heaven.

KEY PHRASE: Let's Worship God on Earth Like They Do in Heaven

SETTING UP THE LESSON   5-7 Minutes

Let's Worship God
Supplies: Kids percussion instruments (Sticks, sand blocks, eggs, tambourines, maracas, castanets, bongo drums, etc—enough for each child to have something) In lieu of instruments, you could clap, snap, or keep beat with hands on the table

PRESENTING THE LESSON   5-10 Minutes

Scripture: Isaiah 6:1-4 & Revelation 4:1-11

MAKING IT REAL TO KIDS TODAY   *(Choose as many as you have time for)*

Game: The Step Race   5-7 Minutes

Craft: Shaker Egg   10 Minutes
Supplies: Plastic eggs OR small "Pringle" cans OR other small plastic container with a lid—Enough for one per person. Colored duct or electric tape, rice, un-popped popcorn, dried peas or plastic confetti. An up-tempo worship song on a CD.

Illustration: Another way to worship   5 Minutes
Supplies: Bibles with the verses marked or copies of the verses on a piece of paper (see the last page of the lesson)

Song: "I Can Only Imagine"   5 Minutes
Supplies: Recording of "I Can Only Imagine" by Mercy Me

WRAPPING IT UP—SENDING IT HOME   5-7 Minutes

Clean Up Time & Prayer Time

KEY PHRASE: Let's Worship God on Earth Like They Do in Heaven

SETTING UP THE LESSON   5-7 Minutes

Let's Worship God
Supplies: Kids percussion instruments (Sticks, sand blocks, eggs, tambourines, maracas, castanets, bongo drums, etc.—enough for each child to have something) In lieu of instruments, you could clap, snap, or keep beat with hands on the table

Teach the kids this simple rhyme. Be sure to have some meter with it so they'll be able to march to it:

Praise God who made the heavens, Praise God who made the trees

Praise God who made the earth, Praise God who made me.

Have all of the kids line up and create a "parade" with the instruments. (This could be done without the parade from a seated or standing position) Encourage the kids to dance and have fun. As they walk around the room a few times give them a beat and then have them repeat their chant while they use their rhythm instruments to keep beat and march around.

ALTERNATE PLAN: you could also pick a couple of songs from a worship CD and either sing along with them, create and use motions to the songs, or use the CD's while the children have their parade.

Teaching Moment: What we just did is called worship. Whenever we spend time focusing on God's goodness and telling God how wonderful He is, that's called worship. We can worship with instruments, words, prayers, songs, dancing or just by being quiet. Anything we do that makes us think about God and shows how important He is in our life is worship.

PRESENTING THE LESSON   5-10 Minutes

Scripture: Isaiah 6:1-4 & Revelation 4:1-11
You do not have to read this directly from the Bible— use the story form below or reword it to fit your personality

God speaks to people constantly. Some hear God's voice. God speaks to others in dreams or visions. Do you know what a vision is? *(Allow for answers.)* A vision is a lot like a dream except usually they come while you're awake. When people have a vision they can picture things God wants to help them see. God gave two men in the Bible very special visions. Their names were Isaiah . . . Can you say Isaiah? *(have kids repeat)* and John. I'll bet you all can say John *(Allow them to repeat to help them remember)*. Isaiah lived more than 700 years before Jesus was born, and John was one of Jesus' disciples. He lived longer than any of the rest of the disciples. Isaiah and John never knew each other, but God gave them both visions of what heaven is like.

Isaiah and John both saw a vision of God seated on a throne. Do you know what a throne is? *(Allow for answers.)* A throne is a very special huge chair made specially for a king or important person. Plus, Isaiah said that the train of God's robe filled the temple. Do you know what a king's robe looks like? *(Allow for answers—if available you could have a long robe or a picture of one. One of the kings from a nativity scene might be a good illustration for this or you could have a kingly looking robe and let the kids try it on)* King's used to wear robes that tied in the front up near the neck. These robes would be long and sometimes the king would have people walk behind him and pick up the back of it to keep the back of it from getting dirty. The part they carried was called the train. Isaiah said he saw the train of God's robe fill the whole temple.

In John's vision he saw 24 leaders from the church sitting in thrones all around God. All of the leaders had crowns on their heads. Both Isaiah and John saw heavenly creatures flying around God's throne. John said the creatures never stopped singing and worshipping God. They always said, "Holy, holy, holy is the Lord Almighty, who was and is and is to come." Can you say that with me? *(repeat "holy, holy holy is the Lord Almighty, who was and is and is to come" …With the children a few times)* John tells us that when the heavenly creatures said those words, the twenty-four leaders of the church who surrounded God, got on their knees in front of God and bowed their head and worshiped God, too. They took off their crowns and threw them in front of God. Then they said, "You are worthy, God. You're worthy of our glory and honor and power. You created

KEY PHRASE: Let's Worship God on Earth Like They Do in Heaven

everything. Everything was created because you wanted it created."

John and Isaiah saw visions of heaven. Both of their visions included heavenly creatures worshipping God every day all day long. We know from Isaiah and John that worship goes on in heaven all the time. In order for God's will to be done "on earth as it is in heaven," God needs to be praised and worshipped here on earth all the time too.

MAKING IT REAL TO KIDS TODAY *(Choose as many as you have time for)*

Game: The Step Race   5-7 minutes

Optional: Mark the floor with thirteen pieces of masking take about one step apart.

If you have a small classroom area, you could give each student a pawn or a button and a ruler to put in front of them on the table. Each time they answer correctly, they can move the button forward one inch.

The Teaching Moment: There are a lot of ways to worship God. Music and words are just a couple of them. Today we're going to play a game to give you a chance to think of ideas of ways to worship God.

Line all the kids up facing you with their feet on the masking tape if you opted to use it. (Or seated around the table if you're using rulers and pawns) Tell the kids you are going to ask questions about ways they can worship God. They'll have just a few seconds to answer, and if they answer correctly, they can move ahead one step.

Beginning with the youngest child, ask each one the first question in the list below. If they have a correct answer, let them move ahead one step. Accept all answers unless someone else has already used it or it's just obviously wrong. Give each child only a few seconds to answer to keep the game moving. After each one has an opportunity to answer, you can ask if anyone has another answer. Kids can move two or more steps for each question. Kids who answer first on one question should answer last on the next question. You can also allow the kids who couldn't answer on the previous question answer the next question first. If a child thinks of something after you pass them, they can give their answer after the last child has had a chance. After you ask the last question, the children that moved the most steps win.

1. Tell me a way you can worship God with words. *(Accept all worship words and words from songs.)*
2. Think of ways you can worship God with your time. *(Anyone they help pleases God and is an act of worship. Singing, reading the Bible, going to church, doing mission work, and more)*
3. What way can you worship God with the things you do? *(Treating friends well, sharing, making things for friends, cleaning bedroom without being asked, doing any chore without being asked—have them specify the chore so everyone has something to add.)*
4. What kind of gifts can you give God? *(money, songs, words of praise, time, hugs to people in the church, smiles for people in church, donating to missions, giving food to food pantries.)*
5. How can you worship God when you are in church? *(sing, follow along in the Bible, listen to the sermon, listen to the lesson, participate in Sunday School, raise hands in praise, pray, clap with the songs, focus on God, dance)*
6. How can you worship God when you are at home? *(Read the Bible, Listen to parents, pray, speak words of praise, tell your parents what you learned in Sunday School, dance to praise songs, listen to praise music, sing with it.)*
7. What about when you are at school? *(Read the Bible during free time, tell friends about Jesus, pray, invite people to church, think about God and Jesus during the day.)*

Craft: Shaker Egg   10 minutes
Supplies: Plastic eggs OR small "Pringle" cans OR other small plastic containers with a lid—one per child. Colored duct or electric tape, rice, popcorn, dried peas or plastic confetti. A fast worship song on a CD.

Give each child a plastic egg or other "holder" as well as enough rice, popcorn, dried peas, or plastic confetti to fill their container a little less than half way. Put the lid on and secure the lid or the egg's middle with colored electric or duct tape. Next, play the CD and let the kids shake their eggs with it. If

KEY PHRASE: Let's Worship God on Earth Like They Do in Heaven

you like to rap, you can use the egg to keep rhythm and let the kids create a rap that worships God.

The Teaching Moment: Did you see how easy that was to make something to help us worship God? We didn't use anything fancy, but it helped us worship. Any time we focus on God, we are worshipping, so everything we make for God or say about God is an act of worship.

Song: "I Can Only Imagine"   5 Minutes
Supplies: Recording of "I Can Only Imagine" by Mercy Me

Today we're going to listen to a song that a group called "Mercy Me" sings about what heaven will be like when we get there. *Play the song. If the kids know it, you could let them sing along.*

The Teaching Moment: Mercy Me sings this song about walking with Jesus in heaven. They know that when we go to heaven we're going to be excited to see Jesus, and heaven will be so beautiful we won't know what to do. We might dance or we might just stand very still, but we will worship Jesus. They remind us that there is no wrong way to worship.

Illustration: Another way to worship   5 Minutes
Supplies: Bibles with the verses marked or copies of the verses on a piece of paper (see the last page of the lesson)

Tell the children: The Bible shows us many ways to worship God. Today we're going to read some scriptures to help us understand that worship is more than just songs. As I read the verses, you can act out the movements and shake your eggs when you hear the word tambourine.

Psalm 63:4 - *I will praise you for as long as I live, and in your name I will lift up my hands.*

Jeremiah 31:4 & 13 - *You can take up your tambourines and go out to dance with the joyful…Maidens will dance and be glad, young men and old as well.*

Psalm 37:7 - *Be still before the Lord and wait patiently on him.*

Psalm 149:3 - *Let us praise His name with dancing and make music to him with the tambourine and harp.*

Psalm 46:10 - *Be still and know that I am God.*

The Teaching Moment: We worship with music most of the time, but it's not the only way to worship. These verses help us learn that we can praise God with our body movements. What other body movements can we use to praise God? *(Allow for answers.)* Everything we do every minute of each day can be worship to our heavenly Father.

KEY PHRASE: Let's Worship God on Earth Like They Do in Heaven

WRAPPING IT UP—SENDING IT HOME 5-7 Minutes

Cleaning Up

We want the children to learn to be responsible, so be sure they help with the clean up, but remind them not to go anywhere, the group is going to talk to God together one more time.

Closing Worship and Prayer

Gather the children in a circle or allow them to sit down to pray. You may take prayer requests if you like. Close with your own prayer or use the one below. Tell the children that today you're going to give them time to praise God during the prayer. They can keep it very simple: *I praise you because you made me.* Remind the children to join you as you pray the Lord's Prayer.

If you need some guidance for your prayer, you can use this:

Father in Heaven. You are a mighty and holy God. The kids and I want to worship you today. *(Share your word of praise then pause to give the children a moment to praise.)* Lord, bless all of the things these kids have mentioned as prayer requests today. We pray all of these things in Jesus' name, who taught us to pray:

Our Father who art in heaven, hallowed be thy Name. Thy Kingdom come, thy will be done on earth as it is in heaven.
Give us this day our daily bread and forgive us our debts as we forgive our debtors.
Lead us not into temptation and deliver us from evil. For thine is the kingdom and the power and the glory forever, Amen.

Let's Worship God on Earth Like They Do in Heaven

Psalm 63:4 - *"I will praise you for as long as I live, and in your name I will lift up my hands."*

Jeremiah 31:4 & 13—*"You can take up your tambourines and go out to dance with the joyful…Maidens will dance and be glad, young men and old as well.*

Psalm 37:7— *Be still before the Lord and wait patiently on him.*

Psalm 149:3— *Let us praise His name with dancing and make music to him with the tambourine and harp.*

Psalm 46:10- *Be still and know that I am God.*

Let's Worship God on Earth Like They Do in Heaven

Psalm 63:4 - *"I will praise you for as long as I live, and in your name I will lift up my hands."*

Jeremiah 31:4 & 13—*"You can take up your tambourines and go out to dance with the joyful…Maidens will dance and be glad, young men and old as well.*

Psalm 37:7— *Be still before the Lord and wait patiently on him.*

Psalm 149:3— *Let us praise His name with dancing and make music to him with the tambourine and harp.*

Psalm 46:10- *Be still and know that I am God.*

Let's Worship God on Earth Like They Do in Heaven

Psalm 63:4 - *"I will praise you for as long as I live, and in your name I will lift up my hands."*

Jeremiah 31:4 & 13—*"You can take up your tambourines and go out to dance with the joyful…Maidens will dance and be glad, young men and old as well.*

Psalm 37:7— *Be still before the Lord and wait patiently on him.*

Psalm 149:3— *Let us praise His name with dancing and make music to him with the tambourine and harp.*

Psalm 46:10- *Be still and know that I am God.*

Jesus, Teach Me How to Pray
A Year in The Lord's Prayer and other Bible Basics

Unit 5: On Earth as it is in Heaven
Week 2: Joy on Earth Like it is in Heaven

Lesson Overview

This week we're going to look at some ways we can express joy on earth like there is in heaven.

Isaiah and Revelation both talk of Heaven being a place where all tears will be wiped from our eyes. John, the writer of Revelation, also shared that he saw a place where there would be no crying or mourning. Obviously Heaven is a joyous place. In the Lord's prayer, we say, "Thy will be done on Earth as it is in Heaven." We'll talk today about talking about having Joy on Earth like it is in Heaven.

KEY PHRASE: Let's Have the Same Kind of Joy on Earth They Have in Heaven

SETTING UP THE LESSON   5-7 Minutes

Symbols of Joy
Supplies: Party noisemakers, smiley stickers, clown noses, trick eyes, etc. You may even bring smiley face cookies, enough for each child. *(if you do, check for food allergies)*

PRESENTING THE LESSON   5-10 Minutes

Scripture: Isaiah 25:6-8; Revelation 7:15-17; Revelation 21:1-8

MAKING IT REAL TO KIDS TODAY   *(Choose as many as you have time for)*

Game: Freeze Dance   5-7 Minutes

Craft: Bookmark   10-15 Minutes
Supplies: Foam or felt cut into rectangles—one for each child and foam or felt letters to spell JOY (or markers to write with)

Song: Go Fish Guys, "I've Got the Joy"   3-5 Minutes
Supplies: This song is also available as a music DVD as well as CD and on YouTube:
https://www.youtube.com/watch?v=jIbNinW7G18

WRAPPING IT UP—SENDING IT HOME   5—7 Minutes

Clean Up Time & Prayer Time

KEY PHRASE: Let's Have the Same Kind of Joy Here on Earth They Have in Heaven

SETTING UP THE LESSON   5-7 Minutes

Symbols of Joy
Supplies: Party noisemakers, smiley stickers, clown noses, trick eyes, etc. You may even bring smiley face cookies, enough for each child. *(if you do, check for food allergies)*

Bring all kinds of "joyful" things— party noisemakers, smiley stickers, clown noses, trick eyes, etc. You may bring smiley face cookies, enough for each child. *(if you do, check for food allergies)* One by one show the kids each item you've brought. Ask them to tell you what each thing is. If you have enough of any item, you can give one to each child. When they've named all the items, ask them what they all have in common. *(Allow for answers.)* The kids should give answers like: they're all happy, smiling, fun, make me laugh, etc. Accept all of these answers. After they've exhausted all possibilities, tell them that all these things are symbols of joy. Ask them if they know what joy is. *(Allow for answers.)*

Teaching Moment: We feel joy deep inside. It's more than just being happy. Happiness comes when good things happen to us, but joy comes from the inside because of our love for Jesus Christ. It's being happy even when things aren't always great. *(If you do bring cookies, you may just want to show one when you're going through your list of items then give them each a cookie in time for the Scripture lesson. They can eat their cookie while you (or the kids) read the scripture—it might help keep them quiet as they listen)*

PRESENTING THE LESSON   5-10 Minutes

Scripture: Isaiah 25:6-10; Revelation 7:15-17; Revelation 21:1-8
You do not have to read this directly from the Bible— use the story form below or reword it to fit your personality

Today we're going to read some scripture. Let's listen carefully because when we're done I want you to tell me what kind of things the verses make you think about. *(If you have several kids who read well, you might let each one read two verses. If you read, be sure to read it with a lot of enthusiasm. Stop after each set of verses and talk to the kids about what they think)*

Isaiah 25:6-10 from *The Message*

6-8 But here on this mountain, the God-of-the-Angel-Armies will
throw a feast for all the people of the world,
A feast of the finest foods, a feast with vintage wines,
a feast of seven courses, a feast lavish with gourmet desserts.
And here on this mountain, God will banish
the pall of doom hanging over all peoples,
The shadow of doom darkening all nations.
Yes, he'll banish death forever.

And God will wipe the tears from every face.
He'll remove every sign of disgrace
From his people, wherever they are.
Yes! God says so!

9-10 Also at that time, people will say, "Look at what's
happened! This is our God!
We waited for Him and he showed up and saved us!
This God, the one we waited for!
Let's celebrate, sing the joys of his salvation.
God's hand rests on this mountain!"

What kind of things do those verses remind you? *(Allow for answers—you may hear things like: Thanksgiving/Christmas Dinner—a happy place where no one cries, etc)* Now, we're going to read some verses in Revelation.

Revelation 7:15-17 "... [God's people will] serve him day and night in his Temple. The One on the Throne will pitch his tent there for them: no more hunger, no more thirst, no more scorching heat. The Lamb on the Throne will shepherd them, will lead them to spring waters of Life. And God will wipe every last tear from their eyes." (The Message)

KEY PHRASE: Let's Have the Same Kind of Joy Here on Earth They Have in Heaven

What kind of things do you think of when you hear these verses? *(Allow for answers—this might be more difficult for younger kids because they don't realize there are really people who don't get to eat. Especially encourage them to notice that every tear will be wiped away)*

Revelation 21:3-4 "Look! Look! God has moved into the neighborhood, making his home with men and women! They're his people, he's their God. He'll wipe every tear from their eyes. Death is gone for good—tears gone, crying gone, pain gone—all the first order of things gone" (The Message)

What did these verses make you think? *(Allow for answers—God will live in our neighborhood—ask them how that will make them feel. God will take all our tears away—there is no crying, tears or pain!!)*

In all these verses, God showed Isaiah and John that heaven is going to be a happy place, a land full of joy. There won't be any crying in heaven—no sickness and no pain. But God will prepare a great feast, and no one will ever be hungry. Heaven will be a place of great joy. When we say the Lord's Prayer, we ask God to have His will be done on Earth as it is in Heaven. So, what we're really asking is God's help for joy to be on Earth like it is in Heaven. But if we really want that, we have to be like Jesus and be joyful as often as possible.

MAKING IT REAL TO KIDS TODAY *(Choose as many as you have time for)*

Game: Freeze Dance   5-7 Minutes
Supplies: Recording of a "joy" song—Go Fish Guys have several

Play the song and have the kids dance as long as the music plays. Let it play six to eight seconds then stop the music. When the music stops all the children should freeze. Their freezing stances should look pretty funny. Anyone who doesn't freeze is "out." Keep playing until only one child remains or time runs out. Let the kids who are "out" judge when someone doesn't freeze.

The Teaching Moment: Was that fun? We love to laugh and have a good time. God likes it when we're laughing and having fun. Do you remember what He said Heaven would be like? *(Allow for answers.)* God said there would be no more tears, there will be a lot of rejoicing. We need to work to try to make Earth like Heaven and create a lot of joy here.

Craft: Bookmark   7-10 Minutes
Supplies: Foam or felt cut into approximately 2x6 to 3x7 rectangles—one for each child; foam or felt letters (or markers) to spell JOY as well as other decorations (smiley faces recommended) for the bookmarks.

Let the children place the letters and decorations on the bookmarks. Consider helping them make the "O" into a smiley face. Ask younger children how to spell joy before you begin, and invite them to repeat the spelling a few times so they will recognize the word after their craft is made.

The Teaching Moment: Today we're making a bookmark that says "JOY" to remind us that God wants us to be joyful here on Earth. Keep your bookmark handy to remind you to always look for the joy in every minute so you can have joy on Earth like it is in Heaven.

Song: Go Fish Guys, "I've Got the Joy"   3-5 Minutes
Supplies: This song is also available as a music DVD as well as CD and on YouTube: https://www.youtube.com/watch?v=jIbNinW7G18

You could sing it twice with the kids or sing it once before the scripture time and again at the end.

The Teaching Moment: Singing brings joy. When we feel like we're losing our joy, singing a song can make us feel the joy of the Lord. So, if you start being sad, sing this song to remind you God wants you to have the joy of Heaven here on Earth.

KEY PHRASE: Let's Have the Same Kind of Joy Here on Earth They Have in Heaven

WRAPPING IT UP—SENDING IT HOME 5—7 Minutes

Cleaning Up

To help the children to learn to be responsible, be sure they clean up and push in their chairs.

Closing Worship and Prayer

Gather the children in a circle holding hands or allow them to sit down to pray. You may take prayer requests if you have time, then close with your own prayer or use the one below for help. They should now be able to pray "The Lord's Prayer" with you instead of repeating after you.

If you need some guidance for your prayer, you can use this:

Father in Heaven. We praise you that you are the God of Joy! We are grateful for the joy you put in our hearts when we follow you. Help us to do your will here on Earth so we can have joy here just like it is in heaven. Lord, bless all the things these kids have mentioned as prayer requests today (*if there's time, you can mention some of their requests*). We pray all of these things in Jesus' name, who taught us to pray: (*Now lead them in the Lord's Prayer.*)

Our Father who art in heaven, hallowed be thy Name. Thy Kingdom come, thy will be done on earth as it is in heaven. Give us this day our daily bread and forgive us our debts as we forgive our debtors.
Lead us not into temptation and deliver us from evil. For thine is the kingdom and the power and the glory forever, Amen.

Jesus, Teach Me How to Pray
A Year in The Lord's Prayer and other Bible Basics

Unit 5: On Earth as it is in Heaven
Week 3: Beautiful on Earth Like it is in Heaven

Lesson Overview

God created Heaven and Earth. Heaven is still perfect just like He made it. Earth, on the other hand, has become much less than perfect and a lot less beautiful. Today we're going to share what the Bible has to say about making the earth beautiful and appreciating the beauty that God has put in it.

KEY PHRASE: Let's Make Earth Beautiful Like it is In Heaven

SETTING UP THE LESSON   5-7 Minutes
Just Look at This Mess

PRESENTING THE LESSON   5-10 Minutes
Scripture: Revelation 21:9-22:5 & 4:2-6
Supplies: (Optional) you could bring gemstones to show the children as you describe heaven. Additionally, you could use about forty Legos™ to show them how a foundation would be laid, and how big the foundation for heaven is.

MAKING IT REAL TO KIDS TODAY   (Choose as many as you have time for)

Song/Video: Heaven Song   5-7 minutes
Supplies: "Better is One Day" by Matt Redman, "There Will Be a Day" by Jeremy Camp, "I Can Only Imagine" by Mercy Me or another Christian song that talks about what Heaven will be like—several are on YouTube

Game: Balloon Soccer   10 Minutes
Supplies: A few balloons and masking tape

Craft: Jewel Mosaic   15 Minutes
Supplies: Heavy tagboard (like the back of a notebook) cut to 8.5"x5.5," copies of the rainbow and flower at the end of this lesson, glue, small paintbrushes to spread the glue (optional), and small to medium craft jewels– at least 75 per child, and glue. Your could alternately provide bright colored construction paper and glue sticks.

WRAPPING IT UP—SENDING IT HOME   5—7 Minutes
Clean Up Time & Prayer Time

KEY PHRASE: Let's Make Earth Beautiful Like it is in Heaven

SETTING UP THE LESSON   5-7 Minutes

Just Look at This Mess

Before the kids arrive make a huge mess of your class area. Crumble paper and newspaper, scatter old cereal boxes, turn chairs over, put chairs on top of the tables. If no one else uses your area throughout the week, ask the janitor to leave the mess from last week. If you don't have carpet, you might take some dirt and put it in a small bucket and tip the bucket so it spills a bit.

When the kids arrive, make a big deal about the mess. Say something like: *Look at this place, it's a mess. We better straighten it up a bit.* Give the kids a couple of garbage bags or bins and spend a few minutes cleaning up. As you clean, tell the children: *It's important to keep things neat and nice. God gave us all that we have, and it's not right to let it be such a mess.* As you finish up: *Today we're going to talk about how keeping things beautiful is doing God's will here on Earth like it is in Heaven.*

PRESENTING THE LESSON   5-10 Minutes

Scripture: Revelation 21:9-22:5 & 4:2-6

You do not have to read this directly from the Bible— use the story form below or reword it to fit your personality

If you have diamonds, pearls, sapphires, topaz, amethyst, etc, you could take them to show the kids as you tell the story. If you ask around the church, there may be folks who have birthstones they'd let you borrow.

Almost 2000 years ago God showed one of Jesus' disciples what Heaven looks like. John recorded everything he saw, and we call his vision the book of Revelation. Does anyone know where the book of Revelation is in the Bible? *(Allow for answers.)* Revelation is the last book in the Bible. Today we're going to hear a little of what John told us about Heaven.

John said that when he saw Heaven it "shone with the glory of God." What do you think it might be like, to shine like the glory of God? *(Allow for answers.)* It would have been unbelievably bright. God's glory is even brighter than the Sun, and we can't look directly at the Sun. John described it as brilliant, like a very precious jewel. Do you know what a precious jewel is? *(Allow for answers.)* A diamond is one kind of precious jewel. *(Show the jewels if you brought them.)* When the light hits a diamond or another precious jewel it sparkles. John said Heaven sparkled in the same way.

John also told us that Heaven is huge—1500 miles square. Do you know how far 1500 miles is? *(Allow for answers.)* To drive 1500 miles would take more than twenty-four hours. It would be like driving almost all the way to Florida and back. John said the walls of the city were more than two hundred feet thick. Wow! Do you know how wide that is? *(Allow for answers.)* Imagine fifteen mini-vans sitting in a line. And the walls were made out of clear jasper. Fifteen hundred miles high and two hundred feet thick—all jasper.

The city of Heaven had three gates on each side, and an angel stood at each gate. Can you guess what each gate was made of? *(Allow for answers.)* Each gate was made of a pearl. Do you know what a pearl is? *(Allow for answers.)* Pearls are round white beads. They are precious and beautiful. John wrote that each gate was made out of one huge, beautiful, precious pearl. Can you imagine how big the pearl would have to be to fill in the gate of a city? *(Allow for answers.)*

The walls of Heaven sat on a huge foundation. It had twelve layers. *(If you have Legos, you could put three or four on each layer and use the color of the gem if you have them as you talk about the foundation. Explain that even though the Legos are plastic, the walls are made of precious jewels).* Each layer was covered with expensive jewels, like jasper *(any color)*, sapphire *(blue)*, agate *(any color)*, emeralds *(green)*, onyx *(black)*, ruby *(red)*, chrysolite *(green)*, beryl *(clear or any color)*, topaz *(orange)*, turquoise *(teal)*, jacinth *(brown)*, and amethyst *(purple)*. These twelve layers sat underneath the city. And on top of these layers are streets are made of pure gold. Can you imagine how beautiful that will be?

John said God was all the light the city needed. He and Jesus shine so bright the Sun didn't have to shine anymore. He told us that a river runs right through the middle of the street. He said it is the River of Life. And the Tree of Life stands on each bank of the river providing twelve different kinds of fruit.

The river flowed out of a huge throne. Do you remember what a throne is? *(Allow for answers.)* A throne is a

KEY PHRASE: Let's Make Earth Beautiful Like it is in Heaven

big chair for the king. This throne that had the River of Life flowing out of it was for God and Jesus to sit on. And John said he saw a rainbow all around God's throne.

John also said nothing impure will be allowed into Heaven, so it will be always be a perfect place.

So, what do you think about Heaven? *(Allow for answers.)* Doesn't it sound beautiful? Everything is perfect in Heaven and absolutely beautiful.

What do we say in our prayer about Heaven? *(Allow for answers.)* We tell God, "Thy will be done on Earth as it is in Heaven." If we really mean it, we need to do our part to make Earth as beautiful as we can. Just like we cleaned up our room this morning, if we do our part, then God can do the rest. Just think how wonderful the Earth would be if everyone was trying to make it as beautiful as Heaven.

MAKING IT REAL TO KIDS TODAY *(Choose as many as you have time for)*

Song/Video: Heaven Song   5-7 minutes
Supplies: "Better is One Day" by Matt Redman, "There Will Be a Day" by Jeremy Camp, "I Can Only Imagine" by Mercy Me, or another Christian song that talks about what Heaven will be like—several are on YouTube

Play the recording for the kids. Help them sing the Chorus if it's an easy one.

The Teaching Moment:

(Better is One Day) This song comes from Psalm 84:10 in the Bible—The people who wrote the Psalms knew that being in God's presence is the best place to be. The Psalmist also knew being in God's house, could mean either Heaven or church. God's heavenly home is lovely, and here on earth we should do our best to help keep God's house and the world He created lovely.

(There Will Be A Day) This song reminds us that Heaven will be a perfect place. Nothing will make us sad or hurt us. Without the evil from the devil, no one will cry. Wouldn't it be wonderful if we had that king of Heaven here on Earth? If we do our best to be like Jesus and treat others like Jesus wants us to, we can make Earth a bit more like Heaven.

(I Can Only Imagine) This song reminds us that even after all John told us, we will still be amazed in Heaven. Heaven is bigger, and Jesus is more wonderful, than we can imagine. We will be so mesmerized when we see Jesus, we will just want to worship Him. It would be wonderful if we worshipped Jesus here on Earth like we will in Heaven.

Game: Balloon Soccer   5-10 minutes
Supplies: Balloons and masking tape

Put two 4' pieces of masking tape on the floor about 15-20 feet apart (more or less depending on your space and the number of kids you have). Divide the kids into two teams with an equal number of older and younger kids on each team. You should only need one balloon, but you may want to have a few ready in case the one in play breaks. Tell the kids that we're going to play Balloon Soccer. Remind them they can't touch the balloon with their hands. There will be no goalie, but they need to try to get the balloon across the other team's line (and keep it from going across their line). Allow the kids to play for 10 minutes or as long as you have time.

If you have a smaller space, have the students take two sides of the room or table and use their hands to keep it from hitting the floor on their side of the room. You can call it "Hand Soccer" so it fits with the teaching moment.

The Teaching Moment: We played Soccer (or Hand Soccer) today just to have some fun. But did you know that Soccer is sometimes called the "Beautiful Game" because it's such a simple game. Almost anything can be beautiful. It doesn't have to be fancy or difficult to be beautiful. Like Soccer, the simplicity of it makes it beautiful. When we take care of things here on Earth, we can make things beautiful and help make God's will be done here on Earth like it is in Heaven.

KEY PHRASE: Let's Make Earth Beautiful Like it is in Heaven

Craft: Jewel Mosaic   15 Minutes

Supplies: Heavy tagboard (like the back of a notebook) cut to 8.5"x5.5," copies of the rainbow and flower at the end of this lesson, glue, small paintbrushes to spread the glue (optional), and small to medium craft jewels– at least 75 per child, and glue. Your could alternately provide bright colored construction paper and glue sticks.

Give each child one piece of tagboard, their choice of a rainbow or flower, and their choice of jewel colors. They can also use the construction paper and rip it into 1/2" pieces. For younger children, put the glue on a small plate and let them use a tiny paintbrush or foam brush. Glue sticks will work well with the construction paper. Have them glue the jewels and/or construction paper to fill in all the rainbow or flower area. Allow the children to make a beautiful mosaic.

The Teaching Moment: Our mosaics are beautiful, but they're still not nearly as beautiful as Heaven. Take this home and hang it in your room or on your refrigerator to help you remember that Heaven is beautiful and to have God's will done on Earth as it is in Heaven, we should be careful to help keep Earth beautiful because Heaven is beautiful.

WRAPPING IT UP—SENDING IT HOME   5—7 Minutes

Cleaning Up

We want the children to learn to be responsible, so be sure they help with the clean up.

Closing Worship and Prayer

Gather the children in a circle holding hands or allow them to sit down to pray. If you choose to join hands, remember that it's OK if some children prefer not to join the circle. Ask them to be respectful of others as they pray and not make any noise.

As you close, and if there is time, ask the children for prayer requests. Though no prayer is too small, children will tend to keep going and be "inspired" by other prayer requests, so feel free to cut them off and tell them they pray quietly to God themselves while you're praying. You may close with your own prayer or use the one below for help. Invite them to pray "The Lord's Prayer" with you.

If you need some guidance for your prayer, you can use this:

Father in Heaven, we praise you that you made a beautiful Heaven and a beautiful Earth. Forgive us that we don't always keep earth as beautiful as you created it to be. Help us do your will here on Earth and remember how beautiful it is in Heaven so we can keep the Earth beautiful, too. Lord, bless all the things these kids have mentioned as prayer requests today (*if there's time, you can mention some of their requests*). And Lord, we pray all of these things in Jesus' name, who taught us to pray: (*now lead them in the Lord's Prayer*)

Our Father who art in heaven, hallowed be thy Name. Thy Kingdom come, thy will be done on earth as it is in heaven.
Give us this day our daily bread and forgive us our debts as we forgive our debtors.
Lead us not into temptation and deliver us from evil. For thine is the kingdom and the power and the glory forever, Amen.

Page intentionally left blank for printing and copying purposes

Jesus, Teach Me How to Pray
A Year in The Lord's Prayer and other Bible Basics

Unit 6: Give us This Day Our Daily Bread
Week 1: God Provides our Daily Bread

Lesson Overview

God rescued the Israelites from slavery in Egypt. You'd think they'd be grateful, however, it only took about 45 days for them to begin complaining about not having enough food. Because He is gracious, God put up with their grumbling and gave the Israelites manna. Manna was little white flakes, and it tasted like wafers with honey on them. Manna is a symbol of God's provision. He gave the Israelites their daily bread every day for the next forty years. Manna can help remind us that God loves us and wants to provide for us. If you're using this during Lent, it's a good example of how the Israelites sacrificed for the forty years in the wilderness. Many who celebrate Lent sacrifice something for forty days, one day for each year the Israelites wandered. (Lent is also forty days long because Jesus faced temptation after forty days of fasting in the wilderness.)

KEY PHRASE: God Loves Us and Will Provide For Us

SETTING UP THE LESSON   5-7 Minutes

What is Manna?
Supplies: Coriander seeds, thin wafers, (You might see if your pastor has thin communion wafers that he or she serves to shut ins.) honey and napkins—Check ahead of time to be sure no one is allergic to honey or wafers.

PRESENTING THE LESSON   5-10 Minutes

Scripture: Exodus 16

MAKING IT REAL TO KIDS TODAY   *(Choose as many as you have time for)*

Game: Hot Buns   5-10 Minutes
Supplies: One stale bun (you may want a few just in case you need extra)

Craft: Stale Bread Bird Feeder   15 Minutes
Adapted from an idea at http://familycrafts.about.com/cs/birdfeeders/ht/CookieCutBird.htm
Supplies: Stale, hard bread (one or more slices for each child), cookie cutters about the size of a slice of bread, straws cut into 1" pieces and string, Plastic knives, peanut butter, bird seed and baggies

Song: Jehovah Jireh, My Provider   5 Minutes
Supplies: Song is on last page or find it on YouTube: https://www.youtube.com/watch?v=fCsH_TtZReY

WRAPPING IT UP—SENDING IT HOME   5-7 Minutes

Clean Up Time & Prayer Time

KEY PHRASE: God Loves Us and Will Provide For Us

SETTING UP THE LESSON 5-7 Minutes

What is Manna?

Supplies: Coriander seeds, thin wafers, (You might see if your pastor has thin communion wafers that he or she serves to shut ins) honey and napkins—Check ahead of time to be sure no one is allergic to honey or wafers.

Show the children the coriander seeds and give each one or two wafers. Let them to spread honey on them or dip them in honey (remind them not to double dip). Ask (with no wrong answers): What does this taste like? Do you like the sweetness of the honey? The Bible tells us about food that God fed to the Israelites. It looked like coriander, but tasted like wafers and honey. The people called it Manna. *(Have the children repeat MANNA)*

PRESENTING THE LESSON 5-10 Minutes

Scripture: Exodus 16

You do not have to read this directly from the Bible— use the story form below or reword it to fit your personality

The Israelites are the people of God. Thousands of years ago they were slaves in Egypt, but God sent Moses to them to lead them out of Egypt and into the promised land. About forty-five days after they left Egypt, the Israelites started grumbling. Do you know what grumbling means? *(Allow for answers.)* Grumbling means complaining. What kind of things do you complain about? *(Allow for answers.)* The Israelites were grumbling because they didn't have very much to eat. They were getting hungry. What does it feel like to be hungry? *(Allow for answers.)*

God heard their grumbling. He understood that they were hungry from walking around the dessert for forty-five days. He promised to send quail every night so they would have meat to eat. What are quail? *(Allow for answers.)* Quail are small birds, almost like little chickens. In addition to the quail, God told them he would rain bread from heaven every morning.

Sure enough, the next morning the Israelites got up, and found small white flakes that looked like coriander seeds all over the ground. The Bible says they tasted like wafers with honey. They had never seen such a thing. Do you remember what we said it was called? *(Allow for answers.)* The Israelites called it manna. The word manna means, "What is it?" in the Israelites' language, so that's what they called the small white flakes. God told them they should go out every morning and collect only as much as their family could eat that day. On Friday they needed to collect enough for two days so they didn't have to do any work, not even collect manna, on Saturday, the day God called "Sabbath. "

Some people got greedy and gathered more than they needed. When they saved it till the next day, it got all rotten and was filled with maggots. Do you know what maggots are? *(Allow for answers.)* Maggots are fly eggs that smell bad and look like little worms. They tried to save some for the next day, and it didn't work! When the Israelites didn't trust God to give them their daily bread the maggots came.

Other people didn't collect two days worth on Friday. They went out on the Sabbath looking for manna, but God didn't send any on Saturday. Those people were hungry on the Sabbath because they didn't obey God's instructions. The people who did obey God's instructions didn't find maggots on the Sabbath.

God took care of His people. For forty years God gave the Israelites bread from heaven every day. Do you remember what the bread from heaven was called? *(Allow for answers.)* It was called manna. It's the way God showed His love for Israel and provided for them.

When we pray, "Give us this day our daily bread," we ask God to take care of what we need every day. It also means we trust God to take care of our daily needs. We don't want to be like the Israelites who collected too much and didn't trust God to give them food everyday. And we don't want to be like the ones who didn't listen to God when he gave them instructions on when to go pick up their manna. We want to always trust God to provide everything we need. It's important to remember the Israelites' manna and let it remind us that God loves us and will give us what we need each day.

KEY PHRASE: God Loves Us and Will Provide For Us

Lenten Lesson: *If you're using this lesson during lent, tell the kids:* Right now we're celebrating Lent. Lent is a forty day period that begins six Wednesdays before Easter on a day we call Ash Wednesday. We use these days to make sure we trust God to provide for us and obey His instructions. Do you remember how many years the Israelites wandered? *(Allow for answers.)* The Israelites were in the desert for forty years. Lent includes one day for every year the Israelites wandered around the desert. *(NOTE: The forty days of Lent are counted as either all the days between Ash Wednesday and Easter-not including Sundays or all the days between Ash Wednesday and Palm Sunday.)*

MAKING IT REAL TO KIDS TODAY   *(Choose as many as you have time for)*

Game: Hot Buns   5-10 Minutes
Supplies: One stale bun (you may want a few just in case you need extra)

1. Have all the children except the oldest stand in a circle about an arm's width apart with the oldest inside the circle where they can see the bun move.
2. Give the stale bun to the youngest person. When you say "GO" the kids begin passing the bun as fast as they can around the circle (you might want to practice this once). When the bun gets back to the youngest person he or she yells STOP.
3. As soon as you say, "GO," (see step 2) the person in the middle begins to name all the things God provides for them. They have until the youngest person stays "STOP" to complete their list.
4. The leader (you) counts how many things the person in the middle says.
5. Repeat steps 1-4 with the next oldest person in the middle of the circle and the next to the youngest starting the bun.
6. Continue until all children have had a chance in the middle or time is up.
7. When you're all done, the one who named the most things God provided wins. (No prize is necessary, but you can give one if you like)

The Teaching Moment: It's good for us to remember and look for all the things that God provides. God loves us so much. He makes sure we have everything that we need. We need to remember to be thankful for all He's provided.

Craft: Stale Bread Bird Feeder   15 Minutes
Adapted from an idea at http://familycrafts.about.com/cs/birdfeeders/ht/CookieCutBird.htm
Supplies: Stale, hard bread (one or more slices for each child), cookie cutters about the size of a slice of bread, straws cut into 1" pieces and string, Plastic knives, peanut butter, bird seed and baggies

1. Use the cookie cutter to cut a shape out of a slice of stale bread.
2. Use the 1" piece of straw to poke a hole in the bread, leave the straw in the hole.
3. Put a 12" string through the straw and tie it.
4. Allow the kids to use the plastic knives to spread some peanut butter on their bird feeder
5. Sprinkle the bird feeder with bird seed
6. Put the bird feeders in plastic bags to get them home

The Teaching Moment: God gave the Israelites bread from heaven. He provided for them while they were in the dessert for forty years. Today we made these bread bird feeders. You can take them home and hang them in a tree to feed the birds just like God fed the Israelites. Every time you see the birds eat from your bird feeder remember that God loves us and will provide for us.

KEY PHRASE: God Loves Us and Will Provide For Us

Song: Jehovah Jireh, My Provider

Supplies: Song is on last page or find it on YouTube: https://www.youtube.com/watch?v=fCsH_TtZReY

Let the kids sing along. You could let them clap with the song or even play a tambourine or an egg.

The Teaching Moment: This is a really great song for us to learn. It reminds us that God provides everything we need. Sometimes the Israelites forgot that simple truth. It's important we don't forget. Do you remember what happened when the Israelites forgot God provided and collected too much manna? *(Allow for answers.)* The manna got bugs in it. What about on Saturday, the Sabbath, morning? *(Allow for answers.)* There wasn't any manna because it was the day of rest We have to always trust God to provide and obey Him in everything that we do.

WRAPPING IT UP—SENDING IT HOME   5-7 Minutes

Cleaning Up

We want the children to learn to be responsible, so be sure they help with the clean up, picking up as many seeds and crumbs as they can. Remind them to take their feeders with them and to keep the bags closed until they get home.

Closing Worship and Prayer

Either gather the children in a circle holding hands or allow them to sit down to pray. You may close with your own prayer or use the one below for help. Remember to end with the children saying the Lord's Prayer with you.

Father in Heaven, we praise you because you always provide for us. Thank you for all we have, food, a home, clothes and education. Help us to remember you will forever be Jehovah Jireh, our provider. Lord, bless all of the things these kids have mentioned as prayer requests today. *(If there's time, you can mention some of their requests).* And Lord, we pray all of these things in Jesus' name, who taught us to pray: *(Lead them in the Lord's Prayer—see side column.)*

Our Father who art in heaven, hallowed be thy Name. Thy Kingdom come, thy will be done on earth as it is in heaven.
Give us this day our daily bread and forgive us our debts as we forgive our debtors.
Lead us not into temptation and deliver us from evil. For thine is the kingdom and the power and the glory forever, Amen.

Jehovah Jireh

Public Domain

Je-hov-ah Ji-reh My pro-vid-er His grace is suf-fic-ient for me, for me, for me.

Je-hov-ah Ji-reh my pro-vid-er His grace is suf-fic-ient for me. My

God shall sup-ply all my needs a-cord-ing to His rich-es in glo-ry

He will give His an-gels charge ov-er me. Je-ho-vah Ji-reh cares for

me, for me. for me. Je-ho-vah Ji-reh cares for me.

Jesus, Teach Me How to Pray
A Year in The Lord's Prayer and other Bible Basics

Unit 6: Give Us This Day Our Daily Bread
Week 2: We Need More than Just Bread

Lesson Overview

Right after Jesus' baptism, He headed into the desert for forty days. He had nothing to eat the entire time He was there. By the end of the forty days, Jesus had to be weak and very hungry. That's when Satan came to tempt Him. And one of the Satan used was bread. Satan knew Jesus was hungry. He also knew God had the power to make the stones into bread if He wanted to; however, Jesus knew that wasn't God's will for His life at that moment. Jesus laid the groundwork for us to understand that God's word is just as vital as our daily bread. It's important for us to know the words that come out of God's mouth. In much the same way, Jesus told His disciples, "I am the bread of life." When we "feed on Jesus" we will never be hungry.

If you're using this during Lent you can also emphasize that Lent lasts forty days, the same number of days that Jesus was in the wilderness. Lent is also symbolic of Jesus spending forty days without food. It gives us forty days to sacrifice to remind us of all that Christ has done for us.

KEY PHRASE: Jesus Is All the Bread We Need

SETTING UP THE LESSON   5-7 Minutes

Stale Bread
Supplies: You guessed it!! Stale Bread—leave bread out in the air for a few days—You might want to cut it into quarters or pieces before you let it get stale—enough to pass out one piece per child. If you wait till the last minute, try putting the bread in a 200 degree oven for a while. *(check for allergies before you allow them to eat it)* One slice of moldy bread (optional), good bread, cinnamon rolls or donuts (optional)

PRESENTING THE LESSON   5-10 Minutes

Scripture: Matthew 4:1-11 & John 6:30-59

MAKING IT REAL TO KIDS TODAY   *(Choose as many as you have time for)*

Craft: Daily Bible Reading Cards   10-15 Minutes
Supplies: Index cards, copies of the "Bread of Life" sheets—1 for every 3 kids, markers, pens or pencils, hole punch, ribbon

Game: Hot Cross Buns   5-10 Minutes

Song: "Jehovah Jireh, My Provider"   5 Minutes

WRAPPING IT UP—SENDING IT HOME   5-7 Minutes

Clean Up Time & Prayer Time

KEY PHRASE: Jesus Is All the Bread We Need

SETTING UP THE LESSON　　　　　　　　　　　　　　　　　　5-7 Minutes

Stale Bread

Supplies: You guessed it!! Stale Bread—leave bread out in the air for a few days—You might want to cut it into quarters or pieces before you let it get stale—enough to pass out one piece per child. If you wait till the last minute, try putting the bread in a 200 degree oven for a while. *(check for allergies before you allow them to eat it)* One slice of moldy bread (optional), good bread, cinnamon rolls or donuts (optional)

Tell the kids you have a snack for them today. Pass out the stale bread. If there aren't any allergies, allow the kids to taste the bread. (If it's just stale, it won't hurt anyone—make sure it doesn't get moldy)

Ask So what do you think about our snack? *(Some may like it, but most will think it's too dry).* What's wrong with it? *(Allow for answers.)* How do you think it got so dry? *(Allow for answers.)*

Bread doesn't last very long. After a week, it will get stale or moldy. *(Show the piece of moldy bread if you have one).* Even though the bread we eat doesn't last more than a week, Jesus said there is a kind of bread that lasts forever.

If you'd like, you could have some good bread, banana bread, cinnamon rolls, etc., for the kids to munch on while you move on to the lesson. If you do, ask the kids if they'd like to have a good piece of bread while you tell them the Bible Story.

PRESENTING THE LESSON　　　　　　　　　　　　　　　　　　5-10 Minutes

Scripture: Matthew 4:1-11 & John 6:30-59

You do not have to read this directly from the Bible— use the story form below or reword it to fit your personality

There are a couple of places in the Bible where Jesus talks about bread that never goes bad. His bread never gets stale, and it never gets moldy. One of the times Jesus talked about bread was right after He was baptized. Do you remember or know what it means to be baptized? *(Allow for answers.).* Baptism is when we make a public announcement of our faith in Jesus Christ by having water put on our heads. Right after John baptized Him, Jesus went into the wilderness for forty days. Do you know what a wilderness is? *(Allow for answers.)* A wilderness is miles and miles of land with no houses or stores, not very many plants and nothing to eat. Jesus had been in the wilderness for forty days when the devil decided to tempt Him.

After forty days with no food or water, Jesus was extremely hungry. What do you think you would feel like if you didn't eat for forty days? *(Allow for answers.)* That's how Jesus felt when the devil came to tempt Him. The very first thing the devil told Jesus was that if He was really the Son of God, He should turn the stones into bread. If you were Jesus, would you want to turn the stone into bread after forty days with no food? *(Allow for answers)* That would have been very tempting for Jesus. But Jesus knew God didn't want Him to listen to Satan, so He told the devil, "People don't live only by eating bread, but by believing every word that God speaks." In other words, Jesus knew that food wasn't nearly as important as reading and learning the Bible and doing what God said.

Later Jesus told His disciples He was the bread of life. He said this because if we have Jesus in our life there is nothing else we need. Jesus never goes stale. God doesn't ever get moldy. The Word of God, the Bible, is never old. It's always fresh and good for us.

Jesus knew that eating food wasn't enough to make us everything God wants us to be. Meat, fruit and vegetables will make our muscles and body strong, but to make our spirit strong—the part of us that looks most like God—we need to have a little bit of God's bread everyday. And what is God's bread? *(Allow for answers.)* God's bread is Jesus and the Bible.

How often do you need to eat? *(Allow for answers.)* We need to eat several times every day in order to stay healthy. What do we need to eat? *(Allow for answers.)* What happens if we eat too much junk? *(Allow for answers.).* If we eat too much junk and don't eat food that is good for us everyday, we'll get sick. If we don't think about Jesus and read the Bible everyday, we will get spiritually sick. When we get spiritually sick, we don't obey God, and we do things that make God very sad. We need Jesus to be our "bread of life" so we can become the best

KEY PHRASE: Jesus Is All the Bread We Need

version of what God created us to be.

Lenten Lesson: Do you remember from last week how many days we said Lent lasted? (*Allow for answers.*) Lent is forty days long. And how many days did we talk about Jesus being in the desert? (*Allow for answers.*) We learned that Jesus wandered in the wilderness for forty days. Lent is a good time to remember that Jesus died for us. It's a good time to make sure we are following Jesus like we should.

MAKING IT REAL TO KIDS TODAY *(Choose as many as you have time for)*

Craft: Daily Bible Reading Cards — 10-15 Minutes
Supplies: Index cards, copies of the "Bread of Life" sheets (at the back of this lesson) — 1 for every 3 kids, markers, pens or pencils, hole punch, ribbon

Give each child seven cards and a piece of ribbon. Let the kids share the "Bread of Life" sheets to copy one verse on each card. Help the younger children or allow them to draw pictures to remind them of the verses. You could alternately allow younger children to paste copies of the verses on their cards. Punch a hole in each card and tie them together with the ribbon.

The Teaching Moment: It's important that we read and learn God's word. We should try to memorize some of the Bible so we can tell other people about God's Word. Today we're writing seven verses, one for each day of the week. So each day, read the verse on the card, and in a few weeks, you'll have seven verses memorized.

Game: Hot Cross Buns — 5-10 Minutes

Have the children sit in a circle on the floor (or in chairs) with one child in the center. Give each child in the circle a chance to ask the child in the center any "serious" question. For instance, "What is your favorite color?" Or "When is your birthday?" or "Where did you go on vacation?" The child in the center will always answer, "HOT CROSS BUNS" without laughing. The kids in the circle need to try to ask a question that will make the center person laugh. Whoever succeeds gets to be in the center of the circle. Play continues until all kids have a chance to be in the center or you run out of time

The Teaching Moment: We just had a fun game, but we were talking about bread. That's because today is all about bread. Do you remember who is the Bread of Life? (*Allow for answers.*) Jesus is all the bread we need.

Song: Jehovah Jireh, My Provider (music on last page of this lesson) — 5 Minutes

You can find this song on most music sites. YouTube offers several good versions. Let the kids sing along. You could let them clap with the song or even play a tambourine or an egg.

The Teaching Moment: The Old Testament of the Bible was written in Hebrew. Can you say Hebrew? (*Allow for repeating*) The word Jehovah means God in Hebrew, and the word Jireh means provider. So Jehovah Jireh means God is my provider. Do you know what the word provider means? (*Allow for answers.*) A provider is someone who gives you something. If I give you a pencil, I'm your pencil provider. God provides for everything we need, so he's our Jehovah Jireh.

KEY PHRASE: Jesus Is All the Bread We Need

WRAPPING IT UP—SENDING IT HOME   5-7 Minutes

Cleaning Up

We want the children to learn to be responsible, so be sure they help with the clean up.

Closing Worship and Prayer

Gather the children in a circle holding hands or allow them to sit down to pray. If you choose to join hands, it's OK if some children prefer not to join the circle. Ask them to be respectful of others as they pray and not make any noise. If you have time, ask the children for prayer requests. You may close with your own prayer or use the one below for help. Don't forget to finish by leading the children in the Lord's prayer.

If you need some guidance for your prayer, you can use this:

Father in Heaven, we praise you that you sent Jesus to be the bread of life. Thank you for the Bible and your Word that is better than bread. Help us to remember that your word will make us strong. We need it as much as we need breakfast every day. Lord, bless all of the things these kids have mentioned as prayer requests today (*If there's time, you can mention some of their requests*). And Lord, we pray all of these things in Jesus' name, who taught us to pray: *(now lead them in the Lord's Prayer)*

Our Father who art in heaven, hallowed be thy Name. Thy Kingdom come, thy will be done on earth as it is in heaven. Give us this day our daily bread and forgive us our debts as we forgive our debtors.
Lead us not into temptation and deliver us from evil. For thine is the kingdom and the power and the glory forever, Amen.

Bread of Life Verses

SUNDAY

God says, "I will never leave you or turn my back on you.

Don't be afraid." Deuteronomy 31:8

MONDAY

Don't worry about anything.

Tell God everything you need. Philippians 4:6

TUESDAY

If you hope in God, He will make you strong again.

Isaiah 40:31

WEDNESDAY

Love the Lord your God with

All your heart, with all your soul, with all your strength

And with all your mind.

Luke 10:27 (NIV)

THURSDAY

Every good and perfect gift is from God.

James 1:17

FRIDAY

Jesus said, "I have come to give you a full life."

John 10:10

SATURDAY

The gift of God is eternal life in Jesus Christ

Romans 6:23 (NIV)

Jehovah Jireh

Public Domain

Jesus, Teach Me How to Pray
A Year in The Lord's Prayer and other Bible Basics

Unit 6: Give us This Day Our Daily Bread
Week 3: Jehovah Jireh, My Provider

Lesson Overview

Today we're going to look at two separate but similar stories. Most folks have heard the story of Jesus feeding the 5000 with two loaves of bread and five fish. Most don't realize He also fed 4000 people with seven loaves and a few small fish on a different day. On both occasions the small lunch fed the entire crowd and supplied leftovers. Jesus provided the daily bread for his followers.

KEY PHRASE: Jesus Makes Sure There Is Enough

SETTING UP THE LESSON — 5-7 Minutes

How Many Can we Feed?
Supplies: Five hoagie rolls and 2 cans of tuna (or 2 pieces of fish)

PRESENTING THE LESSON — 5-10 Minutes

Scripture: Matthew 14:13-22 & 15:29-39 - John 6:1-13

MAKING IT REAL TO KIDS TODAY *(Choose as many as you have time for)*

Illustration: Wants vs. Needs — 10-15 Minutes
Supplies: Paper and writing utensils for each child, bread from the introduction, a doll house or a picture of a house, a bottle or cup of water, fruit or veggies, a piece of clothing, a picture of a TV, a game or toy, a DVD, any other items that the kids may need or NOT need

Game: Spread the Love — 10 Minutes
Supplies: Spring clothes pins, spring chip clips OR binder clips, enough for each child to have five

Song: Jehovah Jireh, My Provider — 5-10 Minutes

WRAPPING IT UP—SENDING IT HOME — 5-7 Minutes

Clean Up Time & Prayer Time

KEY PHRASE: Jesus Makes Sure There Is Enough

SETTING UP THE LESSON   5-7 Minutes

How Many Can we Feed?
Supplies: Five hoagie rolls and 2 cans of tuna (or 2 pieces of fish)

Show the children the bread and the fish. Ask: Do you think there enough food here to feed your family? *(Allow for answers.)* Well, then do you think there's enough for our group here? *(Allow for answers.)* Do you think we can feed everyone in the church? *(Allow for answers.)* What if we tried to feed everyone in your whole school, would this be enough? *(Allow for answers.)* How many do you think we can feed with this? *(Allow for answers.)*

You're probably right, we probably won't be able to feed very many people with these few rolls and a little bit of fish. We might be able to feed our family, but not our whole school. Today we're going to hear about how Jesus fed many people with just such a menu.

PRESENTING THE LESSON   5-10 Minutes

Scripture: Matthew 15:29-39 and John 6:1-13
You do not have to read this directly from the Bible— use the story form below or reword it to fit your personality

The Bible tells about two different times when Jesus provided lunch for a lot of people with just a little food. The first time, Jesus had been preaching for so long, He was exhausted. Plus, He had just found out that King Herod had killed John the Baptist. Do you think Jesus wanted to be with a big crowd after all that? *(Allow for answers.)* He really just wanted to rest. So Jesus and his disciples took a boat across the lake.

But when the people in the nearby towns heard Jesus was so close, they all came out to see Him. Even though Jesus was exhausted, He felt bad that they had walked so far to see Him, that He spent the rest of the day healing the sick among them.

When evening came, the disciples knew the people had to be getting hungry. They told Jesus He should send the people home. But Jesus surprised them. He said, "You give them something to eat." But the disciples didn't have any food! Can you guess how many people came to see Jesus? *(Allow for answers - you might do a little "higher/ lower" to make it interesting)* There were about 5,000 men plus their wives and children. That would be about 10,000 people. *(Give an example of 10,000 or more that your kids will understand—perhaps a football stadium or all the people in your town or two towns.)* Jesus told the disciples to feed that many people.

Andrew, one of Jesus' disciples brought a boy with five loaves of bread and two fish, just like we have today. Do you think they could feed more than 10,000 people with this little bit of food? *(Allow for answers.)* I don't think so either. But Jesus took those five small loaves and two fish and lifted it up, thanked God for it and had his disciples start passing it around. *(If no one has bread or yeast allergies, you can lift the bread when you say lift it up and then break it in half and pass it around to the kids so they can each take a piece of it.)*

So, the disciples gave it to the people, they just kept passing and passing and passing. Finally, everyone in the whole crowd had enough to eat. When everyone finished, the disciples picked up the scraps and collected twelve small baskets of leftovers!

On another day, Jesus was near the Sea of Galilee again. This time a crowd of 4,000 men came out to hear Jesus preach and watch Him heal. That means there were probably more than 8000 people there that day. This time Jesus had seven loaves of bread and a few fish. And He did it again! Jesus knew the people were hungry and really wanted to hear everything He had to say, so he provided their daily bread, and the disciples picked up seven big baskets full of leftovers.

These people wanted to hear and see Jesus so badly they didn't care if they ate. The didn't expect Jesus to give them bread and fish. They didn't know Jesus promised to be our provider.

God promised to always provide for our needs. When we pray "Give us this day our daily bread" it should remind us that Christ can feed thousands with just a little bit when those thousands are willing to make sure they are doing God's will.

KEY PHRASE: Jesus Makes Sure There Is Enough

Lenten Lesson: The people in the Bible were willing to go without food in order to hear Jesus speak. Lent is a time that begins six weeks before Easter. During those forty days some people give up things to get to know God better. People all over the world fast. Do you know what fasting is? *(Allow for answers.)* Fasting is giving up food or some other thing so that a person can grow closer to Christ. Some people give up lunch every day and then read their Bible when they normally would eat lunch. Others give up all desserts or chips. This sacrifice reminds them of Jesus' sacrifice on the cross.

MAKING IT REAL TO KIDS TODAY   *(Choose as many as you have time for)*

Illustration: Wants vs. Needs   10-15 Minutes
Supplies: A piece of paper and pencils or crayons for each child, bread from the introduction, picture of a house or a doll house, a bottle or cup of water, fruit or veggies, a piece of clothing, a picture of a TV, a game or toy, a DVD, any other items that they kids may need or NOT need.

Give each child a piece of paper and something to write with. Have them draw a line down the middle of the page and write the word "WANTS" on one side of the line and "NEEDS" on the other. *(You could do this on a chalk or white board if you like so they can copy.)* Then show the kids each of the items you've brought. Have them write or draw (depending on their age) the item on either the WANTS or NEEDS side of the line.

The Teaching Moment: *After you've shown all the items, go back over each one and ask the kids which column they put it in. Then say:* Sometimes we confuse wants and needs. Food, water, clothing and a home are NEEDS. We would die without them. Everything else are WANTS because we could live without them. Jesus always makes sure we have enough, just like he did with the people who came to hear Him speak. Sometimes we're blessed to have things we WANT too, and we should be extra thankful when God blesses us with more than we need.

Game: Spread the Love   5-10 Minutes
Supplies: Spring clothes pins, spring chip clips OR binder clips, enough for each child to have five

Give each child five clips. Have them clip them to their own clothing. Tell them they have 5-10 minutes (Or as much time as you have.) Tell them they need to walk around the room and find out each person's birthday, their favorite color, their telephone number or address. Any questions they can think of. They should ask politely, "When is your birthday?" and wait for the other person to ask them. As they walk around, they should be very sneaky and put their clothespins on others. If the other person sees them passing along their clothespin, they have to take one from that person. The first one to lose all their clothespins sits down in their chair and is declared the winner. (You can have a prize ready if you like - not necessary)

The Teaching Moment: We had fun passing around our clothespins. But how would life be different if we tried everyday to give things away instead of getting things, like our clothespin game? We don't have to be pushy or even let people know we're doing it. What if we gave stuff away, and no one ever noticed we were doing it?. If we give more, we learn to worry only about what we need, not all the extras that we "want." And we don't really have to worry about our needs, because Jesus makes sure we have everything we need.

Song: Jehovah Jireh, My Provider (chords on last page of lesson 1 in this unit)   5 Minutes

You can find this song on most music sites. YouTube offers several good versions. Let the kids sing along. You could let them clap with the song or even play a tambourine or an egg.

The Teaching Moment: Do you remember what Jehovah means? *(Allow for answers.)* What about Jireh? *(Allow for answers.)* Jehovah means God, and Jireh means provider. So Jehovah Jireh means, "God is my

KEY PHRASE: Jesus Makes Sure There Is Enough

provider." Let's always remember that God wants to give us good things, everything that we need. It's our job to realize that everything we want isn't always everything we need.

So what do you think it means when we pray the Lord's Prayer and say, "Give us this day our daily bread?" (*Allow for answers.*) That part of the prayer reminds us to ask God every day to take care of our every need, and it reminds us that all our wants aren't always our needs.

WRAPPING IT UP—SENDING IT HOME   5-7 Minutes

Cleaning Up

Remind the children to help with the clean up and push in their chairs.

Closing Worship and Prayer

Gather the children in a circle holding hands or allow them to sit down to pray. As you close, and if there is time, ask the children for prayer requests. You may close with your own prayer or use the one below for help. Lead them in the Lord's Prayer as you finish praying today.

If you need some guidance for your prayer, you can use this:

Father in Heaven, we praise you that you have the power to provide for us. Thank you for always making sure we have enough. Help us to always remember that you will forever be Jehovah Jireh, our provider. Lord, bless all the things these kids have mentioned as prayer requests today (*if there's time, you can mention some of their requests*). And Lord, we pray all these things in Jesus' name, who taught us to pray: (now lead them in the Lord's Prayer)

Our Father who art in heaven, hallowed be thy Name. Thy Kingdom come, thy will be done on earth as it is in heaven. Give us this day our daily bread and forgive us our debts as we forgive our debtors.

Lead us not into temptation and deliver us from evil. For thine is the kingdom and the power and the glory forever, Amen.

Jehovah Jireh

Public Domain

116—Unit 6: Give Us This Day Our Daily Bread   Lynne Modranski

Jesus, Teach Me How to Pray
A Year in The Lord's Prayer and other Bible Basics

Unit 7: Forgive us our Trespasses as we Forgive Those who Trespass against us
Week 1: We Forgive Because God Forgave Us

Lesson Overview

Today's story is a familiar one. A man who was forgiven a large debt refused to forgive someone who owed him much less and faced the penalty. Jesus used the parable to help us understand that God has not only forgiven us, but He also gave Jesus Christ as the sacrifice to cover our debt. Without the blood of Jesus, our sins would still be very visible to God, and we could never go to heaven. When we pray the Lord's Prayer, we ask God to forgive us to the same degree we forgive others. This should make adults preparing for this lesson really think about our lives. Even if the children don't completely understand this lesson, it's an excellent chance for us to examine our lives and see if we've forgiven others so we can be forgiven.

KEY PHRASE: Forgive Others Like God Forgives Us

SETTING UP THE LESSON   5-7 Minutes
How much would you charge?

PRESENTING THE LESSON   5-10 Minutes
Scripture: Matthew 18:23-35

MAKING IT REAL TO KIDS TODAY   *(Choose as many as you have time for)*

Game: Settling Accounts   10-15 Minutes
Supplies: Monopoly money and index cards

Illustration: Skit   5-7 Minutes

Craft: IOU's   5-10 Minutes
Supplies: Copies of the Craft page at the end of this lesson - one page for each child, scissors and pens or pencils

WRAPPING IT UP—SENDING IT HOME   5-7 Minutes
Clean Up Time & Prayer Time

KEY PHRASE: Forgive Others Like God Forgives Us

SETTING UP THE LESSON   5-7 Minutes

How much would you charge?
Supplies: Newsprint or whiteboard

SAY: Today we're going to make a list of nice things others do for us. (*Allow the children to name things that people do for them that are nice. Be sure to suggest things you know they don't reciprocate, things like laundry, cooking dinner, taking them to friend's house, teaching them, etc. In addition to parents and family members, consider bus drivers, custodians, teachers, librarians—even though these are paid professionals, the kids don't pay them. After you get a pretty good list, continue*) How much are these things worth each time someone does them? $50, $100, $500? Let's put a price beside each item. (*Take a moment and list amounts.*) Do you have enough money to pay the people who do these nice things? Do you do anything in return for what these people do? When people do things for us and we don't pay them or do something in return, we are indebted to them. When we owe someone something, it's called a debt. Jesus told a parable about a man who owed a large debt.

PRESENTING THE LESSON

Scripture Basis: Matthew 18:23-35
You do not have to read this directly from the Bible—use the story form below or reword it to fit your personality

Jesus told his disciples a story about a man who owed a lot of money to the king. The king called the man to come see him and told him he had to pay his whole bill. This man owed 10,000 talents of gold - today he would have owed the king about two hundred million dollars. Do you know how much two hundred million dollars is? (*Allow for answers.*) I can't even imagine that much money. But that's how much the man owed the king. Do you think he could pay his debt? (*Allow for answers.*) Nope, he couldn't. Even if he sold everything he owned, he couldn't pay what he owed the king.

The king had a solution. He ordered that the man and his whole family be sold. They would become slaves, and the king would get all the money to pay the man's debt. Do you know what it means to be a slave? (*Allow for answers.*) That means that the man and his wife and even his children would belong to someone else. They might not get to live together anymore, and they'd have to do whatever their owner said everyday. They wouldn't be allowed to go anywhere. They'd just work every minute of every day, and if they didn't do it right, the owner might beat them with a whip. Do you think you'd like to be a slave? (*Allow for answers.*)

The man didn't want to be a slave, and he didn't want his wife and children to be slaves either. So the man got down on his knees and begged the king to give him more time to pay. The king felt sorry for the man and his family, so he told the man to forget the debt. He cancelled it. Now the man didn't owe anything anymore. How do you think that made the man feel? (*Allow for answers.*)

As the man was leaving the king's castle, he ran into someone he worked with who owed him about fifty dollars. After being forgiven for two hundred million dollars, what do you think the man did when he saw the man who owed him fifty dollars? (*Allow for answers.*) Since the king had been so nice to the man, I thought the man would be so grateful he would cancel the other man's debt, but instead he told the man he wanted his fifty dollars right that minute. The worker didn't have fifty dollars, so he begged the first man to give him some time to pay. That seems reasonable. What would you do if you'd been forgiven so much and someone asked you for a little time to pay you back? (*Allow for answers*). The man who'd been forgiven by the king wasn't so kind. He called the police, and a policeman took the second man to jail until he could pay the fifty dollars. What do you think about that? (*Allow for answers.*)

Word got back to the king about how the first man treated his co-worker, so the king called the man back in. The king told the man, "You're terrible. I forgave you all that money, and you couldn't even give your co-worker some time to pay his debt to you." The king was so mad he called the police and threw the man in jail.

The Bible says that's what it will be like for us. God will forgive us everything if we just ask. When we pray and ask Him, God will cancel everything we owe—unless we don't forgive others. If we won't forgive others, then God says He won't forgive us.

KEY PHRASE: Forgive Others Like God Forgives Us

Lenten Lesson: *If you're using this lesson during Lent, you can add this:* Christians use lent as a time to do a checkup. We look at our lives and see if there's anything that we need to change, anyone we've done something mean or wrong to, or anything we've done that would make God sad. We should ask God for forgiveness each time we don't act like Christians, but during Lent we take extra time to make sure we're growing to be more like Christ.

MAKING IT REAL TO KIDS TODAY

Illustration: A Skit to Help with today's lesson

4 CHARACTERS: (recruit some adults or teens to visit Children's Program today. If they can memorize the skit it would be better—or you might use older kids in Children's Program) Option: Ask four of your older students to read the play with much emotion.

Kerry—Important Rich Guy/Girl

Jailer—no words—just drags Jay around when necessary guy/girl

Jay—Indebted poor Guy/Girl

Jesse—another indebted poor

KERRY, Someone who looks like an important person——stands or sits on a high chair. Jailer drags in JAY

KERRY *(looking at a clipboard):*—OK, Jay, I see here you owe me ten billion dollars. You're going to have to pay up today or go to jail. I just can't wait any longer for you to pay me.

JAY: *(on knees begging)* - Come on, Kerry, I just don't have any money right now. Can you give me a few more weeks. I really want to pay you, honest I do. I just don't have it now. So, how 'bout it, can I have a few extra days?

KERRY: I'll tell you what, Jay. Let's just forget it. We'll call it even. You don't owe me a penny anymore.

JAY: *(standing up)* Really? Wow! That's exciting! How can I ever thank you, Kerry? You're the best. I'll see you around.

(Jay walks toward Jesse—Kerry stays where he is)

JAY: *(meets Jesse on the street)* Hey Jesse! How are you? It's really good to see you. Do you happen to have that $10 you owe me? I really need it.

JESSE: I'm so sorry, Jay. I just don't have anything right now. *(pull out pockets if you can)* I can probably get it to you next week. Would that be all right?

JAY: *(getting angry)* Come on, Jesse. I have to have it, and I have to have it now! Hand it over! You have to have something—a Wal-Mart gift card, something!

JESSE: But I don't have any... *(Jay interrupts)*

JAY: No, you can't say that! *(really angry now).* That's it! I'm calling the cops. You're going to jail!

The jailer comes in and drags out Jesse

KERRY: *(calling from across the room)* Hey Jay!

JAY: *(in a really friendly tone)* Yeah, Kerry, what 'cha need, good friend?

KERRY: Come here a minute, please.

JAY: *(walks over to Kerry)* So, what' cha need, Kerry?

KERRY: I noticed you were talking to Jesse.

JAY: Yeah. We had a few words.

KERRY: I can't believe you treated him/her that way.

JAY: Well, he does owe me ten bucks. And I'm really hard up for money right now.

KERRY: But I just forgave your whole debt, and it was a lot more.

JAY: Yeah, but you have lots of money. I don't have anything.

KERRY: It doesn't matter, Jay. If you can't forgive Jesse ten dollars, then I want my ten billion.

JAY: *(Sounding very sad)* But I don't have ten billion dollars, Kerry.

KERRY: I'm sorry to hear that, Jay. *(he motions for the jailer)* But you're going to jail.

(The jailer comes in and drags jay off to jail)

KEY PHRASE: Forgive Others Like God Forgives Us

The Teaching Moment: That's exactly what happened in the Bible story today. Jay was forgiven, but he wasn't willing to forgive someone who owed him. What happened when he wouldn't forgive? (Allow for answers.) If Jay wouldn't forgive, he couldn't be forgiven. The same thing happens to us. If we won't forgive others, God can't forgive us.

Game: Settling Accounts   10-15 Minutes
Supplies: Monopoly money and index cards

1. Create enough index cards, one for each child, that have various monetary amounts on them, $20, $50, $200 & $500.
2. Fold the index cards in half, seal the cards with tape or stickers. You could write on the back, "My Debt"
3. Divide children into two teams and let each child each choose one index card but don't open it.
4. Ask the kids all kinds of Bible questions alternating between teams. *(see the page after the lesson for questions)*
5. If the child answers incorrectly, they must go to "jail" until they have $20 to pay their way out.
6. If they answer correctly, they get a piece of monopoly money. Make the harder questions worth a bit more.
7. After one or two rounds of questions, children will open their cards and see how much debt they have to pay. Collect their money and give change.
8. Children with enough money to cover their "debt" can play again. Those who are short must pay what they can and then go to jail until they come up with the rest. They can't answer questions while in jail!
9. Children may use any extra money to help pay their teammates debt plus their $20 jail fee so they can get out of jail.
10. The game ends when only one person is left out of jail or time runs out. The team with the most people out of jail the winning team.

The Teaching Moment: When we owe someone something, we call that a debt. It doesn't have to be money. We can owe time or a favor. God said we always owe love to each other. There is a cost to get into heaven and have a relationship with God. The cost is being perfect. Since we can't be perfect, Jesus paid our debt by being a sacrifice for all the bad things we do. Because God forgave our debts and because of what Jesus did for us, we need to always forgive others.

Craft: IOU's   5-10 Minutes
Supplies: Copies of the Craft page at the end of this lesson - one page for each child, scissors and pens or pencils

1. Give each child one page of IOU's and allow them to cut them apart. (They can do more if they'd like.)
2. Have them write their name on the first blank of each one
3. On the second blank, have them write the name of someone who has done nice things for them
4. On the last blank have them write something they want to do for that person to partially pay the debt for the nice thing they did.
5. Encourage them to give the IOU to the person whose name they wrote on the paper. Remind them to thank the person for the nice things they do.

KEY PHRASE: Forgive Others Like God Forgives Us

The Teaching Moment: We can never repay every debt we owe. Many people do nice things for us and don't expect any repayment, but that doesn't mean we shouldn't be appreciative. We need to always pay attention to what people do for us and thank those people and God for sending them to us. We should also do nice things for other people because people were nice to us. This will remind us to forgive because God forgives us.

WRAPPING IT UP—SENDING IT HOME   5-7 Minutes

Cleaning Up

We want the children to learn to be responsible, so be sure they help with the clean up.

Closing Worship and Prayer

Gather children in a circle holding hands or allow them to sit down to pray. If you choose to join hands, remember that it's OK if some children prefer not to join the circle. Just ask them to be respectful of others as they pray and not make any noise.

As you close, and if there is time, ask the children for prayer requests. You may close with your own prayer or use the one below for help. Children should now be able to pray "The Lord's Prayer" with you instead of repeating after you.

If you need some guidance for your prayer, you can use this:

Father in Heaven, we praise you that you are a forgiving God. Thank you for sending Jesus to pay all our debts. Forgive us for the things we do each day that make you sad. Lord, be in all of the things these kids have mentioned as prayer requests today (*if there's time, you can mention some of their requests*). And Lord, we pray all of these things in Jesus' name, who taught us to pray: *(now lead them in the Lord's Prayer)*

Our Father who art in heaven, hallowed be thy Name. Thy Kingdom come, thy will be done on earth as it is in heaven.
Give us this day our daily bread and forgive us our debts as we forgive our debtors.
Lead us not into temptation and deliver us from evil. For thine is the kingdom and the power and the glory forever, Amen.

KEY PHRASE: Forgive Others Like God Forgives Us

Questions to use for the Game (or make up your own)

1. What was the name of the first woman? — EVE $50
2. What was the name of the first man? — ADAM $50
3. Who built an ark? — NOAH $50
4. Whose wife looked back and turned into salt — LOT $300
5. Who heard a voice from a burning bush? — MOSES $100
6. What were God's people called? — ISRAELITES $500
7. Where was Jesus Born? — BETHLEHEM $100
8. Who was the first king of Israel — DAVID $100
9. Tell me one commandment (use this 5 x) — $100-$500
   - $100 for 1st -
   $200 for 2nd, etc
10. Tell me one line from your favorite song about Jesus. — $20
    - accept all answers - use many times
11. What was it called when Jesus got wet in the Jordan river? — BAPTISM $100
12. Name one of Jesus' disciples (use this 5x) — $100 - $500
    $100 for 1st - $200 for 2nd, etc
13. How many people will be crying in heaven? — NONE $300
14. What was the name of the angel who talked to Mary? — GABRIEL $200
15. How many days was Jesus in the wilderness? — Forty days $50
16. Name one thing you're thankful for (use only for the littlest kids) — $10 - use many times
17. How many did Jesus feed when He was preaching? — 4000 or 5000 men - $400
18. What do we call the day we celebrate Jesus' Birthday? — CHRISTMAS $50
19. What do we call the day we celebrate Jesus' death? — GOOD FRIDAY $100
20. What do we call the day we celebrate Jesus' raising from the dead? — EASTER $100
21. What is the bread called that God fed the Israelites? — MANNA $100

Repeat questions that were missed the first time
If Necessary - Repeat correctly answered questions at 1/2 the value

IOU

NAME
_____

Owes

_____

_____

IOU

NAME
_____

Owes

_____

_____

IOU

NAME
_____

Owes

_____

_____

IOU

NAME
_____

Owes

_____

_____

IOU

NAME
_____

Owes

_____

_____

IOU

NAME
_____

Owes

_____

_____

Page intentionally left blank for printing and copying purposes

Jesus, Teach Me How to Pray
A Year in The Lord's Prayer and other Bible Basics

Unit 7: Forgive us our Trespasses as we Forgive Those who Trespass against us
Week 2: We Forgive Because Christ Asks Us

Lesson Overview

For today's lesson you can read the entire passage of scripture. This is part of Jesus' "Sermon on the Mount" and talks about relationships, as well as the way that we should treat others and interact with them. For the kids sake we're going to focus on verses 21-26. These verses help us see that God is very concerned about how we treat others. The three things Jesus specifically tells us in these few verses are 1. don't call people names 2. making things right with people is more important than giving offerings to God 3. If you're fighting with someone, settle it, don't let it go on. These are great lessons for kids. It's good for them to realize that not only their parents or teachers have these expectations for them, God sets these standards too. Plus this is a great lesson for adults!

KEY PHRASE: God Cares About How I Treat Others

SETTING UP THE LESSON   5-7 Minutes

No Trespassing
Supplies: A few no trespassing signs-see printables at the end of the lesson

PRESENTING THE LESSON   5-10 Minutes

Scripture: Matthew 5:17-48

MAKING IT REAL TO KIDS TODAY   *(Choose as many as you have time for)*

Game: No Trespassing   5-10 Minutes
Supplies: Masking tape

Illustration: Don't Bully the Apple   5 Minutes
Supplies: Two Apples (One dark and one light would be a plus, but not required) and a knife
A day or two before your class time, drop the darker apple on the floor multiple times without breaking the skin or damaging it too much but enough to bruise it well.

Craft: Bracelet Reminder   10-15 Minutes
Supplies: Black, Red and White 1/4" pony beads (about 20-25 per child) and Elastic String OPT: Small charms, crosses or nails, that can be strung (one per child)

WRAPPING IT UP—SENDING IT HOME   5—7 Minutes

Clean Up Time & Prayer Time

KEY PHRASE: God Cares About How I Treat Others

SETTING UP THE LESSON   5-7 Minutes

No Trespassing
Supplies: A few no trespassing signs-see printables at the end of the lesson

Place the "No Trespassing" signs on several chairs in your lesson area. As kids come in, act like the signs aren't there. Greet the children as usual, ask them how their week was. If no children sit in the "No Trespassing" seats, ask the kids why they didn't sit there. If someone does sit in one of those chairs ask that child why they did sit there. Accept all their answers as reasonable. Ask the group what "No Trespassing" means. Use the next paragraph to help them understand.

Trespassing means crossing a boundary without permission. For instance, if someone comes in your bedroom without permission that person is trespassing. In our lesson area, because that sign was on the chair, when someone sits on that chair they are trespassing, they've gone past the boundary that's been set. If mother says no cookies before dinner and you eat a cookie before dinner, you've trespassed because you went beyond the boundary that was set. Trespasses are usually committed against another person.

PRESENTING THE LESSON   5-10 Minutes

Scripture: Matthew 5:17-48
You do not have to read this directly from the Bible—use the story form below or reword it to fit your personality

When Jesus started traveling around the country telling others about God, He spent a few days preaching out on a hill. People from all over came out to hear him. He talked to them about murder. Do you know what murder is? *(Allow for answers.)* Murder is when someone kills someone on purpose. That's pretty bad, don't you think? *(Allow for answers.)* Jesus said, "You know murder is bad, right?" Then Jesus told the people that when they get mad at their friends or call them names, it's just as bad. Do you ever get mad at your friends or family? *(Allow for answers.)* What makes you angry? *(Allow for answers.)* Do you call people names? *(Allow for answers.)* How do you think Jesus feels when we get mad at people or call them names? *(Allow for answers.)* Jesus said that when we do those things they are just as bad as murder.

It's important to God that we work to get along with each other. It's so important that Jesus said if we're bringing our offering to God and remember that someone is upset with us, whether we did something wrong or not, we should put our offering down and go talk to our friend. Do you know what an offering is? *(Allow for answers.)* When we put money in the plate during church, that's an offering. But when we give our time or other things to God those are all offerings. God values our relationships with others so much, he doesn't want our offerings if we are angry or others are angry with us. God wants us to go talk to the person who is upset with us, apologize and try to be friends with them again. Then after we've done our best to apologize, we can take our offering to God. Jesus wants us to get along with each other. He said that is even more important than what we give to God.

Finally, Jesus told the people He wanted them to get along with their enemies. He said if their enemy accused them of something, they should work hard to settle it. Have you ever had someone tattle on you. *(Allow for answers.)* What do you do when you hear that? *(Allow for answers.)* Have you ever said, "I'm sorry," and tried to work it out with the person? *(Allow for answers.)*

We can't always work it out every time someone gets mad at us or plans to tell on us. Sometimes the person will still be mad. A lot of times they'll still tell on us. But lucky for us, God doesn't hold us responsible for the way others act, only the way we act. Have you ever been punished for something someone else did? *(Allow for answers.)* That happens here on earth. Sometimes we get in trouble for something we didn't do, and we end up being responsible for someone else's actions. But with God, it's not like that. He only punishes us for what we've done, not what others have done.

God is very clear. He really meant it when He told us to pray, "Forgive us our trespasses as we forgive those who trespass against us." Jesus cares about how we treat others. He set an example when He died for us and forgave us. He wants us to forgive.

KEY PHRASE: God Cares About How I Treat Others

MAKING IT REAL TO KIDS TODAY
(Choose as many as you have time for)

Game: No Trespassing
Supplies: Masking tape
5-10 Minutes

This game is best played in a long room or hall

1. Place a masking tape line on the floor at one end of the room with about three feet behind it.
2. One child (the guard) stands behind the masking tape with all the other children at the other end of the room.
3. The guard says "GO" and turns his back to the rest of the kids. The other children have to sneak up on the guard with a goal to cross the line. They aren't allowed to run.
4. The guard can say "STOP" and turn back around whenever he or she wants. It can be just a second after they start or a few. Just be careful not too long because those coming from the other end might cross the line.
5. When the guard says stop, the kids have to stop. If the guard catches someone still moving that person has to go back to the beginning (adults should monitor to be sure only those really still moving are sent back).
6. The guard repeats steps #3 - #5 until someone crosses the line. Then that person is the guard, and everyone else tries to cross her line.

The Teaching Moment: We had a lot of fun playing this, but the reason we used this game was to help you understand trespassing. The guard's job was to protect the goal and keep everyone else from getting across. When we cross the line that someone sets for us that's trespassing. We need to be sure we never cross the line that God has set for us.

Illustration: Don't Bully the Apple
5 Minutes
Supplies: Two Apples (one dark and one light would be a plus, but not required) and a knife.

Originally posted on Facebook by Mum in the Moment

A day or two before your class time take the darker of the apples (even if they appear to be close to the same the darker won't show the bruises as much) and drop it repeatedly. Try not to damage the outside, but bruise it well.

During your class, show the children both apples, but hold up the darker apple and tell the children

I don't like this apple. It's kind of ugly, don't you think? I think you should help me tell this apple how horrible it is. *Pass the apple to the oldest child and encourage him or her to say something bad to the apple. The children will probably look at you strange. If they have trouble thinking of something, ask them to tell the apple whatever the last mean thing was that they said to someone. Tell them to talk to the apple and pass it to the next person. After everyone has had a turn, show the children both apples.*

I kind of like this other apple, what do you think about it? *Again they'll probably look at you strange.* But I want to show you the inside of both apples. *First cut the lighter apple in half.* That is definitely a beautiful apple. *Then cut the bruised apple in half. The bruise should have grown significantly overnight.* But what happened to this apple? It doesn't look much different on the outside. *(Allow for answers.)*

The Teaching Moment: This is what unkind words do to our friends and family. Even though you can't tell the difference on the outside, nastiness hurts us on the inside. Jesus told us treating others well is important to him. Each time we forgive, we help people look more like this good apple and we help others to feel better inside.

KEY PHRASE: God Cares About How I Treat Others

Craft: Bracelet Reminder 10-15 Minutes
Supplies: Black, Red and White 1/4" pony beads (about 20-25 per child) and Elastic String
OPT: Small charms, crosses or nails, that can be strung (one per child)

1. Give each child about 10" of elastic string and an equal number of black, red and white beads as well as one small charm if you use that option.
2. Allow children to string the beads on the elastic string. They can put them in any order, but be sure they don't use all one color.
3. When there are enough beads that it will go around their wrist, pull the elastic a little tight and tie it together.

The Teaching Moment: These bracelets can remind you of what Jesus said. The black beads remind us that everything does things we shouldn't do—we sin. When we do things we shouldn't do, it makes us look dirty to God, so we use black to remind us of the dirt. These things separate us from God. That's why Jesus died on the cross. The red beads remind us of what Jesus did for us. He bled and died on the cross so we could be forgiven. The red reminds us of Jesus' blood. The white beads remind us we are forgiven. Jesus' sacrifice allows us to be just like we'd never sinned. White is a symbol for perfect, and when we accept Jesus' blood as payment for our sins, all our dirt is gone, and we look perfect to God.

WRAPPING IT UP—SENDING IT HOME 5-7 Minutes

Cleaning Up

To help children learn to be responsible, remind them they need to help clean up and push in their chairs.

Closing Worship and Prayer

Gather the children in a circle holding hands or allow them to sit down to pray. It's okay if some children prefer not to join the circle or join hands. Remind them to be respectful of others as they pray and not make any noise.

As you close, and if there is time, ask the children for prayer requests. Have the children pray "The Lord's Prayer" with you.

If you need some guidance for your prayer, you can use this:

Father in Heaven, we praise you that you care about the way we treat others. Thank you for sending Jesus so we can see the way we should treat other people. Forgive us that we don't always treat others the way you would. Lord, watch over these children and be with all the things they have mentioned as prayer requests today (*if there's time, you can mention some of their requests*). And Lord, we pray all of these things in Jesus' name, who taught us to pray: (*now lead them in the Lord's Prayer*)

Our Father who art in heaven, hallowed be thy Name. Thy Kingdom come, thy will be done on earth as it is in heaven.
Give us this day our daily bread and forgive us our debts as we forgive our debtors.
Lead us not into temptation and deliver us from evil. For thine is the kingdom and the power and the glory forever, Amen.

NO TRESPASSING

Page intentionally left blank for printing and copying purposes

Jesus, Teach Me How to Pray
A Year in The Lord's Prayer and other Bible Basics

Unit 7: Forgive us our Trespasses as we Forgive Those who Trespass against us
Week 3: We Forgive Because We Are Forgiven

Lesson Overview

Today's lesson is the foundation of the Christian faith. Our celebration of Christmas and Easter, as well as our assurance of salvation, all hinge on this one event in history. Jesus' arrest in the garden, his questioning by Pilate, Peter's denial, the crowd's call for His death, and finally His crucifixion are all a part of today's lesson. Since we know that Jesus rose from the dead, sometimes we don't truly appreciate the sacrifice Jesus made on the cross. It's difficult to help children understand that a blood sacrifice was needed to make us right with God and that Jesus came to be that final sacrifice once and for all, but today we'll attempt to help them see the magnitude of the sacrifice Jesus made.

KEY PHRASE: Jesus Died to Pay For Our Sins

SETTING UP THE LESSON   5-10 Minutes

Game: Missing the Mark
Supplies: Plastic or children's putters (a yard stick or straight stick would work also), practice golf balls and either a disposable cup or a practice putting cup

PRESENTING THE LESSON   5-10 Minutes

Scripture: Luke 22:47-23:46

MAKING IT REAL TO KIDS TODAY   *(Choose as many as you have time for)*

Craft: Cross and Bead Bible Bookmark   10-15 Minutes
Supplies: Small metal craft or scrapbooking cross, one for each child; 2-10 beads for each child and one very thin shoe lace or 1/8" cord for each child.

Song: "By His Wounds" by Mac Powell and others   5 Minutes
Supplies: Recording or YouTube Video of this song-you might write the chorus on a piece of paper

Illustration: What is salvation?   5 Minutes
Supplies: Clear glass about 3/4 full of water, tsp. of baking powder, spoon, food coloring, 1/4 c. ble

WRAPPING IT UP—SENDING IT HOME   5-7 Minutes

Clean Up Time & Prayer Time

KEY PHRASE: Jesus Died to Pay For Our Sins

SETTING UP THE LESSON 5-10 Minutes

Game: Missing the Mark
Supplies: Plastic or children's putters (a yard stick or straight stick would work also), practice golf balls and either a disposable cup or a practice putting cup—You could alternately toss ping pong balls into a cup to make the same point.

Divide the children into two or more teams (about 5-10 kids per team—or children could play individually).

Set the cup or putting cup about 5 feet from where the kids will putt. Let each child have three chances to putt into the cup. (be sure that the children are well supervised and don't swing the club too far)

Keep track of how many balls make it into the cup for each team. Go through the line two or three times depending on your time. The team who makes the most shots wins.

The Teaching Moment: Did anyone here make every shot? (Allow for answers.) It's hard to get every ball in the cup. It's just as hard to be like Jesus in everything we do. When we act badly instead of like Jesus, it's just like missing the cup. In fact, the word sin means missing the mark. Jesus set a high standard for us, and when we don't measure up, when we "miss the mark," that's called sin. Sin separates us from God. But today we're going to talk about how Jesus made a way for us to be able to talk to God and get to heaven someday.

PRESENTING THE LESSON 5-10 Minutes

Scripture: Luke 22:47-23:46
You do not have to read this directly from the Bible—use the story form below or reword it to fit your personality

One night many years ago, Jesus ate a very special dinner with his disciples. After they finished, they went to a garden called Gethsemane. Can you say Gethsemane (Geth - **sem** - uh - nee)? *(Allow them to repeat)* This garden was on the Mount of Olives, a place where a lot of Olive Trees grew. While they were there in the garden, guards from the temple came with some of the temple leaders. One of Jesus' disciples led them. Does anyone know his name? *(Allow for answers.)* Judas seemed confused about what it meant for Jesus to be the Messiah, so he agreed to help the guards find Jesus and arrest Him. Do you know what guards are? *(Allow for answers.)* The temple guards were like our security guards or policemen, but they guarded the church.

Judas had told the temple guards he would show them Jesus by kissing Him on the cheek. So, when Judas walked into the garden, he greeted Jesus with a kiss on His cheek just like friends did back then. The guards immediately arrested Jesus and took Him to the house of the High Priest.

While the High Priest asked Jesus questions, another of Jesus' disciples, Peter, stood outside waiting to see what would happen. While he kept warm at the fire, someone asked him if he knew Jesus. Peter was afraid they'd arrest him too, so he lied and told them he'd never met Jesus. Two more times people asked him about knowing Jesus, and he told them, "no." Right after that third time, a rooster started to crow. How many of you know what a rooster sounds like? *(Allow for "Cock-a-doodle-do")* That rooster reminded Peter that Jesus was his good friend, and it was wrong to lie about knowing Him. Peter felt really bad. He went away from the crowd and cried because he felt so horrible.

Just about that time, the guards brought Jesus out of the house and started to beat him and spit on him. They made fun of him and teased him. Finally they took Jesus to see Pilate, the governor of the area. They told lies about Jesus to make Him look bad. Even with all the lies, Pilate couldn't find any reason to arrest Jesus, but because the governor didn't want to make the temple leaders mad, he asked the crowds standing outside his palace what he should do. He promised to release one prisoner, either Jesus or Barabbas. Can you say Barabbas (Buh-RAB-bus)? *(Allow the kids to repeat)* Barabbas was a terrible man who'd done a lot of bad things, but that didn't matter, the people yelled they wanted Barabbas released. Pilate wanted to let Jesus go, so he asked them again, but they kept yelling, "Crucify him, crucify him." So Pilate released Barabbas and sent Jesus to be crucified.

KEY PHRASE: Jesus Died to Pay For Our Sins

Jesus was hurt so badly from the guards beating him He couldn't even stand up and carry the cross to the hill. So the Roman soldiers pulled a man named Simon from the crowd and made him carry Jesus' cross. When they got out to the hill, a place called "the Skull," they hung Jesus on the cross and put His cross between two others. That's what crucify means. When the Romans hung people on crosses to punish them, they called it crucifixion.

While Jesus was on the cross, He prayed and asked God to forgive the men who nailed Him to the cross. Even though He was in terrible pain and had been treated so badly, He asked God to forgive those who'd made Him feel bad. Jesus hung on the cross for three hours, and the sky got very dark. As He was about to die, Jesus told God that He was in God's hands. Just then the heavy curtain that was in the temple ripped right in two from the top to the bottom *(you might rip a piece of paper or something heavy to emphasize what you just said and to get the kids attention)*. After Jesus died, a soldier stabbed him with a large sword to be sure He was dead.

The curtain that ripped had been used to keep everyone out of the special place where God lived in the temple. Jesus dying on the cross caused the curtain to rip showing that now everyone was allowed to go and talk to God. Jesus had lived perfectly on the Earth so his death on the cross makes up for all our mistakes. Because Jesus died on the cross we can ask God to forgive all of our sins.

The Lenten Lesson: *If you're teaching this lesson during lent, tell the children:* In just a few weeks we'll be celebrating Good Friday. Good Friday is the day we celebrate Christ's death on the cross. Why do you think we call it "good?" *(Allow for answers.)* It's good because without Jesus' death on the cross we'd either still have to offer animal sacrifices each day or we wouldn't be able to go to heaven.

MAKING IT REAL TO KIDS TODAY   *(Choose as many as you have time for)*

Craft: Cross and Bead Bible Bookmark   5-10 minutes
Supplies: Small metal craft or scrapbooking cross (be sure it has an eye), one for each child; 2-10 pony beads for each child and one very thin shoe lace or 1/8" cord for each child.

1. Give each child a small metal cross, 24" - 30" of cord and as many beads as they'd like (up to 10)

2. Fold the cord in 1/2 put it through the eye of the cross, then put the ends of the cord through the loop made when you folded it in half.

3. Add 1-3 beads to the folded cord and slide them up to the cross. Tie a knot directly under the beads.

4. Tie the two ends into another knot about 3" from the end of the doubled cord. Add a few more beads on each strand of the cord and make a large knot on each cord to hold those beads on teh bottom.

The Teaching Moment: This is a bookmark, you can put it in your Bible or another book you're reading. The cross at the end is to remind you that Jesus died on the cross so our sins can be forgiven.

Song: "By His Wounds" by Mac Powell and others   5 Minutes
Supplies: Recording or YouTube Video of this song-you might write the chorus on a piece of paper

Play a recording of this song. Ask the kids to listen closely. During the final chorus turn the volume down and ask them if they know what the words mean:

He was pierced for our transgressions The soldier stabbed Jesus with a sword that's what pierced Him- transgressions are the same as sins.

He was crushed for our sins - another way to say that He was killed for our sins

The punishment that brought us peace was upon Him - death on the cross was punishment and because of it we have peace with God.

By His wounds we are healed - Jesus was wounded. The beatings He took, the stabbing and being crucified all made wounds, and because of those wounds, we can have all of our sins forgiven.

KEY PHRASE: Jesus Died to Pay for Our Sins

Illustration: What is Salvation? 5 Minutes
Supplies: Clear glass about 3/4 full of water, tsp. of baking powder, spoon, food coloring, 1/4 c. bleach

Ask the Kids: What is salvation? Why do we need to be saved?

Show them your glass of water and say: When God created Adam and Eve, they had no sin. Just like this cup of water, they were completely clean. But when Satan came looking like a snake, he talked Eve into disobeying God. It seemed like a harmless thing, but it was still sin. *(Stir 1 teaspoon of baking powder into your water.)* We do things that look harmless everyday, but they're still sin. We tell little lies or don't listen to our parents when they ask us to clean our room. But God told Isaiah that even the good things we do look dirty to Him. *(Squirt in enough food coloring to change the color of the water.)*

Jesus died on the cross because the only way we can be good enough for God is to have no sins. We either have to be perfect or have a sacrifice as a substitute for our sins. Jesus died to be that substitute. If we keep the sin, we have to live with Satan forever, but the blood Jesus shed on the cross cleans up all our sin. *(Pour the bleach into the water)* Just like the stuff in this glass cleaned up the water, Jesus makes us sinless and saves us from living with Satan forever if we ask him.

All we have to do is accept the gift of his death on the cross, pray, and thank Him for dying on the cross. Then, we ask Him to forgive our sins, and we promise to try our best to live for Him. We're going to say a prayer today. If any of you would like to accept Jesus' gift on the cross, you'll be able to pray with me.

WRAPPING IT UP—SENDING IT HOME 5-7 Minutes

Cleaning Up

We want the children to learn to be responsible, so be sure they help with the clean up.

Closing Worship and Prayer

Either gather the children in a circle holding hands or allow them to sit down to pray. Remember it's OK if some children prefer not to join the circle. Ask them to be respectful of others as they pray and not make any noise.

As you close, and if there is time, ask the children for prayer requests. You may close with your own prayer or use the one below for help. Encourage them to pray "The Lord's Prayer" with you.

If you need some guidance for your prayer, you can use this *(you might encourage the kids to repeat after you in case they want to ask Jesus to be their Savior)*:

Heavenly Father, thank you for giving us the gift of your life on the cross. Forgive us for those times when we miss the mark you set for us. We don't want to sin and make you sad, but we have a hard time always being like Jesus. Help us live like Jesus did more everyday. Jesus, I accept the gift you gave when you died on the cross. Thank you for your gift. Lord, bless all the things these kids have mentioned as prayer requests today *(if there's time, you can mention some of their requests)*. And Lord, we pray all of these things in Jesus' name, who taught us to pray: (now lead them in the Lord's Prayer)

Our Father who art in heaven, hallowed be thy Name. Thy Kingdom come, thy will be done on earth as it is in heaven. Give us this day our daily bread and forgive us our debts as we forgive our debtors.
Lead us not into temptation and deliver us from evil. For thine is the kingdom and the power and the glory forever, Amen.

Tell the children if they accepted Jesus' gift on the cross and asked Him for salvation, they should be sure to tell someone. Encourage them to tell you. Give them an opportunity to stay behind and pray with you individually if they'd like. Suggest they talk to the pastor and tell their parents and grandparents if they've accepted Jesus' gift of salvation. If you aren't comfortable praying or talking to a child about Salvation, ask another adult to "assist" in your children's ministry today so they will be there to help with this most important aspect of today's lesson.

Jesus, Teach Me How to Pray
A Year in The Lord's Prayer and other Bible Basics

Unit 8: Lead Us Not Into Temptation
Lesson 1: The Very First Temptation

Lesson Overview

Today's lesson goes back to the very beginning. Temptation is nothing new. It's something that humans have struggled with since time began. We always think there's something more or better than what God has for us. By the time we discover God really does know best, we've usually messed it up pretty badly. This might be a good time for the adults teaching this lesson to take a look at the things that tempt them and be sure they trust God to help get through the temptations.

KEY PHRASE: People Have Been Tempted Since The Beginning of Time

SETTING UP THE LESSON — 5 Minutes

Carrots or Tootsie Rolls
Supplies: Carrots and Tootsie Rolls and bowls to put them in

PRESENTING THE LESSON — 10 Minutes

Scripture: Genesis 3:1-19

MAKING IT REAL TO KIDS TODAY — *(Choose as many as you have time for)*

Game: Throw Away the Things That Tempt You — 5-7 Minutes
Supplies: Scrap paper

Craft: Lead Me Not Into Temptation Wheel — 10 Minutes
Supplies: Paper plates, copies of the craft page at the end of this lesson, poster board or the back of notebooks, hole punch, brass fasteners (split pins), glue

Special: Memory Verse - 1 Corinthians 10:13 — 5 Minutes

WRAPPING IT UP—SENDING IT HOME — 5 Minutes

Clean Up & Prayer Time

KEY PHRASE: People Have Been Tempted Since the Beginning of Time

SETTING UP THE LESSON   5 Minutes

Carrots or Tootsie Rolls
Supplies: Carrots and Tootsie Rolls (or a variety of candy) - Check with parents about food allergies or diabetes and plan accordingly (you could use chips instead of candy)

Put the Carrots and Tootsie Rolls in several bowls all around where the children will be sitting. As they enter tell them they can eat the carrots, but they aren't allowed to have the candy. Go around the room and ask each child which they like best, the carrots or the candy, or if there is anything else they just can't resist. (You may have a few who actually like the carrots better).

Ask them these questions and have them to raise their hands if they would say yes:

1. How many of you think it's hard to look at the candy and not be allowed to eat it?
2. If I (and all the adults) left the room, how many would be tempted to take a piece of candy?
3. How many have taken a cookie or a piece of candy when their mom told them not to?

SAY: In today's Bible story the people had a hard time resisting when God told them not to eat something. *(At this point they may ask for the candy or chips, but continue to tell them they can't have those)*

PRESENTING THE LESSON   10 Minutes

Scripture: Genesis 3:1-19

You do not have to read this directly from the Bible—use the story form below or reword it to fit your personality

The story we're going to share today might be one that many of you know. I'll tell you what, before we tell the story, let's see if you can answer some questions about today's lesson. *(Allow for answers after each question)*

1. What was the name of the first man? *Adam*
2. What was the name of the first woman? *Eve*
3. Where did they live? *The Garden of Eden*
4. What was the Garden like? *It was perfect.*

The Garden of Eden was beautiful. It had every kind of fruit and vegetable. The food grew without anyone planting anything. God took care of making it grow. Imagine all the trees growing fruit and nuts. Tell everyone your favorite fruit. *(Give each child a moment to share.)*

There were also two special trees in the garden. Do you know what they were called? *(Allow for answers.)* One was the Tree of the Knowledge of Good and Evil and the other was the Tree of Life. God told Adam and Eve they should eat from the Tree of Life. They could eat as much as they wanted from that tree, and the fruit would make them live forever. But God told them they could not eat from the Tree of Knowledge of Good and Evil. Can you say that? *(Allow them to repeat)* They had one the only rule in the garden. They could eat as much as they wanted from all the other trees. How do you think they felt about not getting to eat from that tree? *(Allow for answers.)* Does that remind you of our Carrots and Tootsie Rolls?

One day while Eve walked in the garden, she came across a snake. Do you like snakes? *(Allow for answers.)* This snake could walk and talk, and it asked Eve, "Did God really say you couldn't eat any of the fruit from any of the trees in the garden?" What do you think? Is that what God said? *(Allow for answers)* God hadn't told them they couldn't eat from ANY tree, just the one tree. But the snake was trying to trick Eve. Did anyone ever try to trick you? *(Allow for answers.)*

And that's when the trouble started. Eve told the snake that if they ate it or even touched The Tree of the Knowledge of Good and Evil they would die. God didn't say they couldn't touch it. He only said they couldn't eat it. But Eve exaggerated a bit, and that was her first mistake. Do you know what it means to exaggerate? *(Allow for answers.)* Exaggeration is when we say something that's not quite true. If you have six marbles, and you say you have sixteen, you exaggerated. Exaggerations are lies about things that don't matter, so they're the silliest lies to tell.

KEY PHRASE: People Have Been Tempted Since the Beginning of Time

The snake told Eve God didn't know what He was talking about. He made Eve believe God was cheating them out of the best fruit. He said that the fruit was good and wouldn't kill them. And Eve believed him. He convinced her to eat from the tree of Knowledge of Good and Evil. So she ate some fruit from the tree that God said not to eat. Then she took some to Adam. And even though Adam knew He shouldn't eat it, he took some fruit and ate it too.

While they lived in the Garden of Eden, God walked with and talked to Adam and Eve every day in person just like you and I talk to each other. So God came into the Garden the next morning like always. But this time, Adam and Eve hid. They were afraid that God would find out what they'd done. What had they done? *(Allow for answers)* But hiding didn't help, God knew they had eaten from the Tree of Knowledge of Good and Evil. He called out to them, but God knew right where they were. Because they had listened to the snake and eaten from the tree God told them not to, they had to move out of the beautiful garden.

This is the very first time anyone ever faced temptation. Can you say temptation? *(Allow for answers.)* Temptation is what it's called when we know the right thing to do, but something or someone tries to talk us into doing the wrong thing. Have you ever done the wrong thing? *(Allow for answers.)* What happens when you do the wrong thing? *(Allow for answers.)* Do you get punished when you do things your mom and dad tell you not to? *(Allow for answers.)* How did Adam and Eve get punished for not listening to God? *(Allow for answers.)* Adam and Eve had to leave the beautiful garden where everything was perfect. They had to start working for their food instead of just having it grow in the garden.

But the temptation isn't the bad thing. Everyone faces temptation. Temptation is not sin. It's only when we listen to the temptation that we have to face the consequences.

Part of the prayer that we pray, The Lord's Prayer, is asking God to "lead us not into temptation." What do you think that means? *(Allow for answers.)* The Bible says that God never tempts us. *(James 1:13)* But when we pray this we're asking God to help us stay away from things that tempt us and help us choose to do right. It's not always easy to do the right thing, but if we ask, God will help us.

MAKING IT REAL TO KIDS TODAY
(Choose as many as you have time for)

Game: Throw Away the Things that Tempt you 5-7 Minutes
Supplies: Scrap Paper

1. You'll need at least as many sheets of scrap paper as you have children (more would be better - if you have time, allow each child to write one or more things they do that get them into trouble) Allow the kids to crumple the paper into balls.

2. Put a piece of masking tape on the floor about 8 feet long or use a table in the middle of the room.

3. Divide the group into two teams. (try to get an even number of older and younger kids on each team)

4. Put one team on each side of the masking tape or table.

5. Divide the paper wads and put half on each side of the masking tape or table.

6. When you say, "go" the kids begin to throw the paper wads across the line. The goal is to try to get all the wads on the other side of the tape. When one team has no paper wads on their side of the tape, they will win. Allow the kids to throw the paper for about five minutes or until one team can get all the paper on the other side. Chances are that won't happen. If it does, you could do the best two out of three. Repeat the game if you have extra time.

The Teaching Moment: These pieces of paper are like the things that tempt us. No matter how much we try to get away from them or throw them away, there are always more coming our way. It's been happening ever since Adam and Eve lived. We can't get away from temptation, but with God's help we can be 'led away' from it. That's why we pray "lead us not into temptation."

KEY PHRASE: People Have Been Tempted Since the Beginning of Time

Craft: Lead Me Not Into Temptation Wheel 10 Minutes
Supplies: Paper plates, copies of the craft page at the end of this lesson, poster board or the back of notebooks, hole punch, brass fasteners (split pins), glue

1. Give each child a paper plate, a copy of the craft page and a brass fastener. If you don't have brass fasteners, cut out two inch circles from card stock or paper plates, then cut two slits on each side of the circle. (See image) Cut a small hole in the arrow and paper plate then put the ends of the circle that you cut through the arrow and plate and bend back the ends
2. Children may color the triangles different colors if they'd like (light colors)
3. Have children cut out the circle and trace the arrow on the poster board or back of notebook and then cut it out.
4. Glue the circle onto the paper plate. Use the brass fastener to attach the arrow to the plate.

The Teaching Moment: Everyone is tempted every day. We can stay away from temptation by remembering verses from the Bible. God wants to help us stay away from temptation, and one of the things he gave us to help with it is the Bible. The next time you are tempted to do the wrong thing, spin this wheel and read the verse. Keep doing that until you feel like you are able to do the right thing.

Memory Verse: 1 Corinthians 10:13 5 Minutes
Supplies: Large Index Cards or 1/2 sheets of Card Stock

During the three weeks of this unit, we're going to help the kids learn a verse about temptation. Each week they'll have a different activity to help them remember this important verse.

Week 1: This week the kids will copy the verse on a card to take home. Plus, they'll repeat after you several times to begin to learn the verse.

Write the verse on a poster board, chalkboard or white board. Give each of the kids an index card or card stock. Have the kids write the verse below on the card. You'll probably need to help the younger kids. After they've written it, have them repeat after you several times. Read one line at a time to make it easier for the kids to repeat.

You are tempted just like everyone.
But God is faithful.
He won't let you be tempted too much.
When you are tempted
God will give you a way to do what is right.

I Corinthians 10:13

The Teaching Moment: This verse reminds us that everyone faces temptation. Your parents and teachers are tempted to do the wrong thing. Even the pastor is tempted. But this verse reminds us that God is faithful and will help us when we are tempted.

KEY PHRASE: People Have Been Tempted Since the Beginning of Time

WRAPPING IT UP—SENDING IT HOME   5-7 Minutes

Cleaning Up

We want the children to learn to be responsible, so be sure they help with the clean up.

Closing Worship and Prayer

Gather the children in a circle holding hands or allow them to sit down to pray. You may choose to ask for prayer requests. Close with your own prayer or use the one in the margin for help. Be sure to end with the Lord's Prayer.

Heavenly Father, forgive us for the times we give in to temptation. We know that people have been tempted since the very beginning. Every time we're tempted to not follow you, help us remember your words from the Bible and choose the right thing. Lord, bless all of the things these kids have mentioned as prayer requests today (*if there's time, you can mention some of their requests*). And Lord, we pray all of these things in Jesus' name, who taught us to pray: (*now lead them in the Lord's Prayer*)

Our Father who art in heaven, hallowed be thy Name. Thy Kingdom come, thy will be done on earth as it is in heaven.
Give us this day our daily bread and forgive us our debts as we forgive our debtors.
Lead us not into temptation and deliver us from evil. For thine is the kingdom and the power and the glory forever, Amen.

Verses to help me when I'm tempted

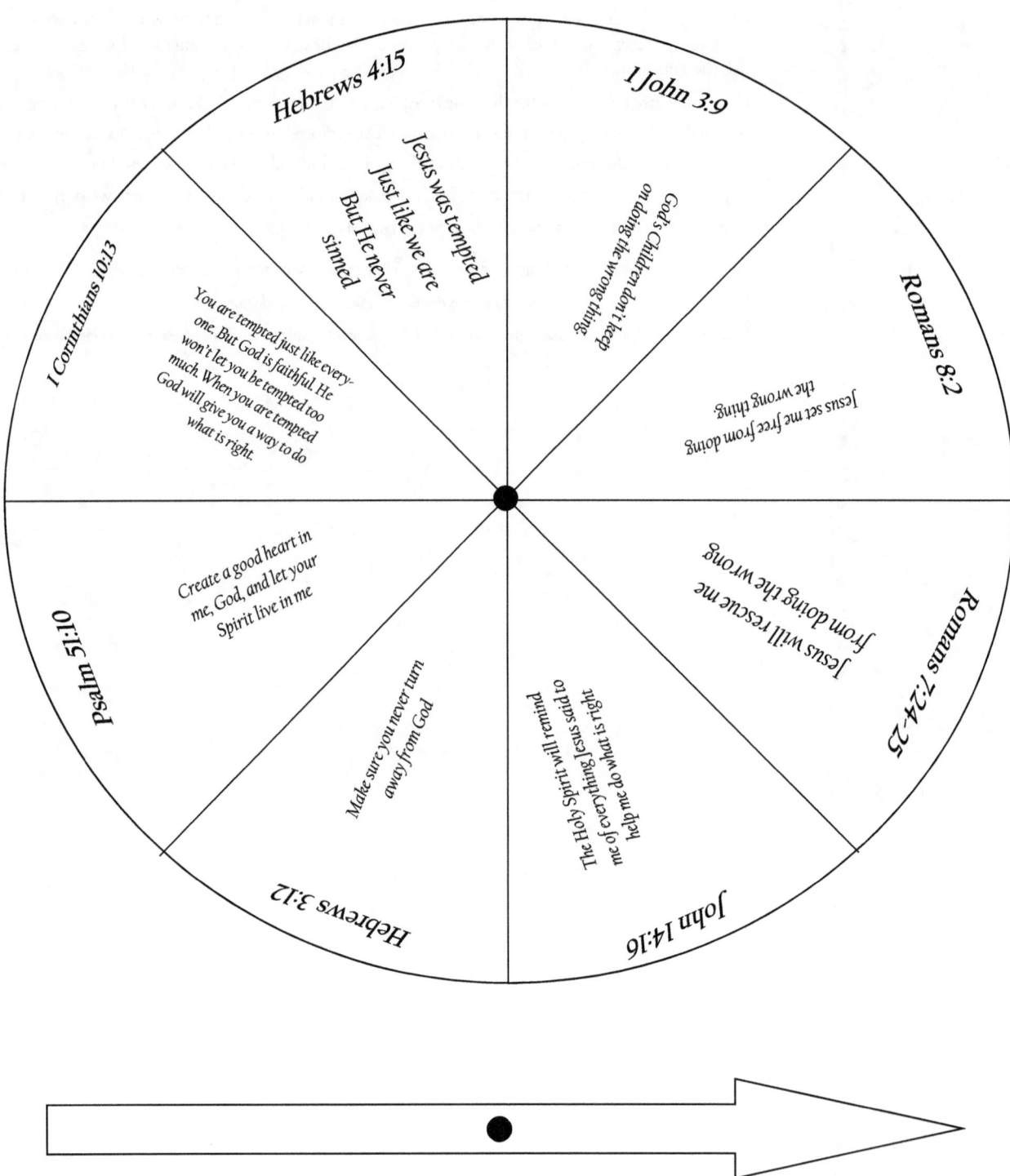

Jesus, Teach Me How to Pray
A Year in The Lord's Prayer and other Bible Basics

Unit 8: Lead Us Not Into Temptation
Lesson 2: Tempted to Be Like Everyone Else

Lesson Overview

Until the time of Samuel, God was the King of Israel, and the Creator appointed men to speak for Him. They were called priests and judges. Prior to Samuel, the judges were hand picked by God; He raised them up to lead the people, and they were not always priests. Samuel was called by God when he was eight. Raised by Eli the priest, Samuel became priest and judge. Because the line of priests was handed down, Samuel's sons were destined to become the next priests, and some feared they'd take on the role of judge, too. But Samuel's sons didn't take after their father, they were dishonest and evil, so the people didn't want them ruling over them. The people went to Samuel and asked him to find them a King instead. As we read, we discover their real motive—they wanted to be like all the nations around them. They didn't trust God to raise up another godly judge to speak for Him.

Like Israel, we often want things everyone else has rather than trust God to always pour out what's best for us. Sometimes it's material possessions, other times it's a job or a lifestyle. Whatever it is, when we want to be the same as someone else, rather than desiring what God wants for us, we've given in to temptation and not trusted God.

KEY PHRASE: Don't Be Tempted to Be Like Everyone Else

SETTING UP THE LESSON   5 Minutes
God is Good

PRESENTING THE LESSON   5 Minutes
Scripture: 1 Samuel 7:15-8:22

MAKING IT REAL TO KIDS TODAY   *(Choose as many as you have time for)*

Game: Mirror   5-15 Minutes

Craft: Crown   10 Minutes
Supplies: Construction paper, markers, jewels or sequins, glue, tape, scissors, stapler
OPTIONAL: Copies of last page of this lesson or ask Burger King ® for crowns and allow students to decorate.
Depending on the time, you can use the Memory Verse Activity for the craft

Memory Verse: 1 Corinthians 10:13   10-15 Minutes
Supplies: Copies of the picture at the end of this lesson, card stock or heavy tagboard, glue, crayons or markers, scissors and plastic bags

WRAPPING IT UP—SENDING IT HOME   5-7 Minutes
Clean Up and Prayer Time

KEY PHRASE: Don't Be Tempted to Be Like Everyone Else

SETTING UP THE LESSON   5 Minutes

God is Good

On a piece of paper, chalkboard, white board or newsprint, have the children help you make a list of all the things God has given as well as His wonderful attributes.

Here are some ideas:

God loves us	God forgives us	God wants to be our friend
He gives us food, clothes, families	He gives us teachers to help us learn	
God is powerful	God is everywhere	
God sends rain, snow, sunshine	God made the moon and stars	God made the Sun

Allow the kids to give you all their ideas. Then tell them: God is wonderful. He knows just what we need. Sometimes we think we need more, but when we think we need more, we're not trusting God to know what's best for us.

PRESENTING THE LESSON   5 Minutes

Scripture: 1 Samuel 7:15-8:22

You do not have to read this directly from the Bible—use the story form below or reword it to fit your personality

There was a man in the Bible named Samuel. The Bible called him a judge. In fact, Samuel was the last judge of Israel. The people of Israel came to him when they needed to know God's opinion. Samuel was a great judge for a long time. He listened to God and always told the people the truth about what God said. Because Samuel was also the priest, the people expected his sons to take over for him when he got too old. However, when Samuel's sons grew up, they didn't do follow God like Samuel did. They liked to cheat people and steal. When Samuel got old and it was time for him to quit being the judge, the people of Israel decided they didn't want Samuel's sons to be their next judges. So, they told Samuel to ask God to give them a king.

This was a huge problem. The people already had a king. Do you know who Israel's king was when Samuel and the other judges lived? *(Allow for answers.)* God told the people of Israel HE himself would always be their king. God planned to always be in charge of Israel. He wanted to choose good leaders for them, men and women who obeyed God and did what He asked them to do. Samuel felt rejected, but God told Samuel that by asking for a king, they were really rejecting God. They wanted a human king and this told God they didn't want Him to be their king anymore. God warned them a human king wouldn't be good for them. It would cost them more money, and they wouldn't be free anymore. The king would rule them, and when humans get that much power and leave God out it can be disastrous.

But it didn't matter, the people still wanted a human king. They didn't trust God to find new judges for them that would do what God asked. And Samuel pointed out one other problem. The reason they wanted a king was because everyone else had one. They didn't want to be different from everyone else. The people of Israel saw what all the other nations had and they were tempted to want the same thing. It never turns out well when we do things just because everyone is doing it.

Have you ever wanted what other people had or wanted to do what other kids were doing? *(Allow for answers.)* Maybe you want to watch television shows or listen to music your mom says are bad for you because your friends do. Or perhaps you see your friends have fancy things your family can't afford, and you want them so much you break rules to get them. When we want things other people have or go get things we can't afford just because someone else does it, it's the same as telling God we're not thankful for what we have. It's tempting to want everything our friends have. But when we think about all the good things God has given us and how wonderful God is, we can do what is right and not want what other people have.

KEY PHRASE: Don't Be Tempted to Be Like Everyone Else

MAKING IT REAL TO KIDS TODAY *(choose as many as you have time for)*

Game: Mirror — 5-15 Minutes

You or another adult should be the leader. Tell the children they need to do everything the adult does. When the adult rubs his head, the children should rub their heads.

Begin by moving your hands or feet slowly. Use slow purposeful motions so the kids can follow. As you progress, speed the motions up and make them more difficult. When someone misses a move, they must sit down where they are. When only one is left standing, allow that child to lead the group. Use as many leaders as you have time for.

The Teaching Moment: Sometimes it's fun to be just like everyone else. Today you were trying to be just like the leader, and even though we were having fun, it was hard sometimes wasn't it? *(Allow for answers.)* It's like that in real life, too. It's hard to always be like someone else. Sometimes it's fun when we begin, but it will get eventually get difficult. Jesus wants us to be who He made us to be. That means we won't be exactly like anyone else. So, always be yourself and Don't be Tempted to Be Like Someone Else.

Craft: Crown — 10 Minutes
Supplies: Construction paper, markers, jewels or sequins, glue, tape, scissors, stapler
OPTIONAL: Copies of last page of this lesson or ask Burger King ® for crowns and allow students to decorate.
Depending on the time, you can use the Memory Verse Activity for the craft

Give each child a sheet of construction paper in their favorite color. Fold the construction paper in half on the long side and cut down the center. Tape the two pieces together at the short end. Allow the kids to cut a pattern at the top that will resemble a crown (they could use the pattern on the last page if desired and you might roughly fit it to their heads and make marks to indicate safe placement of jewels). Have them decorate it with markers, jewels and/or sequins. Remind them to leave the ends free of jewels and sequins so you can fasten it. When they've finished decorating, fit it around their head and staple the ends together.
Alternately, you could ask Burger King® for enough crowns and decorate them with jewels

The Teaching Moment: These crowns can remind us that Israel wanted a king. Why did they want a king? *(Allow for answers.)* They wanted a king because all the other nations had a king. They wanted to be like everyone else. God doesn't want us to be just like everyone else. He created each of us special and unique, and He wants us to follow Him and let Him be our king. Don't be tempted to be like everyone else.

Memory Verse: Puzzle - 1 Corinthians 10:13 — 10-15 Minutes
Supplies: Copies of the picture on the last page of this lesson on card stock or heavy tagboard, crayons or markers, scissors and plastic bags

During this unit, we're going to help the kids learn a verse about temptation. Each week they'll have a different activity to help them remember this important verse.

Week 2: Give each child a copy of the verse at the end of this lesson with markers or crayons. Let the kids decorate the page. After decorated, have them cut the picture in 10-15 pieces. Remind them not to cut the pieces too small. Give each child a plastic bag to put their puzzle in. If you have time allow them to work the puzzle a few times.

The Verse: You are tempted just like everyone. But God is faithful. He won't let you be tempted too much. When you are tempted God will give you a way to do what is right.
I Corinthians 10:13

KEY PHRASE: Don't Be Tempted to Be Like Everyone Else

The Teaching Moment: Take your puzzle home and work it often so that you can remember that God is in control. We have to remember that He is our King. We should follow Him and not any one here on earth and not let what others have or do tempt us to be like everyone else.

WRAPPING IT UP—SENDING IT HOME   5-7 Minutes

Cleaning Up

We want the children to learn to be responsible, so be sure they help with the clean up.

Closing Worship and Prayer

Gather the children in a circle holding hands or allow them to sit down to pray. If you choose to join hands, remember that it's OK if some children prefer not to join the circle.

As you close, and if there is time, ask the children for prayer requests. Remember that no prayer is ever too small, however, children will tend to keep going and be "inspired" by other prayer requests, so feel free to stop taking requests and tell them they can say anything that didn't get said out loud quietly to God themselves while you're praying. You may close with your own prayer or use the one below for help. Be sure to end with the Lord's Prayer

If you need some guidance for your prayer, you can use this:

Heavenly Father, sometimes we want to be like other people. We like to have the same things our friends have. Forgive us when we want those things so badly we forget to be like you or be the person you created us to be. Help us to always listen to and follow you. Help us to not worry about what others have. Lord, bless all of the things these kids have mentioned as prayer requests today (*if there's time, you can mention some of their requests*). And Lord, we pray all of these things in Jesus' name, who taught us to pray: *(now lead them in the Lord's Prayer)*

Our Father who art in heaven, hallowed be thy Name. Thy Kingdom come, thy will be done on earth as it is in heaven. Give us this day our daily bread and forgive us our debts as we forgive our debtors.
Lead us not into temptation and deliver us from evil. For thine is the kingdom and the power and the glory forever, Amen.

You are tempted just like everyone. But God is faithful. He won't let you be tempted too much. When you are tempted God will give you a way to do what is right.

I Corinthians 10:13

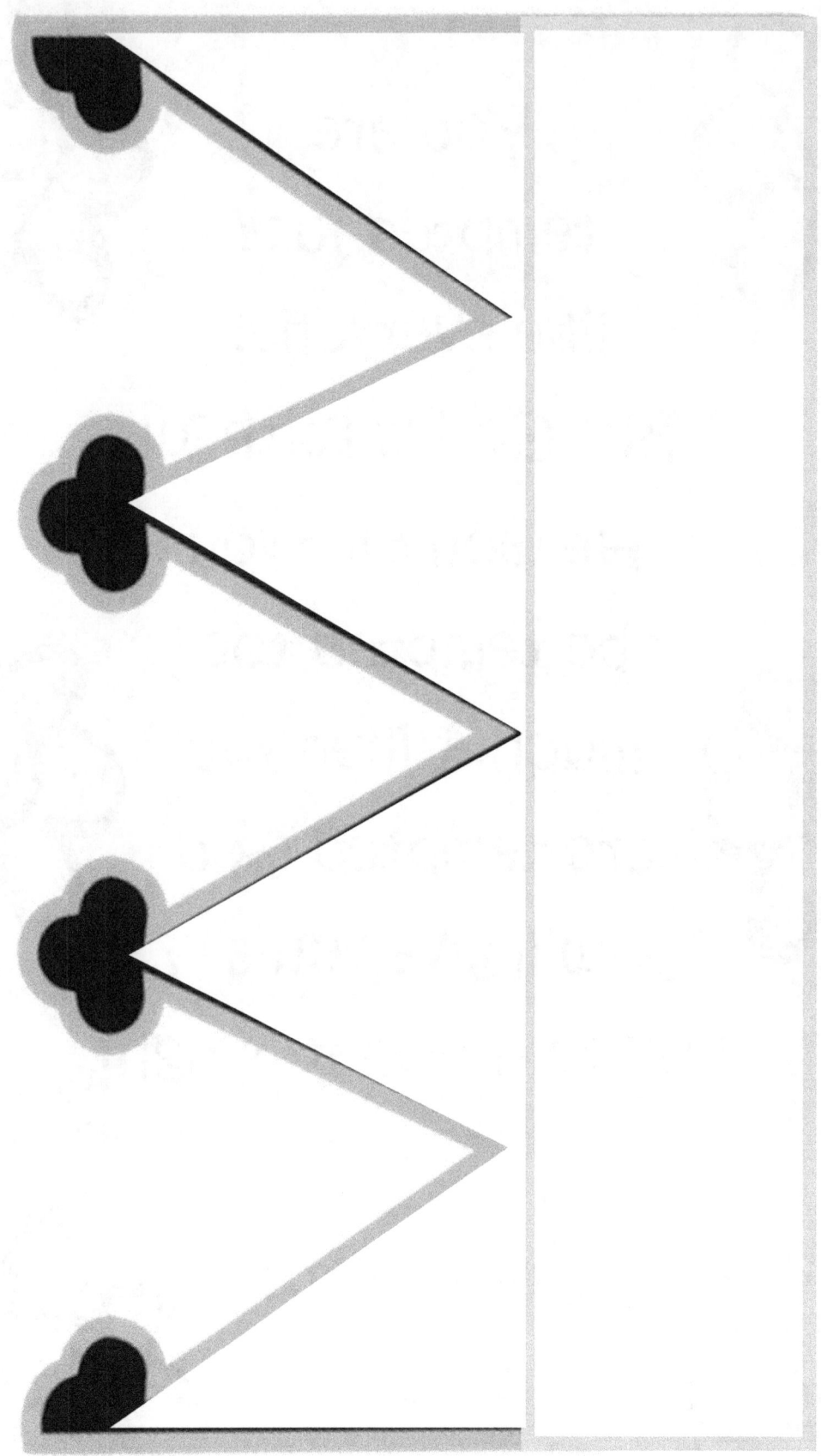

Jesus, Teach Me How to Pray
A Year in The Lord's Prayer and other Bible Basics

Unit 8: Lead Us Not Into Temptation
Lesson 3: Being Close to God Keeps Us From Falling into Temptation

Lesson Overview

Daniel was a man of God who passed one of the ultimate tests of faith. In an attempt to trap him, his colleagues talked the king into creating a rule for one whole month that any person who prayed to anyone besides the king would be thrown in the lion's den. Because Daniel loved God, he resisted the temptation to save his own life and prayed to Yahweh daily and publicly.

Not many could do what Daniel did, and if we managed to pull it off, when God allowed us to be thrown in the lion's den, we'd probably feel betrayed. But Daniel trusted God even as he landed with the jungle beasts. But God gave Daniel the strength to keep praying and trusting Him even though it meant he might end up dead.

Daniel had the strength to resist temptation because he stayed close to God. When we read the Bible and pray constantly, we'll have the strength to resist temptation too.

KEY PHRASE: The Closer We Get to God, the Easier It Is To Resist Temptation

SETTING UP THE LESSON — 5 Minutes
Are You Afraid?

PRESENTING THE LESSON — 10 Minutes
Scripture: Daniel 6:1-28

MAKING IT REAL TO KIDS TODAY — (Choose as many as you have time for)

Video: Veggie Tales, "Where's God when I'm Scared" — 10 Minutes
Supplies: Tablet or TV to play the video and https://www.youtube.com/watch?v=P7EELrP4muA

Game: Do the Right Thing — 5-10 Minutes
Supplies: One copy of scenarios on last page per group and three index cards or 3" squares of construction paper for each student

Craft: Leo the Lion — 15 Minutes
Supplies: For Each Child You will need: Brown construction paper, orange or yellow construction paper, markers, glue or glue sticks, scissors, wiggly eyes, pipe cleaners

Memory Verse: 1 Corinthians 10:13 — 5-10 Minutes

WRAPPING IT UP—SENDING IT HOME — 5-7 Minutes
Clean Up and Prayer Time

KEY PHRASE: The Closer We Get to God, the Easier it is to Resist Temptation

SETTING UP THE LESSON   5 Minutes

Are You Afraid?

Ask the children: What are you afraid of? *(Allow for answers.)* Are you afraid of snakes or lions or tigers? *(Allow for answers.)* What if a lion was chasing you, would you be afraid of that? *(Allow for answers.)* What would you do if a lion was chasing you? *(Allow for answers.)* If I told you to stand still when the lion was chasing you, would you? *(Allow for answers.)* What if your mom told you to stand still? *(Allow for answers.)* Is there anything that would make you stop running if a lion was chasing you? *(Allow for answers.)* Well, listen to this story and see if you could be like Daniel.

PRESENTING THE LESSON   10 Minutes

Scripture: Daniel 6:1-28

You do not have to read this directly from the Bible—use the story form below or reword it to fit your personality

Daniel was a true follower of God. When he was a teenager, the enemies of Jerusalem took Daniel and his friends to live in Babylon. Can you say Babylon? *(Allow for repeating)* As Daniel grew to be an adult, the rulers of Babylon liked Daniel and gave him important jobs. They could see Daniel's wisdom and respected him a great deal. Even though the people of Babylon worshipped many other gods, Daniel always followed God and did things that made God happy. The leaders in Babylon who followed other gods grew jealous of Daniel because God watched over him. Do you know what it means to be jealous? *(Allow for answers.)* Jealous is when we get angry because someone else does well or has more than we do. If you get angry when someone else gets an "A" in school and you get a bad grade that's jealousy.

These other leaders were also jealous of Daniel because the king liked him best of all. So the other leaders came up with a plan to get Daniel in trouble. Have you ever tried to get someone else in trouble? *(Allow for answers.)* Do you think God likes it when we do that? *(Allow for answers.)* I don't think God liked it when those other leaders tried to get Daniel in trouble either. They went to the king and convinced him to make a new law. They told the king that anyone who prayed to God anytime in the next month should be put in with the lions.

Because Daniel loved God and followed God, he prayed every day. In fact he prayed on his knees three times every day with his windows open. Do you remember what the law was? *(Allow for answers.)* No one was allowed to pray during the month. And what would happen if someone prayed to God? *(Allow for answers.)* The person caught praying would be thrown in with the lions. When Daniel heard the new law, what do you think he did? *(Allow for answers.)* What would you be tempted to do? *(Allow for answers.)* I might be tempted to quit praying because I would be afraid. Even though the new law meant Daniel could be put in with the lions, Daniel never quit praying. Every day he entered his room, opened his windows and prayed. The other leaders knew that Daniel wouldn't quit praying to God. So they watched for him to break the new law, and as soon as he did, they told the king . The King was sad when he found out Daniel had broken the law because he really liked Daniel. But it was the law, so the King told the soldiers to throw Daniel in with the hungry lions, and he put a stone over the opening. What do you think happened while Daniels was in the lion's den? *(Allow for answers.)*

The king was so worried about Daniel that he didn't sleep all night. The next morning the King ran to the where they kept their lions. He had the soldiers take the stone off the den and yelled for Daniel. The king was sure the lions had eaten Daniel, but to his surprise Daniel answered. He said, "I'm alright king. God sent an angel to be with me, and the angel held the mouths of the lions shut so they couldn't hurt me." The king was very excited to hear Daniel's voice. He ordered that Daniel be pulled out from the lions. Then he sent a message to everyone in Babylon telling them Daniel's God was a powerful and real God.

God rescued Daniel because he didn't give into temptation and kept doing what God wanted him to do. Daniel stayed close to God by praying and letting people know that he was God's follower. When we follow God and obey Him, he always helps us find a way to do what is right.

KEY PHRASE: The Closer We Get to God, the Easier it is to Resist Temptation

MAKING IT REAL TO KIDS TODAY
(use as many as you have time for)

Video: Veggie Tales, "Where's God When I'm Scared" (Part 3) — 10 Minutes
Supplies: Tablet or TV to play the video and https://www.youtube.com/watch?v=P7EELrP4muA

Part of this video (beginning at 5:10 –end at 12:01) is the Veggie Tales version of Daniel and the Lion's Den. You could show this instead of "Presenting the Lesson" if you don't have time to do both

The Teaching Moment: What would you have done if you'd been Daniel? Do you think you would have prayed to God or the king? *(Allow for answers.)* It's hard to do the right thing when we're scared. Sometimes, when we're afraid, we'll be tempted to do things we shouldn't do. But Daniel prayed all the time. He was very close to God and trusted God. The more we pray and read the Bible, the easier it is to do the right thing.

Craft: Leo the Lion — 15 Minutes
Supplies: For Each Child You will need: Brown construction paper, orange or yellow construction paper, markers, glue or glue sticks, scissors, wiggly eyes, pipe cleaners

Instructions

1. Cut a ten inch circle out of brown construction paper and six inch circle out of the orange or yellow.
2. Glue the six inch circle in the center of the brown circle.
3. Cut the brown circle in quarter inch increments all around to look like a mane (OPTIONAL: use the scissors to curl the mane)
4. Glue the wiggly eyes on.
5. Use the markers to draw a triangle nose in the center (encourage older children to round the edges of the nose) then draw a straight line down from the center of the nose and draw a smile at the bottom of the line.
6. Cut the pipe cleaners into 2 inch lengths and let each child glue two or three on each side of the nose.

The Teaching Moment: Use this lion to remind you that Daniel was afraid because he knew they would throw him in with the lions, but even when he was afraid, he still trusted God and did the right thing and we can do it too!

Game: Do the right thing — 5 Minutes
Supplies: One copy of scenarios on last page per group and three index cards or 3" squares of construction paper for each student

On the last page of this lesson you'll find some scenarios of situations. Give each child three blank index cards. Have them write the numbers 1, 2 and 3 on the three cards. (one number on each) As you read the scenarios give them the two possible answers and then ask them if they have a third. Allow the kids to vote on which of the two or three answers are best.

The Teaching Moment: Each scenario will be a teaching moment. Help the kids see why one answer may be the best one.

Memory Verse: 1 Corinthians 10:13 — 5-10 Minutes
Supplies: Index Cards or 3" construction paper squares and marker

During this unit, we're going to help the kids learn a verse about temptation. They've probably already worked on this verse during the last two weeks.

Week 3: The kids should know the verse well enough by now to put it together.

Before class write one or two sentences of the memory verse below on individual index cards or squares of construction paper. Create one set for each student. Shuffle all the cards and give two to each student. Place the rest in a pile in the middle. Beginning with the youngest student have him or her pick up a card

KEY PHRASE: The Closer we get to God, the Easier it is to Resist Temptation

from the pile. If they already have that card, have them put the card back in the pile. If they don't already have that part of the verse, they should put it in the correct order with their other two cards. If a student got two cards that match, they may use one turn to exchange cards. Each student gets to pick one card. The first person to get all the cards of the verse and put them in the right order wins. You could play until a few students complete the verse.

The Verse: You are tempted just like everyone. But God is faithful. He won't let you be tempted too much. When you are tempted God will give you a way to do what is right. I Corinthians 10:13

The Teaching Moment: This verse reminds us that God always gives us a way out. He wants us to do what is right, and if we are following Him, He'll show us how we can do what is right even when it seems impossible.

WRAPPING IT UP—SENDING IT HOME   5-10 Minutes

Cleaning Up

Encourage children to clean up their mess.

Closing Worship and Prayer

Gather the children in a circle holding hands or allow them to sit down to pray. If you choose to join hands, some children may prefer not to join. Remind them to be respectful of others as you pray.

As you close, and if there is time, ask the children for prayer requests. You may close with your own prayer or use the one below for help. Be sure to close with the Lord's Prayer

If you need some guidance for your prayer, you can use this:

Heavenly Father, thank you that you promise to never let me be tempted more than I can resist. I praise you that you always give us a way out of doing the wrong thing. Lord, bless all of the things these kids have mentioned as prayer requests today *(if there's time, you can mention some of their requests)*. And Lord, we pray all of these things in Jesus' name, who taught us to pray: *(now lead them in the Lord's Prayer)*

Our Father who art in heaven, hallowed be thy Name. Thy Kingdom come, thy will be done on earth as it is in heaven. Give us this day our daily bread and forgive us our debts as we forgive our debtors.
Lead us not into temptation and deliver us from evil. For thine is the kingdom and the power and the glory forever, Amen.

SCENARIOS FOR THE GAME

A. The teacher had to walk to the office on a short errand and told the class to read while she was gone. Someone immediately begins talking, and pretty soon nearly everyone is chatting. What would you do?

   1. Begin to whisper to the person next to you

   2. Keep reading your book. *Listening to what the teacher says is always right*

   3. (KID'S IDEA)

B. You didn't finish your lunch, and mom said you get nothing to eat until dinner. But at basketball practice someone passes out cupcakes. What should you do?

   1. Eat a cupcake and hope mom doesn't find out

   2. Tell your friend "thank you, but no" and explain what your mom said. *Obeying mom, even when she's not there, is always right*

   3. (KID'S IDEA)

C. There are some kids getting ready to write on all the walls on the back of the school. They invite you to come with them. What will you do?

   1. Go in the school and stay away from where they are *Treating property with respect is always right*

   2. Go with the kids so they'll think you're cool, but don't write on the wall

   3. (KID'S IDEA)

D. Your mom told you to clean your room before you can play your video games. You really wanted to play it soon. What should you do?

   1. Get busy and get everything picked up and put away. *Doing what mom says is always right*

   2. Push everything under the bed or into the closet

   3. (KID'S IDEA)

E. You have a note from your teacher to give your mom. You know that it says you behaved badly at school today, and you'll be in all kinds of trouble if you give it to her. What will you do?

   1. Don't give it to your mom, and if the teacher calls her, tell mom you lost the note.

   2. Apologize to your teacher for behaving so badly and give your mom the note as soon as you get home. *Apologizing to the teacher will surprise her, but apologizing and giving the note to mom will be the right thing.*

   3. (KID'S IDEA)

Notes

Jesus, Teach Me How to Pray
A Year in The Lord's Prayer and other Bible Basics

Unit 9: Deliver Us From Evil
Lesson 1: God Delivered Noah from Evil World

Lesson Overview

The story of Noah's ark is one of the most familiar of all time. Even those who've never been in church have most likely heard this story.

Some facts most don't know:

- It may have taken 100 years to build the ark.
- Some think it may have never rained on the earth before this time because in the creation account it says the garden was watered from under the ground.
- Noah and his family were on the boat for an entire year
- Though there were two of every unclean animal, there were either seven or seven pair of every clean animal

In this lesson, we're going to focus on the evil of the people on the earth during Noah's time. Make sure the kids understand that these people weren't just "bad" (like when they disobey their parents) These people were beyond that. They had complete disregard for everyone and everything including God. But God saved Noah from the evil in the world.

KEY PHRASE: God Wants to Deliver Us From Evil

SETTING UP THE LESSON   3-5 Minutes
What Do You Do on a Rainy day?

PRESENTING THE LESSON   5-10 Minutes
Scripture: Genesis 6:1-9:17

MAKING IT REAL TO KIDS TODAY   *(Choose as many as you have time for)*

Game: Pair Up   5-10 Minutes
Supplies: Prepared index cards, scissors

Craft: Noah's Ark   10 Minutes
Supplies: Copies of the ark on the last page of this lesson

Craft Option Two: WWJD Bracelet   10 Minutes
Supplies: Craft Foam cut in 1"x5" strips, hole punch, markers, string

Song: Arky Arky   5 Minutes

WRAPPING IT UP—SENDING IT HOME   5-7 Minutes
Clean Up Time & Prayer Time

KEY PHRASE: God Wants to Deliver Us From Evil

SETTING UP THE LESSON   3-5 Minutes

What Do You Do On a Rainy Day?

This will be an especially easy setup if you've had a lot of rain or snow recently - Ask the kids:

What do you do on a rainy day? *(Allow for answers.)* What about when it rains for two days? *(Allow for answers.)* Three days? *(Allow for answers.)* What would you do if it rained really hard all day long every day for ten days? *(Allow for answers.)* We hardly ever see it rain all day every day with no stop. Usually it quits for a few minutes so we can run to the car without getting wet. But what if it rained so hard you couldn't ride your bike or play ball or even play in the rain? What if rained and poured like that for forty days straight? *(Allow for answers.)* I think I would get very tired of the rain. I'd want to go outside and do SOMETHING! But did you know that someone in the Bible had just that—forty days of rain? I was a non-stop downpour for forty days! Do you know who it was that saw that kind of rain? *(Allow for answers - some of them may know)*

PRESENTING THE LESSON   5-10 Minutes

Scripture: Genesis 6:1-9:17

You do not have to read this directly from the Bible—use the story form below or reword it to fit your personality

Noah lived more than 3000 years ago. We read his story in the very first book of the Bible. Do you know what the first book of the Bible is called? *(Allow for answers.)* The first book is Genesis, and in chapter six God tells us what the world was like when Noah was alive.

The Bible says that the people who lived on the earth when Noah was alive were "wicked." Another word for wicked is evil. Do you know what "wicked" or "evil" means? *(Allow for answers.)* Wicked is worse than bad. The people who lived on the earth were the worst they'd ever been. They didn't care about anyone but themselves. They treated others badly, cheated everyone, lied, stole and killed people. God said their hearts were evil all the time. They never thought about God or cared about Him. These people were worse than anyone you've ever met! God was very sad that the people he created had become so evil. The Bible says his heart was full of pain. The people were that bad. And everyone in the entire world was that way.

Everyone except Noah. The Bible says Noah was the only one on the whole earth who followed God and the only one who ever did anything good. Do you think it would be hard to be the only one who does the right thing? *(Allow for answers.)* What's it like at school when everyone else wants to do the wrong thing, but you still do what's right? *(Allow for answers.)* It's usually very difficult to behave when everyone else is disobeying. But Noah didn't follow everyone else, he kept doing the things God wanted him to do. The Bible says he walked with God. What does it mean to "walk with God?" *(Allow for answers.)* When we walk with God it means we learn what pleases God and do it. It means we talk to God often and listen to Him. It means every step we take, we think, "what would Jesus do?" Noah walked with God.

So when God told Noah to build a boat longer than a football field, even though he lived no where near a lake or an ocean, Noah began to build the boat. Do you know what the boat was called? *(Allow for answers.)* Noah's boat was called an ark. An ark is a big box to put something in. This ark was supposed to float on water. Noah built the ark and then painted the outside of it with tar so it wouldn't leak. Do you know what tar is? *(Allow for answers.)* Tar is black and sticky. It's the stuff they paint on parking lots and roads to seal the cracks.

When Noah finally finished the ark, God told him to take his family inside. Then, God brought animals to Noah to bring into the ark. God brought a pair of each of some kind of animals and seven pairs of some of the other kinds of animals. When Noah, his family, and all the animals were in the ark, God shut the door, and that's when it started to rain.

And it rained and rained and rained. Do you remember how many days I said it rained? *(Allow for answers.)* It rained for forty days. It rained until the whole earth was flooded. What do you think it means that the whole

KEY PHRASE: God Wants to Deliver Us From Evil

earth was flooded? *(Allow for answers.)* It means that every part of the earth had deep water on it. God was very sad because all the people he had created and all of the animals that didn't go on the ark died in the flood. But God sent the flood because the people were so bad, it was the only way he could help Noah stay away from evil.

It's important to remember the people who lived on the Earth with Noah were more than just bad. Everyone does bad things sometimes. These people were evil. They never felt bad for doing wrong and they spent every moment thinking only of themselves. They didn't care about anybody, and didn't care about God. These people *never* did the right thing. It was more than just messing up sometimes.

When we say "The Lord's Prayer" we ask God to "deliver us from evil." When we say that, we're asking God to help us be like Noah. We want help doing the right thing even when everyone else is doing the wrong thing. Because Noah walked with God, God helped him to always do the right thing, and then God saved him and his whole family from drowning in the flood. God wants to save us from evil, so when we pray "deliver us from evil" and then walk with Him, God will always help us stay away from evil and do the right thing.

MAKING IT REAL TO KIDS TODAY

(Choose as many as you have time for)

Game: Pair Up 5-10 Minutes
Supplies: Prepared index cards, scissors

To Prepare: Before children arrive, write the name of an animal on each end of an index card and cut the card in half. Create enough for each child to draw one half of a card. You could make extra so you can play a few times without repeating any animals. If you have a very large group, you could take the name of one "clean" animal (like a cow) and write it on seven cards (fourteen in all) to represent the extra clean animals Noah had to take into the ark.

To Play: Have each child draw a card, then tell them to begin walking around the room acting out what their animal would look like. They shouldn't make any noise at this point. The goal is for the child to find their "pair." Tell them that when they find their match they should sneak their cards to you so no one sees and keep walking around to throw off the other teams. After a few minutes tell the kids they can add a sound as they walk around. When all kids find their match, announce the first three pairs, then you can play again if you have time.

The Teaching Moment: God told Noah to take two of each animal and seven pairs of the kinds of animals that they were allowed to eat. It's fun to pretend to be animals, but God even saved animals from the evil and brought them on the ark so there would be animals after the flood.

Craft: Noah's Ark 10 Minutes
Supplies: Copies of the ark pattern on the last page of this lesson. Follow directions on the page

The Teaching Moment: Noah's ark was huge. It had three levels and completely filled it with animals, Noah, his wife and three sons and their wives, and enough food to feed them for a year. Yes, even though it only rained for 40 days, they were on the ark for a whole year. It took that long for all the water to dry up. The flood made God sad because so many people drowned, but it made God happy to save Noah from the evil that was in the world.

Craft Option Two: WWJD Bracelet 10 Minutes
Supplies: Craft Foam cut in 1"x5" strips, hole punch, markers, string

Give each student one strip of foam. Punch holes in each end. Help the children write WWJD on it in wide letters. Add strings to each hole so kids can tie the bracelet around their wrist.

The Teaching Moment: A long time ago people wore bracelets with WWJD on them to remind them of four words: What Would Jesus Do? Every time they saw those letters, they asked themselves, "What Would Jesus Do." When we face evil, we should always ask "What Would Jesus Do?" to help us stay out of evil.

KEY PHRASE: God Wants to Deliver Us From Evil

Song: Arky, Arky   5 Minutes

There is a lead sheet for this song on the last page of the lesson. This is an old song that's very fun. You might copy these words or put them on a big sheet for everyone to see. If you need help with the song, you will find it on YouTube: https://www.youtube.com/watch?v=wHcypSv4ltY&t=31s

Here are motions for the chorus:

Rise: Everyone stands

Shine: hands frame your face and wiggle fingers

Give God the Glory, Glory: Hands up and shaking excitedly. Sit during verses

The Teaching Moment: This song can help us remember the story of Noah and the ark he built. Can you remember why God told Noah to build the ark? *(Allow for answers.)* God wanted to save Noah from the evil in the world.

WRAPPING IT UP—SENDING IT HOME   5-7 Minutes

Cleaning Up

Always set expectations high! Invite the children to clean up and push their chairs in when their done.

Closing Worship and Prayer

Gather the children in a circle holding hands or allow them to sit to pray. If you choose to join hands, remember that it's OK if some children prefer not to join the circle. Just ask them to be respectful of others as they pray and not make any noise.

As you close, and if there is time, ask the children for prayer requests. You may close with your own prayer or use the one below for help. Remember to close with the Lord's Prayer

If you need some guidance for your prayer, you can use this:

Father in Heaven, You are so wonderful to us. We praise Your name. We thank You for the way You lead and guide, and we are grateful that You keep us from evil when we follow You. Help us to always walk with You and ask for Your help. Lord, bless all of the things these kids have mentioned as prayer requests today *(if there's time, you can mention some of their requests)*. And Lord, we pray all of these things in Jesus' name, who taught us to pray: *(now lead them in the Lord's Prayer)*

Our Father who art in heaven, hallowed be thy Name. Thy Kingdom come, thy will be done on earth as it is in heaven.
Give us this day our daily bread and forgive us our debts as we forgive our debtors.
Lead us not into temptation and deliver us from evil. For thine is the kingdom and the power and the glory forever, Amen.

Noah's Ark

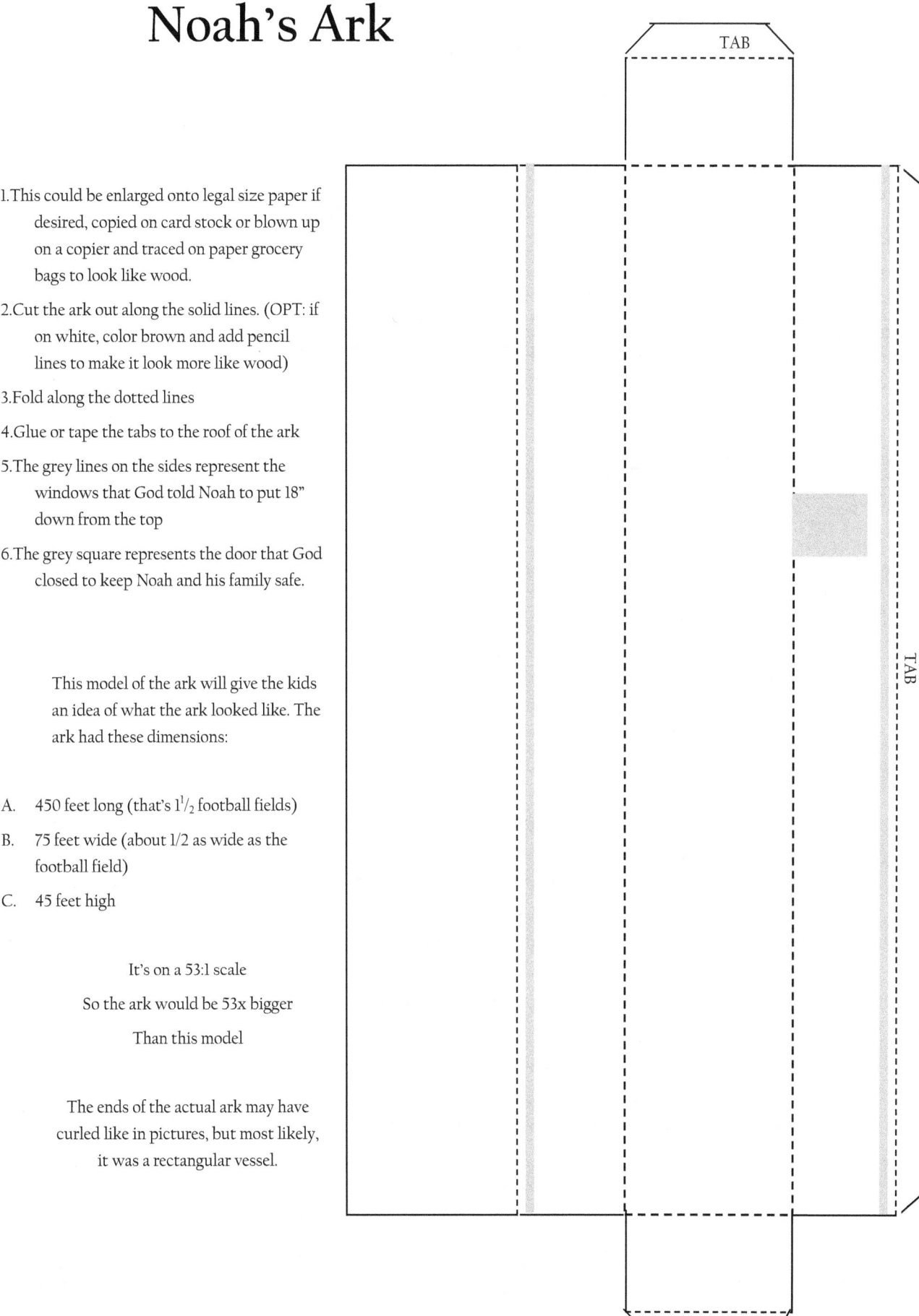

1. This could be enlarged onto legal size paper if desired, copied on card stock or blown up on a copier and traced on paper grocery bags to look like wood.
2. Cut the ark out along the solid lines. (OPT: if on white, color brown and add pencil lines to make it look more like wood)
3. Fold along the dotted lines
4. Glue or tape the tabs to the roof of the ark
5. The grey lines on the sides represent the windows that God told Noah to put 18" down from the top
6. The grey square represents the door that God closed to keep Noah and his family safe.

This model of the ark will give the kids an idea of what the ark looked like. The ark had these dimensions:

A. 450 feet long (that's $1^1/_2$ football fields)
B. 75 feet wide (about 1/2 as wide as the football field)
C. 45 feet high

It's on a 53:1 scale
So the ark would be 53x bigger
Than this model

The ends of the actual ark may have curled like in pictures, but most likely, it was a rectangular vessel.

Arky, Arky

Public Domain

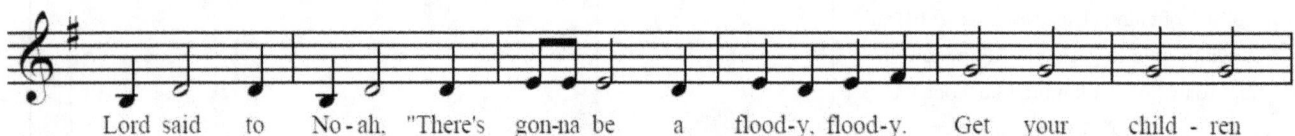

Chorus Has Same Melody as Verse

1. The Lord said to Noah, there's gonna be a floody, floody (2x)
   Get your children Out of the muddy, muddy, children of the Lord

   CHORUS So, Rise and shine and give God the glory, glory (3x)
   Children of the Lord

2. The Lord said to Noah, you'd better build an arky, arky (2x)
   Build it out of Cypress barky, barky, Children of the Lord. (CHORUS)

3. The animals they came on board, two by twoey, twoey (2x)
   Elephants and Kangarooey, rooyees children of the Lord. (CHORUS)

4. The dark clouds came over and shut out the lighty, lighty (2x)
   Forty days and Forty nighty nighties, children of the Lord.

5. The rain came down for forty long day-sy, day-sys, (2x)
   Almost drove old Noah crazy, crazy, children of the Lord (CHORUS)

6. The sun came out and dried up the landy, landy (2x)
   Everything was fine and dandy, dandy, children of the Lord. (CHORUS)

7. This is the end of, the end of our story, story (2x)
   Everything was hunky dorey, dorey children of the Lord (CHORUS)

Lynne Modranski

Jesus, Teach Me How to Pray
A Year in The Lord's Prayer and other Bible Basics

Unit 9: Deliver Us From Evil
Lesson 2: Thankful that God Delivers Us from Evil

Lesson Overview

The book of Job is the story of man who loved God with all his heart. In fact he was so good at serving God, that when the devil showed up at God's throne with the angels, God started bragging about him. The devil told God if Job faced trials, he would turn his back on God. The devil took away everything Job had, and when that didn't cause Job to curse God, the devil inflicted severe pain on him personally. Even with boils all over his body, Job would not quit giving praise to God. When four of his friends showed up and tried to figure out what kind of mistake Job had made that would cause such terrible things happen to him, Job insisted he was faithful to God and would continue to be despite his sorry state.

When God saw Job's faithfulness, He delivered Job from the evil that the devil was inflicting upon him. Additionally, God gave him back all of his flocks and fields as well as his servants. What's more he gave Job children to take the place of the ones that had been killed. When we pray "deliver us from evil" we need to be sure to follow God and be faithful to Him even when life seems unbearable because God wants to deliver his people from evil.

KEY PHRASE: We Should Be Thankful that God Delivers Us From Evil

SETTING UP THE LESSON   5-7 Minutes
Bad Things Happen

PRESENTING THE LESSON   5 Minutes
Scripture: Job 1-2 & 42:12-17

MAKING IT REAL TO KIDS TODAY   *(Choose as many as you have time for)*

Game: Thankful Game   5-10 Minutes
Supplies: Something to pass - a squishy ball or stuffed animal will work - and the following words each on a small slip of paper: Home, School, Friends, Toys, TV Shows, Songs, Family, Games

Craft: Thank You Cards   10-15 Minutes
Supplies: Construction paper and old greeting cards (a few for each child), markers or crayons

Memory Verse: 1 Thessalonians 5:16-18   5 Minutes

WRAPPING IT UP—SENDING IT HOME   5-7 Minutes
Clean Up Time & Prayer Time

KEY PHRASE: We Should Be Thankful that God Delivers Us From Evil

SETTING UP THE LESSON   5-7 Minutes

Bad Things Happen

On the last page of this lesson you'll find pictures of bad things that might happen. Be sensitive that some kids may have experienced fire, flood, tornado or robbery—the topics of the four pictures. If you know one of these happened recently to a child, you might want to leave that example out or talk to the parent before the lesson to see if the child can handle the picture and to allow the parent to be prepared for any emotions the pictures might cause.

As you show the kids the pictures, talk about the damage that each can cause. Ask how they'd feel if those things happened to them. Explain that evil things happen in our world. We can't help it, and no one is to blame. Because sin and evil are in the world, bad things happen. These are just a few things that can happen. Today we're going to talk about a man who had a lot of evil in his life.

PRESENTING THE LESSON   5 Minutes

Scripture: Job 1-2 & 42:12-17

You do not have to read this directly from the Bible—use the story form below or reword it to fit your personality

Job was a very good man who lived a long time ago. Job did everything God asked him to do. He prayed every day and loved God. One day when all the angels came to meet with God, the devil came too. God was so proud of Job, He bragged about Job. God said, "Have you ever seen anyone as good as my servant Job?" God was proud of Job. The devil told God that Job was only good because nothing bad happened to him. The devil said, "If something bad happens to Job, he won't be so good. I'll prove it to you." So the devil went out into the world and cause evil to fall on Job.

The devil caused fire, soldiers and a great wind—like a tornado—to kill all of Job's cows and sheep and all of Job's children. His whole farm was destroyed. But Job kept praising God. So, the devil did more. He made Job very sick and did all kinds of evil things to Job.

Job was terribly sad because of all the bad things that happened. He tore his clothes and dressed in rough cloth to show how sad he was. Job even sat in ashes and put ashes on his head to show how sad he was. But Job kept on loving God and praising Him. Even when Job's wife told him to give up on God, Job wouldn't. He told her he believed in God and loved Him and would never give up on God.

Some of Job's friends came to visit him to try to make him feel better. But they thought Job must have done something wrong to make all the bad things happen, so they only made Job feel worse. And even when his friends made him feel bad, Job still praised God and loved Him.

This made God even more proud of Job. God was so proud of Job that He told Job's friends they were wrong to say bad things about Job. Then God returned to Job all of the things the devil had taken away. God gave Job even more cows and sheep. He gave Job a wonderful farm and ten more children.

The devil did evil to Job, but because Job never gave up on God, God delivered him from the evil the devil wanted to do. Job knew that God never causes bad things to happen to us. He knew that because evil and sin are in the world, bad things happen even to good people sometimes. God blessed Job and gave him good things. God wants to help us when evil things happen, too, but we have to always rely on God, love God praise God, and trust Him even when evil comes.

KEY PHRASE: We Should Be Thankful that God Delivers Us From Evil

MAKING IT REAL TO KIDS TODAY *(Choose as many as you have time for)*

Game: Thankful Game   5-10 Minutes
Supplies: Something to pass - a squishy ball or stuffed animal will work - and the following words each on a small slip of paper: Home, School, Friends, Toys, TV Shows, Songs, Family, Games

1. Have the children sit in a circle. Choose the oldest child to be "it" first. This person can be in the middle of the circle or to the side depending on the setup of your room. Give an older child in the circle the ball or toy.

2. Allow "it" to pick out a slip of paper with one of the words on it. (Slips may be returned to the bowl to be reused.)

3. *Tell the children in the circle:* When I say "GO," whoever has the ball or toy will pass it to the person next to them. And you will all pass it around. When it gets back to the first person, you should yell, "I'm Thankful too!"

4. *Tell It:* When I say "GO," you will name all the things they are thankful for that go with the word on the paper you drew. I will count how many you name, and you must stop when they hear the person with the toy say, "I'm Thankful too!" *You may need to help younger children come up with the first couple things they are thankful for. If you have a small group, you might want to take it around the circle twice before the person says "I'm Thankful too!"*

5. Continue allowing children to name things they are thankful for until everyone has had a turn or you run out of time.

6. If everyone has a chance to share, the one who names the most things they are thankful for could be the winner.

The Teaching Moment: Just like Job we should always be thankful to God for everything, even when evil comes our way. Remember all these things we talked about today and give thanks whenever you can to let God know you appreciate all He does.

Craft: Thank You Cards   10-15 Minutes
Supplies: Construction paper and old greeting cards (a few for each child), markers or crayons

(if this lesson falls near Mother's/Father's Day or some other holiday, you could make these cards holiday appropriate and have the children be thankful for their mother/father etc.)

Gather old greeting cards from the congregation. Give each child a piece of construction paper and allow them to choose one or two cards. Tell the kids to choose one person for whom they are thankful.

1. Help the kids fold the construction paper in 1/2 (or 1/4's for a smaller but sturdier card)

2. Have the children cut designs from the greeting cards.

3. Glue the cut out designs on their construction paper.

4. On the front let the kids write "I'M THANKFUL FOR YOU" They could also add stickers or color pictures if they like. Older children might write a message that says why they are thankful.

The Teaching Moment: Job was always thankful even when bad things happened to him because he knew that God would deliver him from evil. Even when a lot of bad things were happening, Job remembered to be thankful and praise God. So take this card and give it to someone who you are thankful to God for.

KEY PHRASE: We Should Be Thankful that God Delivers Us From Evil

Memory Verse: 1 Thessalonians 5:16-18   5 Minutes

This is a great passage for you and the kids to memorize!

Always be joyful; pray all the time; give thanks no matter what happens

Break this into three lines and say it like a cheer or rap with the emphasis on the capitalized word:

1. ALWAYS be joyful
2. PRAY all the time
3. Give THANKS no MATTER what happens

Repeat this several times. Get the kids to really get into it with some rhythm and clapping.

The Teaching Moment: You now know three more verses from the Bible. What does it mean to always be joyful? *(Allow for answers.)* In every situation, we should look for the positive so we can be joyful. What does it mean to pray all the time? *(Allow for answers.)* This means we won't close our eyes every time we pray because we will pray when we take spelling tests and when we're walking. We'll ask God to be with us every moment of the day. How do you Give thanks no matter what happens? *(Allow for answers.)* Even when things seem to be going all wrong, we should thank God that He is with us delivering us from evil.

WRAPPING IT UP—SENDING IT HOME   5-7 Minutes

Cleaning Up

Make sure your area is cleaned up before you leave so children learn the importance of cleaning up after themselves.

Closing Worship and Prayer

Gather the children in a circle holding hands or allow them to sit down to pray. If you choose to join hands, remember that it's OK if some children prefer not to join the circle.

As you close, and if there is time, ask the children for prayer requests. You may close with your own prayer or use the one below for help. Remember to close with the Lord's Prayer.

If you need some guidance for your prayer, you can use this:

Father in Heaven, You are so wonderful to us. We praise your name. We feel bad when evil happens to us or people we know, God. It makes us very sad. Help us to always remember that you don't cause the evil. Help us to be thankful even in the midst of all the bad things like Job was. Lord, bless all of the things these kids have mentioned as prayer requests today *(if there's time, you can mention some of their requests)*. And Lord, we pray all of these things in Jesus' name, who taught us to pray: *(now lead them in the Lord's Prayer)*

Our Father who art in heaven, hallowed be thy Name. Thy Kingdom come, thy will be done on earth as it is in heaven.
Give us this day our daily bread and forgive us our debts as we forgive our debtors.
Lead us not into temptation and deliver us from evil. For thine is the kingdom and the power and the glory forever, Amen.

Page intentionally left blank for printing and copying purposes

Jesus, Teach Me How to Pray
A Year in The Lord's Prayer and other Bible Basics

Unit 9: Deliver Us From Evil
Lesson 3: God Wants to Deliver Us From Evil

Lesson Overview

By the time the kids get to this lesson hopefully they'll realize that following God doesn't exempt us evil. However, because we follow Him and pray, God will save us and walk with us when evil comes our way. As dedicated as Paul was to following Christ, he still managed to find himself in prison often. In this particular instance, Paul was imprisoned for being a follower of Jesus Christ. But the earthquake God sent delivered them from the evil of prison. And Paul used the opportunity to show the jailer how to become a follower of Jesus Christ. Today we'll look not only at "deliver us from evil," but our response to God's gift of deliverance.

KEY PHRASE: God Wants to Deliver Us From Evil

SETTING UP THE LESSON   5-7 Minutes
INTRO GAME: Earthquake

PRESENTING THE LESSON   5-10 Minutes
Scripture: Acts 16:16-40

MAKING IT REAL TO KIDS TODAY   *(Choose as many as you have time for)*

Craft: F.R.O.G. (Fully Rely On God)   10 Minutes
Supplies: Green and White construction paper or foam, scissors, markers, copies of the final page of this lesson

Game: F.R.O.G. Race   5-7 Minutes

Illustration: What must I do to be saved?   5 Minutes
Allow some extra time today for the prayer time so you can be sure to include this element in the lesson.

WRAPPING IT UP—SENDING IT HOME   10 Minutes
Clean Up Time & Prayer Time

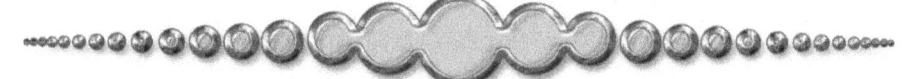

KEY PHRASE: God Wants to Deliver Us From Evil

SETTING UP THE LESSON   5-7 Minutes

INTRO GAME: Earthquake

Divide the kids into groups of three or more so you'll have one to three kids left over to be jailers. For instance, a group of nine will have two groups of four and one jailer; a group of twelve could have three groups of three and three jailers. (If a very small group, use two groups of two, and let and adult be the first jailer.)

Have each group hold hands. Tell them their hands linked together represent chains. They can't let go because they are chained together. The extra kids are the jailers. When one of the jailers yells, "Earthquake" the groups holding hands should start shaking and shaking. Then the jailer will yell, "Jailbreak" When the kids hear Jailbreak, they will break groups and create new groups. The jailers will then try to get into a group. New groups must have at least one new person (two if the groups have four) and be the same size as the original group. The children who can't get into a group are then the "jailer(s)." Play can continue for as long as you have time.

The Teaching Moment: We had fun pretending we were chained up. The earthquake loosened our chains, but we never totally escaped. Today we're going to hear a story from the Bible about chains, jails and earthquakes.

PRESENTING THE LESSON   5-10 Minutes

Scripture: Acts 16:16-40
You do not have to read this directly from the Bible—use the story form below or reword it to fit your personality

Paul is one of the most famous people from the Bible. In fact he wrote thirteen books in the New Testament. He traveled all over the world by foot and boat. There were no cars or motors when Paul lived. It took him a long time to get from place to place, but everywhere he went, he told people about Jesus. However, sometimes Paul got in trouble for telling others about Christ.

One time Paul and his friend, Silas, were in Philippi *(like the name Philip with a long "I" at the end)* Can you say Philippi? *(Allow for response.)* One girl in Philippi had an evil spirit. She was a slave and the people who owned her liked the evil spirit because she used it to tell fortunes. Paul and Silas felt bad for her and commanded the evil spirit to leave. But this made her owners really mad. So they had Paul and Silas arrested, and the police dragged them off to jail.

Paul and Silas were chained up in jail. Jails were a lot different when Paul lived than they are today. It was awful, very dark and damp. With no windows and doors, the jail cell probably had a dirt floor to sit on. How would you feel if you were in a place like that? *(Allow for answers - then share how you would feel.)* Do you think you would sing songs of praise to God if you were in a place like that? *(Allow for answers - then share your answer.)*

But that's what Paul and Silas did. They sat in their jail cell and sang church songs and prayed. One night as they sang, all the other prisoners were listening to them. Suddenly a huge earthquake hit the jail! Every door in the prison came open, and all the chains came loose. The earthquake woke the prison guard. When he saw all the doors opened, the jailer panicked. What do you think the jailer thought happened when he saw the doors open? *(Allow for answers.)* The jailer thought all of his prisoners had escaped. If they were gone, he was going to be in huge trouble! He would lose his job for sure, and the city leaders might put him in prison or even kill him if the prisoners weren't there. The guard pulled out his sword. He was going to kill himself because he thought all the prisoners had escaped, but Paul yelled out, "Don't do it! We're all here!"

The jailer was so grateful that Paul and Silas and all the prisoners hadn't escaped, he ran in to Paul and Silas' cell. He had heard Paul and Silas singing songs to God, and he knew God sent the earthquake to allow Paul and Silas to escape.

The jailer asked Paul and Silas, "What do I have to do to be saved?"

Paul and Silas told him, "You have to believe in Jesus." Then Paul and Silas told the jailer all about

KEY PHRASE: God Wants to Deliver Us From Evil

Jesus—about His death on the cross and his resurrection. The jailer was so grateful that he took them home with him. The jailer cleaned their wounds—the places where they'd been hurt when they were dragged into jail—and he fed them a nice dinner.

The next morning, the jailer got a message that he should release Paul and Silas. They didn't have to go back to prison. God delivered them from evil. Jail is not a nice place at all. It's not a place we want to go, and it certainly wasn't a place Paul and Silas wanted to be.

In the past few weeks we've heard about Noah, Job, and now Paul. All three had to go through some hard times. When we pray "deliver us from evil," it doesn't mean that God will never let anything bad happen to us. Just like Noah had to live in the evil world before God delivered him and Job lost everything before God replaced his animals and family, sometimes bad things will happen to us. Just like Paul had to go to prison, sometimes we'll have to go places we don't want to go. But in the same way God helped Noah, Job, and Paul and brought them out of these bad things, God will deliver us from evil when we rely on him for everything, follow him, and pray.

MAKING IT REAL TO KIDS TODAY *(Choose as many as you have time for)*

Craft: F.R.O.G. (Fully Rely On God)   10 - 15 Minutes
Supplies: Green and White construction paper or foam, scissors, markers, and copies of the frog pattern on the last page of this lesson

1. Give each child a 5x5 piece of white construction paper or foam, 1/2 sheet green construction paper or foam as well as a copy of the last page of this lesson.
2. Trace each of the two bigger shapes onto the green paper/foam. Cut them out
3. Cut out the eyes (You could just print them on white card stock or have the children color them.)
4. Draw the nose and mouth as shown with black markers.
5. Glue the head of the frog onto the legs and then add the eyes
6. Glue the whole frog onto a piece of white or other color paper/foam.
7. Above the frog write "Fully Rely On God (F.R.O.G.)"

The Teaching Moment: This fun little frog can remind us that God wants to deliver us from evil, but in order for Him to do that we have to Fully Rely on Him. We have to trust God and follow Him in all we do. God wants to deliver us from evil.

Game: F.R.O.G. Race   5 Minutes

1. Divide the children into two or three teams (or they can race as individuals).
2. Make two lines on the floor as far apart as you have room for
3. Put the teams into lines behind one of the marks
4. Have the first person in each team hop like a frog down to the second mark and back. When they return to the line, they should gently tap the second person who can then begin his or her hop down and back. Continue until one teams gets all players down and back.
5. VARIATION: set a timer and have the lines move as described above until the timer goes off or you say stop. The team whose players went down and back the most times wins.

The Teaching Moment: Today we pretended to be frogs hopping down and back to remind us to Fully Rely on God. Paul relied on God to save him from every evil that came his way. Every time we hear or see a frog, we need to remember to "F," what does the "F" stand for? (FULLY) "R," what does the "R" stand for? (RELY) "O," what does the "O" stand for? (ON) "G," what does the "G" stand for? (GOD)

KEY PHRASE: God Wants to Deliver Us From Evil

Illustration: What must I do to be saved? — 5 Minutes

You may want to have the children clean up before you move into this illustration. Today, we will offer the children an opportunity to ask Jesus to be their Savior. If you're uncomfortable sharing the way of salvation, talk to your pastor or another person in your church who you can see without a doubt knows Christ. You might even invite someone to come and share this part of the lesson. You or your guest should tell the children your salvation story. Then move into this short description and prayer.

In today's story the jailer asked Paul and Silas "What do I have to do to be saved?" That's a very important question. This may be the most important question in the whole Bible. Do you know what it means to be saved? *(Allow for answers.)* We are saved from our sin. The Bible says that sin separates us from God. It says that sin will keep us from heaven. So, we have to do something to get rid of our sin. But on our own, we can't. Some people try to be good enough and do good things, but since we can't be as good as Jesus, we can't be good enough. We can't ever be perfect. So Jesus died on the cross to pay for our sin. To be saved we have to accept Jesus' gift. We have to say to God, "I'm sorry for the times when I make you sad with my sin. I am glad you sent Jesus to die to take away my sin. I accept Jesus' gift on the cross. I want Jesus to be my Savior."

WRAPPING IT UP—SENDING IT HOME — 5 Minutes

Cleaning Up

Hopefully, you did this earlier.

Closing Worship and Prayer

Today we're going to pray a prayer that will help you ask Jesus to be your Savior. That's the best way for Jesus to "deliver us from evil." If you'd like Jesus to be your Savior, you can pray this prayer with me.

If you need some guidance for your prayer, you can use this. You might want to encourage the kids to repeat after you in case they want to ask Jesus to be their Savior:

Father in Heaven, You are so wonderful to us. We praise your name. We've learned that bad things happen to everyone. But we also learned that if we trust in you, you will help us when those bad things come our way. Help us to always rely on you and trust that you will help us. Jesus, we want to be like Paul and Silas and the jailer. We want to be saved. We want you to be our Savior. I'm sorry for all the times I sin and make you sad. Thank you for dying on the cross to take away my sin. I accept the gift Jesus gave us when He died on that cross. Jesus you are my Savior. And Lord, we pray all of these things in Jesus' name, who taught us to pray: (now lead them in the Lord's Prayer)

Our Father who art in heaven, hallowed be thy Name. Thy Kingdom come, thy will be done on earth as it is in heaven. Give us this day our daily bread and forgive us our debts as we forgive our debtors.

Lead us not into temptation and deliver us from evil. For thine is the kingdom and the power and the glory forever, Amen.

After you finish praying, ask children to tell you if they've made a decision for salvation and encourage them to tell their parents and your pastor.

Make a F.R.O.G

Make a F.R.O.G

Page intentionally left blank for printing and copying purposes

Jesus, Teach Me How to Pray
A Year in The Lord's Prayer and other Bible Basics

Unit 10: For Thine is the Kingdom, Power & Glory. Amen.
Lesson 1: The Power of God

Lesson Overview

Today's lesson covers several chapters of Exodus. Before God freed the Israelites from the rule of Egypt, He showed Pharaoh his power through many miracles and plagues. First Aaron's staff became a snake, then he turned the Nile to blood. This was followed by a plague of frogs and a plague of gnats. Even though by this time his advisors told him it had to be God, Pharaoh still wouldn't let the Israelites go. So in came swarms of flies, and then all of Egypt's livestock died. Even the boils and hail that destroyed crops wouldn't convince Pharaoh. Locusts that ate all the rest of the crops and darkness so black they couldn't see their hand in front of their face made the Egyptian advisors think that Egypt was doomed for destruction, but it didn't deter Pharaoh. Only when his firstborn son (and the firstborn of every Egyptian) died, did Pharaoh finally let the Israelites leave Egypt. But the story of the power of God doesn't end there, because Pharaoh changed his mind and chased down the Israelites. To save them God made a path through the Red Sea. It stood like walls on either side of Israel, and they safely walked across on dry ground. Meanwhile, God stayed behind the nation of Israel and detained the Egyptians. When Pharaoh and his army finally tried to cross behind them, the river closed back up and the army was destroyed. This is a marvelous story and testimony to the power of God.

KEY PHRASE: We serve a Powerful God

SETTING UP THE LESSON — 1-2 Minutes

Questions and Answers

PRESENTING THE LESSON — 7-10 Minutes

Scripture: Exodus 7-14

MAKING IT REAL TO KIDS TODAY — *(Choose as many as you have time for)*

Review: Name the Plagues — 5-7 Minutes
Supplies: Newsprint or Index Cards or both

Craft: God's Power Book — 5-10 Minutes
Supplies: Copies of the booklet on the final pages of this lesson, crayons and stapler

Game: Power of God Word Search — 5-10 Minutes
Supplies: Copies of the Puzzle

Song: Pharaoh, Pharaoh — 5 Minutes

WRAPPING IT UP—SENDING IT HOME — 5-7 Minutes

Clean Up Time & Prayer Time

KEY PHRASE: We Serve a Powerful God

SETTING UP THE LESSON   1-2 Minutes

Questions and Answers

Ask the kids: What's the yuckiest thing you can think of? *(Allow for answers.)* Are you afraid of snakes? *(Allow for answers.)* How do you feel about frogs? *(Allow for answers.)* Do you think snakes or frogs could show how powerful God is? *(Allow for answers.)* Well, let's hear what the Bible has to say about it.

PRESENTING THE LESSON   5-10 Minutes

Scripture: Exodus 7-14

You do not have to read this directly from the Bible—use the story form below or reword it to fit your personality

The Israelites lived in Egypt for about 400 years. They'd been slaves almost that entire time. They prayed and prayed that God would save them. Finally God sent Moses to rescue them, but in order to get them out of Egypt, Moses had to convince Pharaoh to let the Israelites leave. Pharaoh knew if the Israelites left, He would lose all his free help. Can you say Pharaoh? *(Allow for answers.)* Do you know what a Pharaoh is? *(Allow for answers.)* Pharaoh is what the Egyptians called their kings. So, Pharaoh was in charge. Though it seemed impossible, Moses and his brother, Aaron, had to convince Pharaoh that God wanted the Israelites to leave and then get the king to let them go.

Well Pharaoh was not going to let the Israelites out of their slavery. So God decided to show Pharaoh just how powerful He is. Aaron and Moses visited Pharaoh and told him, "God said, 'Let my people go.'" Pharaoh wanted to know why he should care what God said. So Aaron took his walking stick and threw it down. It turned into a snake! What would you think if a walking stick turned into a snake? *(Allow for answers.)* Pharaoh wasn't impressed. He didn't care, and he wouldn't let them go.

So God told Aaron to take his walking stick and use it to touch the water in the Nile river. When he did, God caused the water to turn into blood. Do you think the Egyptians could drink the water after it turned into blood? *(Allow for answers.)* No, they couldn't drink it! Plus, all the fish died, and the river started to stink! But still Pharaoh didn't think God was the most powerful, so he wouldn't let the Israelites go.

The next week God sent frogs all over Egypt. Frogs filled Pharoah's house and every house in Egypt. Everywhere they walked, they stepped on frogs. How would you feel about so many frogs? *(Allow for answers.)* Even though Pharaoh asked Moses to pray and ask God to take the frogs away, the king still didn't think God was the most powerful. He kept the Israelites as slaves.

Next, Aaron took his walking stick and hit the ground and stirred up the dust. As soon as the dust hit the air, it turned into gnats. Gnats surrounded all the people and all the animals. Dust all over Egypt turned into gnats. Do you know what gnats are? *(Allow for answers.)* They are those tiny bugs that are usually outside near trees or weeds. Gnats hang out near rotten food too. Hundreds of gnats would be awful. You'd get them in your mouth and they'd stick in your hair! Pharaoh's wisest men tried to tell him that God must be mad at them, but Pharaoh wouldn't listen.

Next, God sent flies. Every person and every house had flies all over them. There were flies on all the animals and all over the ground. What would you think if you saw that many flies? *(Allow for answers.)* Do you think you could get that many with a fly swatter? *(Allow for answers.)* I don't think I could! Pharaoh finally promised to let the Israelites go. So Moses prayed and every single fly left. But as soon as all the flies left, Pharaoh changed his mind.

Next God sent a terrible disease on all the animals that belonged to the Egyptians that caused all of their animals to die. Every cow and horse, every pig and chicken, every single animal died. But none of the Israelite animals died. Next God told Moses to take ashes and throw them in the air. Do you know what ashes are? *(Allow for answers.)* Ashes come from a fire. It's the dust that's left over after the fire is done burning. When Moses threw the ashes in the air, it caused sores all over the Egyptians. They had big sore places all over them called boils. They could hardly walk because it hurt so bad. But still Pharaoh was stubborn and wouldn't allow the Israelites to leave.

KEY PHRASE: We Serve a Powerful God

God told Pharaoh He was going to show the Egyptians how powerful He was. This time God sent hail all over Egypt. Do you know what hail is? *(Allow for answers.)* Hail is huge chunks of ice. Sometimes hail look like golf balls or softballs. The big chunks create big dents in our cars, but in Egypt, the huge ice balls destroyed crops. Even more animals died, and the fields were ruined.

Then God sent locust. Do you remember what locust look like? *(see picture on Unit 4 - 11)* Locusts look a lot like a fat brown grasshopper. Even though they're small bugs, they eat everything. So, all the Egyptians' crops that the hail didn't destroy were ruined by the locust. But even with all the animals killed and the crops destroyed, Pharaoh would not let the Israelites leave Egypt.

So, do you think God gave up? *(Allow for answers.)* He'd already done a lot to show how powerful He was, but God wasn't done yet. What do you think God did next? *(Allow for answers.)* God made it dark. Even where it was supposed to be light, it was dark. And it wasn't just dark like when you go to bed, it was so dark they couldn't see their hand when they held it up by their face. For three days it was dark. The sun never came up. Pharaoh got very angry, but still he wouldn't let the people go.

God had just one more way to show His power. The last thing that God did was cause the oldest son in every house to die in the middle of the night. Every house in Egypt woke up crying because someone had died in their house. It was a very sad time. Even in Pharaoh's house the oldest son died. Pharaoh was very sad. He told the people they could leave, and this time he let them go.

God led the Israelites out of Egypt. They headed out with all their families, their animals and many gifts from the Egyptians. God went ahead of them in a cloud and took them toward the Red Sea. By this time, Pharaoh remembered he wouldn't have any slaves any more! He headed out, chasing the Israelites with his army. They caught up with Moses and the Israelites just as they reached the Red Sea. Pharaoh thought he had the Israelites trapped. But God had saved the best for last. He still had one more way to show Pharaoh how powerful He is. God told Moses to hold up his walking stick and point it toward the water. Who knows what happened? *(Allow for answers.)* When Moses held up his staff, the water stopped and made a path. The water was piled up on each side of the path. The Israelites walked right through the Red Sea and the ground was dry!

And while the Israelites were walking through, God caused the cloud that was in front of them to move behind them to keep the Egyptians confused and to hold them back. They couldn't get past the cloud. After all the Israelites made it through the sea, God moved the cloud and let the Egyptians continue to chase the Israelites. But when the Egyptians entered the sea, God told Moses to lower his walking stick, and the water came back over top of all the Egyptians.

God is very powerful. He loved the Israelites a lot. So He showed Pharaoh His power so Pharaoh would leave the Israelites alone. If we trust God, he will rescue us. Sometimes it takes longer than we want it to, just like the Israelites. But God is Powerful!

MAKING IT REAL TO KIDS TODAY   *(Choose as many as you have time for)*

Review: Name the Plagues
Supplies: Newsprint or Index Cards or both

With a list of plagues and miracles this long it's a good idea to review them. Use the newsprint to list them as the kids remember them, then use another sheet (or another column) to put them in order. Instead or additionally, write the names of the plagues on thirteen index cards. Create at least two sets—more sets if you have a large group.

Divide the class into as many groups as you have card sets. Then have them put the cards in order. You could declare a winner when the first group gets them in the correct order.

1. Walking Stick became a Snake
2. Water turned into Blood
3. Frogs everywhere
4. Gnats
5. Flies
6. Livestock Disease
7. Sores/Boils
8. Hail
9. Locust
10. Darkness
11. Death of the oldest son
12. Dry Land in the Red Sea
13. Closed the Red Sea over the Egyptians

KEY PHRASE: We Serve a Powerful God

The Teaching Moment: How many of the plagues would you have put up with before you let the Israelites go? *(Allow for answers.)* Which of these do you think is the worst (besides the death of the oldest son)? *(Allow for answers.)* Which do you think shows God's power the best? *(Allow for answers.)* God really wanted Pharaoh to let the Israelites go, so He showed Pharaoh how powerful He is. Because God is Powerful!

Craft: God's Power Booklet 10-15 Minutes
Supplies: Copies of the booklet on the final pages of this lesson, crayons and stapler

1. Copy the last four pages one sided.
2. Have the children fold on the heavy lines first and then the dotted lines, with the dotted lines on the inside.
3. Put the pages in order and staple together
4. Allow the children to color the pictures, draw what is on the description or add to the picture (IE: Gnats-draw dots, hail - draw circles, dark - color black, flies - add a fly or two)

The Teaching Moment: Take this booklet home and use it to tell your parents or some other grownup about the power of God that Pharaoh saw.

Game: Power of God Word Search 5-10 Minutes
Supplies: Copies of the bottom of puzzle on the next page

Allow the children to complete the puzzle

The Teaching Moment: This is a fun way for us to remember all the ways that God showed His power to Pharaoh. You can use the words on this puzzle to remind you of the power of God.

Song: Pharaoh, Pharaoh 5 Minutes

Copy words for older children. Go over the words of the chorus for younger children. Sing to the tune of Louie, Louie

CHORUS Pharaoh, Pharaoh, Oh baby, let my people go. Yeah, Yeah, Yeah, Yeah, Yeah, Yeah
Pharaoh, Pharaoh, Oh baby, let my people go. Yeah, Yeah, Yeah, Yeah, Yeah, Yeah

Well a burnin' bush told me just the other day, that I should come over here and say,
"Gotta get my people out of Pharoah's hand and lead 'em on over to the Promised Land." Singin'

CHORUS

Well, me an' God's people headed to the Red Sea, but all of Pharoah's army was a comin' after me
So I raised my rod, and I stuck it in the sand, and all of God's people walked upon the dry land. Singin'

CHORUS

Well all of Pharoah's army was a comin' too. So, what do you think that I did do?
I raised my rod, and I cleared my throat. And all of Pharoah's army did the dead man's float. Singin'

CHORUS

Motions:

Pharaoh, Pharaoh - "walk like an Egyptian" to the left and then the right (look left with left arm bent up at elbow with hand bent forward in front of you while right hand is face up behind you - then switch)

OH baby - Big "O" above your head then swing it down like you're rocking a baby

Let my people go - Thumbs point over shoulder

(In this break insert a powerful, from the gut, "UGH" and push elbows back)

KEY PHRASE: We Serve a Powerful God

Yeah, Yeah, Yeah, Yeah - Hands over head shaking fingers while bending knees gradually O

(In the verses raise your rod, stick it in the sand, clear your throat and do the dead man's float)

Song ends with one extra "Yeah"

The Teaching Moment: This is a really fun song that can help us remember that God made dry ground in the Red Sea and then closed it up over the Egyptians to show His power.

WRAPPING IT UP—SENDING IT HOME 5-7 Minutes

Clean Up Time

We want the children to learn to be responsible, so be sure they help with the clean up, but remind them not to go anywhere, the group is going to talk to God together one more time.

Closing Worship and Prayer

Gather the children for prayer and ask for prayer requests if you have time. Close with your own prayer or use the one below for help. Remember to end with the Lord's Prayer so the kids will practice saying it again.

If you need some guidance for your prayer, you can use this:

Father in Heaven, You are so powerful. It's exciting for us to see how great and mighty You are. We praise You that You showed Pharaoh Your power, and we can see Your power here on earth. Lord, bless all of the things these kids have mentioned as prayer requests today *(if there's time, you can mention some of their requests)*. And Lord, we pray all of these things in Jesus' name, who taught us to pray: *(now lead them in the Lord's Prayer)*

Our Father who art in heaven, hallowed be thy Name. Thy Kingdom come, thy will be done on earth as it is in heaven.
Give us this day our daily bread and forgive us our debts as we forgive our debtors.
Lead us not into temptation and deliver us from evil. For thine is the kingdom and the power and the glory forever, Amen.

Power of God Word Search

```
X S S S A S S C E L L W S K R L O C U S T S G C O
E K R A E S D E R K C R A O K P T R E O S R S L C
F A S R E E Y S N L F E I L G D W K L I L O I D U
I T S E E E T L S K L E E N K W A S R S O E A E E
S S I T I S L D D O I A S E N I I N S A S D O E A
S S R R H L A D D S S T Y D R E N O H A D T I E S
L S P A E I F E H K F L O N N S S G G S N G O G A
S O D E E T A I L T W O A L I A E D S F S L R D Y
T N F B E L A A D N L L G U I R L S Y T L E K I E
S T S F L U I W S B Y S I G E D A M O I I S E I E
E N E R U D E T S E T G S G R S S S H M A C K M K
I G G R A A L N E A P A W S E Y T N F K T S K K I
E C E T I A A A N S S P S S N C N B P O L M R T N
K I R R T K S G R K G Y O N K A R F H A R A E S K
A H O H E N E E S R T T S K T A I T A R S O S T S
R N A O H R A L S R C S Y R E L A T D S R I A E L
G I K I S I O K R L G H O S O I A F P R A T N H B
S G D E L C H S E K E E R K G E E I A Y O D N A T
L B I D U O P E E T F E G E T A L R G H G S F H D
A F R S I R R B T D N S A G A R R O R H S E O G R
I I T E R S U S E O I A A N A L K N O M A A R E G
A S K N G S S C T K B I S K S I L E R F R E D F S
E S T O S E T N L K S H R E S S N B S A O S S K E
W E R S S G S W S H L S F S E E L S H K E E G D I
L F D B E R K L L K E S D B A T E P P A G E R D M
```

FIND THESE WORDS

SNAKE	MOSES
WATER	FROGS
BLOOD	HAIL
WALKING STICK	LOCUST
GNATS	DARK
FLIES	RED SEA
SORES	EGYPTIANS
PHARAOH	ISRAELITES

Name _____

God Showed His Power to Pharaoh

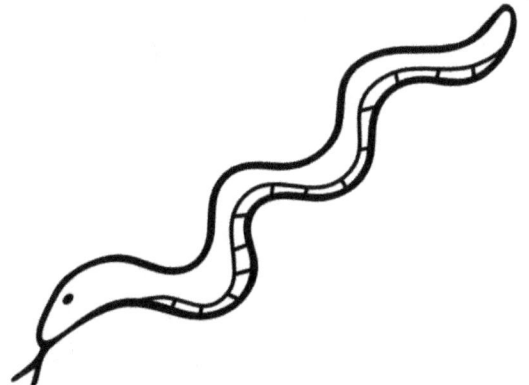

God Showed His Power to Pharaoh by Turning a walking stick into a snake

God Showed His Power to Pharaoh by

Bringing the Red Sea over the Egyptians

God Showed His Power to Pharaoh by

Turning all the water into blood

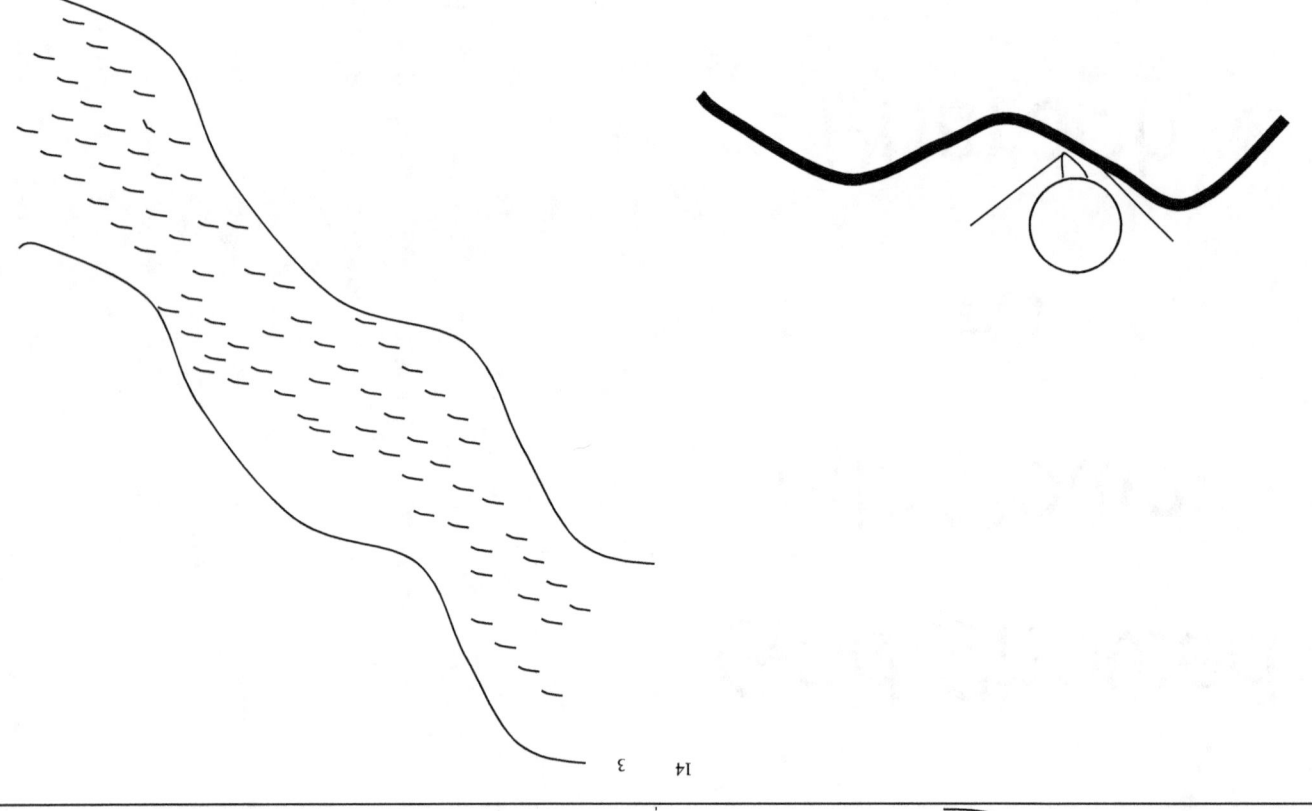

God Showed His Power to Pharaoh by

Putting Frogs Everywhere

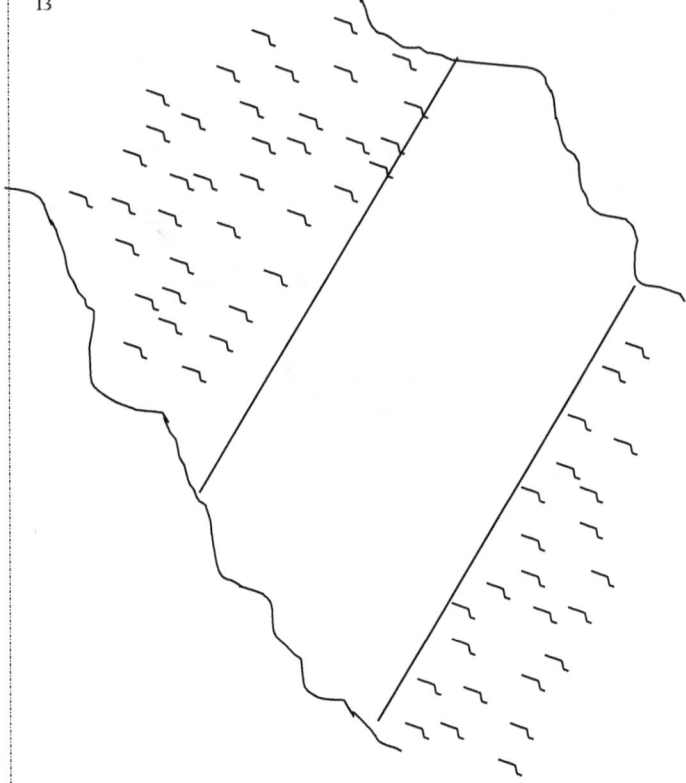

God Showed His Power to Pharaoh by

Making a dry path in the Red Sea

God Showed His Power to Pharaoh by
Changing all the dust into Gnats

God Showed His Power to Pharaoh when
The oldest son in every house died

God Showed His Power to Pharaoh by

Making flies go everywhere!

God Showed His Power to Pharaoh by

Making it dark even in the day

God Showed His Power to Pharaoh by
Letting locust eat all the crops

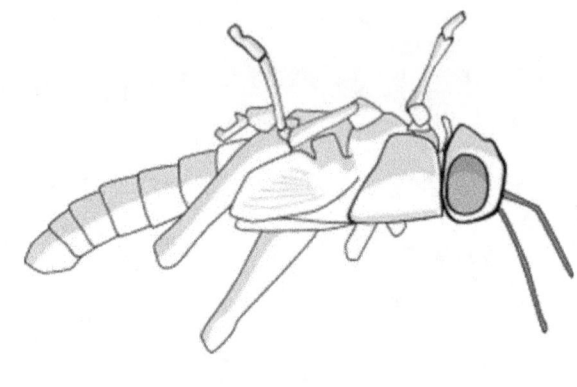

God Showed His Power to Pharaoh by
Letting all the animals die of a disease

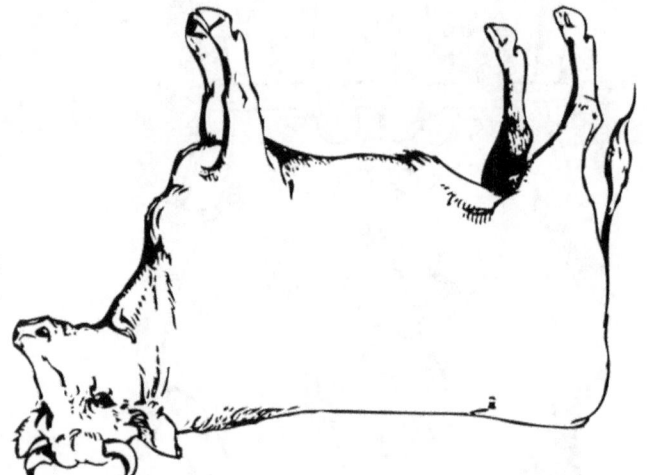

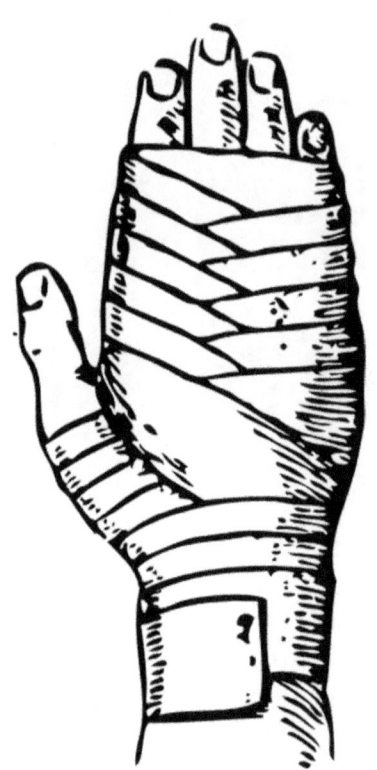

God Showed His Power to Pharaoh by
Spreading ashes to create sores on the skin

God Showed His Power to Pharaoh by
Sending Hail that destroyed crops

Jesus, Teach Me How to Pray

A Year in The Lord's Prayer and other Bible Basics

Unit 10: For Thine is the Kingdom, Power & Glory. Amen.
Lesson 2: The Glory of God

Lesson Overview

To be perfectly honest, the glory of the Lord is a difficult concept even for adults. Today we're going to share a couple of stories of how God showed His glory in the Bible. The first is in Exodus. Moses often saw the glory of God. The glory of God appeared to the people in a cloud. Then in Luke we read about Jesus being transformed, and Peter and John seeing God's glory in Jesus himself. Glory is unspeakable magnificence. It is great splendor and beauty. Glory is often thought of as a radiating light. The difficult part is we don't really know what this glory looked like. It's just described as the glory of the Lord. This might be hard to help the kids see, but just continue to express how wonderful, beautiful, and magnificent God is. He is more glorious than words can express.

KEY PHRASE: God Appeared to His People in Glory

SETTING UP THE LESSON — 5-7 Minutes

   Video: Space video from YouTube
   Supplies: There are three video choices from YouTube in the lesson or choose your own.

PRESENTING THE LESSON — 5-10 Minutes

   Scripture: Exodus 24:15-18, 34:29-35 & Luke 9:28-36

MAKING IT REAL TO KIDS TODAY — *(Choose as many as you have time for)*

   Game: Flashlight Tag — 5-10 Minutes

   Craft: Luminary — 10-15 Minutes
   Supplies: Jelly jars, votive candles, sand or kitty litter, brown paper bags or construction paper

   Song w/video: "Show me Your Glory" by Third Day — 5 Minutes
   or "God of Wonders" by Third Day and Caedman's Call

WRAPPING IT UP—SENDING IT HOME — 5-7 Minutes

   Clean Up Time & Prayer Time

KEY PHRASE: God Appeared to His People in Glory

SETTING UP THE LESSON   5-7 Minutes

Video: Scenes from Space
Supplies: Choose one of the videos below from YouTube or choose one of your own

Photos from the Webb Telescope - https://www.youtube.com/watch?v=65ExK0XYNFg

Universe- Nebula - https://www.youtube.com/watch?v=fkWrjrdT3Zg (about 3 minutes)

The Hand of God: Images of the Cosmos - http://youtu.be/bbr8nNYGMZA (about 3:59)

The YouTube videos listed above were made from pictures of the universe. The James Webb photos are even more amazing than the Hubble photos. Today we're going to talk about God's glory, but it's a concept difficult to depict. These stars, Nebula, and galaxies are a good beginning. Start the video just before the kids come in. As they enter have them come in quietly, gather them around the screen and encourage them to watch quietly. Show as much as you have time for. As the video ends move directly into the lesson.

PRESENTING THE LESSON   5-10 Minutes

Scripture: Exodus 19:16-20:21; 24:15-18, 34:29-35 & Luke 9:28-36
You do not have to read this directly from the Bible—use the story form below or reword it to fit your personality

So what did you think about that video? *(Allow for answers.)* That was video of stars and planets, galaxies and the universe. All things that God created. These things are great pictures of the glory of God. At the end of the Lord's Prayer, we say, "For Thine is the Kingdom, the Power and the Glory, Forever. Amen" Last week we talked about the Power of God. Today we're going to learn about the Glory of God.

Does anyone remember who Moses was? *(Allow for answers.)* Moses led the Israelites out of Egypt. He was good at listening to God and always did what God asked. Three months after they left Egypt, God called all the people to gather around Mount Sinai. He wanted to speak to them and give them the Ten Commandments. But the glory of the Lord was too much for the Israelites. A great cloud covered the top of the mountain, and lightning flashed all around. Finally, a trumpet sounded from the mountain top and God began talking. But the sound was so loud and the glory of God so big, the people trembled in fear. The asked God to quit talking to them because the they couldn't handle the glory of God.

Later, when Moses climbed the mountain to get the Ten Commandments, the cloud on the mountain began to glow. The Israelites said the cloud looked like fire on top of the mountain. No one would go near the mountain while God's glory rested on top. God's glory was in the cloud. The fire and the sound of God's voice frightened everyone except Moses and Aaron.

After Moses got the Ten Commandments, He came down from the mountain, but the Bible tells us Moses' face was radiant because he'd been near God's glory. Do you know what radiant means? *(Allow for answers.)* It means Moses' face was glowing. In fact, it glowed so brightly that Moses put a scarf over his face so the Israelites wouldn't see it and be frightened. Every time Moses talked to God his face started glowing again.

Jesus showed God's glory in the Bible, too. One time Jesus took Peter, James, and John up on a mountain with Him to pray. While Jesus was praying, His face changed, and His clothes became as bright as lightening. Peter, James and John were surprised at what Jesus looked like. They'd never seen Jesus look like that before. They'd never seen God's glory that way. Peter wanted to stay in God's glory forever, but Jesus told them

When the Bible talks about God's glory, it means people saw things that were magnificent and beautiful. Usually it means that something beautiful is bright or glowing, a lot like the fire in the cloud that the Israelites saw on the mountain with Moses. When we tell God that the glory is His, we praise Him for how wonderful He is and remember that God is magnificent and beautiful and full of light.

KEY PHRASE: God Appeared to His People in Glory

MAKING IT REAL TO KIDS TODAY
(Choose as many as you have time for)

Game: Flashlight Tag   5 Minutes
Supplies: One or two flashlights and a CD player with a Christian CD for the small group game

For a Large Group or a Large Room: Make the room as dark as possible. Identify a rug or spot in the room as "base." Make one or two children "it" (one for every 7-10 children). Have those children ("it") cover their eyes while the rest of the children hide.

The children who hide will try to get to base without having a flashlight shined on them. Those holding the flashlight must stay away from the base and try to find the hiders. When they find one, they must shine the flashlight on the hider. When someone is caught by the flashlight, they are "out" until all kids are either out or make it to base. The first one or two kids to make it to base will be "it" next.

For a Small Group or a Small Room: Make the room as dark as possible with the kids sitting in a circle. Give the flashlight to one student (two if you have more than ten in your class). When you turn the music on the student should shine the light on the student next to them and then move the light around the circle while the music plays. Have them keep the light moving slowly from student to student until you stop the music. When the music stops, the light should stop. The person who has the light on him or her will be the next person to shine the light. Play for as long as you have time.

The Teaching Moment: It's fun to play with flashlights, but every time we see a flashlight we can remember that Jesus is the Light. Flashlights can also remind us of God's glory because almost every time God showed His glory, He did it with light. So, the next time you use a flashlight remember God appeared to His people in all His glory.

Craft: Luminary
Supplies: Jelly or bouillon jars, votive candles, sand or kitty litter, brown paper grocery bags or construction paper

Give each child a lunch bag OR piece of brown paper grocery bag OR piece of construction paper. (If they use a piece of brown paper bag or construction paper, be sure it will fit around the jelly jar)

Allow the kids to decorate the bag or paper. Then let them cut out stars or other shapes for the light to show through. Remind them not to cut to the edge. You might have them fold before they make their cuts.

Put a bit of sand or kitty litter in the bottom of the jelly jar. Add the candle to the jar. Put the jar in the bag or wrap the jar with the paper bag or construction paper.

The Teaching Moment: We made this luminary to remind us of God's glory. The light shining through is beautiful. God is beautiful and makes things beautiful. Jesus said He is the light. The light can remind us of His glory.

Song w/video: "Show me Your Glory" by Third Day or "God of Wonders" by Third Day and Caedman's Call

You could play one or both of these songs while the kids are doing their luminaries. The YouTube videos for these songs (listed below) are much like the one at the beginning and could be substituted for "Setting Up the Lesson"

The songs can be found on iTunes, Rhapsody or other online music service.
These are the YouTube links:
https://www.youtube.com/watch?v=Z_e3aJLRsdc
https://www.youtube.com/watch?v=TTXBLspw_Z0

WRAPPING IT UP—SENDING IT HOME　　　　　　　　　5-7 Minutes

Clean Up Time

Don't forget to use this time to help the kids learn that it's important to clean up our messes. Encourage them to push in chairs also.

Closing Worship and Prayer

Gather the children for prayer. If you have time, you could ask for prayer requests. Use the prayer below or prayer spontaneously and then end with the Lord's Prayer so the kids will practice saying it again.

If you need some guidance for your prayer, you can use this:

Father in Heaven, You are amazing and magnificent. We are glad you showed Moses and the Israelites your glory. Forgive us for those times when we don't listen to you the way Moses did, and help us learn to do what you ask so we can see your glory. Lord, bless all of the things these kids have mentioned as prayer requests today (*if there's time, you can mention some of their requests*). And Lord, we pray all of these things in Jesus' name, who taught us to pray: *(now lead them in the Lord's Prayer)*

Our Father who art in heaven, hallowed be thy Name. Thy Kingdom come, thy will be done on earth as it is in heaven. Give us this day our daily bread and forgive us our debts as we forgive our debtors.

Lead us not into temptation and deliver us from evil. For thine is the kingdom and the power and the glory forever, Amen.

Jesus, Teach Me How to Pray
A Year in The Lord's Prayer and other Bible Basics

Unit 10: For Thine is the Kingdom, Power & Glory. Amen.
Lesson 3: Why Do We Say "Amen" at the End

Lesson Overview

The word "Amen" is a Hebrew word that means, "So be it." It's a word of affirmation and can mean "it is true" or "truthfully." When we say Amen, we are saying we agree with the words we just said or heard someone else say. It is truly correct to say, "Amen" when someone else is praying when you agree with them. Today the kids will look at just two verses of scripture. Matthew 18:19-20 tells us how important it is to share our prayers with other Christians. God wants us to pray together and agree in prayer.

KEY PHRASE: That's Right!

SETTING UP THE LESSON — 5 Minutes
What Does it Mean

PRESENTING THE LESSON — 5-10 Minutes
Scripture: Matthew 18:19-20

MAKING IT REAL TO KIDS TODAY — (Choose as many as you have time for)

Game: Amen — 5-7 Minutes

Craft: My Lord's Prayer — 10 Minutes
Supplies: Copies of the last page and pencils or crayons

Song: "Yes, Lord" — 5 Minutes

Memory Verse: Matthew 18:19 — 5 Minutes

WRAPPING IT UP—SENDING IT HOME — 5-7 Minutes
Clean Up Time & Prayer Time

KEY PHRASE: That's Right!

SETTING UP THE LESSON   5 Minutes

What Does it Mean?

There are a lot of words we say and read in the Bible that not everyone knows the meaning. I'm going to say some words, you tell me what you think they mean. *(Allow for answers, if they don't get it right, help them out with the answer in parenthesis)*

- Blessed - *(holy or made special by God)*
- Redeemer - *(A person who buys something back - Jesus is our redeemer - he paid the price for our sin on the cross)*
- Grace - *(a gift we don't deserve or that is given for no reason - Jesus' death on the cross is an act of grace)*
- Mercy - *(not being punished for something bad we've done - Jesus keeping us from getting what we deserve for our sins is an act of mercy)*
- Saved - *(rescued—when we accept Jesus' gift of forgiveness on the cross we are saved from our sins)*
- Thine - Like "for Thine is the Glory, Power . . . " *(yours)*

The Teaching Moment: It's important to understand the words we say. Today we're going to look at the very last word in The Lord's Prayer. In fact, it's the last word in just about every prayer we pray.

PRESENTING THE LESSON   5-10 Minutes

Scripture: Matthew 18:19-20
You do not have to read this directly from the Bible—use the story form below or reword it to fit your personality

What is the last word we say when we say "The Lord's Prayer"? *(Allow for answers.)* We end with the word, "Amen." But do you know what the word, "Amen" means? *(Allow for answers.)*

Amen is a Hebrew word. Can you say Hebrew? *(Allow children to repeat)* Abraham was a Hebrew, and the Israelites were Hebrews. In Israel they still speak Hebrew today. Amen means "it is true" or "I believe it" or "I agree with you." When we say "Amen" we say "That's right, God can do it!"

Today we're going to hear just two verses of scripture. *(you may want to have the verses on a piece of paper to pass out to all the kids or a board or newsprint and allow them to read it all together - You can use any version you prefer - this is the passage as found in "The Message")*

> When two of you agree on anything at all on earth and make a prayer of it,
> my Father in heaven goes into action.
> And when two or three of you are together because of me,
> you can be sure that I'll be there.
> Matthew 18:19-20 The Message

When we say "Amen" it means we agree. What does our scripture today tell us happens when we agree in prayer? *(Allow for answers.)* This verse says God goes into action. God wants to go into action for us!

But, we can't just say "Amen." To really put God into action, we have to mean it. We have to really mean, "I believe it. God can do it."

These verses also tell us we should always ask people to pray for us and with us. What does the verse say about that? *(Allow for answers.)* Jesus said that when "two of us" agree on anything, God goes in action. So, we should always look for someone to share our prayer with.

Jesus also made us another promise to remind us God wants us to get together with other Christians. Do you see what He said? *(Allow for answers.)* Jesus said when we get together because of Him, He shows up too. Today, because we have gathered in this place to honor Him, Jesus is here. Do you believe that? If you do, then say, "Amen"! *(Encourage kids to say "Amen")*

KEY PHRASE: That's Right!

MAKING IT REAL TO KIDS TODAY

(Choose as many as you have time for)

Game: Amen 5-7 minutes

Have each child think of their favorite ‹*choose a category*›. This can be candy, TV Show, class at school, teacher, toy, etc. Go around the room and let each child say, "My favorite ‹*category*› is ‹whatever it is›." All kids who also like the thing that was mentioned should say, "AMEN" and stand up. Keep track of how many kids respond positively. You can do this with as many topics as you have time for. The child with the most positive responses at the end could be congratulated.

The Teaching Moment: What did we say when we agreed with the favorite? *(Allow for answers.)*. Do you remember what Amen means? *(Allow for answers.)* I hope this little game helps you always remember that Amen means we agree or that's the truth!

Craft: My Lord's Prayer
Supplies: Copies of the last page and pencils or crayons

Help children write the lines of the Lord's Prayer in their own words. Very young children might be want to draw pictures that help them remember what they might say. Encourage the children to avoid using words they don't understand.

The Teaching Moment: Jesus taught His disciples the Lord's Prayer as a model of how to pray. It's not important that we pray these exact words everyday. But it is important that we pray often. Thessalonians tells us to never stop praying. The Lord's Prayer helps us to know how to pray. We don't have to pray the exact words of this prayer, but our prayers should include praising God, remembering to ask for God's will to be done and asking for what we need, for forgiveness, and help to live like Jesus did.

Song: "Yes, Lord" (I'm Trading My Sorrows) 5 Minutes

You can find this song on YouTube or a music service. Some folks use hand motions with the chorus, thumb up on every "yes" and index finger pointing up on "Lord." Others clap on the beat then three straight claps on "Yes, Yes Lord."

The Teaching Moment: This is a fun song to sing! When we say, "Yes, Lord" we are actually saying, "Amen" This song says we believe we can trade our sorrows and pain and shame for God's joy. When we sing songs, it's important that we know what the words mean. Do you believe you can trade your sorrows, pain and shame for God's joy? *(if they do, encourage the kids to say, "Amen")*

Memory Verse: Matthew 18:19 5 Minutes

Whenever two or three of you
agree on anything at all here on earth and make a prayer of it,
my Father in Heaven goes into action
Matthew 18:19

Repeat this verse a few times then ask:

- How many people does this verse talk about? *(2 or 3)*
- What do we need to do? *(agree on something and prayer about it)*
- What does God do? *(God goes into action)*
- Where is that in the Bible? *(Matthew 18:19)*

After you ask the questions, repeat the verse several times again pausing for a moment at the end of each line. You can substitute God for "Father in Heaven"

KEY PHRASE: That's Right!

The Teaching Moment: *This verse is it's own teaching moment - helping kids memorize scripture is a great life skill. They'll be able to come back to this for years once they've learned it here.*

WRAPPING IT UP—SENDING IT HOME   5-7 Minutes

Clean Up Time

Don't forget that it's good for the kids to learn the responsibility of cleaning up after themselves. Encourage them to push in chairs too.

Closing Worship and Prayer

You may close with your own prayer or use the one below for help. You could ask the children for prayer requests if you have time. Remember to end with the Lord's Prayer so the kids will practice saying it again.

If you need some guidance for your prayer, you can use this:

Father in Heaven, we thank you for all of your promises. Thank you that you promised to hear us when we pray, and you always want to be with us. Lord, we believe it when you say that if two of us agree on anything you'll begin to act. *(If you took prayer requests:)* So we ask that you bless all of the things these kids have mentioned as prayer requests today *(Today would be a perfect opportunity to mention the kids requests out loud)*. And Lord, we pray all of these things in Jesus' name, who taught us to pray: *(now lead them in the Lord's Prayer)*

Our Father who art in heaven, hallowed be thy Name. Thy Kingdom come, thy will be done on earth as it is in heaven. Give us this day our daily bread and forgive us our debts as we forgive our debtors. Lead us not into temptation and deliver us from evil. For thine is the kingdom and the power and the glory forever, Amen.

Name_____

My Lord's Prayer

Many people pray the Lord's Prayer often, even every day. But Jesus gave us this prayer to show us how to pray. We don't have to say these words exactly. Today we're going to write a prayer in our own words using the Lord's Prayer as a guide.

Our Father who art in Heaven

_____

_____

Hallowed Be Thy Name

_____

_____

Thy Kingdom Come, Thy Will be done, on earth as it is in Heaven.

_____

_____

Give us this day our daily bread

_____

_____

And forgive us our debts as we forgive our debtors

_____

_____

Lead us not into temptation, but deliver us from evil

_____

_____

For Thine is the Kingdom and the Power and the Glory forever. Amen.

_____

_____

Page intentionally left blank for printing and copying purposes

Jesus, Teach Me How to Pray
A Year in The Lord's Prayer and other Bible Basics

Unit 11: Psalm 23
Lesson 1: The Lord is My Shepherd, He Gives Me Everything I Need

Lesson Overview

One of the most familiar passages of scripture, the 23rd Psalm is a favorite of many. Most adults who attended church as a youngster have at least part of this scripture memorized. The first few verses of this beloved chapter remind us that God gives us everything we need. When some read, "I shall not want," they think it means new cars, boats, trains, planes and more. But this word "want" is best defined as *"to be in a state of destitution or poverty."* (check it out on dictionary.com) For many in developed countries like America, it's difficult to imagine what it really means to "want."

Today we're going to look at the prophet Elijah. Elijah told King Ahab a drought would hit the country. When his prophecy came true, all of Israel eventually ran out of food. God sent Elijah to a widow who only had enough flour and oil left to bake a bit of bread. She expected it to be her last loaf before she and her son would die. Because the widow was willing to help Elijah, her last jar of flour and oil didn't run out until it started to rain again. God provided for Elijah as well as the widow and her son.

KEY PHRASE: God Will Make Sure We Have Everything that We Need

SETTING UP THE LESSON   5-10 Minutes

What do you need?
Supplies: A variety of old magazines, catalogs or newspapers (including store ads) for the children to use.

PRESENTING THE LESSON   5-10 Minutes

Scripture: Psalm 23:1-3 and 1 Kings 17:1-16
(you might want to have a shepherd's crook for these next three weeks)

MAKING IT REAL TO KIDS TODAY   *(Choose as many as you have time for)*

Game: Money, Money, Money   10 Minutes
Supplies: Monopoly Money, paper and pencils

Craft: Everything I need collage   10-15 Minutes
Supplies: Magazines, Newspapers, Catalogs and advertisements, construction paper, scissors & glue

Memory Verse: Psalm 23:1-3a   5-7 Minutes

Song: "Jehovah Jireh" or "I Just Want to be a Sheep" by Brian Howard   3-5 Minutes

WRAPPING IT UP—SENDING IT HOME   5-7 Minutes

Clean Up Time & Prayer Time

KEY PHRASE: God Will Make Sure We Have Everything That We Need

SETTING UP THE LESSON
5-10 Minutes

What do you need?
Supplies: A variety of old magazines, catalogs or newspapers (including store ads) for the children to use.

Give the children a few minutes to cut out three pictures of things they need. Encourage them to look in more than one book or paper. After they've cut out their pictures (or three or four minutes have passed by), give each child a chance to share at least one of their pictures. Without commenting on whether or not the pictures are actual needs, move into the Bible lesson.

PRESENTING THE LESSON
5-10 Minutes

Scripture: Psalm 23:1-3 & 1 Kings 17:1-16

You do not have to read this directly from the Bible—use the story form below or reword it to fit your personality

Today we're going to start learning the 23rd Psalm. It's a special song King David wrote. These six verses are in the Bible and can help us know about God. Repeat these words after me: *(stop after each line so the kids can repeat)*

> The Lord is my Shepherd;
> I shall not want.
> He makes me lie down in green pastures.
> He leads me beside the still waters.
> He restores my soul.
> He guides me on the right path for His name's sake.

God is our shepherd. That means He takes care of us, just like a shepherd takes good care of the sheep. Because God takes good care of us, he makes sure we have everything we need. What do you think it means that God as our shepherd will take us to green pastures and still waters. *(Allow for answers.)* God wants to give us food, a great place to rest and everything that is good for us. Today we're going to hear about a time in the Bible when God took good care of a man.

Elijah was a man who loved God. He did everything God told him to do. When King Ahab wouldn't listen to God, God told Elijah to tell the King it wasn't going to rain anymore in Israel. And sure enough, on that day it stopped raining and didn't rain again for three years. Because there was no rain, nothing would grow, so there was no food in the whole country.

When there's no rain and no food grows, it's called a famine. Can you say famine? *(Allow kids to repeat)* At the beginning of the famine God provided for Elijah. He sent a bird to him everyday to bring him food, and he was able to drink from a little stream of water that ran nearby. But with no rain the water soon dried up.

By now there was very little food in the country. But God sent Elijah to a widow in Zarephath. Do you know what a widow is? *(Allow for answers.)* A widow is a woman who was married, but her husband died. This widow had a son, and she was almost out of food. She only had enough flour and oil left to make one last loaf of bread for her and her son to share. So when Elijah came to her, she didn't really have anything to feed him.

But because Elijah asked her, and he was from God, the widow went home and made the bread and brought some to Elijah. Because she took care of Elijah, God protected the widow and her son. Even though she only had one jar of flour left and one jar of oil, they never ran out. Every time she went to make food for herself, her son and Elijah, there was more flour and oil in the jars. Every day until after the rain came the widow had flour and oil to make bread.

God was the widow's shepherd. He made sure she had just what she needed so she wouldn't be hungry or die during the famine. She didn't have a lot of food, but she had what she needed to make bread during the famine. We should always remember that God is our shepherd. He wants to give us everything we need.

KEY PHRASE: God Will Make Sure We Have Everything That We Need

MAKING IT REAL TO KIDS TODAY *(Choose as many as you have time for)*

Craft: Everything I need collage   10 Minutes
Supplies: Magazines, newspapers, catalogs and advertisements, construction paper, scissors & glue

As you begin, ask each child if the pictures they cut out before the Bible lesson are really pictures of things they need. Remind them that the widow only had flour and oil. She didn't have anything else to eat. Help them to understand that we only "need" food, water, clothing and a dry place to live.

Give each child a piece of construction paper, as well as glue, scissors and access to the magazines, etc. Before the kids begin cutting, ask them what kinds of things they NEED. When they say things like TV or games, toys or other "nice" things, ask if they "need" those things or "wish they had" them. Encourage them to find pictures of food, clothes and shelter. Have the kids write "The Lord is my Shepherd, I shall not want" on the construction paper and then glue their pictures around this verse of scripture. If the pictures they had at the beginning are appropriate, they can use them in their collage.

The Teaching Moment: Sometimes we think the things we wish we had are really what we need. But we only "need" food, water, clothing and a place to keep dry and warm. There are a lot of other things that we want, and many we think we need, but we can live without them. Use this picture to remind us that God makes sure we have everything we need.

Game/Illustration: Money, Money, Money   10-15 Minutes
Supplies: Monopoly Money, paper and pencils

Before your class, put Monopoly money in several envelopes with different amounts between $50-$500 in each envelope. Seal the envelopes. Divide the kids into teams of one to three (be sure your non-readers are on a team with readers)

Give each team a piece of paper and pencils along with one sealed money envelope. Tell them not to open the envelopes. Have the kids write a list of things they need to live for one day and the amount they think it would cost for the three of them to get each thing. Tell them in addition to all the normal things they need, on this day they will be doing their school shopping, so they should list all the things they'll have to have to start school. Allow them to work for a few moments and encourage them to let everyone on their team include the things they would buy.

After they've had some time to work, ask the kids what they have on their lists. Make sure that they have these things on the list:

Housing ($10-$30/day for rent if they all live together- or more if your area is higher)

Food ($15-$30/day for three people depending on what they eat)

Gas or bus fare ($5/day or more depending on how far they go)

After they've shared some of what's on their list, tell them to write these amounts (or those above) next to the items on their list. (adjust them for current prices you've seen) If kids put games or other items on their list, make sure they have them priced appropriately.

Notebooks ($1 each)	Pencils ($3/pack)	New shoes ($15)
New Pants ($15)	New shirt ($15)	Underwear ($8)
Socks ($5)		

After they write down all their amounts and add them up, have the kids open their envelopes. Ask them if they have enough money for everything on their list. Allow them to cross off things they don't need so they can balance their budget. If kids who have more money than they need want to, they can give away some of their money to teams who have less.

KEY PHRASE: God Will Make Sure We Have Everything That We Need

The Teaching Moment: Did you think the amount of money you got was fair? *(Allow for answers.)* That's kind of how life is. We don't always have enough to get everything we want. Some people get more than others, and some get more than they need. This Psalm reminds us that God will always make sure we have as much as we NEED. Sometimes we want more than we actually need, things like games and toys. Sometimes God uses other people to help us get the things that we need. *(if some children gave their money to help others, use them as an example)* God wants to always make sure we have everything that we need.

Memory Verse: Psalm 23:1-3a   5-10 Minutes

Write these first few words on a white board or poster. Go around the circle of kids and have each one say one word. Encourage them to go faster and faster. Optionally, when someone misses a word they could be "out." Repeat it over and over until one or two kids are left. Be prepared to help non-readers or give younger kids exemption from being out.

The Lord is my shepherd, I shall not want.
He makes me lie down by still waters, He restores my soul.
He guides me on the right path for His name's sake.

Song: Jehovah Jireh   3-5 Minutes

Chords and words are on the last page of this lesson or you could download a YouTube version

The Teaching Moment: One of God's names is Jehovah, and Jireh is a Hebrew word that means provider. God wants to provide for all of our needs. When we follow him, He will be our shepherd and take care of what we need.

Optional Song: "I Just Want to Be a Sheep" by Brian Howard

This song is protected by Copyright, so I can't reprint it on this page, but you can find it here:

http://www.butterflysong.com/index.cfm/PageID/32/index.html

The Teaching Moment: We want to be a sheep because then God can be our Shepherd and care for us.

WRAPPING IT UP—SENDING IT HOME   5-7 Minutes

Clean Up Time

Don't forget that it's good for the kids to learn the responsibility of cleaning up after themselves. Encourage them to push in chairs too.

You might copy the next page with Psalm 23 on it and let the kids take it home to memorize.

Closing Worship and Prayer

Even though we're moving on to the 23rd Psalm, we'll continue to pray the Lord's Prayer during these final weeks. Again, if there is time, ask the children if there's anything that they would like you to pray about for them. Remember that no prayer is ever too small, however, children will tend to keep going and be "inspired" by other prayer requests, so feel free to stop taking requests and tell them they can say anything that didn't get said out loud quietly to God themselves while you're praying. You may close with your own prayer or use the one below for help. Remember to end with the Lord's Prayer so the kids will practice saying it again.

If you need some guidance for your prayer, you can use this:

KEY PHRASE: God Will Make Sure We Have Everything That We Need

Father in Heaven, we thank you for all of Your promises. We are glad that You want to be our Shepherd. Thank You that You give us everything that we need. Help us to always trust You to be our Provider. Today we want to ask You to bless all of the things these kids have mentioned as prayer requests today *(Today would be a perfect opportunity to mention the kids requests out loud)*. And Lord, we pray all of these things in Jesus' name, who taught us to pray: (now lead them in the Lord's Prayer)

Our Father, who art in heaven, hallowed be Thy name Thy Kingdom come, Thy will be done On earth as it is in heaven.

Give us this day our daily bread and forgive us our debts as we forgive our debtors.

Lead us not into temptation, but deliver us from evil

For thine is the Kingdom and the Power and the glory forever and ever. Amen.

PSALM 23 from "The Message"

The Lord is my shepherd, I shall not want

He makes me lie down by still waters, He restores my soul

He guides me on the right path for His name's sake

Even though I walk through the valley of the shadow of death, I will fear no evil

For You are with me, your rod and staff comfort me

You prepare a table before me in the presence of my enemies

You anoint my head with oil and my cup overflows

I know goodness and mercy will follow me all the days of my life.

And I will live in God's House forever.

NOTE TO PARENTS: We'll be learning the 23rd Psalm during the next couple of weeks. Your children will be encouraged to memorize this passage of scripture. Feel free to help them with it at home.

PSALM 23 from "The Message"

The Lord is my shepherd, I shall not want

He makes me lie down by still waters, He restores my soul

He guides me on the right path for His name's sake

Even though I walk through the valley of the shadow of death, I will fear no evil

For You are with me, your rod and staff comfort me

You prepare a table before me in the presence of my enemies

You anoint my head with oil and my cup overflows

I know goodness and mercy will follow me all the days of my life.

And I will live in God's House forever.

NOTE TO PARENTS: We'll be learning the 23rd Psalm during the next couple of weeks. Your children will be encouraged to memorize this passage of scripture. Feel free to help them with it at home.

Jehovah Jireh

Public Domain

Notes

Jesus, Teach Me How to Pray

A Year in The Lord's Prayer and other Bible Basics

Unit 11: Psalm 23
Lesson 2: The Lord is My Shepherd, I Will Never Be Afraid

Lesson Overview

Today we're going to read a poem from the book of Isaiah to help us see how special we are to God. Because God is always watching over us, we don't need to be afraid. No matter what happens to us, there is no need to fear.

KEY PHRASE: When We Trust God, We Don't Need to Fear

SETTING UP THE LESSON — 5-7 Minutes

What are you afraid of?
Supplies: Blank paper and crayons

PRESENTING THE LESSON — 5-10 Minutes

Scripture: Psalm 23:3b-4 and Isaiah 43:1b-5a (a shepherd's crook might be handy)

MAKING IT REAL TO KIDS TODAY — *(Choose as many as you have time for)*

Game: Afraid from A to Z — 7-10 Minutes

Craft: No Fear Zone door hanger — 10 Minutes
Supplies: Copies of the last page of this lesson on card stock or heavy paper, crayons, stickers or other decorations

Memory Verse: Psalm 23:1-4 Puzzle — 5-10 Minutes

Song/Video: Veggie Tales "God is Bigger Than the Boogie Man" — 5 Minutes

Optional Song: "I Just Want to be a Sheep" by Brian Howard — 5 Minutes

WRAPPING IT UP—SENDING IT HOME — 5-7 Minutes

Clean Up Time & Prayer Time

KEY PHRASE: When We Trust God, We Don't Need to Fear

SETTING UP THE LESSON   5-7 Minutes

    What are you afraid of?
    Supplies: Blank paper and crayons

Give each child a piece of blank paper and crayons. Have them each draw a picture of what they are afraid of.

OK, let me see your picture and tell me what is it that you are afraid of? *(Allow for answers.)* Why are you afraid of that? *(Allow for answers.)* What do you do when the thing you are afraid of happens or comes near? *(Allow for answers.)* Did you know that God doesn't want us to be afraid? *(Move into the lesson)*

PRESENTING THE LESSON   5-10 Minutes

        Scripture: Psalm 23:4 and Isaiah 43:1b-5a

You do not have to read the first part of this directly from the Bible
use the story form below or reword it to fit your personality
Make copies of the Isaiah passage printed on one of the following pages of this lesson
so the kids can read it together.

Last week we learned the first part of the 23rd Psalm. Today we're going to learn the next two verses. Do you remember how the first part, the part we learned last week, goes? *(Allow for answers.)*

        The Lord is my shepherd, I shall not want
        He makes me lie down by still waters, He restores my soul
        He guides me on the right path for His name's sake

The next two verses say,

        Even though I walk
        through the valley of the shadow of death,
        I will fear no evil.
        For you are with me.
        Your rod and your staff comfort me.

Repeat that part after me. *(Now say the verses one line at a time so the kids can repeat.)*

In other words, we don't have to be afraid because God is always with us. These verses remind us again that God is our shepherd. And just like a shepherd uses his shepherd's crook to keep the sheep safe, God has a plan to keep us safe. So, God makes sure we have everything we need. Plus, He's always there for us so we don't have to be afraid.

There are a lot of places in the Bible where God shared His plan to keep us safe so we don't need to be afraid. One of those is Isaiah 43. Today we're going to read this and talk about it a bit. (Pass out copies of the scripture on the last page of this lesson. It's taken from "The Message." If your church prefers a different translation, you may want to copy that instead. Begin reading this out loud. Have the children read it with you.)

What does Isaiah say about being afraid? *(Allow for answers.)* He said we shouldn't be afraid. Why not? *(Allow for answers.)* How did Jesus pay for us? *(Allow for answers.)* How much does God love us? *(Allow for answers.)*

Let's read this from Isaiah one more time. This time you may each take turns reading a line. We'll read it a couple of times through so that everyone who'd like a turn reading can do that. If you'd prefer not to read, just tap the person next to you, so they'll know to go ahead. *(Now allow the kids to do just what you said. Make sure kids know they don't have to read if they really don't want to. Go ahead and read it a couple of times. Keep going until the every person has been able to read one or two lines. It's OK to repeat it a few times)*

Be aware that you may have kids in your program who are abused. They may wonder why God isn't protecting them. If any of the children were afraid of a parent or other adult during the preparation stage or seem to withdraw or struggle with these verses, be very sensitive. Be sure to discuss concerns you have with the Pastor or church staff.

KEY PHRASE: When We Trust God, We Don't Need to Fear

MAKING IT REAL TO KIDS TODAY   *(Choose as many as you have time for)*

Game: No Fear from A to Z   7-10 Minutes

Have the kids sit in a circle. The first student should say "I see an A_____, but I'm not afraid" Have him fill in the blank with something that begins with the letter "A" that he might be afraid of. (If the kids can't think of anything, allow them to say something silly.) The second person says, "I see a B_____ and an A____, but I'm not afraid." This student should come up with a word that begins with "B" and then repeat the "A" word that the previous person said. Help the kids as it gets tougher. Continue until you get to Z.

The Teaching Moment: This was a lot of fun. It reminds us that we are afraid of a lot of things, but when we trust in God we don't have to be afraid of any of those things. God wants us to trust Him. He doesn't want us to fear!

Craft: No Fear Zone Door hanger   10 Minutes
Supplies: Copies of the last page of this lesson on card stock or heavy paper, crayons, stickers or other decorations

Make copies of the final page of this lesson on heavy paper or card stock. Cut the pages in half. Allow the students to decorate the door hanger with crayons, stickers, etc. You could seal these with clear contact paper if you like. *(You could also use foam pre-made door hangers)*

The Teaching Moment: Because Jesus is our shepherd, we don't have to be afraid. He is always with us. Hang this on your bedroom door so that every time you enter or leave your room you'll remember that with Jesus we never have to be afraid.

Memory Verse: Psalm 23:1-4   7-10 Minutes

On the next to the last page of this lesson you'll find a puzzle with these verses. Give the kids a copy of this puzzle and have them fill in the blanks using the key at the bottom of the page. If you have non-readers, pair up the oldest with the youngest so that all the non-readers have a reader to work with. Here's the answer for those who need help:

The Lord is my shepherd, I shall not want
He makes me lie down by still waters, He restores my soul
He guides me on the right path for His name's sake
Even though I walk through the valley of the shadow of death,
I will fear no evil, for you are with me; your rod and your staff, they comfort me.

Song/Video: "God is Bigger than the Boogie Man" by Veggie Tales   5 Minutes

This song is available on several Veggie Tales CD's, DVD's, YouTube and most music services. The kids will be able to pick up the chorus rather quickly.

The Teaching Moment: This is a good song for us to learn. Every time we begin to be afraid, we can sing it to remind us that when we trust God, we don't have to be afraid.

Optional Song: "I Just Want to Be a Sheep" by Brian Howard

This song is protected by Copyright, so I can't reprint it here, but you can find it here:

http://www.butterflysong.com/index.cfm/PageID/32/index.html and as a video on YouTube

The Teaching Moment: We want to be a sheep because then God can be our Shepherd and care for us.

KEY PHRASE: When We Trust God, We Don't Need to Fear

WRAPPING IT UP—SENDING IT HOME   5-7 Minutes

Clean Up Time

Don't forget that it's good for the kids to learn the responsibility of cleaning up after themselves. Encourage them to push in chairs too.

Closing Worship and Prayer

Even though we're moving on to the 23rd Psalm, we'll continue to pray the Lord's prayer during these final weeks. Again, if there is time, ask the children if there's anything that they would like you to pray about for them. Remember that no prayer is ever too small, however, children will tend to keep going and be "inspired" by other prayer requests, so feel free to stop taking requests and tell them they can say anything that didn't get said out loud quietly to God themselves while you're praying. You may close with your own prayer or use the one below for help. If you're using this unit following the Lord's Prayer units, remember to end with the Lord's Prayer so the kids will practice saying it again.

If you need some guidance for your prayer, you can use this:

Father in Heaven, we are so glad that You are always with us. Forgive us when we become afraid. We know we shouldn't because You promised to always watch out for us, but sometimes we still have fear. Help us, Jesus, to trust You more, and help us always remember if we trust You, we don't have to be afraid. Today we want to ask You to bless all of the things these kids have mentioned as prayer requests today. (*Today would be a perfect opportunity to mention the kids requests out loud*) And Lord, we pray all of these things in Jesus' name, who taught us to pray: (now lead them in the Lord's Prayer)

Our Father, who art in heaven, hallowed be Thy name Thy Kingdom come, Thy will be done On earth as it is in heaven.
Give us this day our daily bread and forgive us our debts as we forgive our debtors.
Lead us not into temptation, but deliver us from evil
For thine is the Kingdom and the Power and the glory forever and ever. Amen.

Isaiah 43:1b-5a (The Message)

God says, "Don't be afraid, I've paid the price for you.
  I've called your name. You're mine.
When you're in over your head, I'll be there with you.
  When you're in rough waters, you will not go down.
When you're between a rock and a hard place,
  it won't be a dead end—
Because I am God, your personal God,
  The Holy of Israel, your Savior.
I paid a huge price for you:
  all of Egypt, with rich Cush and Seba thrown in!
That's how much you mean to me!
  That's how much I love you!
I'd sell off the whole world to get you back,
  trade the creation just for you.
So don't be afraid: I'm with you."

Psalm 23:1-4

The Lord is my shepherd, I shall not want
He makes me lie down by still waters, He restores my soul
He guides me on the right path for His name's sake
Even though I walk
through the valley of the shadow of death,
I will fear no evil.
For you are with me.
Your rod and your staff comfort me.

Isaiah 43:1b-5a (The Message)

God says, "Don't be afraid, I've paid the price for you.
  I've called your name. You're mine.
When you're in over your head, I'll be there with you.
  When you're in rough waters, you will not go down.
When you're between a rock and a hard place,
  it won't be a dead end—
Because I am God, your personal God,
  The Holy of Israel, your Savior.
I paid a huge price for you:
  all of Egypt, with rich Cush and Seba thrown in!
That's how much you mean to me!
  That's how much I love you!
I'd sell off the whole world to get you back,
  trade the creation just for you.
So don't be afraid: I'm with you."

Psalm 23:1-4

The Lord is my shepherd, I shall not want
He makes me lie down by still waters, He restores my soul
He guides me on the right path for His name's sake
Even though I walk
through the valley of the shadow of death,
I will fear no evil.
For you are with me.
Your rod and your staff comfort me.

The Lord is my shepherd; I shall not want.

He maketh me to lie down in green pastures:

he leadeth my soul; he leadeth me in the

paths of righteousness for his name's

sake. Yea, though I walk through the

valley of the shadow of death, I will fear

no evil; for thou art with me; thy rod

and thy staff they comfort me.

Psalm 23:1-4

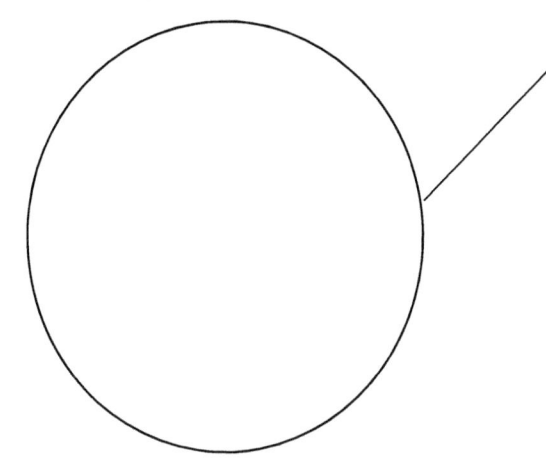
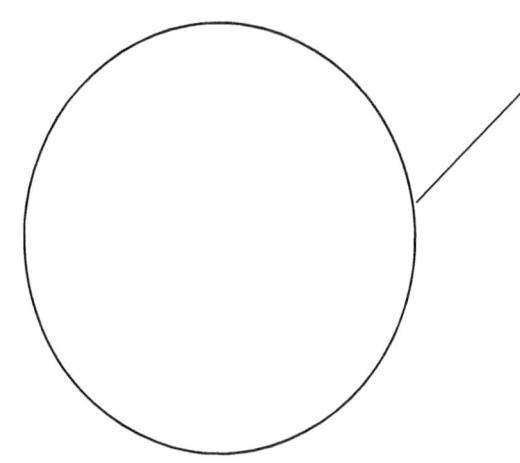

Jesus is my Shepherd . . . So, even when it gets dark at night I will NOT FEAR	Jesus is my Shepherd . . . So, even when it gets dark at night I will NOT FEAR

Page intentionally left blank for printing and copying purposes

Jesus, Teach Me How to Pray
A Year in The Lord's Prayer and other Bible Basics

Unit 11: Psalm 23
Lesson 3: The Lord is My Shepherd, I Don't have any Worries

Lesson Overview

The last two verses of the 23rd Psalm talk about all the blessings we receive because we follow Christ. God wants our enemies to see how He blesses us. He wants to give us good things and take care of us. God is our shepherd. We are His sheep. He knows what's best for us, and He wants to provide for us and protect us. Because God is watching out for us, we have nothing to worry about.

KEY PHRASE: When We Trust in God, We Have No Worries

SETTING UP THE LESSON — 5-7 Minutes
Finding the Food

PRESENTING THE LESSON — 5-10 Minutes
Scripture: Psalm 23:5-6 & Numbers 13:17-14:9

MAKING IT REAL TO KIDS TODAY — *(Choose as many as you have time for)*

Game: Sheep Hunt — 7-10 Minutes
Supplies: Stuffed animals to represent the sheep

Craft: I want to be a sheep — 5-10 Minutes
Supplies: Copies of the craft page at the end of the lesson, crayons, cotton balls, glue

Memory Verse: Psalm 23 — 5 Minutes

Video: The Lion King - Hakuna Matata section — 5 Minutes
Supplies: Video or YouTube clip: *http://www.youtube.com/watch?v=ejEVczA8PLU*

Optional Song: "I Just Want to be a Sheep" by Brian Howard — 5 Minutes

WRAPPING IT UP—SENDING IT HOME — 5-7 Minutes
Clean Up Time & Prayer Time

KEY PHRASE: When We Trust God, We Have No Worries!

SETTING UP THE LESSON   5-7 Minutes

Finding the Food

Before the kids arrive, prepare one zip sandwich bag half full of popcorn or pretzels for each child *(be aware of food allergies)*. Put them in a basket or box. Cover the snacks so they're "hidden," then sit the box or basket right in front of the kids. After the kids arrive, tell them you have a snack for them and then ask if they see it. Let them guess where it may be. One of them should guess easily.

Say: You did a good job finding your snack. Did you know that farm sheep can't usually find their food? *(Allow for answers.)* Except for grass that's right on the ground in front of them, sheep can't usually find water or food. Generally, the shepherd leads them to their food or sits it in front of them. *(Pass out the snacks)*

Farm sheep could never make it without a shepherd? They would die without someone to take care of them. In the Bible, Jesus called us His sheep. He said, "I am the Good Shepherd." Sheep never worry because they trust their shepherd to take care of them. They follow anywhere their shepherd leads them. Jesus wants us to follow Him like that so he can give us everything we need and protect us. When we trust God and let Jesus be our Shepherd, we have no worries. *(Allow them to eat the snack while you share the lesson)*

PRESENTING THE LESSON   5-10 Minutes

Scripture: Psalm 5-6 & Numbers 13:17-14:9

*You do not have to read this directly from the Bible—
use the story form below or reword it to fit your personality*

How many of you were here last week? *(ask for show of hands)* Do you remember the verses we've learned in the last two weeks? *(Allow for answers.)* So far we've learned the first four verses of the 23rd Psalm *(have them repeat each line)*:

The Lord is my shepherd, I shall not want.
He makes me lie down by still waters, He restores my soul.
He guides me on the right path for His name's sake.
Even though I walk through the valley of the shadow of death,
I will fear no evil. For you are with me. Your rod and your staff comfort me.

We've heard that God will provide for all of our needs, and we should have no fears. Today we're going to learn the last two verses of the 23rd Psalm. These verses remind us to trust God and not worry. These verses say:

You set a table for me right in front of my enemies, You put oil on my head.
I know your goodness and love will stay with me all of my life.
And I will live in God's house forever.

King David wrote this Psalm. He was thankful to God because God always took care of His needs. He knew that God would always love Him, so He didn't have to worry.

There are two other men in the Bible who trusted God and didn't worry even when every one else was afraid. Joshua and Caleb were leaders in Israel. Moses sent them with ten other men to scout out the land God promised to give them. For forty days they spied on the people in the Promised land. When they returned, they told Moses about everything they saw. Ten of the men told Moses and the Israelites that the people in the land were huge. They said the people there made them feel like grasshoppers. They were afraid and didn't think they could get the land God promised.

But Joshua and Caleb weren't worried at all. God had promised them they would live in that land and Joshua and Caleb believed God. They told Moses about the country's beauty. The crops grew strong, and they would have plenty to eat. They were sure they could go into the new country and take over. These two men

KEY PHRASE: When We Trust God, We Have No Worries!

trusted God completely. They trusted God to give them everything they needed, and they weren't afraid. So they had no worries.

All the people in Israel believed the ten men who were afraid. They told Moses they wanted to go back and be slaves in Egypt again. It upset God when they didn't trust Him. God said since they were worried and didn't trust Him, only Joshua and Caleb would be allowed to live in the wonderful land that God was giving to them.

The Israelites, including Joshua and Caleb, wandered in the desert for forty more years because they didn't trust God. Finally after all of those who didn't trust God had died, Joshua and Caleb, along with all the people who had been kids back then, got to go live in the beautiful country that God had promised for them.

The 23rd Psalm is important because it helps us know that God wants to take care of us and protect us. Because God is our shepherd, we don't ever have to worry. Sheep never worry. They know their shepherd will feed them and keep them safe. They never even go look for food. They know their shepherd will take them right to the food. We should be like sheep and trust God to take care of us.

MAKING IT REAL TO KIDS TODAY   *(Choose as many as you have time for)*

Game: Sheep Hunt   7-10 Minutes
Supplies: Stuffed animals to represent sheep (1 or 2 per child)

Before the kids arrive, hide the stuffed animals. Tell the kids there are sheep lost all over the room, and they will be the shepherds. They need to find the sheep. If you have a great age span in your group, allow the younger kids to start first for 30-60 seconds. You may want to give four and five-year-olds a head start and then six and seven-year olds and last the oldest kids. Make a big deal about the kids who find the most or have each child come to a home base after they've found one sheep.

The Teaching Moment: You were all good shepherds. You found the sheep before anything bad could happen to them. When we aren't where God wants us to be, He looks for us. He wants us to know that He will always watch out for us, and even when things aren't going the way we want them to, He is there for us. When we trust Him, we'll have no worries.

Memory Verse: Psalm 23   5 Minutes

Have the kids repeat after you one line at a time:

The Lord is my shepherd, I shall not want.

He makes me lie down by still waters, He restores my soul.

He guides me on the right path for His name's sake.

Even though I walk through the valley of the shadow of death, I will fear no evil.

For You are with me, your rod and staff comfort me.

You prepare a table before me in the presence of my enemies.

You anoint my head with oil, and my cup overflows.

I know goodness and mercy will follow me all the days of my life.

And I will live in God's House forever.

KEY PHRASE: When We Trust God, We Have No Worries!

Craft: I want to be a Sheep 5-10 Minutes
Supplies: Copies of the Sheep on the last page of this lesson, crayons, cotton balls, glue

Give each child a copy of the sheep. Allow them to color the head (and words) and glue cotton balls on the body and top of the head.

The Teaching Moment: God is our shepherd. A shepherd takes good care of his sheep. He makes sure his sheep have food and a place to sleep, and He protects His sheep from the things that want to hurt the sheep. A sheep has a shepherd, so it has no worries. God wants to be our shepherd so we'll have no worries.

Video & Song: The Lion King - Hakuna Matata section 5 Minutes
Supplies: The Lion King on Video or DVD
or YouTube clip: *http://www.youtube.com/watch?v=ejEVczA8PLU*

Let the kids watch this four minute clip. Most will probably have seen it before. You might encourage them to sing with it.

The Teaching Moment: Hakuna Matata really is a Swahili phrase that means "There are no worries." It's a phrase they use every day in Africa. We think it's fun to say. But when we follow God and allow Him to be our shepherd, we really can live a life with no worries. God wants to give us everything we need and protect us. When we trust God, we can really sing Hakuna Matata.

Optional Song: "I Just Want to Be a Sheep" by Brian Howard 5 Minutes

You'll find the words here: *http://www.butterflysong.com/index.cfm/PageID/32/index.html*
and the video here: *https://www.youtube.com/watch?v=rzZDU4tFuKs&t=6s*

The Teaching Moment: We want to be a sheep because then God can be our Shepherd and we'll have no worries.

WRAPPING IT UP—SENDING IT HOME 5-7 Minutes

Clean Up Time

Don't forget that it's good for the kids to learn the responsibility of cleaning up after themselves. Encourage them to push in chairs too.

Closing Worship and Prayer

Even though we're learning the 23rd Psalm now, we'll continue to pray the Lord's prayer during these final weeks. Again, if there is time, ask the for prayer requests. You may close with your own prayer or use the one below for help. Remember to end with the Lord's Prayer so the kids will practice saying it again.

If you need some guidance for your prayer, you can use this:

Father in Heaven, thank you for being our shepherd. Thank you for making sure we have all that we need. We praise you that you watch over us, and when we trust you, we have no worries. Today we want to ask you to bless all of the things these kids have mentioned as prayer requests. *(Today would be a perfect opportunity to mention the kids requests out loud).* And Lord, we pray all of these things in Jesus' name, who taught us to pray: *(now lead them in the Lord's Prayer)*

Our Father, who art in heaven, hallowed be Thy name Thy Kingdom come, Thy will be done On earth as it is in heaven.
Give us this day our daily bread and forgive us our debts as we forgive our debtors. Lead us not into temptation, but deliver us from evil
For thine is the Kingdom and the Power and the glory forever and ever. Amen.

I Want to Be A Sheep

A Sheep Has No Worries!

Picture courtesy of clker.com

Page intentionally left blank for printing and copying purposes

Jesus, Teach Me How to Pray
A Year in The Lord's Prayer and other Bible Basics

Unit 12: The Greatest Commandments & The 10 Commandments
Week 1: Love the Lord & Your Neighbor

Lesson Overview

Today's lesson uses some very familiar verses. We'll begin with the "Golden Rule," *Love your neighbor as yourself and Love God with all your might.* Jesus said, "All of the law and the commandments are summed up" in these two verses. Next, we'll look at a few verses that help us understand what it means to truly show God that we love Him. Finally, we'll end with the story of the Good Samaritan. Kids will begin to understand it's not who we are or what we look like that makes us a good person, but the way we love God and treat others.

KEY PHRASE: Love God and Love Others

SETTING UP THE LESSON — 5-7 Minutes
Who is my Neighbor?

PRESENTING THE LESSON — 5-10 Minutes
Scripture: Mark 12:30-31; 1 John 4:19-5:3; Luke 10:29-37

MAKING IT REAL TO KIDS TODAY *(Choose as many as you have time for)*

Game: Do You Love Your Neighbor? — 5-10 Minutes

Craft: Bloom Ball: Part 1 — 5-10 Minutes
Supplies: Copies of the final page of this lesson, crayons or markers

Memory Verse: Mark 12:30-31 — 5 Minutes

Song: "Love the Lord Your God" by Lincoln Brewster — 5 Minutes

WRAPPING IT UP—SENDING IT HOME — 5-7 Minutes
Clean Up Time & Prayer Time

KEY PHRASE: Love God and Love Others

SETTING UP THE LESSON   5-7 Minutes
Who is my neighbor?

Ask the kids to tell you about their neighbors. Be prepared to curtail any discussions that might get too graphic (you never know what kind of neighbors kids might have). If this happens ask them to share some good things about their neighbors. You might also ask if they like their neighbors and if they ever do anything for their neighbors.

The Teaching Moment: Today we're going to hear what God has to say about our neighbors and what it means to God that we get along with our neighbors

PRESENTING THE LESSON   5-10 Minutes

Scripture: Mark 12:30-31; 1 John 4:19-5:3; Luke 10:29-37
You do not have to read this directly from the Bible—
use the story form below or reword it to fit your personality

Pass out Bibles or copies of Mark 12:30-31 & 1 John 4:19-5:3 to 3-6 of the better readers in your group.

The Bible tells us to love God with all we have. Let's listen as some of us read some Bible verses that tell us about loving God and others. *(Allow your readers to read Mark 12:30-31 & 1 John 4:19-5:3 - you might use the New Century Version or Contemporary English Version to make it easier for the children to understand).*

How does this say God knows we love Him? *(Allow for answers.)* Here it says if we love God, we will believe in Jesus as God's Son, love Jesus, and obey God's commands. If we do these things, then God knows we really do love Him. It also says if we love God, we'll love our brothers and sisters. That means we'll love other people. It means we'll be kind to our family and the people we go to school with. In fact, in our memory verse today, God says we'll love our neighbors.

(You could recruit 4-6 volunteers - adults or the older kids - to act this out as you read for a little extra fun.)

Jesus told a story to help the people understand how to show love to their neighbors. Jesus said one time a man was walking on a very dangerous road. Sure enough, some robbers attacked him, beat him up and took all of his money. They left him in bad shape lying beside the road.

A short time later a preacher walked by. The preacher saw the man lying by the road. Do you think the preacher helped the man? *(Allow for answers.)* He probably should have, but he had a lot to do. He didn't think he had time to help, so he walked on the other side of the road so he could pretend he didn't see him. It wasn't too long before a person from the church walked by. Do you think this man helped? *(Allow for answers.)* It's a shame, but this man didn't want to get messy so he walked on the other side of the road too.

Finally a third man came walking down the road. But this man was the enemy. No one liked him. In fact, even the man who was injured didn't really like the man. He was from a different country. He may have even looked different. They called this man a Samaritan. Can you say Samaritan? *(Allow for answers.)* Do you think this man helped? Most Samaritans wouldn't, but being different didn't matter to this Samaritan. He saw the man lying beside the road and felt bad for him. He picked the man up, put bandages and medicine on him and put him on his donkey. He took the man to the next town, found a place that would take care of the man and paid them to take care of him.

After Jesus told the people this story, he asked them, "Which of these three men was a neighbor to the man? The preacher, the church man or the Samaritan?" What do you think was the right answer? *(Allow for answers.)* Jesus said it was the Samaritan. He said that if we want to "Love our Neighbor" like God said we should, we have to be like the Samaritan and be nice to everyone, even people we don't like. We should be nice to them and help them. Do you think you can do that? *(Allow for answers.)* It will be very hard, but if we love God with all our heart and soul and mind we can do it!

KEY PHRASE: Love God and Love Others

MAKING IT REAL TO KIDS TODAY
(Choose as many as you have time for)

Game: Do you Love Your Neighbor   5-10 minutes

1. Have the children sit in chairs or stand in a circle with the oldest in the center as the caller. (An adult could be the first caller to show the children what to do.)
2. You or another adult says, "‹name of child in the center› do you love your neighbor?"
3. The child in the center says, "Yes, I love my neighbors ‹name a child› and ‹name a child›, but I really love everyone who has ‹name a trait - like shoe color, eye or hair color, buttons, zippers, pants, etc.› (For example, Yes, I love me neighbors, John and Betsy, but I really love everyone who has pink socks on)
4. The two people named as well as everyone with that trait should change spots. They can't move to the spot next to where they are now, and they can't take the same spot back. The child in the center should try to get a spot. Whoever is left with no space is the next caller. If a child has a hard time getting a chair after two times being a caller, announce it's someone else's turn and give someone who hasn't been caller a chance to volunteer.
5. Game continues for as long as you have time. No winners, just fun!

The Teaching Moment: The Bible tells us that we must love God and our neighbor. This is a fun game to remind us that we should love everyone. It doesn't matter what color their eyes or hair are or what kind of clothes they are wearing. God tells us to treat everyone with love.

Craft: Bloom Ball-Part 1   5-10 Minutes
Supplies: Copies of the final pages of this lesson, crayons or markers

Today's Craft is the first of an eight part craft -
be sure to collect the pieces so that you can use them again next week
You'll use the piece marked "TOP" during the next several weeks -
the one marked "BOTTOM" won't be used until you attach all the top pieces,
so be sure to put it someplace where it won't get lost

Give each child a copy of the last two pages of this lesson. Have them draw a picture that will remind them of the commandment listed on the piece. They can cut out the circles and write their names on the back. (Make sure they put their names on these.)

Eventually they will attach these pieces to other pieces they'll make during the next eight weeks. The twelve pieces they complete will make a ball with the 10 commandments and these two "greatest" commandments.

Since this is an eight week long craft, be sure to create a couple extra for kids who miss today.

The Teaching Moment: Today we created two pieces of a craft that we're going to be working on for the next eight weeks. Jesus told his disciples that these two were the greatest of all the commandments. We'll use this craft to remind us that God has given us instructions to help us have a great life.

Song: *Love the Lord Your God* by Lincoln Brewster or *Love God Love People* by Danny Gokey   5 Minutes

You can get recordings of these from iTunes, Amazon Music, Spotify or another music service.

Lincoln Brewster's song will help the children memorize the first of these two commandments, while Danny Gokey's song will emphasize the Key Phrase for today. Use either or both depending on your time. Both have very singable choruses, so have the children sing along when possible.

KEY PHRASE: Love God and Love Others

The Teaching Moment: If we Love God as much as we possibly can, we will get closer to God and become more like Him. This way we can grow to be the best that we can possibly be.

Memory Verse: Mark 12:30-31   5 Minutes

Love the Lord Your God * with all Your Heart * and all Your Soul * and all Your Mind *
and all Your Strength *and Love your Neighbor * as Yourself.

Have the kids repeat after you in phrases (pausing at the *)

OR

Teach the children some sign language to go with this memory verse - to see actual signs visit www.lifeprint.com

Love = Hug yourself

Lord = make an "L" shape with your right thumb and index finger. Put your hand palm down at your left shoulder and bring it across to your right hip

God = hold your hand in front of your face with your thumb in front of your nose. Bring your hand straight down in the center of you

All = hold your hands in front of your chest, left fingers pointing right and right fingers pointing left. With your left palm in front of your right, move the right hand all the way around the left hand.

Heart = draw a heart on your chest where your heart would be

Soul = make a fist - thump it on your chest 2x with the thumb near your chest (at lifeprint see self)

Mind = point to your brain

Strength = make muscles with both hands (at lifeprint see strong)

Neighbor = with your hands about 9" apart and at waist level hold them next to you as if indicating a person next to you

Yourself = Make a fist and with your thumb up. Point your thumb at someone twice (at lifeprint see self)

WRAPPING IT UP—SENDING IT HOME   5-7 Minutes

Cleaning Up

We want the children to learn responsibility so be sure they help with the clean up, but remind them not to go anywhere, the group is going to talk to God together one more time.

Closing Worship and Prayer

Either gather the children in a circle holding hands or allow them to sit down to pray. If you choose to join hands, remember that it's OK if some children prefer not to join the circle. Just ask them to be respectful of others as they pray and not make any noise. You can always begin your prayer time with a quiet song if you like.

Even though we've finished with the parts of the Lord's prayer, (or you've chosen to teach this section before the Lord's Prayer) we're going to continue to use it to pray as we close. If there is time, ask the children for prayer requests. Remember, no prayer is ever too small, however, children will tend to keep going and be "inspired" by other prayer requests, so feel free to stop taking requests and tell them they can say anything that didn't get said out loud quietly to God themselves while you're praying. You may close with your own prayer or use the one below for help.

If you need some guidance for your prayer, you can use this :

KEY PHRASE: Love God and Love Others

Father in Heaven, today we just want to tell You how much we love You, Lord. We are thankful for You, and we praise Your name. We love You with our heart, our soul, our mind and our strength. Help us Lord, to love our neighbor and treat them the way we want to be treated. Lord, bless all of the things these kids have mentioned as prayer requests today (*if there's time, you can mention some of their requests*). And Lord, we pray all of these things in Jesus' name, who taught us to pray: (now lead them in the Lord's Prayer)

Our Father who art in heaven, hallowed be thy name. Thy Kingdom come, Thy will be done in earth as it is in heaven. Give us this day our daily bread and forgive us our debts as we forgive our debtors. Lead us not into temptation, but deliver us from evil. For thine is the Kingdom, the Power, and the Glory forever, AMEN.

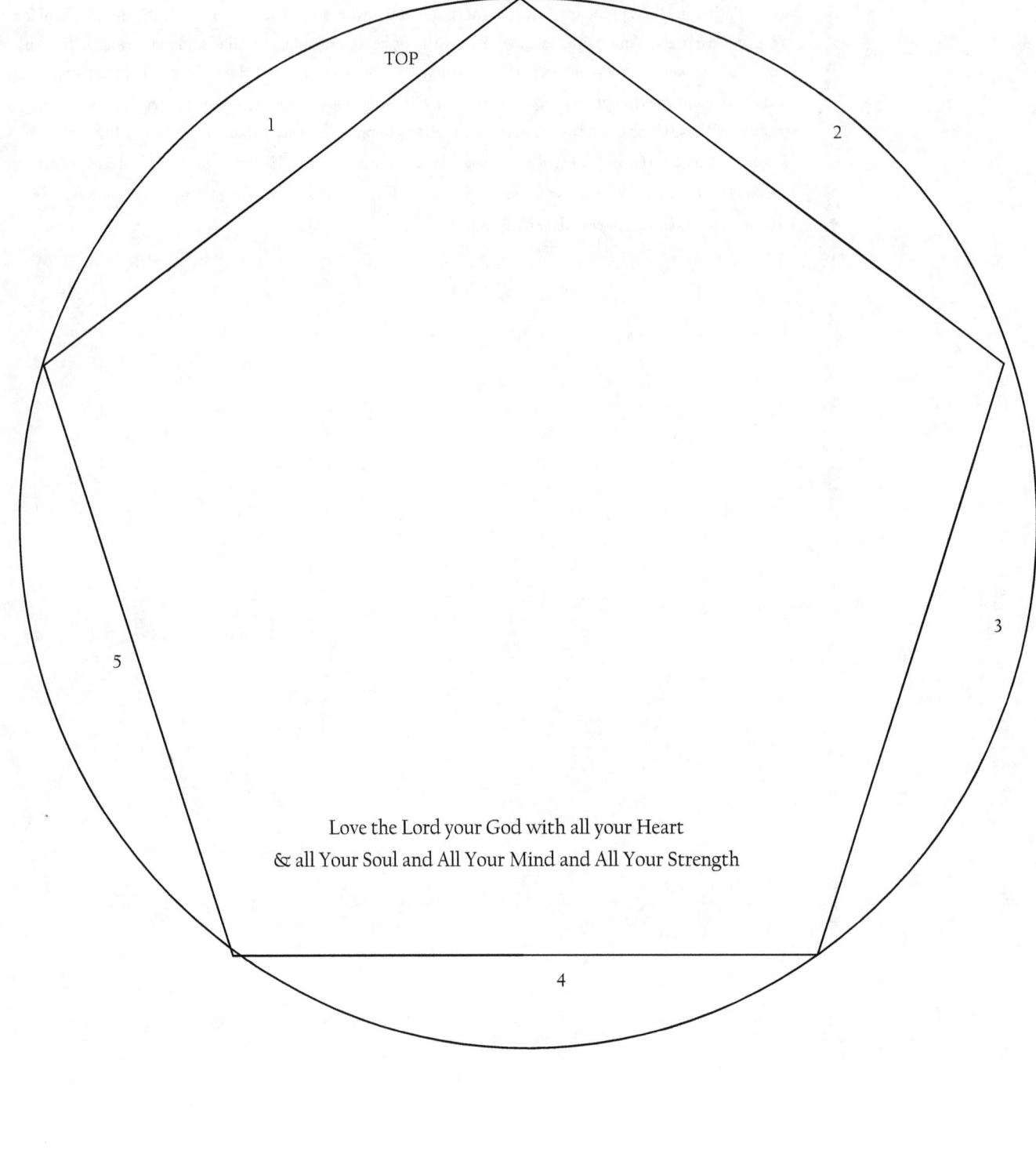

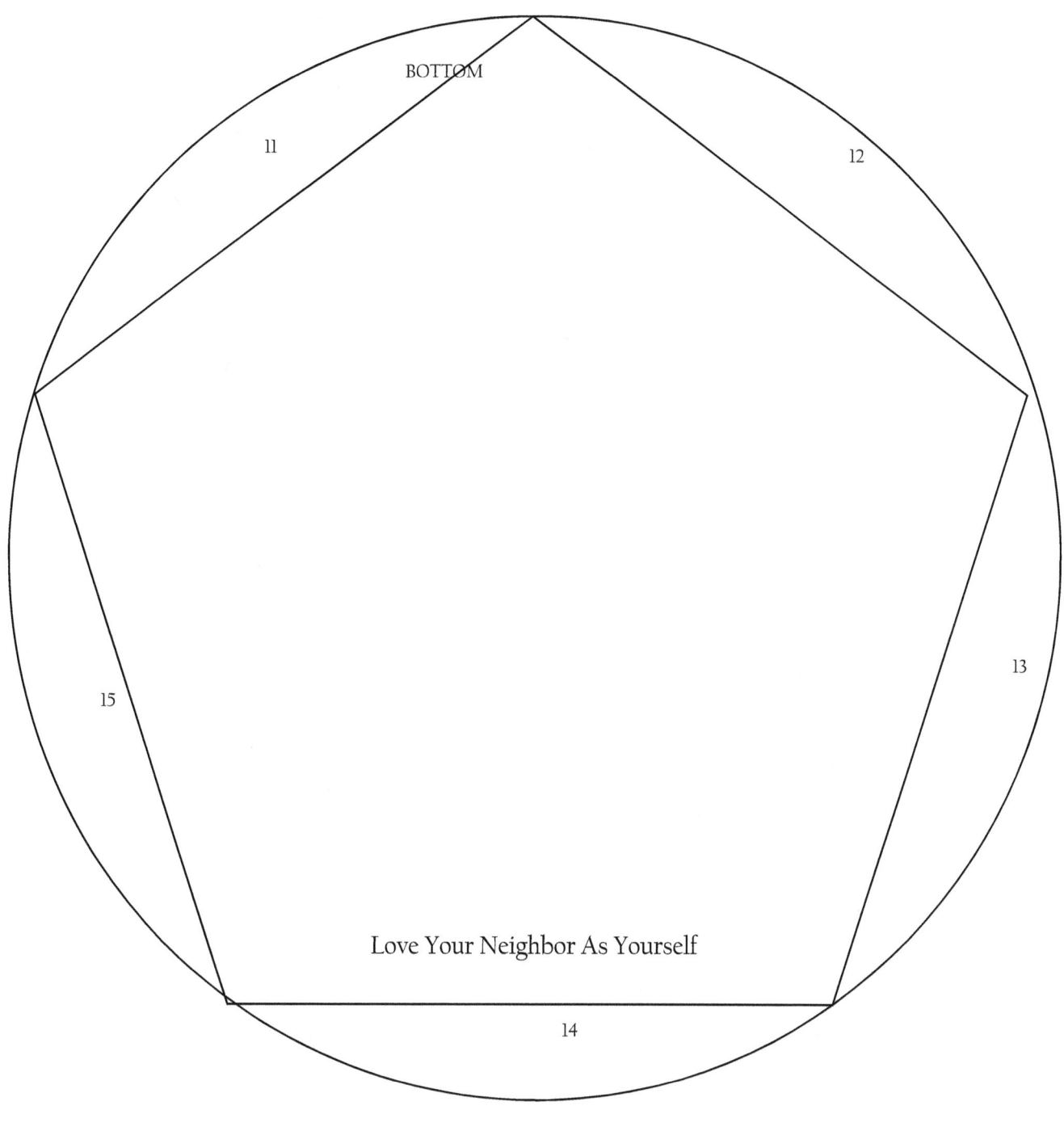

Page intentionally left blank for printing and copying purposes

Jesus, Teach Me How to Pray
A Year in The Lord's Prayer and other Bible Basics

Unit 12: The Greatest Commandments & The 10 Commandments
Week 2: No Gods Except the True God

Lesson Overview

Today is the first of seven lessons to help the children learn the 10 Commandments. The first four (and perhaps five) commandments are summed up in the verse, "Love the Lord your God with all your heart, soul, mind and strength." Today we'll help the kids understand that an idol is like a statue. We'll also help them understand that anything we love more than God is a false god. The True God warns us that we must not worship anyone or thing except Him.

KEY PHRASE: No Gods But the True God

SETTING UP THE LESSON — 5-7 Minutes
Gods and Idols

PRESENTING THE LESSON — 5-10 Minutes
Scripture: Exodus 32:1-15

MAKING IT REAL TO KIDS TODAY *(Choose as many as you have time for)*

Game: Freeze Dance — 10 Minutes
 Supplies: CD Player and Music (could combine this with the Songs)

Craft: Bloom Ball - Part 2 — 5-10 Minutes
 Supplies: Copies of the final page of this lesson, crayons or markers, staplers

Memory Verse: Mark 12:30-31 & Exodus 20:3-6 — 5-10 Minutes

Song: Go Fish Guy's "The 10 Commandment Boogie" — 5-10 Minutes
 and/or Lincoln Brewster's, "Love the Lord Your God."

WRAPPING IT UP—SENDING IT HOME — 5-7 Minutes
Clean Up Time & Prayer Time

KEY PHRASE: No Gods But the True God

SETTING UP THE LESSON   5-7 Minutes

God's and Idols
SUPPLIES: White board, chalk board, or newsprint to make a list

We're going to help the kids see the things that have the potential to become gods or idols today. Ask the kids, "What is your favorite thing in the whole world?" Make a full list of these things so the kids can see them all. Consider keeping a tally of those that are mentioned more than once.

Instruct the children:

1. If you have a favorite thing on this list, stand up
2. If you would give your favorite thing to your parent, sit down
3. If you would trade favorite things with a friend, sit down
4. If you would give your favorite thing to your friend, sit down
5. If you would give your favorite thing to me if I asked, sit down (Hopefully, by now all kids are sitting)

If all kids are sitting, say: I'm glad all of you are willing to give up your favorite thing. Sometimes we love "things" so much they get in the way of our learning to love God. Today we're going to talk about what it means to love things too much.

If there are kids still up, say: We all have favorite things. Thanks for being so honest. You can sit down now. Today we're going to talk about what it means to love things too much.

PRESENTING THE LESSON   5-10 Minutes

Scripture: Exodus 20:3-6 and Exodus 32:1-35
You do not have to read this directly from the Bible
use the story form below or reword it to fit your personality

Today we're going to begin to look at the Ten Commandments. The Ten Commandments were special laws God gave His people. When they followed these laws, it made them different than all other people on earth.

Does anyone know what the first two of the Ten Commandments are? *(Allow for answers - if they answer the memory verse from last week, congratulate them on remembering, but help them understand that those verses sum up the whole Ten commandments, but aren't in the Ten commandments)* The first two commandments go together. They are "You can't have any gods except me" and "You can't ever make any idols." Does anyone know what an idol is? *(Allow for answers.)* An idol is a like statue that people worship. When Moses was alive all the other countries had lots of gods and lots of idols. God who created the earth wanted His people to remember that He was the only true God. No idol and no other pretend god could take His place.

One time Moses went up on the mountain to be with God. While Moses was there, God wrote these Ten Commandments on two big stones. But while he was there, God gave Moses many other instructions. There were so many instructions, Moses stayed on the mountain for forty days. Do you know how long forty days is? *(Allow for answers.)* Forty days is how long it's been since_____. *(Fill in that blank with the holiday that would have been about 40 days ago.)*

While Moses was on the mountain, the rest of the Israelites stayed in their camp. But they got tired of waiting for Moses to come back from talking to God. Moses left his brother Aaron in charge while he was on the mountain. So, the people told Aaron they were tired of waiting, and they wanted a real god they could follow.

Aaron told them to bring all their gold jewelry. He melted it all and molded it into the shape of a calf. Do you know what a calf is? *(Allow for answers.)* A calf is a baby cow. So the Israelites made this big golden calf and started to worship it. They called it their god and had a special holiday for their new god.

KEY PHRASE: No Gods But the True God

When the only real God looked down from the mountain, He saw the Israelites' party. And the sight made him very mad. He told Moses to go back down the mountain. When Moses got to where he could see the people, he saw they were dancing and singing and having a party for this new god. But this god wasn't a god at all! It was just a statue of a cow! Do you know what we call statues like this calf? *(Allow for answers.)* That's what we call an idol.

God punished the Israelites that day because they didn't follow His rules. God wants to be the only God we have. He loves us and knows what's best for us. God said He wants us to always worship Him. We should never have anything that we love more than Him. If we love our "things" more than God, those things are our idols. They are like a golden calf. God doesn't want us to love anything more than Him, not our toys or games, not even our moms and dads. God wants us to love Him the most.

MAKING IT REAL TO KIDS TODAY
(Choose as many as you have time for)

Game: Freeze Dance   5-10 Minutes
Supplies: CD player and music (you could combine this with the song time and use one of those tunes for this game)

Choose one student to be "it." Have the child hit the play button. When the music comes on, the kids can begin to dance. When "it" pauses the music, they should all freeze and become like statues. "It" then can pick his favorite "statue" (Tell "it" he should try to pick someone who froze immediately.) Let this favorite statue be the next "it." Continue for as long as you have time.

The Teaching Moment: We pretended to be statues today. There's really nothing wrong with statues, until we act like the people who waited on Moses. When Moses lived, people prayed to statues and worshipped them. We need to remember that God, who is our Father in Heaven, is the only true God and we shouldn't worship anyone or anything else.

Craft: Bloom Ball-Part 2   5-10 Minutes
Supplies: Copies of the final page of this lesson, crayons or markers, staplers

*Today's Craft is the second of an eight part craft -
You'll need one piece from last week - the one that says "TOP" and the copies from the final page
You could alternately decorate today's pieces and add them to the pile. Then put them together in week eight.*

Give each child a copy of the last two pages of this lesson. Have them draw a picture that will remind them of the commandment listed on the piece. They can cut out the circles and **write their names on the back.**

If you plan to connect one circle each week, after they've cut out the circles, give them the circle from last week that's says, "TOP" and have them fold all three pieces along the six straight lines near the edges of the circle. Then they can match the #1 tab to #1 - #5 to #5 and #10 to #10 and staple these three places along the solid lines.

Collect the pieces so they can add more to them next week. Be sure to have the extras from last week available for kids who may not have been here, plus be sure to leave a few extras from today's craft for next week in case there are children who missed today.

Eventually they will attach these pieces to other pieces they'll make during the next few weeks. The twelve pieces they complete will make a ball with the 10 commandments and the two "greatest" commandments.

KEY PHRASE: No Gods But the True God

Memory Verse: Mark 12:30-31 & Exodus 20:1-6 — 5 Minutes

Love the Lord Your God with all Your Heart and all Your Soul and all Your Mind and all Your Strength, and Love your Neighbor as Yourself. - Mark 12:30-31

And

You shall not have any other God's except the one True God. You shall not worship any idols - Exodus 20:1-6

Each week the kids will review the Mark 12:30-31 verse. Hopefully they'll be able to repeat this verse without much coaching in just a few weeks. Repeat it a few times this week. Ask them to repeat after you. There is also sign language for these verses in last week's lesson if you'd like to use it to reinforce these verses.

Make a huge 1 and 2 out of construction paper. When you hold up the 1 say the first commandment. Do the same with the 2. Then hold up the 1 and have the kids say the first commandment. Do the same with the 2. Save these numbers for next week or hang them on the wall of your class space.

1. No other gods except the real God
2. Don't worship idols or statues or things

Song: Go Fish Guy's "The Ten Commandment Boogie" — 5 Minutes
and/or Lincoln Brewster's, "Love the Lord Your God."

These are available on CD and most online services as well as on YouTube. We'll be using these two songs for the next several weeks. You may want to switch between the two from week to week or use both depending on the amount of time you have.

The Teaching Moment: (whichever song you use) God loves us. He wants us to learn to love Him in return. God gave us these commandments so we would understand how important it is to love Him. We're going to sing these songs (this song) for the next few weeks so you'll learn it well. That way it will be easier for you to remember what God wants you to do.

WRAPPING IT UP—SENDING IT HOME — 5-7 Minutes

Cleaning Up

We want the children to learn to be responsible, so be sure they help with the clean up, but remind them not to go anywhere, the group is going to talk to God together one more time.

Closing Worship and Prayer

Gather the children in a circle holding hands or allow them to sit down to pray. If you choose to join hands, remember that it's OK if some children prefer not to join the circle. Ask them to be respectful of others as they pray and not make any noise. You can always begin your prayer time with a quiet song if you like.

Although you have either finished learning the parts of the Lord's prayer or are using these lessons as a separate unit, we're going to continue to use it to pray as we close. If there is time, ask the children if they have any prayer requests. Remember no prayer is too small, however, children will tend to keep going and be "inspired" by other prayer requests, so feel free to stop taking requests and tell them they can say anything that didn't get said out loud quietly to God while you're praying. You may close with your own prayer or use the one below for help.

If you need some guidance for your prayer, you can use this:

KEY PHRASE: No Gods But the True God

Father in Heaven, you are the only God. We love you more than anyone or anything else. We don't ever want to disobey you by having other gods or idols. Help us to always be faithful to you. Lord, bless all of the things these kids have mentioned as prayer requests today (*if there's time, you can mention some of their requests*). And Lord, we pray all of these things in Jesus' name, who taught us to pray: (now lead them in the Lord's Prayer)

Our Father who art in heaven, hallowed be thy name. Thy Kingdom come, Thy will be done in earth as it is in heaven. Give us this day our daily bread and forgive us our debts as we forgive our debtors. Lead us not into temptation, but deliver us from evil. For thine is the Kingdom, the Power, and the Glory forever, AMEN.

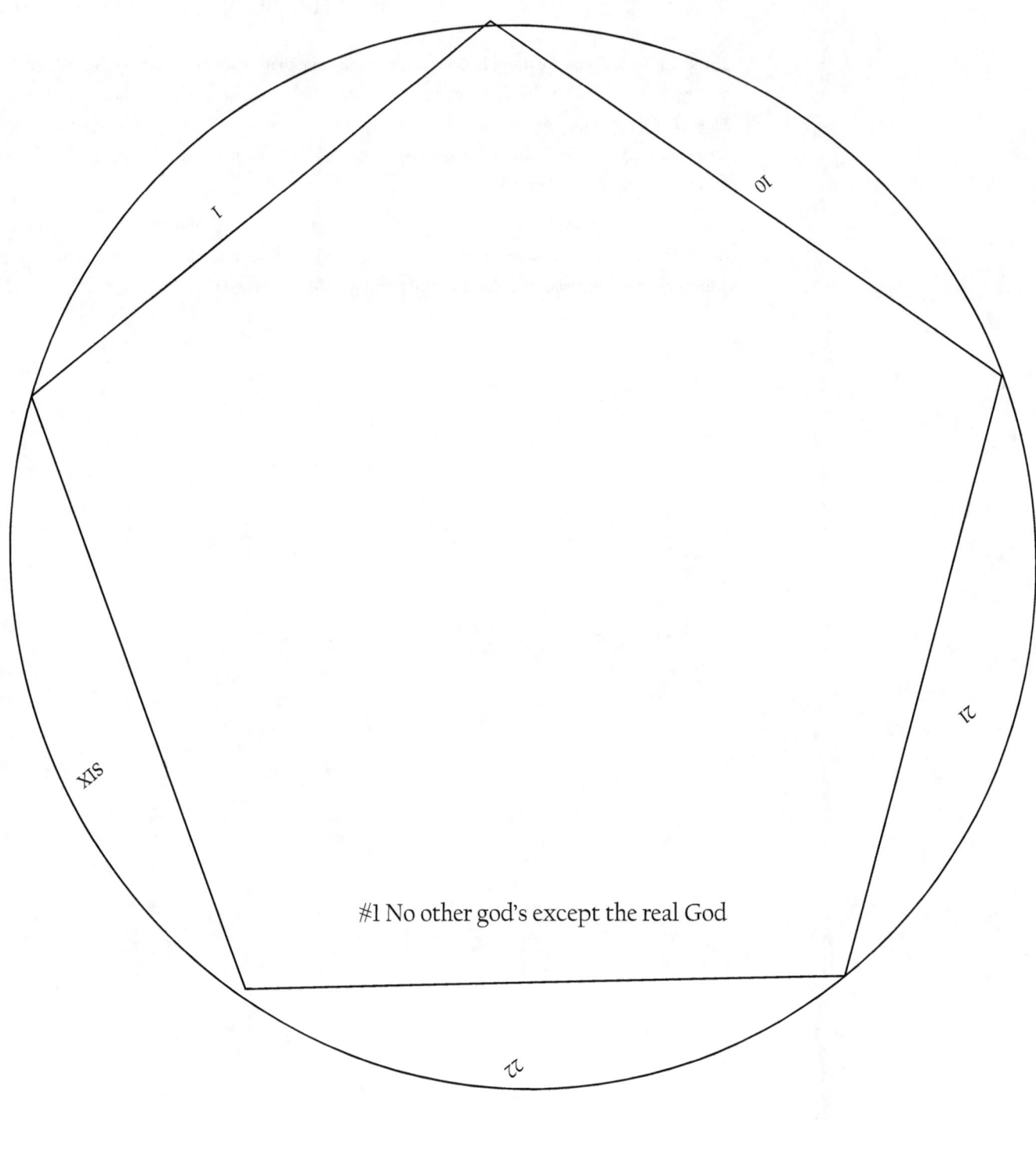

#1 No other god's except the real God

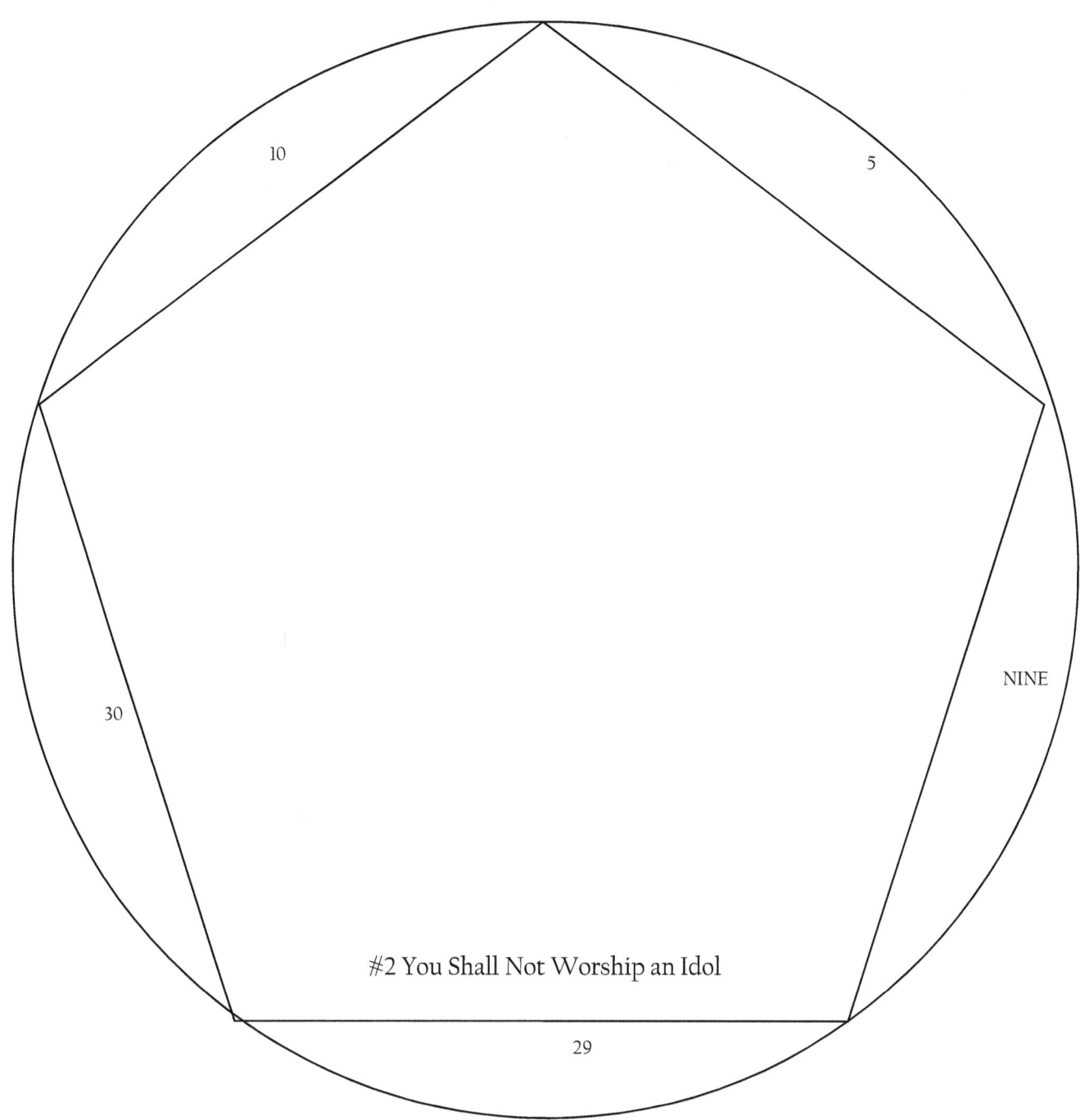

10

5

30

NINE

#2 You Shall Not Worship an Idol

29

Page intentionally left blank for printing and copying purposes

Jesus, Teach Me How to Pray
A Year in The Lord's Prayer and other Bible Basics

Unit 12: The Greatest Commandments & The 10 Commandments
Week 3: Don't Misuse God's Name or God's Day

Lesson Overview

Unfortunately, children hear the name of God used in inappropriate ways every day. Even people who attend church on a regular basis sometimes say "Oh, God" or "Jesus" when things aren't going the way they anticipated. Today we want to help the kids understand that saying God or Jesus' name should be reserved for when they are talking to or about God or Jesus. We will try to do this without condemning adults in their lives who may not have learned this lesson yet. Finally, we'll talk about the Sabbath, another commandment often overlooked by many. Jesus said the Sabbath was made for man, probably because God knew that our bodies need a time of rest. However, in addition to being a time of rest, God also said it was supposed to be a holy day. So the Sabbath needs to be different than the other six days of the week. This will make a good lesson for many adults as well as the children.

KEY PHRASE: Don't Misuse God's Name or God's Day

SETTING UP THE LESSON — 5-7 Minutes
A Review

PRESENTING THE LESSON — 5-10 Minutes
Scripture: Exodus 20:7-11

MAKING IT REAL TO KIDS TODAY — *(Choose as many as you have time for)*

Game: Days of the Week Chairs (a version of Musical Chairs) — 5-10 Minutes

Craft: Bloom Ball-Part 3 — 10-15 Minutes
 Supplies: Copies of the final page of this lesson, crayons or markers, staplers

Memory Verse: Mark 12:30-31 & Exodus 20:17 — 5-10 Minutes

Song: Go Fish Guy's "The 10 Commandment Boogie"
 and/or Lincoln Brewster's, "Love the Lord Your God." — 5-10 Minutes

WRAPPING IT UP—SENDING IT HOME — 5-7 Minutes
Clean Up Time & Prayer Time:

KEY PHRASE: Don't Misuse God's Name or God's Day

SETTING UP THE LESSON
5-7 Minutes

A Review

Who can tell me what we talked about last week, and what we're going to be talking about during these next few weeks? *(Allow for answers.)* For the next five weeks we're going to be learning about the Ten Commandments. What were the two we learned last week? *(Allow for answers.)* Last week we talked about the first two commandments. First we should have no gods except the real God and second, we should never worship idols or statues. Tell me some other gods we could have or idols we could worship. Do you remember? *(Allow for answers - if they don't come readily, ask what their favorite toy is, then "could that be an idol?" After you get several responses move on.)* Anything we love more than our Father in Heaven is another god, and all the things we can see and touch but love or spend more time with than Jesus could be our idols.

Today we're going to look at the next two commandments. *Have a stack of papers very near to where you are - "accidentally knock them off and say, "Oh my 'the name of a child in your class'" - After you get them picked up, '"accidentally" drop them again and say, "Oh, 'name of another child'")* I'm sorry, I seem to be very clumsy today. Like I said, today we're going to look at the next two commandments. *(Pick up a pen or a marker to write with, either drop it or make sure it's a pen or pencil that won't write and say "first and last name of a child" - the goal here is to sound like people do when they use the Lord's name in vain. Do this a few times, then have another adult or older child prepared to interrupt you and scold you for yelling at the kids when they aren't doing anything)*

I'm sorry, was I doing that? I didn't mean to sound like I was yelling at you. I was just getting very frustrated, and it came out. Ask the children whose names you used, "Did it make you feel bad?" *(Allow for answers.)* How do you think it would make you feel if people blamed you like that all the time? *(Allow for answers then move right into the lesson.)*

PRESENTING THE LESSON
5-10 Minutes

Scripture: Exodus 20:7-11

You do not have to read this directly from the Bible—
use the story form below or reword it to fit your personality

God feels bad when we blame Him for things, too. The third commandment God gave was to never use His name "in vain." Do you know what "in vain" means? *(Allow for answers.)* When we do something "in vain," it means that it has no purpose, it's useless and worthless. Every time I said your name, and I wasn't talking to you or about you, it was pointless and mean. That's exactly what it's like when we say, "Oh, God" or say "Jesus" without thinking. Even Gosh or Jeesh can be bad sometimes because they sound so much like God and Jesus.

God's name is special and holy, so it's important for us to only say His name when we are talking to Him or about Him. Another way of saying "Do not take God's name in vain," is to say, "Don't misuse God's name." Can you say that? Don't misuse God's name. *(Allow the kids to repeat)* From today on, we're going to be very careful about how we use God and Jesus' names.

The fourth commandment is another that helps us worship God better. It tells us "Remember the Sabbath Day and Keep it Holy." Do you know what the Sabbath is? *(Allow for answers.)* The Sabbath is a day of rest. God created the earth in six days, and then He took the next day off. He spent six days working hard to make the moon, the sun, the stars, the plants, and everything else, so on the seventh day He took a day of rest. God doesn't really need the day off, but He knew we did. So He told us to set aside one day every week and make it holy. When Moses lived, the Sabbath was the last day of the week, like our Saturday. After Jesus died and then became alive again on a Sunday, Jesus' followers started getting together on Sundays. Today, Sunday is our special and holy day. Do you remember what holy means? *(Allow for answers.)* Holy means we make it special and different.

KEY PHRASE: Don't Misuse God's Name or God's Day

What's one thing you do on Sunday that's different from what you do the rest of the week—something that makes it holy and special? *(Allow for answers - kids might visit grandparents or eat out, encourage them to come up with a lot of ideas.)* One thing we've all done today is come to church. We come here to worship God together. That's something that really pleases God, when we all come together to praise Him and learn about Him.

MAKING IT REAL TO KIDS TODAY *(Choose as many as you have time for)*

Game: Days of the Week Chairs   7-10 Minutes

Set chairs in a circle. Use one chair less than the number of children in your group. Have the kids walk around the inside of the circle of chairs. You (or another adult) should say random names of the week. Each time you say Sunday, the kids will scramble to sit down. The one with no chair can either be out or be the next "caller" (the one to say names of the week). If you let a student be a caller, you may want to create strips of paper with the names of the week on them and let the caller draw them randomly and put them back in the mix. Either way, remove one chair from the circle each time one student is out. If you allow the child to be the caller, you can choose to switch callers every time someone new is out or play a few times and allow a different child to call each time. The caller should not face the chairs when he or she calls out the names of the days of the week. Remind the caller not to say the days in order. The last child remaining wins.

The Teaching Moment: This was a different way to play musical chairs. And every time you heard the words Sunday you stopped walking and sat. The word Sunday was special in our game. In the same way we should try to make our Sundays different and special.

Memory Verse: Mark 12:30-31 & Exodus 20:7-11   5-10 Minutes

*Love the Lord Your God with all Your Heart and all Your Soul and all Your Mind
and all Your Strength and Love your Neighbor as Yourself. - Mark 12:30-31*

Hopefully, this will be the third week the kids have repeated the Mark verses. You will find sign language for these verses in the first lesson of this Unit. Optionally you could have the kids fill in the word when you point to them. Begin on one side of the room and work around. Say a few words of the verse and then leave a hole for the kids to fill in. Go around several times pausing at different words each time through. Keep it moving. If one student misses, move along and point to the next child.

*You should never misuse God's name and be sure to keep the Sabbath holy
Exodus 20:7-11*

For the commandments we're focusing on today:

Let's review the first two commandments: *(hopefully the construction paper 1 & 2 were saved from last week. As you hold them up, help the kids remember the first two commandments)*

1. No other Gods except the real God
2. Don't worship idols or statues

Now let's add the next two: *(create a big 3 & 4 to match last week's numbers. Hold them up and allow the kids to shout out the verse)*

3. Don't misuse God's name
4. Keep the Sabbath Holy

OK, now let's try all four *(hold the numbers up one at a time, let the kids shout them out - mix up the numbers to see if they know them out of order)*

KEY PHRASE: Don't Misuse God's Name or God's Day

Song: Go Fish Guy's "The 10 Commandment Boogie" and/or Lincoln Brewster's, "Love the Lord Your God."   5-7 Minutes

Both are available on CD and most online services as well as on YouTube. The Go Fish Guy's "10 Commandment Boogie" is available as a music video. The dance that goes with it is really cute. These few weeks would be a great time to get your kids up and moving!

The Teaching Moment: Both of these songs will help us remember these important verses from the Bible. Sometimes Bible verses are difficult to remember, so it's important that we find ways to help us memorize. The more of the Bible we can remember, the more it can help us in life.

Craft: Bloom Ball-Part 3   10-15 Minutes
Supplies: Copies of the final page of this lesson, crayons or markers, staplers

Today's Craft is the third of an eight part craft -
You'll need the section from last week - all pieces attach to the one that says "TOP"
or save all pieces and attach them all on the last week

Give each child a copy of the last two pages of this lesson. Have them draw a picture that will remind them of the commandment listed on the piece. Then they can cut out the circles and write their names on the back.

After they've cut out the circles, have them make a forward fold along the six straight lines near the edges of the circle. Then they can match tabs from today's circles with the ones they've already attached. (Tabs 4 & 3 will match the TOP section, match the two 8's from today 9 will match one from last week) Staple the tabs together.

Collect the pieces so that they can add more to them next week. Be sure to have the extras from the last two weeks for kids who weren't here and save a few extras from today for kids who missed.

Eventually they will attach these pieces to other pieces they'll make during the next few weeks. The twelve pieces they complete will make a ball with the Ten Commandments and the two "greatest" commandments.

The Teaching Moment: Ask the kids: Who remembers the first part of our "Greatest Commandments" (Love the Lord your God . . . All your strength). Today we created pieces for the next two commandments. Did you know the first part of this "greatest commandment" is the first four commandments all rolled into one? If you Love the Lord Your God with all your heart, soul, mind and strength, you won't break the first four commandments.

WRAPPING IT UP—SENDING IT HOME   5-7 Minutes

Cleaning Up

We want the children to learn to be responsible, so be sure they help with the clean up, but remind them not to go anywhere, the group is going to talk to God together one more time.

Closing Worship and Prayer

Gather the children in a circle holding hands or allow them to sit down to pray. If you choose to join hands, remember that it's OK if some children prefer not to join the circle. Ask them to be respectful of others as they pray and not make any noise. You can always begin your prayer time with a quiet song if you like.

You may be using these lessons as a separate unit rather than following the Lord's Prayer lessons. Either way, we're going to continue to use it to pray as we close. If there is time, ask the children for prayer requests. You may close with your own prayer or use the one below for help.

If you need some guidance for your prayer, you can use this:

KEY PHRASE: Don't Misuse God's Name or God's Day

Father in Heaven, thank you for always loving us. Forgive us when we use your name foolishly and don't make Sunday any different than every other day of the week. Help us, Lord, to make sure all our words please you, and always keep your day special. Lord, bless all the things these kids have mentioned as prayer requests today (*if there's time, you can mention some of their requests*). And Lord, we pray all of these things in Jesus' name, who taught us to pray: (*now lead them in the Lord's Prayer*)

Our Father who art in heaven, hallowed be thy name. Thy Kingdom come, Thy will be done in earth as it is in heaven. Give us this day our daily bread and forgive us our debts as we forgive our debtors. Lead us not into temptation, but deliver us from evil. For thine is the Kingdom, the Power, and the Glory forever, AMEN.

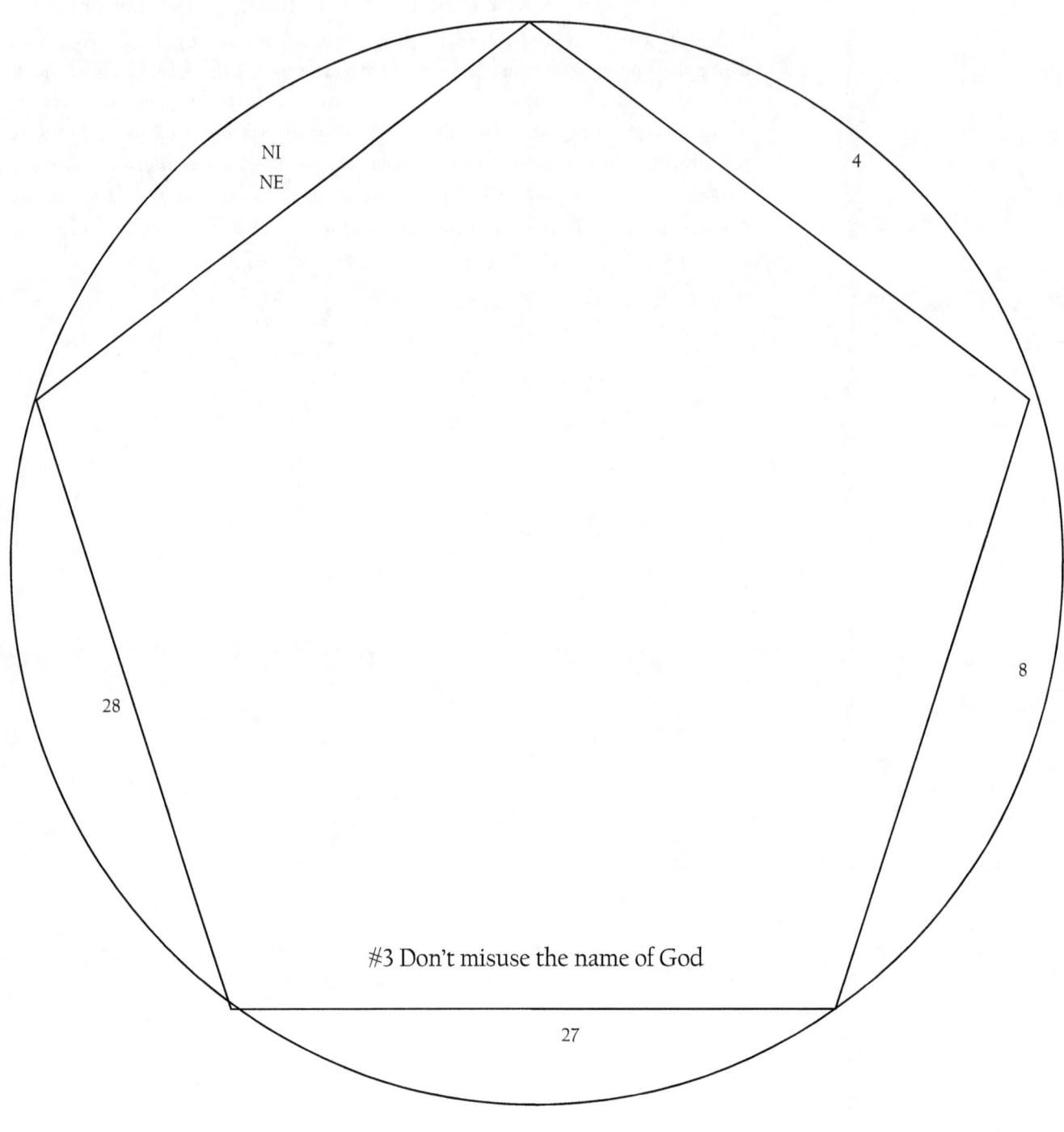

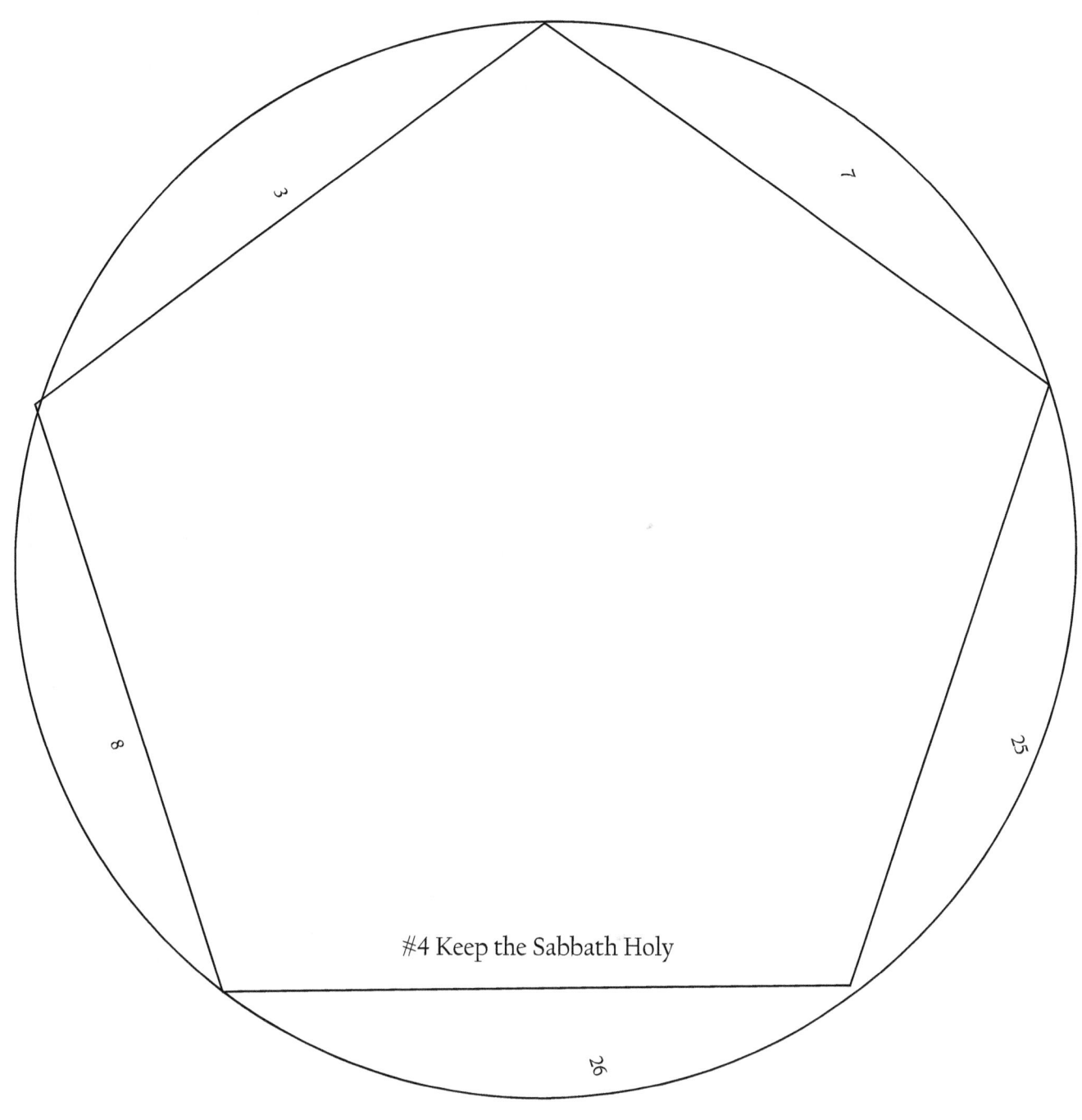

#4 Keep the Sabbath Holy

Page intentionally left blank for printing and copying purposes

Jesus, Teach Me How to Pray
A Year in The Lord's Prayer and other Bible Basics

Unit 12: The Greatest Commandments & The 10 Commandments
Week 4: Honor Your Father and Mother

Lesson Overview

Most of the kids in your children's program will want to honor their parents. Even though they don't always get it right, they will have a desire to make their parents proud. For those kids, this will be an easy lesson. However, you may find at least a few whose parents are not worthy of anyone's respect. They may be abusive or absent. If a child has nothing good to say about his parent, don't force him to come up with something nice. Help them understand that God is also their Father. Plus, there's a good chance they have aunts, uncles, and adults in the church they can respect like they should a father or mother. As these kids grow, we may have to help them understand that God is not like their parents. God, the perfect parent, expects earthly parents to imitate Him. But even the best parents miss the mark. Many children get a poor picture of God because their parents were not God honoring. We won't be focusing on this today, but it's a good concept to remember for everyone who deals with children.

KEY PHRASE: Honor Your Father and Mother

SETTING UP THE LESSON   5-7 Minutes
Bragging on my Mom and Dad

PRESENTING THE LESSON   5-10 Minutes
Scripture: Misc. verses from Proverbs-10:1; 15:20; 19:28; 20:20; 23:22; 23:25 & Matthew 15:3-6
Supplies: Copy of the verses from the end of this lesson

MAKING IT REAL TO KIDS TODAY   *(Choose as many as you have time for)*

Game: Wise and Foolish   10 Minutes
Supplies: Copy of Scenarios from the end of this lesson

Craft: Bloom Ball-Part 4   5-10 Minutes
Supplies: Copies of the final page of this lesson, crayons or markers, staplers

Memory Verse: Mark 12:30-31 & Exodus 20:8   5-10 Minutes

Song: Go Fish Guy's "The 10 Commandment Boogie"   5-10 Minutes
          and/or Lincoln Brewster's, "Love the Lord Your God."

WRAPPING IT UP—SENDING IT HOME   5-7 Minutes
Clean Up Time & Prayer Time

KEY PHRASE: Honor Your Father and Mother
SETTING UP THE LESSON
5-7 Minutes

Bragging on my Mom and Dad

Hey everyone! Have you ever heard your mom telling someone you did a good job or your dad talk about something you did well? *(Encourage kids to raise their hand - hopefully all kids will - if not ask the same question about a grandparent or aunt, etc - and be sure to say good things about those children any time you have a chance!)* Most of us hear nice things from our parents, grandparents, or teachers. Today's your chance to brag on your mom and dad *(or other adult in their life if necessary)*. We're going to go around the room and have each of you say one good thing about your mom or dad *(or aunt or teacher, etc.)* *(Allow each child to share. If a child prefers not to share, don't make him. You may have an abused child or a quiet kid who prefers not to say anything - at the end give anyone you had to skip a second chance, then move into the lesson.)*

PRESENTING THE LESSON
5-10 Minutes

Scripture: Misc verses from Proverbs - 10:1; 15:20; 19:27; 20:20; 23:22; 23:25 & Matthew 15:3-6
Supplies: Copy of the verses from the end of this lesson

This week we're going to have the children read the verses and talk about each one

Who can tell me which commandment we're on? *(Allow for answers.)* We're up to number five. It says, "Honor your father and your mother." Today we're going to read some verses from the book of Proverbs in the Bible. These verses will help us see how God wants us to treat our parents. Let's read a few of these verses. *(Allow the older children to read the Proverbs, stopping to ask the questions)*

Proverbs 10:1 - A wise son brings joy to his father, but a foolish son makes his mother sad.
Proverbs 15:20 - A wise son brings joy to his father, but a foolish man doesn't like his mother.
QUESTION - Are you a wise or foolish child? How does a wise child bring joy to his parents? *(Make sure the kids understand that wise and foolish have nothing to do with getting good grades. Wise children act in respectful ways, listen in school and work hard. Wise means we don't follow the crowd when they are misbehaving. Wise children have good habits that help with good grades, but some kids, even if they are wise, might struggle with a subject in school.)*

Proverbs 19:27 - If you stop listening to instructions, you will be far away from knowing a lot.
Proverbs 23:22 - Listen to your father, he gave you life, and love your mother when she is old.
QUESTION - Have you ever stopped listening to your parent's instructions? What happens when you don't listen to your parents? *(if a child describes a parent who asks him to do things that are not right, help that child understand that they still must respect their parents and not talk back even if their parent's instruction is at fault)*
Proverbs 20:20 - If a person talks badly to his father or mother, his life will be very dark
QUESTION - How would you talk badly to your parents? Do you ever talk back to your parents? Do you tell them, "no"?

In Matthew, Jesus told some grown ups they weren't honoring their mother and father. Honoring our parents is so important that Jesus told the Pharisees they should still be treating their parents with respect and helping them even though they were adults. When you act in a wise way and listen to your mom and dad, you honor your parents. Helping your parents is a part of honoring them. Even when you grow up, you'll need to honor your parents.

We have one more verse from Proverbs to help us know how to honor our mother and father. *(Ask one of your readers to read this last verse)*

KEY PHRASE: Honor Your Father and Mother

Proverbs 23:25 - I hope you make your father and mother glad, and you make your mother rejoice!

QUESTION - What kinds of things do you do that make you mother and father glad? *(We're ending with this verse so the kids can finish on a positive note. Help them think about all they do that make their parents glad - DO NOT allow them to focus on good grades. Some kids have a hard time getting good grades no matter how hard they try, but the key is to helping them understand that doing their best and trying hard is what really matters. When they treat their teachers and other adults with respect, etc. this makes their parents glad)*

When we listen to our parents and make wise decisions, we honor our Father and Mother. Honoring our parents also honors God. It's important for us to make sure we always honor our father and mother.

MAKING IT REAL TO KIDS TODAY *(Choose as many as you have time for)*

Game: Wise or Foolish?   10 Minutes

On the one of the last pages of this lesson you'll find scenarios you can read to the children. After each, allow one child to share what they would do if it happened to them. When the child finishes have all the children who think it's a wise decision to run to one side of the room and everyone who thinks it's a foolish decision to run to the other side of the room.

If everyone thinks it's wise, (including you) congratulate the kids and move to the next scenario. (if this is really not at all wise, offer another solution and allow the kids to move to the other side if they change their mind.)

If some think it's foolish, ask one of the kids who voted foolish to move to a third section of the room and give you a better idea. Those who think this new idea is wise should move to that side of the room. If there are still children in the "foolish" corner, allow one of these kids to come up with another idea and move to another section of the room. Then have all the kids run to the person who they think had the best idea.

Continue with this until all the scenarios are used or as long as you have time.

Craft: Bloom Ball-Part 4   5-10 Minutes
Supplies: Copies of the final page of this lesson, crayons or markers, staplers

Today's Craft is the fourth of an eight part craft -
You'll need the section from last week - all the pieces attached to the one that says "TOP"
unless you plan to attach them all in the final week
Keep the one marked "BOTTOM" someplace where it won't get lost

Give each child a copy of the last page. Have them draw a picture that will remind them of the commandment listed on the piece and cut out the circle. Remind kids to put their names on the back.

If you're building the ball now, after they've cut out the circle, have them make forward folds on the six straight lines near the edges of the circle. Then they can match tabs from today's circle with the ones they've already attached. Help them staple these places. (Tabs 2, 6 & 7)

Collect their project or the new pieces so they can join it to the bottom half in a few weeks.

Today they should complete the top half of their bloom ball. The five pieces they have stapled together are the commandments that help us know how to "Love the Lord your God with all your Heart, with all your Soul with all your Mind and with all your Strength."

Next week they'll begin to build the bottom. Eventually they will attach these pieces to other pieces they'll make during the next few weeks. The twelve pieces they complete will make a ball with the 10 commandments and the two "greatest" commandments. Take extra pieces from the last few weeks and staple them together so that kids who come the last few weeks can have a top to put with their ball.

KEY PHRASE: Honor Your Father and Mother

The Teaching Moment: Today we've finished the pieces for the top half of our ball. What's the commandment on the top of our ball? *(Allow for answers.)* Love the Lord your God with all your heart, soul, mind and strength is the verse on the top. The five pieces that we've attached (or will attach) to the top help us to know how to do just that. What are the five commandments that attach to the top of the ball? *(Allow for answers.)* God tells us to not worship any god but our God, not to have any idols, not to misuse His name and never misuse His special day. Today we added "Honor your father and mother." Since God is our heavenly Father, when we treat our parents with respect, we are also treating God with respect. This ball will help us remember how to *(encourage the kids to repeat this with you)* "love the Lord Your God with all your heart, with all your soul, with all your mind and with all your strength."

Memory Verse: Mark 12:30-31 & Exodus 20:8   5 Minutes

Love the Lord Your God with all Your Heart and all Your Soul and all Your Mind and all Your Strength and Love your Neighbor as Yourself. - Mark 12:30-31

and

Honor your Father and Mother - Exodus 20:8

Review the two greatest commandments. Be sure the kids know these are found in Mark 12.

Create a big 5 on construction paper (be sure the 1-4 are left from the last two weeks) Hold up the 5 and ask the kids if they know what the 5th commandment is. *(Honor your father and mother)* Then hold up the other numbers and have them respond with the correct commandment.

1. No other Gods except the real God
2. Don't worship idols or statues
3. Don't misuse God's name
4. Keep the Sabbath Holy
5. Honor Your Father and Mother

Song: Go Fish Guy's "The 10 Commandment Boogie"   5-10 Minutes
        and/or Lincoln Brewster's, "Love the Lord Your God."

These are available on CD and most online services as well as on YouTube. If you have the DVD for "The 10 Commandment Boogie" encourage the kids to do the motions to the song this week. If not, you might do some dancing to both songs or "freeze dance" with them to add something new with the songs. (Freeze Dance - When the music is playing, the kids dance. When you pause the music, they have to freeze however they are. OPT: If they move after the music stops, they are out)

WRAPPING IT UP—SENDING IT HOME   5-7 Minutes

Cleaning Up

We want the children to learn to be responsible, so be sure they help with the clean up, but remind them not to go anywhere, the group is going to talk to God together one more time.

Closing Worship and Prayer

Gather the children in a circle holding hands or allow them to sit down to pray. If you choose to join hands, remember that it's OK if some children prefer not to join the circle. Ask them to be respectful of others as they pray and not make any noise. You can always begin your prayer time with a quiet song if you like.

Although you have either finished learning the parts of the Lord's prayer or are using these lessons as a separate unit, we're going to continue to use it to pray as we close. If there is time, ask the children if they have any prayer requests. Remember no prayer is too small, however, children will tend to keep going

KEY PHRASE: Honor Your Father and Mother

and be "inspired" by other prayer requests, so feel free to stop taking requests and tell them they can say anything that didn't get said out loud quietly to God while you're praying. You may close with your own prayer or use the one below for help.

If you need some guidance for your prayer, you can use this:

Father in Heaven, we are thankful that you are our Father. We want to always honor our Father and Mother. Sometimes it's hard, so help us to honor them and You in everything we do. Lord, bless all of the things these kids have mentioned as prayer requests today. (*If there's time, you can mention some of their requests.*) And Lord, we pray all of these things in Jesus' name, who taught us to pray: (*lead them in the Lord's Prayer*)

Our Father who art in heaven, hallowed be thy name. Thy Kingdom come, Thy will be done in earth as it is in heaven. Give us this day our daily bread and forgive us our debts as we forgive our debtors. Lead us not into temptation, but deliver us from evil. For thine is the Kingdom, the Power, and the Glory forever, AMEN.

KEY PHRASE: Honor Your Father and Mother

PROVERBS VERSES FOR LESSON

Proverbs 10:1 - A wise son brings joy to his father, but a foolish son makes his mother sad.

Proverbs 15:20 - A wise son brings joy to his father, but a foolish man doesn't like his mother.

Proverbs 19:27 - If you stop listening to instructions, you will be far away from knowing a lot.

Proverbs 20:20 - If a person talks badly to his father or mother, his life will be very dark

Proverbs 23:22 - Listen to your father, he gave you life, and love your mother when she is old.

Proverbs 23:25 - I hope you make your father and mother glad and you make your mother rejoice!

SCENARIOS FOR GAME

Suggested "wise" answers are listed, but use your judgment with other answers. If kids have a hard time figuring out what is wise, talk about the correct answer briefly so they'll understand why it's the "wise thing to do.

1. You saw a man drop $20 in a store. He is walking away quickly. What should you do?
   (Tell mom or dad or the adult you are with, and try to catch the man to return his money. Be sure that "telling an adult" is part of the wise answer. Running after a strange adult without adult supervision is not wise.)

2. The teacher had to leave the room for a minute and told everyone to read their book. Someone starts a paper ball fight. What should you do?
   (Keep Reading - Tattling is not always a "wise" answer - although if an "unwise" teacher asks directly, the children should respectively answer truthfully)

3. All the kids are teasing a boy who spilled his lunch all over the floor. They are laughing and pointing. What do you do?
   (don't laugh, help him clean up the mess, share your lunch or ask a teacher if he can get another)

4. You were too long getting your things out of your locker at school, and you missed the bus. A neighbor from down the road comes by and offers you a ride home. What should you do?
   (Go back in the school and call your mom. She can tell you if it's OK to ride home with the neighbor or she'd rather come to get you herself)

5. Your mom says to never use the phone. The babysitter is at your house with you, and she gets very sick and passes out. What should you do?
   (trick question - the wise thing would be to call 911 - mom and dad probably won't mind when you're trying to help someone who is hurt)

6. Mom said no snacks before dinner. You are at your friends house, and his mom offers you a cookie. What will you do?
   (Say, "No thanks, Mom said no snacks before dinner today.")

7. You wreck your bike into the back of your dad's car. There's a dent and the paint is scratched. What should you do?
   (tell your dad before he sees it)

8. You were playing with your brother's favorite toy and accidentally broke it. What will you do?
   (Go tell your brother and say you're sorry. If you have some money you could offer to replace it)

9. Someone brought their dad's cigarettes to school. You are with a group at recess who are trying the cigarettes. What should you do?
   (Walk away from the group)

10. Your friend takes a book that doesn't belong to her. She asks you not to tell anyone. The teacher asks if you've seen the book or know what happens to it. What do you do?
    (you tell the teacher that your friend has the book)

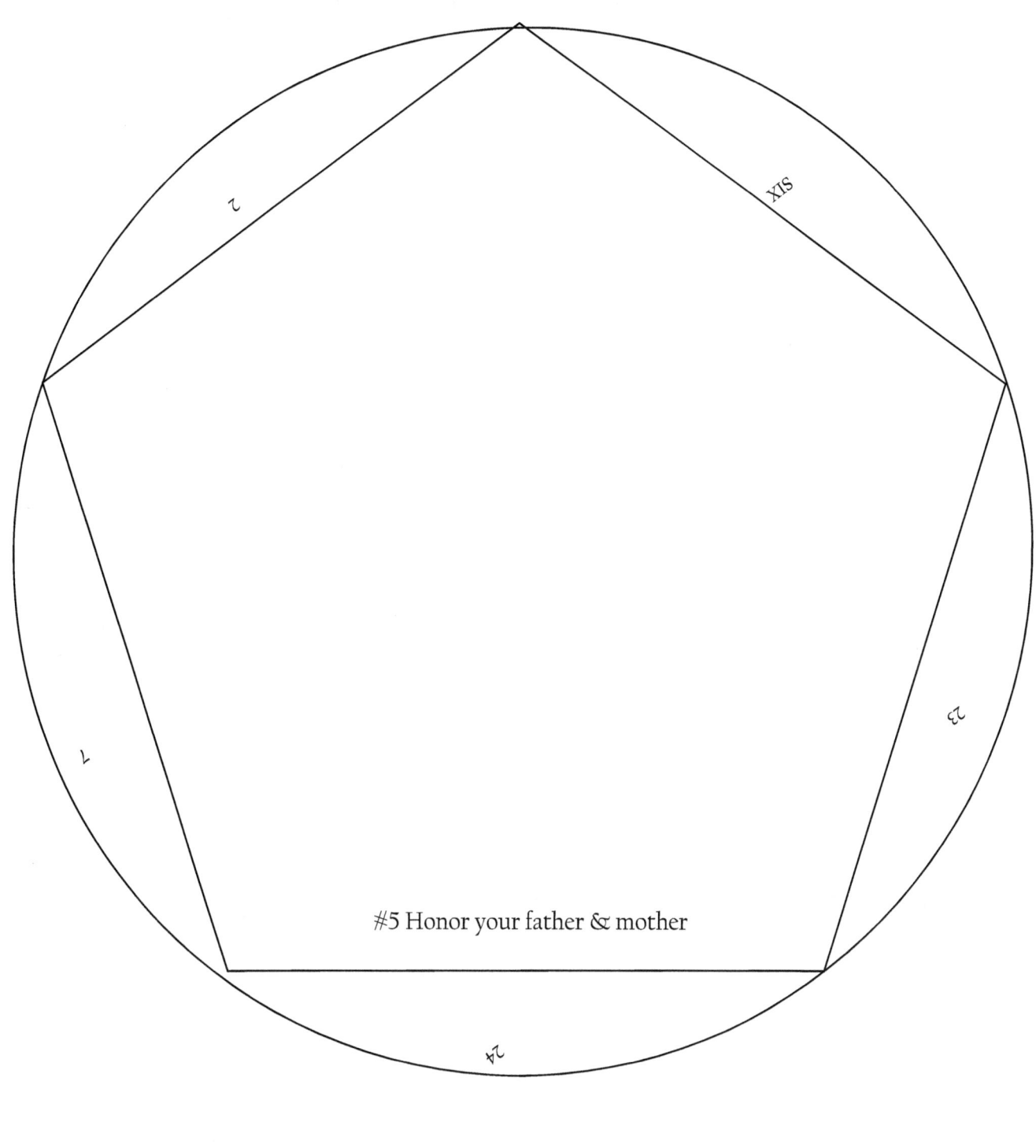

Page intentionally left blank for printing and copying purposes

Jesus, Teach Me How to Pray
A Year in The Lord's Prayer and other Bible Basics

Unit 12: The Greatest Commandments & The 10 Commandments
Week 5: Don't Murder & Be True to Your Marriage

Lesson Overview

The lesson today will focus on the story of Cain and Able. Because Cain was jealous, he took his brother out in the field and killed him. If the children should ask, it's important to understand that accidental killing is different than murder. Accidents are not a sin. Since adultery is a very difficult concept for children to understand, we'll focus primarily on murder. Jesus said that even calling someone a fool was just as serious as murder and looking at someone lustfully was a bad as adultery. As we briefly discuss the sanctity of marriage, we'll also mention that we should dress modestly and not look at magazines and books that show people without all of their clothes on. When we do these things, it makes God very sad.

KEY PHRASE: Don't Murder & Be True to your Marriage

SETTING UP THE LESSON   5-7 Minutes
Have you ever been angry?

PRESENTING THE LESSON   5-10 Minutes
Scripture: Genesis 4:1-16 & Matthew 5:21-28

MAKING IT REAL TO KIDS TODAY   (Choose as many as you have time for)

Game: When I Get Angry   10-15 Minutes

Craft: Bloom Ball-Part 5   5-10 Minutes
 Supplies: Copies of the final page of this lesson, crayons or markers, staplers

Memory Verse: Mark 12:30-31 & Exodus 20:17   5-10 Minutes

Song: Go Fish Guy's "The 10 Commandment Boogie"   5-10 Minutes
and/or Lincoln Brewster's, "Love the Lord Your God."

WRAPPING IT UP—SENDING IT HOME   5-7 Minutes
Clean Up Time & Prayer Time

KEY PHRASE: Don't Murder & Be True to your Marriage

SETTING UP THE LESSON   5-7 Minutes

Have you ever been angry?

Today, we're going to ask the children what it's like when they're angry. Ask: Who do you get angry with, and what do you act like when you're angry? Have you ever hurt someone because you were angry? *(Give every child a chance to share for 30 seconds or so.)* Today we're going to hear about a guy who got really mad at his brother.

PRESENTING THE LESSON   5-10 Minutes

Scripture: Genesis 4:1-16 & Matthew 5:21-28

*You do not have to read this directly from the Bible—
use the story form below or reword it to fit your personality*

Who can tell me the name of the first man and woman God put on the earth? *(Allow for answers.)* Adam and Eve were the first people God created. Did you know they had children? The first two were boys. They named them Cain and Abel. Can you say Cain and Abel? *(Allow them to repeat.)* Cain was a gardener. He raised fruit and vegetables. Abel was a shepherd. He took care of flocks of sheep. Cain and Abel both brought offerings to God. The Bible tells us Abel brought his very best sheep every time he made an offering. Cain brought offerings, too, but it might not have always been his very best. The Bible says Cain brought "some" of his crops to offer them to God.

God likes it when we put him first and give Him our very best. So God liked Abel's offerings better. This made Cain very mad. He wanted God to like his offerings as much as Abel's. He was jealous of Abel and upset that God liked Abel's offerings better. Do you know what the word jealous means? *(Allow for answers.)* Jealous is when you want to be like someone else, and you feel upset because you're not.

Cain got so jealous that one day when he and Abel were out in the field together, he killed his brother. Because Cain had done something so evil, God had to discipline Cain. God told Cain that none of his crops would grow for him anymore. Cain moved away from his family because of what he'd done.

In the Ten Commandments, God said we should never murder. Do you know what it means to murder? *(Allow for answers.)* Murder means to kill someone, not accidentally, but on purpose. And Jesus said even more about murder. He said God doesn't even want us to get angry with someone. Even calling them names is terrible. Have you ever called someone names? *(Allow for answers.)* We need to try to remember to never do that because God says it's just like murder.

Jesus also talked about the next commandment. It's one that most people think doesn't matter to kids because it talks about marriage. But Jesus wants everyone to stay true to their marriage. Today that seems like it's hard for a lot of people. But it was difficult when Jesus lived, too. Being true to your marriage is a good thing to learn when you're kids so when you get old enough to start dating, you'll remember to respect the man or woman you date. Whoever you date will be someone's husband or wife someday. So you should treat him or her like you want someone to treat the person you're going to marry.

Today we're going to do some things that will help us remember the next two commandments: Don't ever murder and stay true to your marriage.

KEY PHRASE: Don't Murder & Be True to your Marriage

MAKING IT REAL TO KIDS TODAY
(Choose as many as you have time for)

Game: When I Get Angry 5-10 Minutes

These are three different activities. Have some fun with them.

1. **Breathe Deep**

   Have the kids stand in a circle. Allow the youngest in the room be the counter. Tell the kids they are going to breathe in very slowly while the counter counts to five. And then they'll blow the air out very slowly while the counter counts to ten. Remind the counter to count nice and slow and even. Let the second youngest and the third youngest have a turn to count - then move into the second exercise.

2. **Melting Popsicle**

   We're going to pretend we're popsicles. Everyone is going to stand very stiff and solid like a frozen popsicle. *Go around and try to move arms on the kids. Encourage them to stay very stiff even when you try to move their arms.* Now tell the kids it's getting hot. Ask if they know what happens when a popsicle gets hot. Tell them they have melted just a little. Coach them to melt little by little until they are puddles on the floor. You can repeat this more than once if you have time.

3. **Balloon Trip**

   Have the children pretend they are a balloon filling up with air. As you count to five, tell them to suck in air like they are filling themselves up. Tell them to start with their arms down by their sides and make their arms go up higher as they fill up so they look like a big "O" when you get to five. Have them hold it while you count to five again so they are like a balloon that's full of air. Finally, count to ten while they let the air out. Have them breathe out and bring their arms down and wiggle down to the ground like a balloon you let the air out of (You might have a balloon there to show them how it looks when you let the air out of a balloon - hold onto the balloon.)

The Teaching Moment: We had a lot of fun breathing and pretending to be popsicles and balloons. But did you know that when you get angry you can do those three things to help you not sin. Remember, Jesus said that when we call people names that's the same as murder. So we want to make sure that when we get mad, we don't hit or call people names. So, the next time you feel mad, try breathing or becoming a popsicle or a balloon so you don't make God sad.

(These activities were inspired by: http://www.goodcharacter.com/GROARK/Anger.html)

Craft: Bloom Ball: Part 5 5-10 Minutes
Supplies: Copies of the final page of this lesson, crayons or markers, staplers

*Today's Craft is the fifth of an eight part craft -
You'll need the other loose piece from the first week - the piece that is marked "BOTTOM"*

Give each child a copy of the last two pages of this lesson. Have them draw a picture on each piece that will remind them of the commandment listed on that piece. These might be more difficult for the kids than some of the other commandments. Help them with ideas of what to draw if necessary. A gun with the standard symbol for no (a red circle with a diagonal line) over it would be good, and a bride and/or groom or a wedding bell could take care of the marriage commandment.

Next, have them cut out the circles, put their names on the back, and fold the edges forward along the six straight lines. Then they can match tabs from today's circle with the one marked "BOTTOM". Help them staple these places. (Tabs 12, 13 & 17) Alternately, you can save them to put the entire ball together during the final week.

Collect their project so they can add more to them next week. Be sure to create extra pieces for kids

KEY PHRASE: Don't Murder & Be True to your Marriage

who miss today.

Eventually they will attach these pieces to other pieces they'll make during the next few weeks as well as the top they finished last week. The twelve pieces they complete will make a ball with the Ten Commandments and the two "greatest" commandments.

Memory Verse: Mark 12:30-31 & Exodus 20:13-14   5-10 Minutes

Love the Lord Your God with all Your Heart and all Your Soul and all Your Mind
and all Your Strength and Love your Neighbor as Yourself. - Mark 12:30-31

By now the kids should know the Two Greatest Commandments well. Ask one or two of the kids who have it memorized to repeat this for you. Challenge them to memorize where it's found: Mark 12:30-31 - You might also let them know it's found in several other places in the Bible.

And

You should never murder and always be true to your marriage - Exodus 20:13-14

Create two more numbers (6-7) on construction paper (1-5 should be left from previous weeks) Tell the kids you're going to hold up a number and the first one to raise their hand and say that commandment correctly gets a point (or you could have tootsie rolls for each student who gets one correct)

1. No other Gods except the real God
2. Don't worship idols or statues
3. Don't misuse God's name
4. Keep the Sabbath Holy
5. Honor your Mother and Father
6. Don't murder
7. Be True to your Marriage

Song: Go Fish Guy's "The 10 Commandment Boogie"   5-10 Minutes
and/or Lincoln Brewster's, "Love the Lord Your God."

These are available on CD and most online services as well as YouTube. The Ten Commandment Boogie is available on *Go Fish Guys* "Superstar" DVD. The kids may have been doing one or both of these songs for several weeks now. If so, they should know them well. So have fun with them! If you don't have a lot of time, use them during the memory verse section.

WRAPPING IT UP—SENDING IT HOME   5-7 Minutes

Cleaning Up

We want the children to learn to be responsible, so be sure they help with the clean up, but remind them not to go anywhere, the group is going to talk to God together.

Closing Worship and Prayer

Gather the children in a circle holding hands or allow them to sit down to pray. If you choose to join hands, remember it's OK if some children prefer not to join the circle. Ask them to be respectful of others as they pray and not make any noise. You can always begin your prayer time with a quiet song if you like.

Although you have either finished learning the parts of the Lord's prayer or are using these lessons as a separate unit, we're going to continue to use it to pray as we close. If there is time, ask the children if they have any prayer requests. Remember no prayer is too small, however, children will tend to keep going and be "inspired" by other prayer requests, so feel free to stop taking requests and tell them they can say anything that didn't get said out loud quietly to God while you're praying. You may close with your own

KEY PHRASE: Don't Murder & Be True to your Marriage

prayer or use the one below for help.

If you need some guidance for your prayer, you can use this:

Father in Heaven, we are thankful that you love us. We didn't know that calling people names was so bad before. Forgive us that we do that sometimes. Help us to treat everyone kindly and always remember to respect others. Lord, bless all of the things these kids have mentioned as prayer requests today (*if there's time, you can mention some of their requests*). And Lord, we pray all of these things in Jesus' name, who taught us to pray: (*lead them in the Lord's Prayer*)

Our Father who art in heaven, hallowed be thy name. Thy Kingdom come, Thy will be done in earth as it is in heaven. Give us this day our daily bread and forgive us our debts as we forgive our debtors. Lead us not into temptation, but deliver us from evil. For thine is the Kingdom, the Power, and the Glory forever, AMEN.

KEY PHRASE: Don't Murder & Be True to your Marriage

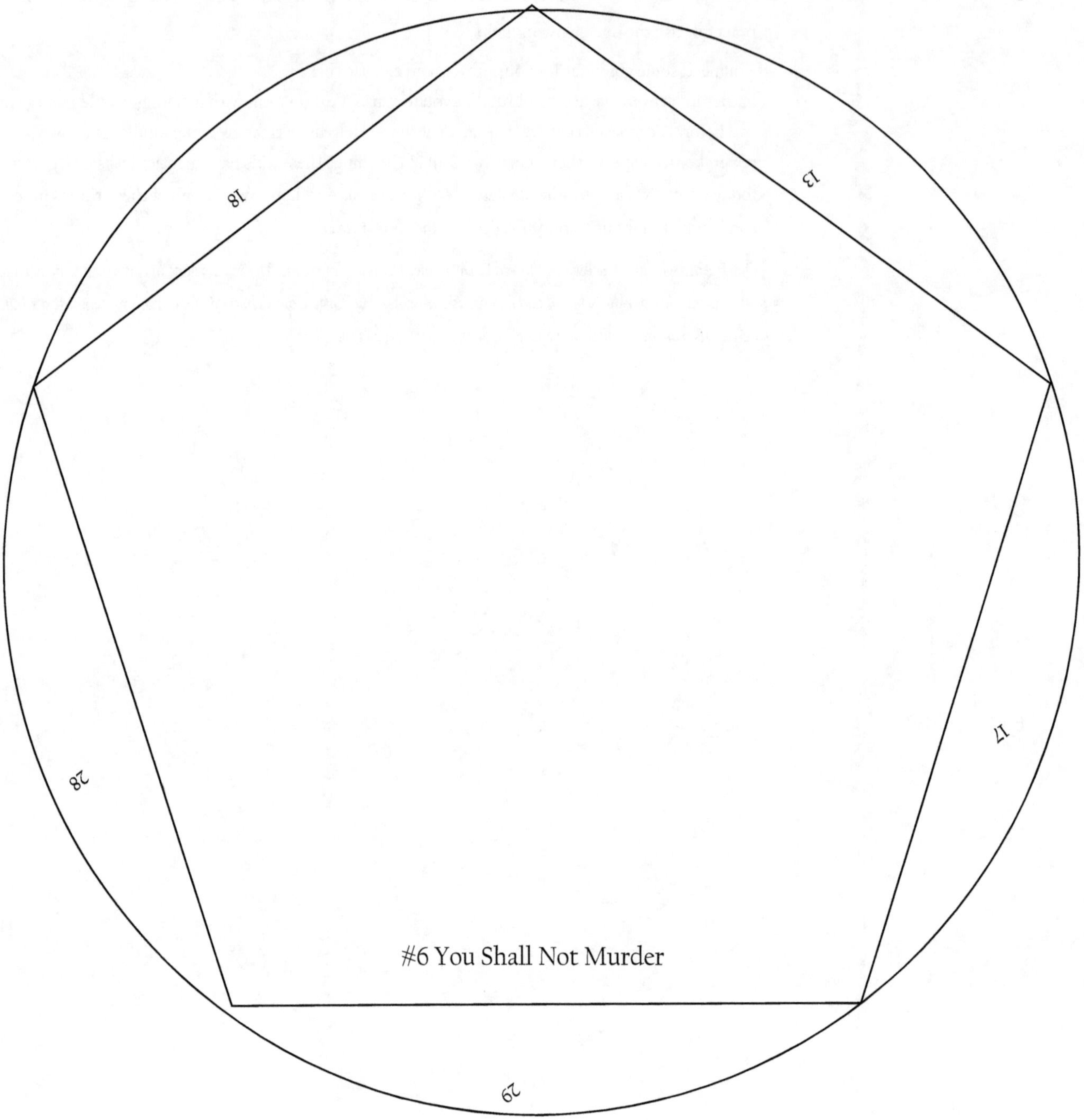

18

13

28

17

#6 You Shall Not Murder

29

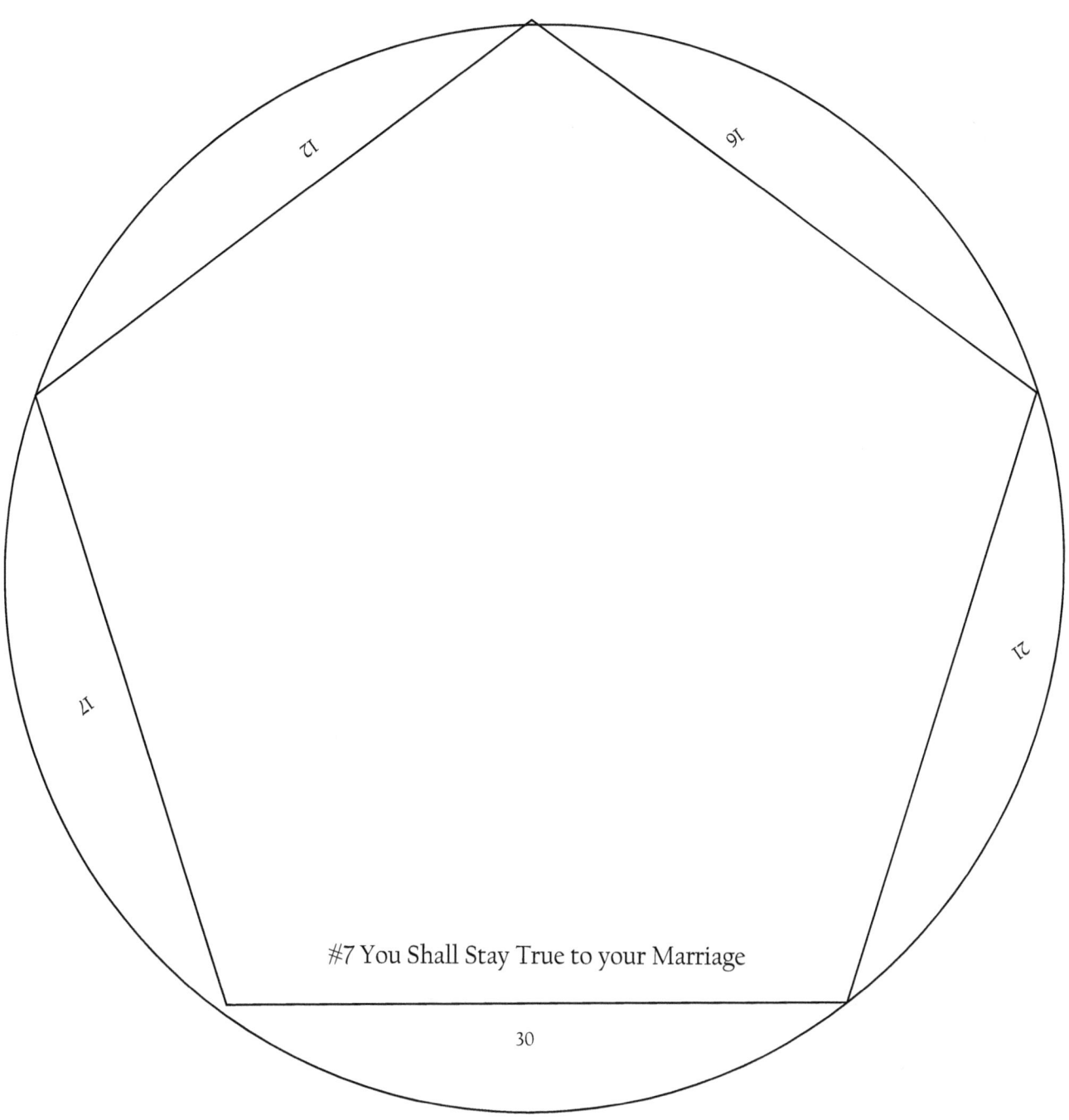

#7 You Shall Stay True to your Marriage

Page intentionally left blank for printing and copying purposes

Jesus, Teach Me How to Pray
A Year in The Lord's Prayer and other Bible Basics

Unit 12: The Greatest Commandments & The 10 Commandments
Week 6: No Stealing

Lesson Overview

The story or Jacob and Esau can help us learn a bit about stealing. Jacob's name fittingly means deceiver. He came out of the womb pulling Esau's leg, and he never stopped. One day, Esau came into the house very hungry. Jacob had cooked some red stew. Esau was so hungry that he traded his birthright (the right of the oldest to twice the inheritance as the rest of the siblings) to Jacob in exchange for something to eat. And while most of us would give our sibling some dinner if they came in hungry, Jacob tricked his brother out of the larger share.

And if that wasn't enough, when his father was near death and ready to give the blessing of the oldest to Esau, Jacob (with his mother's encouragement) tricked Isaac and lied to him to steal Esau's blessing. This is one of the commandments the kids will be able to understand. It's a great opportunity to help them see that taking anything that doesn't belong to them is wrong.

KEY PHRASE: No Stealing!

SETTING UP THE LESSON — 5-7 Minutes

Look what I found!
Supplies: A pen with a bank or someone else's name on it; some change; a book; a couple of cans of veggies, a loaf of bread

PRESENTING THE LESSON — 5-10 Minutes

Scripture: Genesis 27

MAKING IT REAL TO KIDS TODAY — *(Choose as many as you have time for)*

Game: Doggy, Doggy Where's Your Bone? — 5-7 Minutes

Craft: Bloom Ball-Part 6 — 5-10 Minutes
Supplies: Copies of the final page of this lesson, crayons or markers, staplers

Memory Verse: Mark 12:30-31 & Exodus 20:15 — 5-10 Minutes

Song: Go Fish Guy's "The 10 Commandment Boogie" — 5-10 Minutes
and/or Lincoln Brewster's, "Love the Lord Your God."

WRAPPING IT UP—SENDING IT HOME — 5-7 Minutes

Clean Up Time & Prayer Time

KEY PHRASE: No Stealing!

SETTING UP THE LESSON   5-7 Minutes

Look what I found!

Supplies: A pen with a bank or someone else's name on it; some change; a book; a couple of cans of veggies, a loaf of bread

Put all of your "supplies" in a bag. Have another adult come in with the bag of supplies and tell the kids, "Look what I found!" They should be very excited. Now go into this simple skit. (If you don't have a second adult, you could read the part of the other adult and ask the kids about all the things you've found.)

OTHER ADULT: Hey, Look! I found all of this stuff this week. This is great! I found this pen at the bank (or whoever's name is on it). Then, this money was laying on someone's desk at work. No one was around, so I figured no one else must want it. Then after work, this book was lying on a bench at the mall. The guy sitting next to it was sleeping, so he didn't need it. At the grocery store these cans of vegetables and this loaf of bread were sitting right near the door. Why would they put them so close to the door? I figured it must be for me!

YOU: "Wait! Are you sure you just 'found' all these things?"

OTHER ADULT: Well, yes. I found every single thing here

YOU: (to the kids) What do you kids think? (Allow answers from the kids - hopefully they'll recognize that at least the veggies and bread were stolen - if not, you should say, "I think maybe you stole some of those things")

OTHER ADULT: Really? I don't want to be a thief. I honestly thought I just found them.

YOU: Sometimes it's hard to tell the difference between "finding" and stealing, but since none of those things belong to you, my friend, I think they've all been stolen. Whenever we take something that doesn't belong to us without asking, we're stealing. Some people say they "find" things and some people say they're "borrowing,," but unless you have permission to take something, even a pen at a bank, it's really stealing. I think you better take them back!

OTHER ADULT: Wow! I guess you're right

YOU: (to the kids) Well, that's a great lead in to our next commandment. God said, "You should never steal."

PRESENTING THE LESSON   5-10 Minutes

Scripture: Genesis 27

You do not have to read this directly from the Bible—
use the story form below or reword it to fit your personality

Who can tell me the name of the first book of the Bible? *(Allow for answers.)* Genesis is the first book. And in Genesis, we read about a man named Isaac who had two sons. Their names were Esau and Jacob. They were twins. Do you know what twins are? *(Allow for answers.)* Esau and Jacob didn't look alike, but they were both born at the same time. Esau was born first, and the Bible says that Jacob was born with his hand on Esau's heal, just like he was pulling it.

In fact, that's how he got the name Jacob. Jacob's name means holding onto the heal. Kind of like we say today, "Pulling your leg." Do you know what it means when I say, "I was just pulling your leg"? *(Allow for answers.)* Pulling your leg means someone tricked you or played a prank on you by saying something that wasn't true and then laugh and tell them the truth. So, Jacob's name fit him well. Jacob was always "pulling someone's leg." Yep, the other meaning of his name is "deceiver." Do you know what it means to deceive someone? *(Allow for answers.)*

KEY PHRASE: No Stealing!

Deceive means to trick them, and Jacob loved to trick people.

Esau and Jacob were very different. Esau was very hairy and liked to go out hunting, and that made his dad very happy. Jacob had smooth skin and stayed at home and looked after things there, and his mother liked that a lot. One day Esau came in while Jacob was cooking some stew. Esau was so hungry from being out in the field that when he got back in the house, he told Jacob he could have his birthright if Jacob would give him some stew. That means that Jacob would get two shares of everything his father had.

Many years later, Jacob and Esau's father, Isaac, was growing very old. He could hardly see because he was so old. He called for Esau and told him to go hunting and find something to cook for him and then Isaac would give Esau the blessing that goes to the oldest.

Esau and Jacob's mom heard about it and called for Jacob. She said, "Go out and get a goat, and I'll fix it so it will taste just the way your father likes it." Then Jacob dressed in Esau's clothes and put the hair of the goat on his arms. He had to trick his father into thinking he was Esau.

When he took the meal into Isaac, Jacob told his dad that he was Esau. Isaac thought his voice sounded wrong, but as soon as he touched the hair on his arms and smelled Esau's clothes, Isaac thought Esau had brought him the dinner.

So Isaac ate, and then he blessed Jacob with his best blessing. He prayed that Jacob would have riches and servants and be greater than his brother. That blessing was supposed to be for Esau, but since Jacob tricked Isaac, he got Esau's blessing.

After Jacob left, Esau came in. He told Isaac that his dinner was ready. But Isaac told him someone had already brought him dinner and taken his blessing! Esau was very upset. He was mad at Jacob because Jacob stole his blessing.

In fact Esau was so mad, Jacob was afraid so he ran far away from home. He didn't see his family for twenty years all because he stole from his brother! Jacob tricked and lied and stole, but when he was older, he came back to his brother and apologized. Jacob became a close friend of God, and God forgave him for these things he did wrong.

MAKING IT REAL TO KIDS TODAY *(Choose as many as you have time for)*

Game: Doggy, Doggy, Where's Your Bone? 7-10 Minutes

Have the children sit in a semi-circle. Find something to be a "bone" (an eraser or box of crayons would work) Choose one child to be "doggy." "Doggy" sits in the middle at the front of the semi-circle with "Doggy's" eyes closed. Put a "bone" behind "doggy." An adult should choose one child to steal the bone. The selected child should steal the bone, and all the children should put their hands behind their back. Then help all of the children say, *"Doggy, Doggy where's your bone. Someone stole it from your home. Guess who! Maybe you! Maybe monkeys in the zoo. Wake up doggy find your bone."* After the chant is over, "Doggy" get's three chances to guess who stole the bone. If the doggy guesses correctly you can give them a point or a piece of candy. The one who has the bone becomes the "doggy." Continue until all kids get a chance to be the doggy or time is up.

The Teaching Moment: We had fun "stealing" the doggy's bones, but it's really important that we don't take anything that doesn't belong to us. Do you remember what Jacob took from his brother? *(Allow for answers.)* Jacob took Esau's blessing and his birthright—all the things the oldest son gets. What happened to Jacob? *(Allow for answers.)* Jacob ended up living far away from his family for a long time. God said we should never steal. In fact, he said if we did steal, we should return what we stole and give the person we stole from even more than we took.

KEY PHRASE: No Stealing!

Craft: Bloom Ball: Part 6   10 Minutes
Supplies: Copies of the final page of this lesson, crayons or markers, staplers

Today's Craft is the sixth of an eight part craft -
You'll need the section they worked on last week - the piece that is marked "BOTTOM"

Give each child a copy of the last page of this lesson. Have them draw a picture that will remind them of the commandment listed on the piece and cut out the circle.

After they've cut out the circle, have them fold the piece along the six straight lines near the edges of the circle. Then they can match tabs from today's circle with the one marked "BOTTOM". Help them staple these places. (Tabs 11 & 16) Alternately, you can save them to put the entire ball together during the final week.

Collect their project so they can add more to them next week.

Eventually they will attach these pieces to other pieces they'll make during the next few weeks as well as the top. The twelve pieces they complete will make a ball with the 10 commandments and the two "greatest" commandments.

The Teaching Moment: Today we added one more piece to our project. In just a couple of weeks, they'll be all done and connected together to look like a ball. We'll be able to hang them up to remind us that God gave us these commandments because He loves us so much. God wants us to know how to live. He wants us to be happy, and God knows that when we follow His ideas and obey His commandments, we'll be able to have the best life possible.

Memory Verse: Mark 12:30-31 & Exodus 20:15   5-10 Minutes

Love the Lord Your God with all Your Heart and all Your Soul and all Your Mind
and all Your Strength and Love your Neighbor as Yourself. - Mark 12:30-31

Begin with the oldest kids who've been in attendance in weeks past. Have them repeat these verses. You could give a tootsie roll or other small candy to every child who will say it by himself and gets it correct.

And

You Should Never Steal - Exodus 20:15

Create one more number (8) on poster board (1-7 should be left from previous weeks) Hold up the numbers in random order. Have the kids raise their hands to answer and choose one to stand and give their response. If they get it correct, they can remain standing. Keep going through the numbers until all of the children are standing.

1. No other Gods except the real God
2. Don't worship idols or statues
3. Don't misuse God's name
4. Keep the Sabbath Holy
5. Honor your Mother and Father
6. Don't murder
7. Be True to your Marriage
8. Don't Steal

Song: Go Fish Guy's "The 10 Commandment Boogie"   5-10 Minutes
and/or Lincoln Brewster's, "Love the Lord Your God."

Choose one or both of these songs to sing with the group.

The Teaching Moment: Remind them that these songs will help them remember the important verses we're learning during these 8 weeks.

KEY PHRASE: No Stealing!

WRAPPING IT UP—SENDING IT HOME
5—7 Minutes

Cleaning Up

We want the children to learn to be responsible, so be sure they help with the clean up, but remind them not to go anywhere, the group is going to talk to God together one more time.

Closing Worship and Prayer

Gather the children in a circle holding hands or allow them to sit down to pray. If you choose to join hands, remember that it's OK if some children prefer not to join the circle. Just ask them to be respectful of others as they pray and not make any noise. You can always begin your prayer time with a quiet song if you like.

Although you have either finished learning the parts of the Lord's prayer or are using these lessons as a separate unit, we're going to continue to use it to pray as we close. If there is time, ask the children if they have any prayer requests. Remember no prayer is too small, however, children will tend to keep going and be "inspired" by other prayer requests, so feel free to stop taking requests and tell them they can say anything that didn't get said out loud quietly to God while you're praying. You may close with your own prayer or use the one below for help.

If you need some guidance for your prayer, you can use this:

Father in Heaven, thank you, that you are a God of abundance. You give us everything we need. Forgive us, Lord, when we take things that don't belong to us, and remind us whenever we forget. Lord, bless all of the things these kids have mentioned as prayer requests today (*if there's time, you can mention some of their requests*). And Lord, we pray all of these things in Jesus' name, who taught us to pray: (*lead them in the Lord's Prayer*)

Our Father who art in heaven, hallowed be thy name. Thy Kingdom come, Thy will be done in earth as it is in heaven. Give us this day our daily bread and forgive us our debts as we forgive our debtors. Lead us not into temptation, but deliver us from evil. For thine is the Kingdom, the Power, and the Glory forever, AMEN.

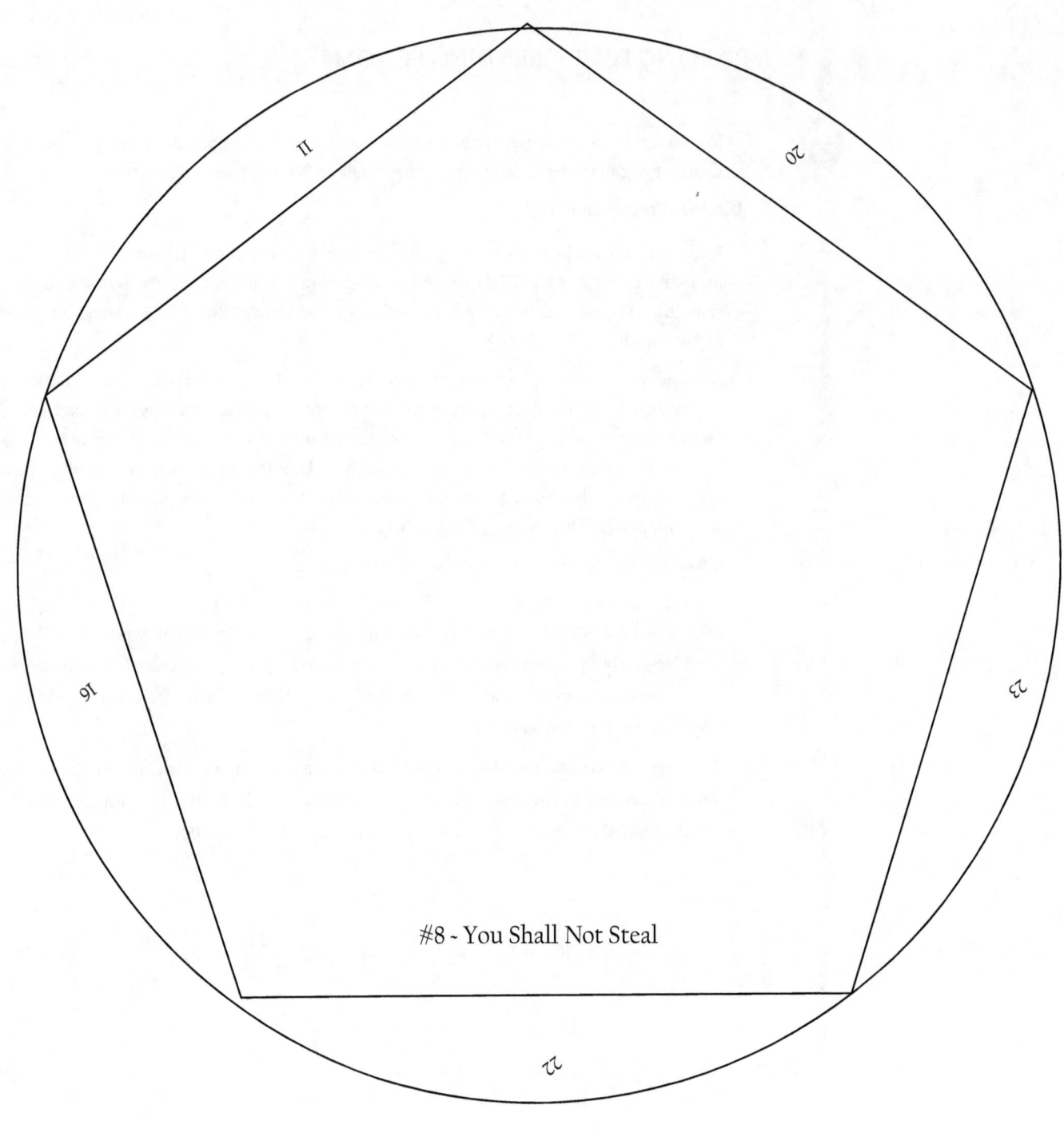

#8 - You Shall Not Steal

Jesus, Teach Me How to Pray
A Year in The Lord's Prayer and other Bible Basics

Unit 12: The Greatest Commandments & The 10 Commandments
Week 7: No Lying

Lesson Overview

Today we're going to look at a one of the most drastic results of lying ever recorded. Annanias (anna-NIE-us) and his wife, Sapphira (like Sapphire with an "a" at the end) wanted to be popular. Many people who had become Christians were selling their property and bringing the money to the apostles to use to help spread the gospel. Annanias and Sapphira didn't want to be left out. So, the couple sold their land and brought a portion of the proceeds to Peter. Not really a big deal. It was their money, they could do anything they wanted with it. The problem arises when they tell Peter that they gave him the entire amount. No one asked them to give all the money, but they chose to lie to make themselves look good. The drastic part is that both fell over dead. If you feel that the story of the couple's death is too difficult for your group to deal with (especially if someone just lost an adult they love), you could say that God punished them. It's important for the kids to realize that when we lie, it's not only doing wrong to other people, we're also letting God down.

KEY PHRASE: No Lying!

SETTING UP THE LESSON — 5-7 Minutes
   Pinocchio

PRESENTING THE LESSON — 5-10 Minutes
   Scripture: Acts 5:1-11

MAKING IT REAL TO KIDS TODAY — *(Choose as many as you have time for)*

   Illustration: When is it hard to tell the truth? — 3-5 minutes

   Game: Who is Lying? — 5-10 Minutes

   Craft: Bloom Ball-Part 7 — 5-10 Minutes
   Supplies: Copies of the final page of this lesson, crayons or markers, staplers

   Memory Verse: Mark 12:30-31 & Exodus 20:16 — 5 Minutes

   Song: Go Fish Guy's "The 10 Commandment Boogie" and/or Lincoln Brewster's, "Love the Lord Your God." — 5-7 Minutes

WRAPPING IT UP—SENDING IT HOME — 5-7 Minutes
   Clean Up Time & Prayer Time

KEY PHRASE: No Lying!

SETTING UP THE LESSON   5-7 Minutes

Pinocchio

Tell me what you know about the story of Pinocchio? *(Allow for answers.)* What was Pinocchio's biggest problem? *(Allow for answers.)* Pinocchio's nose grew every time he lied. He had a really hard time telling the truth. Do you remember what happened when he started telling the truth? *(Allow for answers.)* Pinocchio's nose got shorter, and he finally was able to become a real boy when he remembered to always tell the truth and listen to his father. The story of Pinocchio helps us to know how important telling the truth is. Did you know that telling the truth is very important to God, too? *(Allow for answers.)*

PRESENTING THE LESSON   5-10 Minutes

Scripture: Acts 5:1-11

You do not have to read this directly from the Bible
use the story form below or reword it to fit your personality

Who can tell me what happened on Easter? *(Allow for answers.)* That's right, on Easter, Jesus rose from the dead. What about forty days after Easter? *(Allow for answers—some kids my try Pentecost, but we'll get to that in a minute.)* Forty days after Easter, Jesus disappeared into heaven. Do you know what happened fifty days after Easter? *(Allow for answers)* On the fiftieth day after Easter, God sent His Holy Spirit to everyone who believed in Jesus, and word about Jesus dying for our sins started to spread. But it took a lot of money for the disciples to travel all over, so many of Jesus' followers started selling their fields and everything they owned. They brought all the money to the disciples to help them spread the news about Jesus. Everyone who loved Jesus wanted to get in on it. And Annanias and Sapphira didn't want to miss out.

So, Annanias and Sapphira sold a field they owned, and Annanias took part of the money to Peter. The problem is Annanias told Peter the money they brought was the whole amount they got from the land. They didn't have to give it all to Peter, but they thought if they told him it was the whole amount, it would make them more important. But the Holy Spirit told Peter Annanias was lying.

Peter asked Annanias, "Why would you lie about this? This was your land and your money. You didn't have to give it to us. You didn't lie to me. Since you are giving this money to do God's work, you lied to God." *Just then Annanias fell over and was dead. So they carried him out of the house. (or "Right then, because he lied to God, God punished Annanias)*

About three hours later, Sapphira came to see Peter. She didn't know that Peter found out Annanias had lied. Peter asked her, "Is this the amount of money that you got from that land?" She said, "Yes, it is." Peter said, "Why would you lie to God." *And then Sapphira fell over dead too. (or "God punished her, too")*

Annanias and Sapphira lied, not only to Peter, but they also lied to God. Most of our lies are not just to other people, they are also to God. Even when we tell part of the truth, like Annanias and Sapphira, if it's not the whole truth, we are really lying. It's important to God that we always tell the whole truth all the time. That's why, when God gave us the 10 Commandments, He said, "You should never lie." No one since Annanias and Sapphira *have died suddenly (or been punished this badly)* because they lied, but our lies still make God very sad. It's important that we always tell the truth.

KEY PHRASE: No Lying!

MAKING IT REAL TO KIDS TODAY

(Choose as many as you have time for)

Game: Who is Lying?   5-10 Minutes

Have all the children stand in a line. You will make statements and when the children think you're telling the truth, they will put their finger on their nose. If they think you're lying, they should sit on the floor. After each statement, check with the ones sitting on the floor and ask what they think the truth is. Then reveal the truth. You could give a tootsie roll or some other candy to kids who correctly catch you lying. Use phrases like:

I am wearing blue today (you may use your sock or underwear color to trick them)

I have a new puppy

The pastor has a green car

Have at least twenty statements ready.

The Teaching Moment: Today we told a few lies to have fun. It's important that we learn the difference between playing a game or really telling a lie. When we tease or play a game, people always know we might be saying something that isn't true, and we always tell the truth when we're done. Jesus said He is the truth. If we love Jesus, we need to be sure to always tell the truth.

Craft: Bloom Ball-Part 7   5-10 Minutes
Supplies: Copies of the final page of this lesson, crayons or markers, staplers

Today's Craft is the seventh of an eight part craft -
You'll need the section they worked with last week - the piece that is marked "BOTTOM"

Give each child a copy of the last page of this lesson. Have them draw a picture that will remind them of the commandment listed on the piece and cut out the circle.

After they've cut out the circle, have them fold the piece along the six straight lines near the edges of the circle. Then they can match tabs from today's circle with the one marked "BOTTOM". Help them staple these places. (Tabs 15 & 20) Alternately, you can attach them all in the final week.

Collect their project so they can add more to them next week.

Next week they will attach these pieces to all the other pieces. The twelve pieces they complete will make a ball with the 10 commandments and the two "greatest" commandments.

The Teaching Moment: We have only one piece left to attach to our project. Do you remember how many commandments God gave to Moses? *(Allow for answers.)* There are 10, but all are important to God. He wants us to obey all of His commands.

Memory Verse: Mark 12:30-31 & Exodus 20:16   5-7 Minutes

Love the Lord Your God with all Your Heart and all Your Soul and all Your Mind
and all Your Strength and Love your Neighbor as Yourself. - Mark 12:30-31

The kids should have been reviewing these verses for several weeks now. See how many know they are from Mark 12:30-31. You'll find sign language for these in the first lesson in this Unit, or for a new idea allow the kids to copy this on a piece of paper and decorate it with hearts to remind them that God wants us to love Him and others.

And

KEY PHRASE: No Lying!

You should never lie. - Exodus 20:13

Create one more number (9) on poster board (1-8 should be left from previous weeks) Hold up the numbers in random order and allow the kids to tell you which commandment it is. Or for something different go through the commandments in order and have the kids all shout out the commandment together.

1. No other Gods except the real God
2. Don't worship idols or statues
3. Don't misuse God's name
4. Keep the Sabbath Holy
5. Honor your Mother and Father
6. Don't murder
7. Be True to your Marriage
8. Don't Steal
9. Don't Lie

Song: Go Fish Guy's "The 10 Commandment Boogie" and/or Lincoln Brewster's, "Love the Lord Your God" 5-10 Minutes

Use a CD or DVD (or YouTube) to sing these with the kids. If they've been singing these songs each week, you might speak with the pastor or worship leader to see if they could sing one or both during the church service next week as they finish up this unit on the 10 commandments.

Illustration: When it's hard to tell the truth 3-5 Minutes

When is it hard to tell the truth? *(Allow for answers.)* Is it hard to tell the truth when you know you're going to get in trouble? *(Allow for answers.)* Why is that? *(Allow for answers.)* When we do something wrong, we make God very sad. He loves us and wants us to always choose to do the right thing. What happens when we lie about it? *(Allow for answers.)* When we lie about doing the wrong thing, we make God sad all over again, and if we do it all the time, it might even make God mad. Fortunately, the Bible says that God is slow to anger. That means that he doesn't get mad very easily. So, let's try to make God proud of us and make Him smile by always telling the truth.

WRAPPING IT UP—SENDING IT HOME 5-7 Minutes

Cleaning Up

We want the children to learn to be responsible, so be sure they help with the clean up, but remind them not to go anywhere, the group is going to talk to God together one more time.

Closing Worship and Prayer

You can either gather the children in a circle holding hands or allow them to sit down to pray. If you choose to join hands, remember that it's OK if some children prefer not to join the circle. Just ask them to be respectful of others as they pray and not make any noise.

Even though we've finished with the units focusing on the Lord's prayer, we're going to continue to use it to pray as we close. If there is time, ask the children if they have prayer requests. Remember that no prayer is ever too small, however, children will tend to keep going and be "inspired" by other prayer requests, so feel free to stop taking requests and tell them they can say anything that didn't get said out loud quietly to God themselves while you're praying. You may close with your own prayer or use the one below for help. If you need some guidance for your prayer, you can use this:

Father in Heaven, we are thankful that you love us. We know when we lie, it makes you very sad. We're sorry we lie so easily. Help us, Jesus, to always tell the truth even when it might get us in trouble. Lord, bless all the things these kids have mentioned as prayer requests today. *(if there's time, you can mention some of their requests)* And Lord, we pray all of these things in Jesus' name, who taught us to pray: *(lead them in the Lord's Prayer. You'll find it in the margin.)*

Our Father who art in heaven, hallowed be thy name. Thy Kingdom come, Thy will be done in earth as it is in heaven. Give us this day our daily bread and forgive us our debts as we forgive our debtors. Lead us not into temptation, but deliver us from evil. For thine is the Kingdom, the Power, and the Glory forever, AMEN.

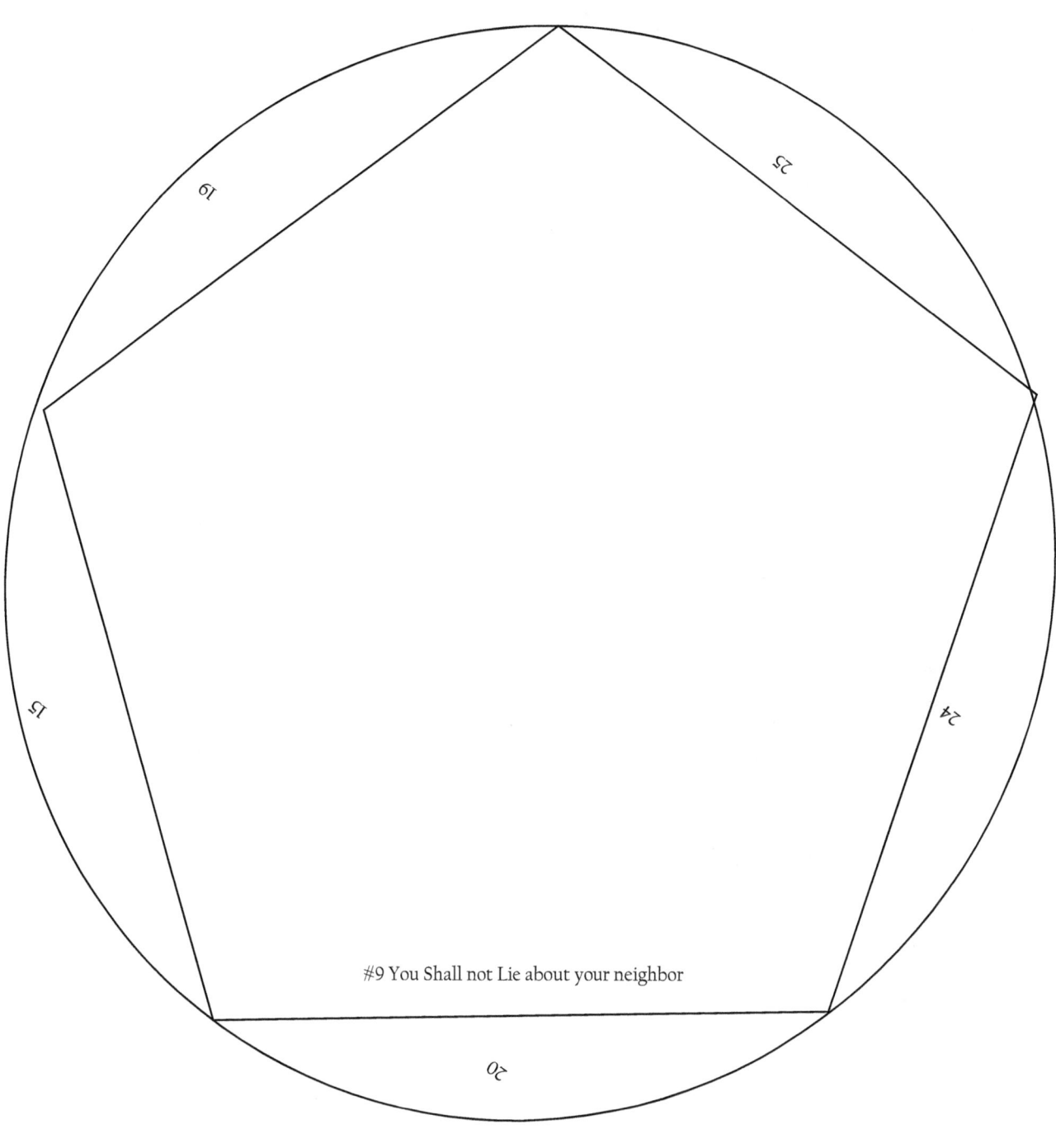

#9 You Shall not Lie about your neighbor

Who is Lying?

Here are some other ideas for your truth/lie statements

1. My favorite color is _____
2. My favorite toy is _____
3. My favorite ice cream is _____
4. The last movie I saw was _____
5. My best friend's name is _____
6. My favorite song is _____
7. I know how to   _____
8. My favorite animal is_____
9. Yesterday I went _____
10. What did you have for breakfast today?
11. What color is your bedroom?
12. What color is your mom's car?
13. The best gift you got for you birthday or Christmas?
14. My phone number is _____
15. I like to _____

Jesus, Teach Me How to Pray
A Year in The Lord's Prayer and other Bible Basics

Unit 12: The Greatest Commandments & The 10 Commandments
Week 8: We Can't Want Our Neighbors Things

Lesson Overview

Most of us know "Joshua fought the battle of Jericho." For six days the Israelites walked around the city, and on the seventh, they walked around it seven times. The walls fell down, and the army took over Jericho. Most don't realize that God had commanded the Israelites to completely destroy everything they found in Jericho. The Bible says they burned the town completely, but it wasn't long before one man's disobedience became evident. Achan (Ake-an) kept a beautiful robe and some silver and gold. No one knew until they decided to go attack Ai (I). What should have been an easy battle, was a terrible loss. When the leaders asked God why He didn't go with them, they discovered Achan's sin. Achan said he coveted the beautiful things. While we won't share the end of the story with the kids, perhaps you'd like to know that Achan was stoned to death as punishment for his sin. Coveting is a difficult concept to understand, but whenever we want things that aren't ours bad enough that we're willing to steal, lie, trick and disobey, we are covetous.

KEY PHRASE: We Should Never Want Our Neighbors' Things

SETTING UP THE LESSON   5-7 Minutes

I want some!
Supplies: M&M's

PRESENTING THE LESSON   5-10 Minutes

Scripture: Joshua 6 & 7

MAKING IT REAL TO KIDS TODAY   *(Choose as many as you have time for)*

Game: Knock down the wall of Jericho   5-10 Minutes
Supplies: small light boxes (cereal boxes will work), lots of scrap paper/newspaper

Craft: Bloom Ball-Part 8   10 Minutes
Supplies: Copies of the final page of this lesson, crayons or markers, staplers

Memory Verse: Mark 12:30-31 & Exodus 20:17   5-10 Minutes

Song: Go Fish Guy's "The 10 Commandment Boogie"   5-10 Minutes
and/or Lincoln Brewster's, "Love the Lord Your God"

WRAPPING IT UP—SENDING IT HOME   5-7 Minutes

Clean Up Time & Prayer Time

KEY PHRASE: We Should Never Want our Neighbors' Things

SETTING UP THE LESSON   5-7 Minutes

I Want Some
Supplies: M&M's or other small candy (make sure there are no food allergies in your group)

Have several bowls of the candy scattered among where the kids will sit. When they want the candy, tell them they can't have any because it belongs to someone else. (You aren't lying - right now it belongs to YOU)

Ask the kids, "What is one thing you don't have that your friend has that you really want?" *(Go around the room and give each child fifteen seconds or so to answer.)* What would you be willing to do to get it? *(Allow for random answers.)* Would you take it from your friend? *(Allow for answers.)* What if you found one, and your parents told you to throw it away? *(Allow for answers.)*

If all the kids said they would throw it away, congratulate them and tell them today we're going to hear about a time when one of the Israelites wanted other people's stuff so bad he didn't listen to God. Then move into the lesson. *(without giving the kids the candy)*

If any kids said they would hide it or not throw it away, ask them what they think God would want them to do. *(Allow for answers.)* Tell them today we're going to hear about what God would want them to do.

PRESENTING THE LESSON   5-10 Minutes

Scripture: Joshua 6 & 7

You do not have to read this directly from the Bible
use the story form below or reword it to fit your personality

How many of you know the story of Jericho? *(Allow the kids to share using the following information to fill in the blanks where they miss some of the story)* Jericho was one of the first cities that Israel attacked when they went into the land God had promised to give them. God gave them special instructions. They were going to take seven days to win the city. There were big walls all around the city. On the first day the whole Israelite army was supposed to march all the way around the city. God told Joshua to lead the army around the city once a day for six days. On the seventh day they were supposed to walk around the city seven times and blow trumpets the entire time. After they were done marching seven times, the priests were going to blow long blasts on the trumpet and then the people had to shout. They did what God said, and when the priests blew the trumpets, the walls of the city fell down. The army of Israel easily went into the city of Jericho and set the town on fire. The whole city burned. God told them they had to destroy everything, they weren't allowed to keep anything they found in Jericho.

That's the part of the story that most people know, but do you know what happened after that? *(Allow for answers.)* Soon after they took Jericho, the Israelites went to the city of Ai. They were sure they could win, so they headed into battle. But they were surprised. The people of Ai attacked them, and they couldn't win. The Israelites were very sad. They bowed down to God and prayed and asked God why he didn't help them win the battle.

God told them He couldn't go with them because they didn't obey him. Some of the Israelites had seen things in the city of Jericho that were really nice. They saw things they wanted. And instead of destroying them like God told them to, they took them. A man named Achan finally told the truth. He said that he'd seen some beautiful clothes and a lot of gold and silver. He told Joshua that he coveted the clothes and the gold and silver. Do you know what covet means? *(Allow for answers.)* Covet means that you want something that doesn't belong to you. It means that you want it so bad you're willing to lie, steal or disobey God or your parents to get it.

How many of you would like to have had some of that candy when you came in? *(Allow for answers.)* Did anyone take a piece without asking or after I said we can't have any? *(Allow kids to answer - if no one took one, you can

KEY PHRASE: We Should Never Want our Neighbors' Things

reward them by allowing them to have the candy since they didn't covet - if someone did take the candy, you can choose to not allow them to have the candy - right now anyway - and tell them that just like the whole nation of Israel lost the battle because one person coveted and disobeyed God, all the kids will be affected because only a few didn't follow directions and coveted the candy.)

MAKING IT REAL TO KIDS TODAY *(Choose as many as you have time for)*

Game: Knock Down the Wall of Jericho 5-10 Minutes
Supplies: Small light boxes (cereal boxes will work well), lots of scrap paper

Set up two or more "walls" made of small boxes (If you have more than 20 children in your program, you may want more walls). Make them as large as you can, but make them even.

Divide the kids into even teams with older and younger kids on both teams (less than 10 kids per team)

Allow the kids to crumple all the paper into balls. Then when you say, "GO" tell them to start throwing the paper balls at the wall to knock down the wall. The team that knocks down the other team's wall first wins.

The Teaching Moment: Did you have fun knocking down these walls? *(Allow for answers.)* Do you remember the name of the city the Israelites knocked down? *(Allow for answers.)* Right, Jericho! Did they throw things at the wall to knock them down? *(Allow for answers.)* No, they didn't, they marched around the wall and on the seventh day, God knocked the wall down! Do you remember what Achan did when he went into Jericho? *(Allow for answers.)* Achan coveted the things that were in the city of Jericho. That means he wanted them for his own. So he took them! When we think of Jericho, we need to always remember to obey God and never want things that don't belong to us. We have to trust God will provide for us.

Craft: Bloom Ball-Part 8 10-15 Minutes
Supplies: Copies of the final page of this lesson, crayons or markers, staplers, string or yarn

*Today's craft is the last of an eight part craft -
You'll need the section they worked with last week and the section marked "TOP"*

Give each child a copy of the last page of this lesson. Have them draw a picture that will remind them of the commandment listed on the piece and cut out the circle. After they've cut out the circle, have them fold the pieces along the six straight lines near the edges of the circle.

Give them the bottom section of their ball that they've been working on for the last 7 weeks. Then they can match tabs from today's circle with the one marked "BOTTOM". Help them staple these places. (Tabs 14, 18 &19) Alternately, you can attach all the numbers today. If you've saved it till the end and have a number of younger children, you may want to enlist an extra helper.

Next give each child the top part of the ball with their name on it (they finished this a few weeks ago - Be sure there are extra top parts for kids who may not have been in your program during the first 4 weeks). Help them match the remaining tabs to attach the bottom of the ball to the top. (Tabs 21-30) Attach a piece of string or yarn to the top of the ball so the kids can take it home and hang it up. Or you might hang them from the ceiling of your children's area for a few weeks as decoration.

Memory Verse: Mark 12:30-31 & Exodus 20:17 5-7 Minutes

*Love the Lord Your God with all Your Heart and all Your Soul and all Your Mind
and all Your Strength and Love your Neighbor as Yourself. - Mark 12:30-31*

Each week the kids have been reviewing the Mark 12:30-31 verse, so begin by asking them what this verse says. Hopefully they'll be able to repeat this verse without much coaching. If they need help, tell

KEY PHRASE: We Should Never Want our Neighbors' Things

them the first couple of words. After you've reviewed this verse, ask the kids about the 10 Commandments. Ask them how many they know. You can use the numbers as in past weeks if you like.

You shall not want your neighbor's things - Exodus 20:17

1. No other gods except God
2. No idols
3. Don't misuse God's Name
4. Keep the Sabbath Holy
5. Honor your parents
6. Don't Murder
7. Stay True to your marriage
8. Don't steal
9. Don't Lie
10. Don't wish your neighbor's things were yours.

Song: Go Fish Guy's "The 10 Commandment Boogie" and/or Lincoln Brewster's, "Love the Lord Your God" 5-10 Minutes

These are available on CD and most online services as well as on YouTube.

The Teaching Moment: (whichever song you use) God has given us commandments. God didn't give us commandments because He is mean, but because he loves us and wants us to have the best. God knows that if we follow these rules He's given us, we can have a wonderful life. If we can remember these using songs or poems or anything, it will help us follow them and have the life that God wants to give us.

WRAPPING IT UP—SENDING IT HOME 5-7 Minutes

Cleaning Up

We want the children to learn to be responsible, so be sure they help with the clean up, but remind them not to go anywhere, the group is going to talk to God together one more time.

Closing Worship and Prayer

Either gather the children in a circle holding hands or allow them to sit down to pray. If you choose to join hands, remember that it's OK if some children prefer not to join the circle. Just ask them to be respectful of others as they pray and not make any noise. You can always begin your prayer time with a quiet song if you like.

Even though we've finished with the units focusing on the Lord's prayer (or you might be using this as a stand alone series), we're going to continue to use it to pray as we close. If there is time, ask the children if they have any prayer requests. Remember that no prayer is ever too small, however, children will tend to keep going and be "inspired" by other prayer requests, so feel free to stop taking requests and tell them they can say anything that didn't get said out loud quietly to God themselves while you're praying. You may close with your own prayer or use the one below for help.

If you need some guidance for your prayer, you can use this:

Father in Heaven, we are thankful that you love us. Forgive us for all the times we want other people's stuff. Help us to be happy with what you give us and not covet. Lord, bless all the things these kids have mentioned as prayer requests today. *(if there's time, you can mention some of their requests)* And Lord, we pray all of these things in Jesus' name, who taught us to pray: *(lead them in the Lord's Prayer)*

Our Father who art in heaven, hallowed be thy name. Thy Kingdom come, Thy will be done in earth as it is in heaven. Give us this day our daily bread and forgive us our debts as we forgive our debtors.
Lead us not into temptation, but deliver us from evil. For thine is the Kingdom, the Power, and the Glory forever, AMEN.

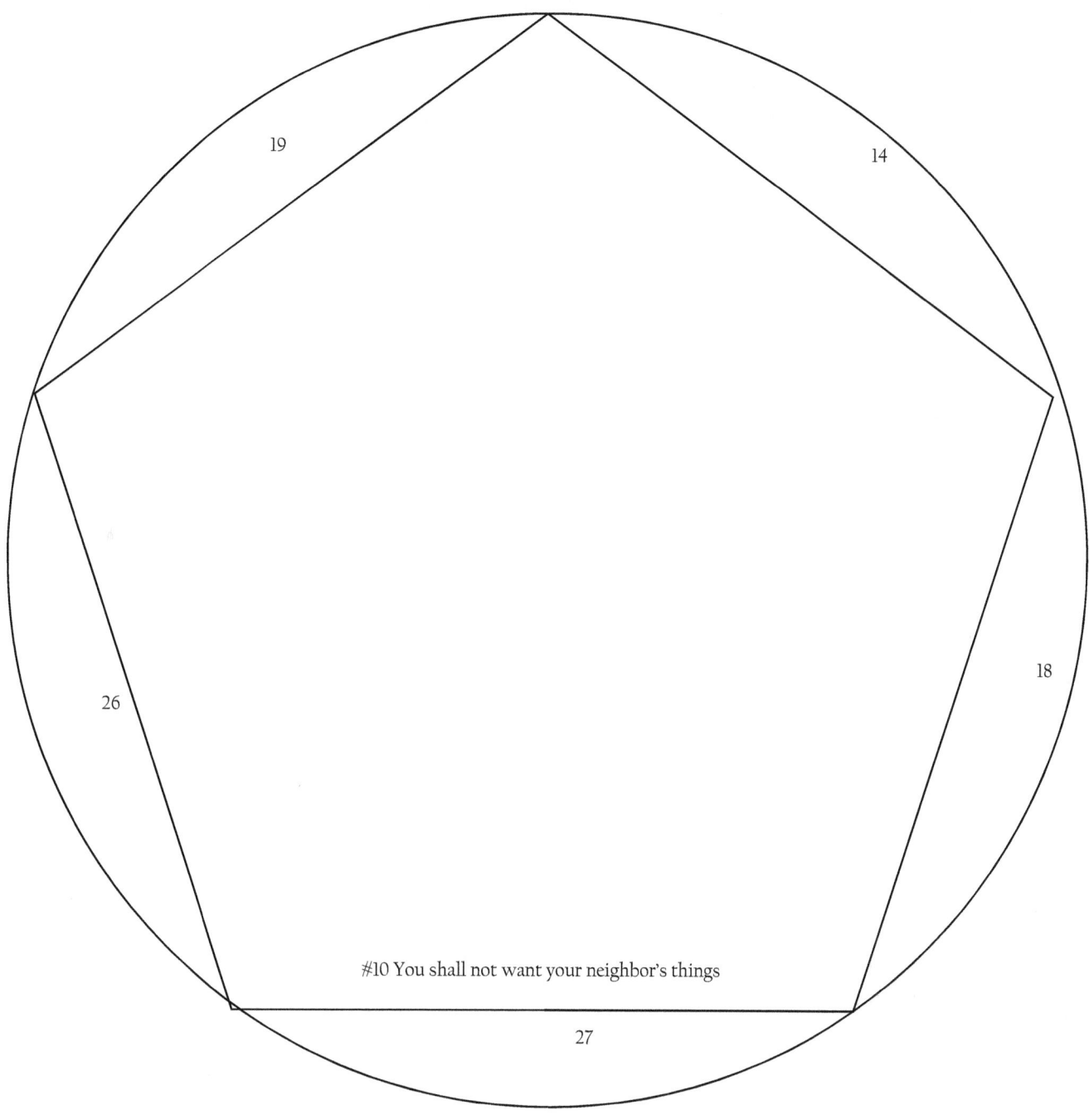

#10 You shall not want your neighbor's things

Jesus, Teach Me How to Pray
A Year in The Lord's Prayer and other Bible Basics

Unit 13: Holidays of the Church
World Communion Sunday

Lesson Overview

This week's lesson is designed for use on World Communion Sunday (the first Sunday in October). Should you be using this on some other Sunday or a mid-week program, just skip the references you'll find to World Communion. God gave us communion so we would never forget the beautiful gift He gave us in the death of Jesus Christ. There are fewer activities with today's lesson so you can take time to reenter the service early and celebrate or observe the sacrament with the rest of the church.

KEY PHRASE: Jesus said, 'Do this and Remember Me'

SETTING UP THE LESSON   10-15 Minutes

Game: Memory   5-10 Minutes
Supplies: Copies of Cards on last pages– Copy on heavy cardstock or print on paper and glue to construction paper.

Introduction: Reminders   5 Minutes

PRESENTING THE LESSON   10-15 Minutes

Scripture: Matthew 26:26-30 & 1 Corinthians 11:23-32

MAKING IT REAL TO KIDS TODAY   *(Choose as many as you have time for)*

Craft: Picture to color   5-10 Minutes
Supplies: Copies of the coloring page, crayons, markers, or colored pencils

Illustration: Observing/Partaking in Communion

WRAPPING IT UP—SENDING IT HOME   5 Minutes

Clean Up & Prayer Time

NOTE TO LEADERS FOR CHURCHES USING THIS DURING CHILDREN CHURCH DURING REGULAR WORSHIP: If you plan to take the children back into the sanctuary during communion, you'll find a letter at the end of this lesson that you can adapt to your congregation. Send it home with the kids the week before this lesson so parents will be aware their children are reentering the service and will be prepared to take their kids for the sacrament if they so choose. If your church doesn't allow kids to take communion until they've been confirmed, explain this during the lesson time.

Be sure to talk to the pastor about what time would be good to bring them in and make him or her aware of the fact you'll be reentering. If you're using this in a mid-week program or Sunday School, try to present it just before a Sunday when Communion will be celebrated so that the children better understand what is happening the next time they see the congregation take part in the Lord's Supper.

KEY PHRASE: Jesus said, "Do this and Remember Me"

SETTING UP THE LESSON   5-10 Minutes

Game: Memory
Supplies: Copies of the cards at the end of the lesson printed on heavy cardstock of on paper pasted onto construction paper

The old fashioned Memory Game. Divide the group into teams to make matches or allow students to play as individuals. Team one picks two cards. If they match, they get to keep the match and choose again, if not, the cards are turned back over, and Team two picks two cards. This process continues until all the matches are made. If it goes quickly, you might want to play again.

If you'd like them to be bigger, these squares have been created so you can also enlarge them at 200% and they'll fit 1 picture (2 cards) per sheet on an 8.5 x 11 sheet of paper.

The Teaching Moment: Sometimes remembering is hard, but we have many things in our everyday lives that help us. *The introduction to the story will be this game's teaching moment.*

Introduction to the Story: Reminders
Supplies: Rainbow, Cross, Wedding ring, Christmas Tree (a picture would work), Small loaf of uncut bread or a piece of tortilla bread, grape juice,

Ask the kids, "Do you have a hard time remembering things sometimes?" *Let them answer, then respond honestly with something like:* "Me too, that's why I like using objects to help me remember. Look at some of these things, and let's see if you can figure out what they help me remember."

Show the kids each item and ask them what they think of when they see it. They may not know the original reason these were set up as reminders, so be sure to give them the real meaning of the symbol. If you have another that's your favorite, add it to the list. Save the bread and juice for last.

Rainbow: After the great flood when Noah God saved by telling him to build an ark, God gave a rainbow as a promise to never flood the earth again

Cross: Jesus' death for our sins

Wedding Ring: Like a ring goes on forever, marriage is meant to go on forever.

Christmas Tree: It's green to remind us that God's love goes on forever

Then bring out the bread and juice—ask them what it reminds them of. Just get their opinion, don't go into too much detail. After they respond say, "Those are good answers. Let's look and see what the Bible says about it."

PRESENTING THE LESSON   5-10 Minutes

Scripture: *Matthew 26:26-30 & 1 Corinthians 11:23-32*
You do not have to read this directly from the Bible— use the story form below or reword it to fit your personality

Today we're going to talk about the bread and the juice. These are some of the most important reminders the church uses. In fact some churches use them every week, and almost every church uses them at least one time every month. Do you know what we call it when we have the bread and the juice during church? *(Allow for answers.)* It is called Communion *(ask them to repeat the word Communion)* or the Lord's Supper *(ask them to repeat those words).* Some churches call it the Eucharist *(have the kids repeat U—ka—wrist),* but here we usually call it _____ *(insert the word your church uses).*

It all started about 2000 years ago. On the night before Jesus died on the Cross, he had a very special meal with his disciples. Do you remember who the disciples were? *(Leave a moment for answers.)* The disciples were twelve men who were Jesus' closest friends. He spent all His time teaching them the things they needed to know to help everyone become a Christian.

The night before the religious leaders hung Jesus on a cross, Jesus and his friends gathered in an upstairs room to celebrate Passover. God created Passover as a reminder, too. It helped the Jews remember when God

KEY PHRASE: Jesus said, "Do this and Remember Me"

helped them escape from Egypt.

I think God must like things that help us remember Him. While the disciples were eating this special meal, Jesus got up and took the bread they were eating, *(pick up your bread)* and He ripped it apart. *(tear the bread apart)* He said to them, "Every time you eat bread, I want you to remember me. Yes, every time you eat bread, I want you to remember that my body was ripped apart like this bread so you can go live with God someday. *(then set the bread back down).* A little later Jesus picked up his cup. *(pick up the juice)* Jesus was drinking wine or grape juice, and when He picked it up, He held it up high. *(raise up the cup)* He probably held His hand over the top of the cup *(cover the cup with your hand)* and said a prayer thanking God for it. Then He said to His disciples, "Every time you get together and drink this juice, I want you to remember me. I want this juice to remind you of my blood that you'll see when I die."

Jesus kept saying, "Do this and Remember Me." It was important to Him that His disciples remembered the real reason He died on a cross. And it's important that we remember too. Every time there is communion in a church, we should be very quiet and think about the things we do wrong, because if we never did anything wrong, Jesus wouldn't have had to die on a cross.

At this point take a moment and describe your mode of taking communion so the kids will have an idea of what's going to happen.

For example, if your church uses intinction (dipping the bread in the cup): Here we take communion by intinction *(Allow the kids to repeat that after you: in - 'tinc - shun).* That means we take a piece of the bread and dip it into the cup. When you get the piece of bread, the pastor will say, "The body of Christ broken for you." Then you hold onto the bread until you get in front of the juice, and as you dip your bread into the juice, you should make sure your fingers don't go in the juice since everybody has to use the same juice. The pastor will say, "The blood of Christ shed for you." Then you eat it. When you eat it, you should make sure you remember why you are eating it. Do you remember why we celebrate communion? *(Allow for answers.)* The bread reminds us of Jesus' body broken on the cross, and the juice reminds us of His blood.

*Today is WORLD COMMUNION SUNDAY - Do you know what that means *(wait for answers)*? That means all over the world, in England and Germany and Africa and even in China and some Middle Eastern countries where people can be punished if they worship Jesus, churches are celebrating communion. In a few minutes we're going to go and watch the adults take communion. We have to be very quiet because a lot of them will be trying to pray, and they'll be remembering what Jesus did for them. When we go into the sanctuary, we're all going to sit together in one place and watch quietly.

NOTE FOR THE LEADER: *Please don't "serve" the kids communion today. We'll take them into the worship area so they can do that. There are two reasons we don't. First, not all parents (or churches) want their kids to have communion until they are older. Second, in most churches only the clergy can bless the bread and juice so that it may be served. This isn't because they are better or more holy, but only to make sure that Communion is always served in a manner worthy of Christ so that the message Paul shared in our Corinthians reading for today is followed.*

MAKING IT REAL TO KIDS TODAY

Craft: On the following pages you'll find a coloring picture in case you have extra time and need to give the kids something to do.

WRAPPING IT UP—SENDING IT HOME

Cleaning Up

We want the children to learn to be responsible, so be sure they help with the clean up.

Closing Worship and Prayer

Before you pass out the coloring sheets, gather the children in a circle holding hands or allow them to sit

KEY PHRASE: Jesus said, "Do this and Remember Me"

down to pray. If you choose to join hands, remember that it's OK if some children prefer not to join the circle. Just ask them to be respectful of others as they pray and not make any noise.

As you close, and if there is time, ask the children if they have prayer requests. While no prayer is ever too small, children will tend to keep going and be "inspired" by other prayer requests, so feel free to stop taking requests and tell them they can say anything that didn't get said out loud quietly to God themselves while you're praying. You may close with your own prayer or use the one below for help. End with "we pray as Jesus taught us to pray" and the Lord's prayer.

If you need some guidance for your prayer, you can use this:

Father in Heaven *(Allow kids to repeat after each phrase)*. Thank you that you give us ways to remember the important things about Jesus. Thank you for the rainbow so we can remember your promise never to flood the whole earth again. Thank you for our cross jewelry so we can remember that Jesus died for us and thank you for communion. Help us to always remember that Jesus' blood was shed and His body was broken so we can go to Heaven someday. Thank you for loving us. Please bless all of these things the kids have asked prayer for today *(or you can mention them individually)* as we pray the way you taught your disciples to pray: *(end with the Lord's Prayer - if you're doing this near the beginning of your Lord's Prayer series have the kids repeat after you one line at a time - if it's more than 10 weeks in, have them say the prayer with you.)*

Our Father who art in heaven, hallowed be thy name. Thy Kingdom come, Thy will be done in earth as it is in heaven.
Give us this day our daily bread and forgive us our debts as we forgive our debtors.
Lead us not into temptation, but deliver us from evil. For thine is the Kingdom, the Power, and the Glory forever, AMEN.

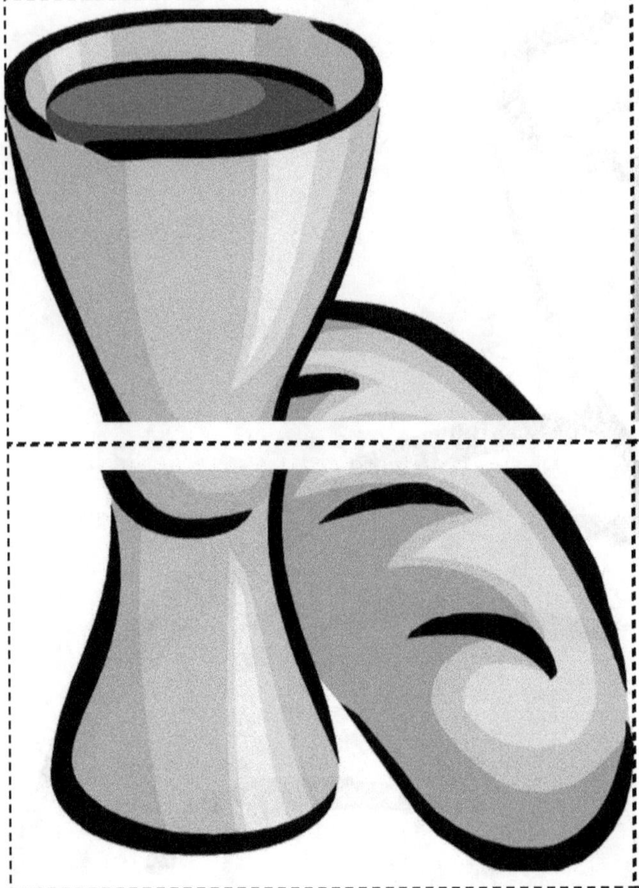

Royalty free pictures found at www.clker.com

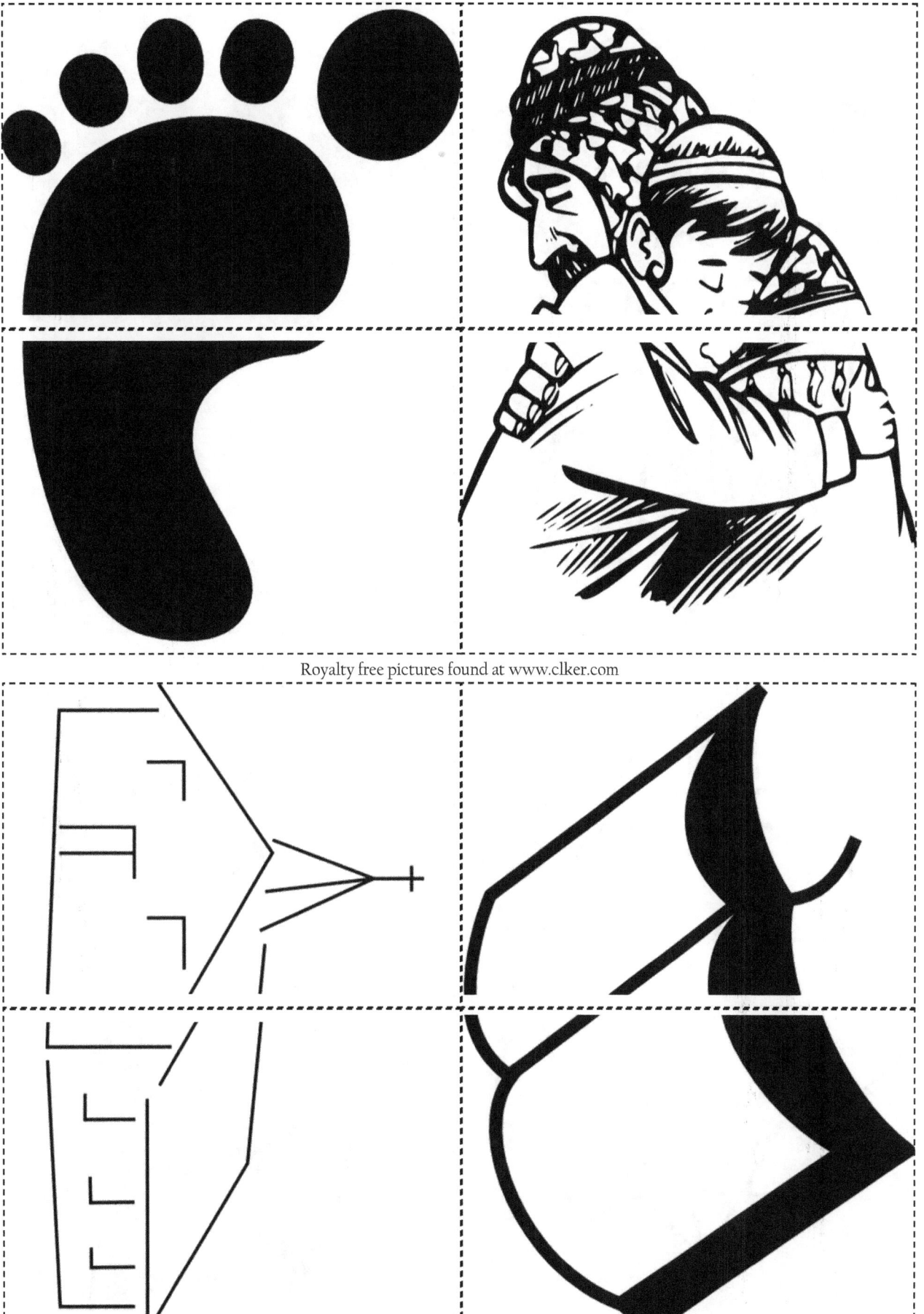

Royalty free pictures found at www.clker.com

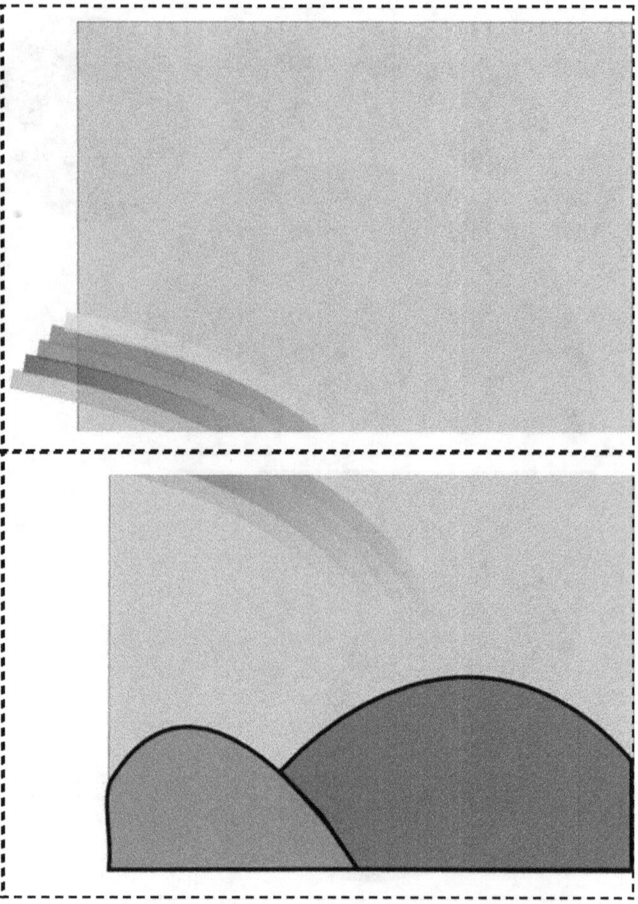

Royalty free pictures found at www.clker.com

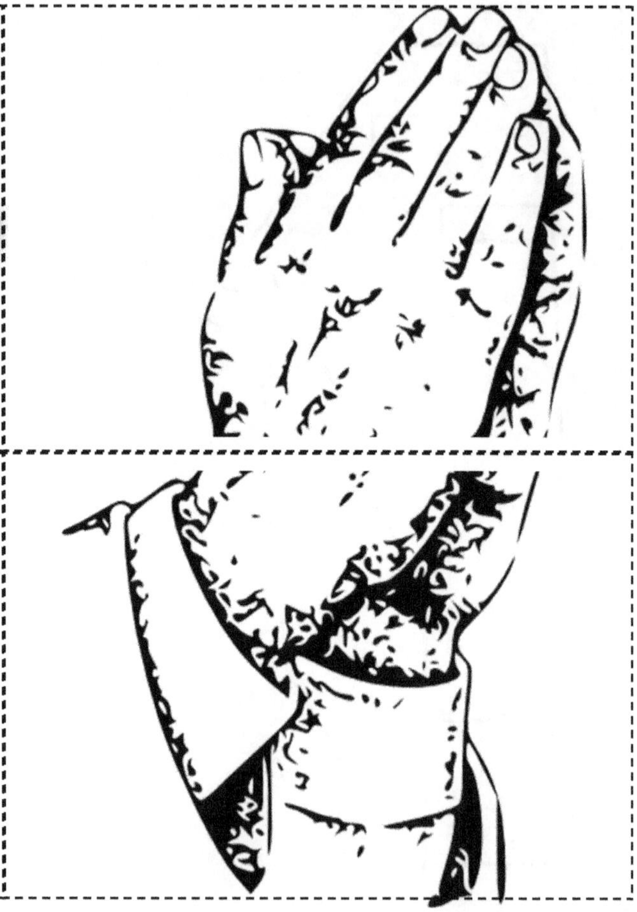

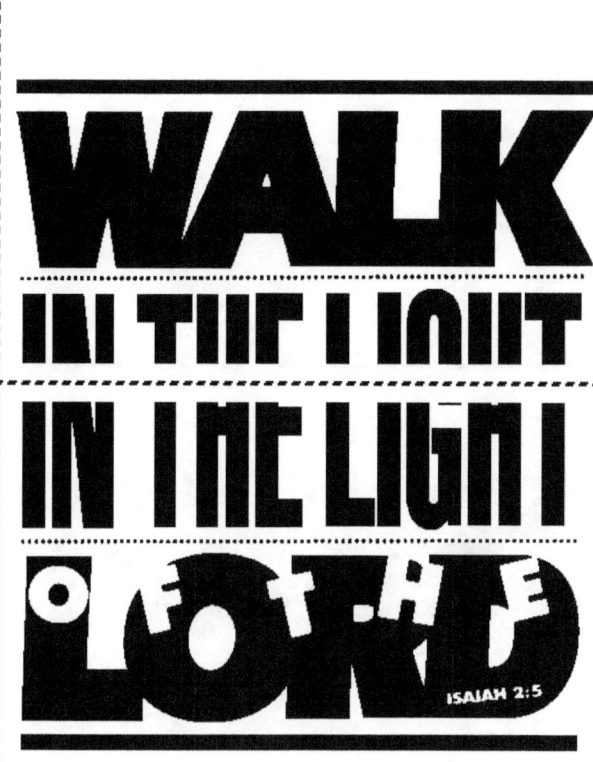

Royalty free pictures found at www.clker.com

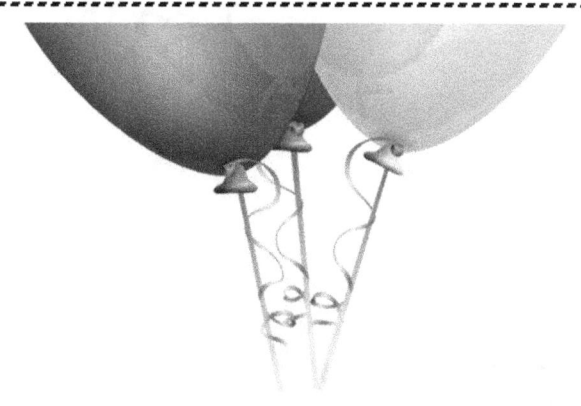

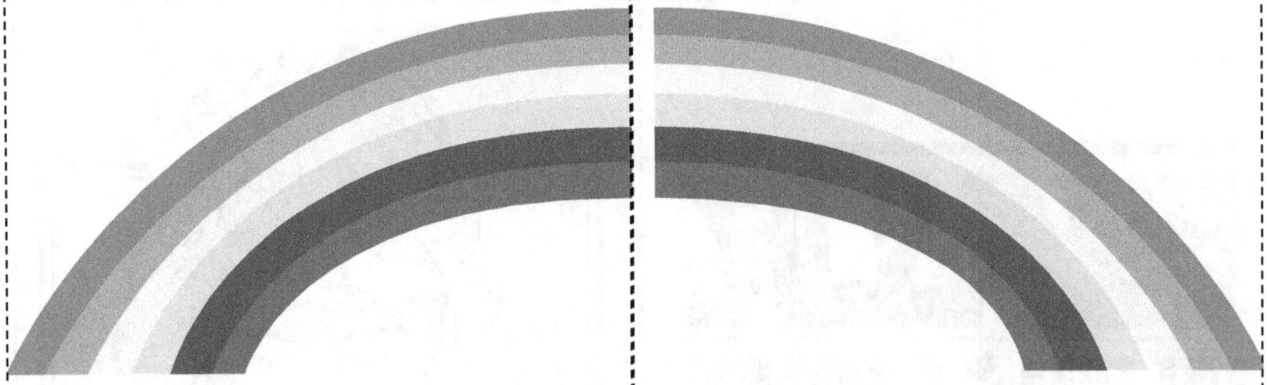

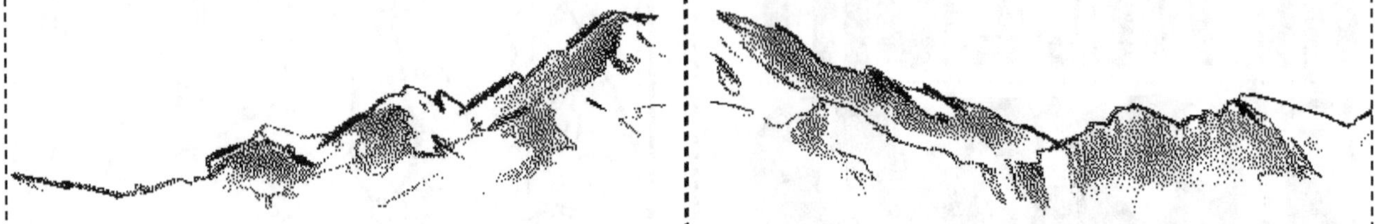

Sample Letter You Can Send to Parents the Week Before you use this lesson
if you will be reentering worship to participate in Communion

Dear Parents,

Next week we have a special lesson for the children in our Children's Ministry. We're going to help them understand Communion a bit better, and at the end of the lesson, we'll bring the kids into the sanctuary in time for Communion.

Since the first Sunday in October is World Communion Sunday, we'll be celebrating communion together. Your child will be learning about the reason we celebrate communion and will be welcome to celebrate communion during worship. However, we understand that some parents prefer their children reach a certain age or maturity before they partake of this Holy Sacrament. To that end we will keep all of the children in one pew, and when you walk by, if you'd like them to take communion, simply stop and motion for them to go with you. Otherwise, you may come back and take them back to sit with you AFTER you are served.

If you choose to have your child not take communion, you shouldn't feel bad or pressured. If you are worried about questions he or she might ask about other kids who do take it, feel free to tell them that in your family you wait until you're older or share any honest answer about why you feel they should wait. Be sure that they know this is OK with God because He has asked you to watch over them and take care of them for Him. If you have any other questions about kids and communion, please be sure to talk to the Pastor or Children's Ministry Leaders. They'll be happy to discuss it with you.

Thanks so much for allowing us to help your kids grow closer to Jesus!

The Children's Ministry Staff

Page intentionally left blank for printing and copying purposes

Jesus, Teach Me How to Pray
A Year in The Lord's Prayer and other Bible Basics

Unit 13: Holidays of the Church
Thanksgiving

Lesson Overview

The Psalms are full of words of thanksgiving to the Lord. In fact, scripture praises our Creator over and over again. Today we're going to focus on thanking God and remembering that He will never stop loving us.

KEY PHRASE: Give Thanks to the Lord—His Love Endures Forever

SETTING UP THE LESSON   5-7 Minutes

Introduction: The First Thanksgiving

PRESENTING THE LESSON   5-10 Minutes

Scripture: Psalm 136:1-16 & 23-26
Supplies: Bibles (the same version for all children) or copies of the second page of the lesson

MAKING IT REAL TO KIDS TODAY   *(Choose as many as you have time for)*

Game: Thankerchief   5-10 Minutes
Supplies: Handkerchief

Craft: Cornucopia Craft   10-15 Minutes
Supplies: Copies of the last page of this lesson (or you could use the template at: http://www.dltk-holidays.com/thanksgiving/mcornicopia.htm scissors, glue, and something to color with. Another Option would be to get Cornucopia kits from Oriental Trading Co. (www.orientaltrading.com)

Song: "Forever" by Chris Tomlin   5 Minutes
Supplies: Download a copy of this song from Amazon, iTunes, or other music service

WRAPPING IT UP—SENDING IT HOME   5-7 Minutes

Clean Up Time & Prayer Time

KEY PHRASE: Give Thanks to the Lord—His Love Endures Forever

SETTING UP THE LESSON

5-7 Minutes

Introduction: The First Thanksgiving

Begin by asking the children what they know about Thanksgiving. Allow them to share their knowledge without interrupting, then share this bit of info:

Almost 400 years ago, only the American Indians or Native Americans lived in the United States. In fact, even where this church sits, there were no houses. But in 1620 that changed forever. 100 people got on a ship in England. Do you know the name of the ship? *(Allow for answers.)* It was the *Mayflower*. There were men and women and even kids and babies on the ship. It took them three months to get the ship from England to America. Do you know how long three months is? *(Allow for answers.)* Three months is about the amount of time you have off from school in the Summer or the time between when school starts and Thanksgiving. When they got here, it was already the beginning of winter, so it was pretty cold. There were no stores to buy food or clothes. There were no houses for them to live in. They had to build them from trees they cut down.

Do you know why the pilgrims came to America? *(Allow for answers.)* The pilgrims wanted to worship God. They didn't want the king to tell them how to pray and worship. That first winter in America was very hard. At least forty-six people died because of disease, lack of good food, and the extremely cold winter. The next summer, the Wampanoag Tribe helped the pilgrims plant gardens and grow crops. One year after they settled they set aside three days of prayer to thank God for all the food he provided, and they invited their new Indian friends. The records from that three day celebration tell us that fifty-three pilgrims and approximately ninety Indians ate the feast together.

Thanksgiving was first celebrated to honor God and thank Him for all their blessings. Even though the winter had been hard and so many people had died, the pilgrims worshipped and thanked God. As people who worship God, it's important we keep our focus on God during the holiday.

So let me ask a few questions: How many will watch the parade on TV or go to a parade around here on or around Thanksgiving? *(Allow for answers)* What's more important: God or Parades? *(Allow for answers.)* God is more important.

What will you eat on Thanksgiving? *(Allow for answers.)* What's more important: God or Turkey? *(Allow for answers.)* God is more important that even the best Thanksgiving dinner.

How many days do you get off from school? *(Allow for answers.)* What's more important: God or days off from school? *(Allow for answers.)* Even though we like to have some days off, God and thanking Him are always more important.

PRESENTING THE LESSON

5-10 Minutes

Scripture: Psalm 136:1-16 & 23-26
Today you'll want to read this pretty much exactly as written.

The Bible records many times when people were thankful for everything God did. The Psalms are full of prayers the Israelites prayed and songs they sang. Today we're going to read Psalm 136 together. It's a Psalm of Thanksgiving. *(Consider passing out Bibles and allowing kids to follow along and read the line that the Israelites would read. You could alternately copy the next page.)*

This is a Psalm the Israelites read together. The priest said a line and then the Israelites would repeat another line. I'll pretend to be the priest, and you all can pretend to be the Israelites. Here's your line: His Love Endures Forever. After every line I say, you say, "His Love Endures Forever." *(Have them repeat that line several times and say it very loud and with meaning. After they can say it well, begin the Psalm—read your part with enthusiasm.)*

KEY PHRASE: Give Thanks to the Lord—His Love Endures Forever

¹ Give thanks to the LORD, for he is good.
His love endures forever.
² Give thanks to the God of gods.
His love endures forever.
³ Give thanks to the Lord of lords:
His love endures forever.
⁴ to him who alone does great wonders,
His love endures forever.
⁵ who by his understanding made the heavens,
His love endures forever.
⁶ who spread out the earth upon the waters,
His love endures forever.
⁷ who made the great lights--
His love endures forever.
⁸ the sun to govern the day,
His love endures forever.
⁹ the moon and stars to govern the night;
His love endures forever.
¹⁰ to him who struck down the firstborn of Egypt
His love endures forever.
¹¹ and brought Israel out from among them
His love endures forever.
¹² with a mighty hand and outstretched arms
His love endures forever.
¹³ to him who divided the Red Sea asunder
His love endures forever.
¹⁴ and brought Israel through the midst of it,
His love endures forever.
¹⁵ but swept Pharaoh and his army into the Red Sea;
His love endures forever.
¹⁶ to him who led his people through the desert,
His love endures forever.
²³ to the One who remembered us in our low estate
His love endures forever.
²⁴ and freed us from our enemies,
His love endures forever.
²⁵ and who gives food to every creature.
His love endures forever.
²⁶ Give thanks to the God of heaven.
His love endures forever.

KEY PHRASE: Give Thanks to the Lord—His Love Endures Forever

MAKING IT REAL TO KIDS TODAY *(Choose as many as you have time for)*

Game: Thankerchief
Supplies: Handkerchief

Arrange chairs in a circle or have children sit in a circle on the floor. Pass a "thankerchief" (handkerchief) around the circle, as everyone recites this poem (be sure to go over the poem a few times with the kids before you begin the game):

Thankerchief, thankerchief, around you go --
Where you'll stop, nobody knows.
But when you do, someone must say,
What they are thankful for this day.

When the poem ends, the player holding the "thankerchief" must say, out loud, one thing for which he or she is thankful. This continues until everyone has had a turn to say something or time runs out

The Teaching Moment: Even when it's not Thanksgiving, we must remember to always give thanks to God because He is good, and His love endures forever.

Craft: Cornucopia
Supplies: Copies of the last page of this lesson (or you could use the template at: http://www.dltk-holidays.com/thanksgiving/mcornicopia.htm scissors, glue, and something to color with. Another Option would be to get Cornucopia kits from Oriental Trading Co. (www.orientaltrading.com)

Tell the children they will be creating a cornucopia. Invite them to say cornucopia a few times. Have the children color and cut out the items on the coloring sheet. Help them cut between the Xs on the horn of plenty. This slit will allow them to slide one or two of the vegetables under the front of the cornucopia giving it a three-dimensional look.

The Teaching Moment: A Cornucopia is a symbol of abundance and blessings. Sometimes it's called a horn of plenty because that's what abundance means—to have plenty. It's always filled with fruit and vegetables to remind us that God has provided good things for us and we should be thankful. It reminds us that God is good and His love endures forever.

This cornucopia is for you and your family to remember all God has given you so you can remember to be thankful for everything God gives us and remember that every gift comes from God.

Song: "Forever" by Chris Tomlin
Supplies: Download this song from Amazon, iTunes, or other music service

Play the first verse for the children then stop the song. Ask: Do you hear some familiar words in this song? *(Allow for answers.)* It repeats His love endures forever many times. So, I'm going to play it again, and every time it says, "His love endures forever," we will sing it with them. *You might also encourage them to sing the chorus:*

Forever, God is faithful

Forever, God is strong

Forever, God is with us

Forever

The Teaching Moment: What does it mean that "God's Love Lasts Forever?" *(Allow for answers.)* It means just that. God's love will never end. No matter what we do, God will never stop loving us. .

WRAPPING IT UP—SENDING IT HOME 5—7 Minutes

Cleaning Up

We want the children to learn to be responsible, so be sure they help with the clean up.

Closing Worship and Prayer

Gather the children in a circle holding hands or allow them to sit down to pray.

Today instead of prayer requests we'll allow the children to be thankful. You will start the prayer *(see below if you need help)*, and then someone in the circle will say "Thank you, God, for ____." Each time someone is thankful, have the kids all say together, "His Love Endures Forever." Ask your oldest student to start after you say what you are thankful for. After kids have had a chance to say thanks to God, close with "we pray as Jesus taught us to pray" and the Lord's prayer. Let the kids know that it's time for them to start saying the prayer with you instead of after you, so you won't wait on them to repeat this week.

(If the Holiday lessons are the first you're teaching, you can omit the Lord's Prayer or have the children repeat "The Lord's Prayer" one line at a time after you)

If you need some guidance for your prayer, you can use this:

Father in Heaven, thank you for all the good things you give to us. "Thank you God for _____," *(Lead the kids in "His love endures forever." After all children have had a chance to share say:)* We pray all this in Jesus' name as He taught us to pray,

Our Father who art in heaven, hallowed be thy Name. Thy Kingdom come, thy will be done on earth as it is in heaven. Give us this day our daily bread and forgive us our debts as we forgive our debtors.
Lead us not into temptation and deliver us from evil. For thine is the kingdom and the power and the glory forever, Amen.

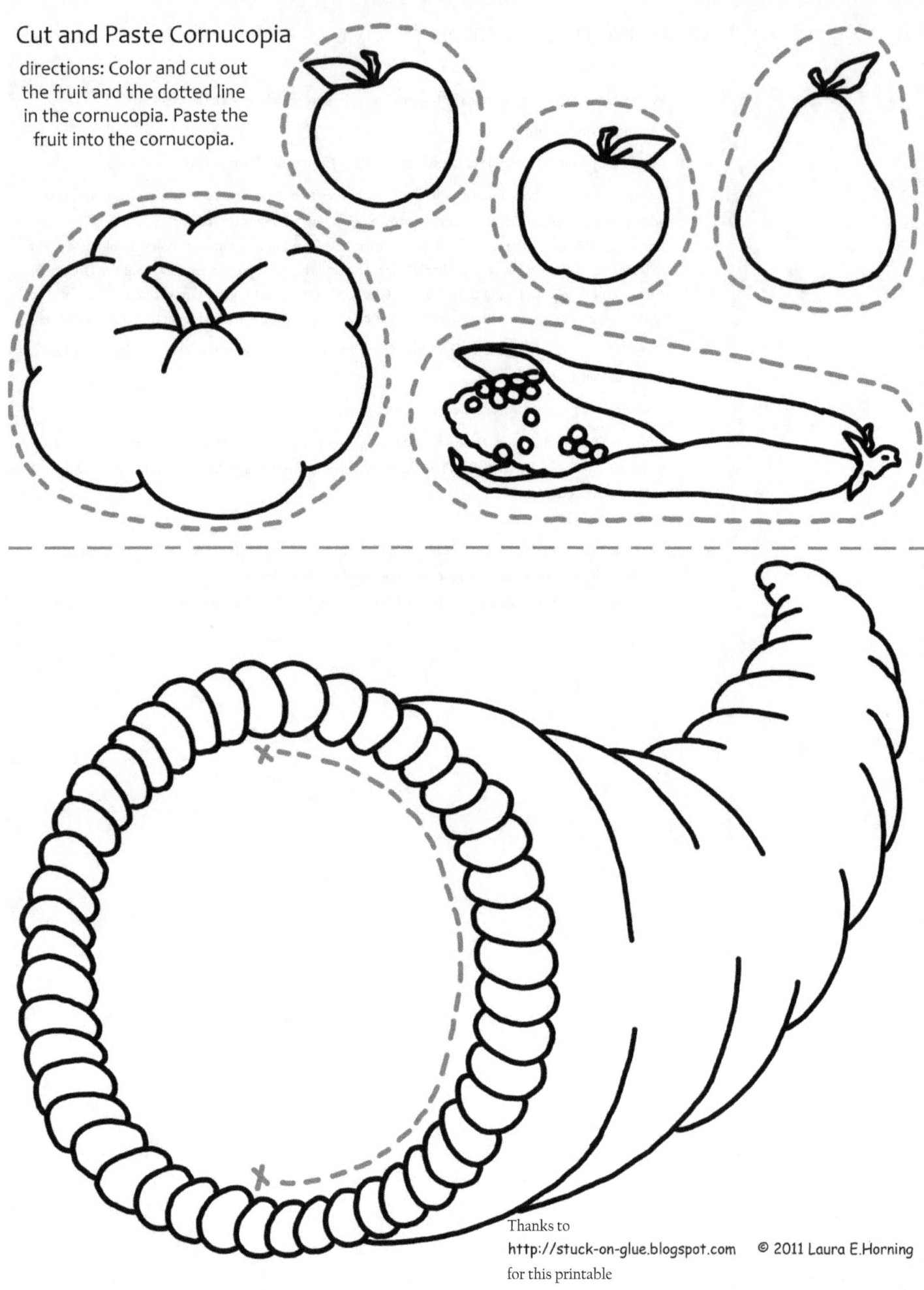

Jesus, Teach Me How to Pray

A Year in The Lord's Prayer and other Bible Basics

Unit 13: Holidays of the Church
Advent 1: What is Advent?

Lesson Overview

This lesson is designed for the first Sunday in Advent—Four Sundays before Christmas

The Word "Advent" comes from Latin "ad" meaning 'to' and "vent" meaning 'come'—So Advent means "to come." We celebrate Advent as a four week period of preparation as we wait for Jesus "to come." The celebration climaxes at Christmas as we remember the "advent" of Christ's coming to earth more than 2000 years ago; however, as Christians, we also look to Christ's second "advent" when he returns at the end of the world. This may seem like an abstract concept to most of our kids, especially the youngest ones; however, by using some illustrations, we can help them understand the basics of the season.

KEY PHRASE: We Celebrate Advent Because Christ is Coming

SETTING UP THE LESSON   5-7 Minutes

Introduction: Making Preparations
Supplies: A basket full of all kinds of cleaning supplies, grab a broom and a sweeper from the church if you can. Include a feather duster, clean sheets, sponges, toilet brush, etc.

PRESENTING THE LESSON   5-10 Minutes

Scripture: Matthew 24:30-25:13

MAKING IT REAL TO KIDS TODAY   *(Choose as many as you have time for)*

Craft: Advent Wreath   15-20 minutes
Supplies: Glue, heavy styrofoam plates (one per child), purple or red votive candles (4 per child) *(traditionally, churches use three purple and one pink)*, white votive candles (1 per child), scraps of green garland, white berries or very small white bulbs or beads, red berries or very small red bulbs or beads (several of each for each child), a set of advent readings or suggested scriptures and "TO PARENTS" letter at the end of the lesson for each child. OPTIONAL: glue gun

Song: "O Come all Ye Faithful"   5 Minutes

Game: Fill it Up   10 Minutes
Supplies: For every two to eight children: 1 bucket, 1 quart container with a piece of masking tape about 2 inches from the top, $1/8$ cup measure or small scoop, 1 towel

WRAPPING IT UP—SENDING IT HOME   5—7 Minutes

Clean Up Time & Prayer Time

KEY PHRASE: We Celebrate Advent Because Christ is Coming

SETTING UP THE LESSON 5-7 Minutes

Introduction: Making Preparations

Supplies: A basket full of all kinds of cleaning supplies, perhaps a broom and a sweeper from the church. Include a feather duster, clean sheets, sponges, toilet brush, etc.

Bring out your basket of supplies. Sounding exasperated, explain to the students that you've been very busy preparing for company. Take out each item and tell what you did with each one: "I dusted my whole house, I scrubbed the bathroom including the toilet, I swept all the floors, got all the dust bunnies out from under the bed, changed the sheets, washed the rugs . . . . Etc." Ask the kids if they've ever worked really hard to get something ready. *(Allow for answers.).* Discuss what kinds of things they did.

Say (*or in your own words*): "We prepare for important people and guests to come. We get everything ready for them. Today we're going to talk about Advent. Can you say "Advent?" *(Encourage children to repeat.)* Advent starts four Sundays before Christmas, and the word means "to come." During Advent we prepare for Christmas, the day we celebrate Jesus' "coming" to earth. Since the word Advent means "to come," it's also a time to celebrate Jesus' promise to someday "come" back to earth. Today we're going to read some verses from the Bible that help us remember that Jesus promised to come back someday.

PRESENTING THE LESSON 5-10 Minutes

Scripture: Matthew 24:30-25:13

You can read this directly from the Bible, use the story form below, or reword it to fit your personality.
If you read this, open your Bible so the children know it came from there.

Jesus told His disciples that someday He would come back to earth. He said an angel would blow a trumpet (*if possible have your helper blow a trumpet here*), then Jesus would gather all the people who follow Him and take them to heaven. He warned them that no one would ever know exactly when He would come back. He told them it would be a big surprise.

Then Jesus told them to make sure they were ready, "prepared," for the time when He would come again. He said to them, "If you knew someone was going to break into your house, you would keep an eye on your stuff so the robber wouldn't be able to take it." We have to keep an eye out for things that help us see Jesus just like you would keep an eye out for a robber if you knew he was coming.

Jesus told them another story about a bride getting ready for her wedding. Do you know what a wedding is? *(Allow for answers—make sure they know that the groom is the man at the wedding, the woman is the bride and the bridesmaids are the bride's friends who are in the wedding).* Jesus said there were ten bridesmaids waiting for the groom to come. The groom took longer than they expected, so the bridesmaids had to wait a long time. Since they didn't have batteries or flashlights back then, all ten had oil lamps so they'd have some light when it got dark . *(You might want to have an oil lamp to show the kids.)*

Five bridesmaids brought extra oil with them. *(You could have a jar of oil to show them.)* They didn't want to run out. But the other five bridesmaids weren't prepared. They didn't bring any extra oil.

What do you think happened to all the bridesmaids' lamps since the groom took so long? *(Allow for answers—hopefully someone will say they ran out of oil).* Eventually, they ran out of oil. The first five took their oil jars, filled up their lamps, and had plenty of light. But the other five had to leave to buy oil.

Can you guess what happened while they were gone? *(Allow for answers.)* While they were buying more oil, the groom showed up. The first five bridesmaids went into the wedding with the groom, and they shut the door. *(Demonstrate slamming a door.)* Jesus called them wise. When the other five returned, they discovered they'd been left behind. They missed their friend's wedding because they weren't prepared.

This story is one of Jesus' parables. That means it's a story about earthly things that has a heavenly meaning.

KEY PHRASE: We Celebrate Advent Because Christ is Coming

In this parable, Jesus is the groom, the church is the bride, and we are all the bridesmaids. Jesus told this story to help us see that we need to always be prepared for the day when He comes back. What do you think we need to do to be ready when Jesus returns? *(Allow for answers—affirm anything remotely correct)* First we have to ask Jesus to be our Savior and then follow Him. We need to learn what the Bible says and pray often. We also need to tell others about Jesus so they'll be prepared when Jesus comes too.

MAKING IT REAL TO KIDS TODAY *(Choose as many as you have time for)*

Craft: Advent Wreath   15-20 Minutes

Supplies: Supplies: Glue, heavy styrofoam plates (one per child), purple or red votive candles (4 per child), *(traditionally, churches use three purple and one pink)*, white votive candles (1 per child), scraps of green garland, white berries or very small white bulbs or beads, red berries or very small red bulbs or beads (several of each for each child), a set of advent readings or suggested scriptures and "TO PARENTS" letter at the end of the lesson for each child. OPTIONAL: glue gun

You may want to cover the tables as this craft could use a lot of glue. Have the kids place the four candles around the outside edge of the plate at the 12, 3, 6 & 9 o'clock positions and the white candle in the center. Then let them put glue over the rest of the plate and cover it with the green garland. They can add the white and red berries, bows and/or bulbs as desired.

The Teaching Moment: This is an advent wreath. We use an advent wreath to help us prepare for Christmas and Jesus' coming. Every day, you and your family can light one of the candles to remind you that Jesus is the light of the world. What color are the candles? *(Allow for answers. Depending on the colors you chose, use the script below.)*

Purple (or Red or Navy) is the color of a King, so the purple candles remind us that Jesus is a King.
If you added a pink candle: Pink is the color of peace and hope, so during the third week of advent we light a pink candle.

The white candle reminds us that Jesus is holy. Do you remember what holy means? *(Allow for answers.)* Yes, holy means special and perfect for God. Then we put the green garland around. The green reminds us that just like a pine tree, God's love goes on forever. What do you think the white berries *(or ornaments or bows)* remind us of? *(Allow for answers.)* Just like the white candle they represent the holiness of Jesus, and the red decorations remind us of the blood of Jesus because he died for us.

Game: Fill it up   7-10 Minutes

Supplies: For every two to eight children: 1 bucket, 1 quart container with a piece of masking tape about 2 inches from the top, $1/8$ cup measure or small scoop, 1 towel

Line the children up from oldest to youngest. Have them count off 1—2 -1—2 to divide them into teams. (Or 1, 2, 3 etc. if you need to divide them into three or more teams). Give each team a bucket about 1/2 full of water. Set an empty pitcher/container on the other side of the room.

Each team member must dip their measuring cup into their bucket and carefully walk to the quart container and dump the water in. Then they must WALK back to their bucket and hand the scoop to the next team member. The team that fills their container to the line wins. Place the tape lower if you have less time. If water is spilled, it must be cleaned up with the towel before the next person takes their turn. Tip: Tell them not to fill their scoop to the top to avoid taking time to clean up.

The Teaching Moment: Today we had fun filling up our containers. We worked together to try to get them full. Do you remember what happened to the bridesmaids that didn't keep their lamps full of oil? *(Allow for answers.)* Those bridesmaids weren't ready when the bridegroom came, and they got left out of the party. This is a fun game, but it can help us remember that we have to be prepared for Jesus. Much like we tried to keep the water off the floor, we don't want to rush through our preparations. Followers of Jesus need to stay prepared and always be ready for Jesus.

KEY PHRASE: We Celebrate Advent because Christ is Coming

Song: "O Come all Ye Faithful" (1st Verse) — 5 Minutes or less

You can sing this with our without accompaniment or use a track of some kind. So that the children learn one song, we'll use the same one each week. If there's another carol you'd rather use feel free. Team teachers should communicate with the other leaders so the same carol is used throughout the season. If you have some time, you might want to define a few words or review them: Ye, Faithful, Triumphant, Bethlehem, Adore

> O Come, All Ye Faithful, Joyful and Triumphant
> O Come, Ye, O Come, Ye to Bethlehem
> Come and behold Him, Born the King of angels
> O come let us adore Him, O come let us adore Him,
> O come let us adore Him, Christ the Lord

WRAPPING IT UP—SENDING IT HOME   5-7 Minutes

Cleaning Up

We want the children to learn to be responsible, so be sure they help with the clean up, but remind them not to go anywhere, the group is going to talk to God together one more time.

Closing Worship and Prayer

Gather the children in a circle holding hands or allow them to sit down to pray. If you choose to join hands, remember that it's OK if some children prefer not to join the circle. Remind them to be respectful of others as they pray and not make any noise.

As you close, and if there is time, ask the children for prayer requests. Remember that no prayer is ever too small, however, children will tend to keep going and be "inspired" by other prayer requests, so feel free to stop taking requests and tell them they can say anything that didn't get said out loud quietly to God themselves while you're praying. You may close with your own prayer or use the one below for help. They should now be able to pray "The Lord's Prayer" with you instead of repeating after you. *(If you are starting with this Bonus section and haven't done any of "the Lord's Prayer" lessons yet, have the children repeat "The Lord's Prayer" after you.)*

Use this prayer or pray spontaneously:

Father in Heaven. We praise you that you promised to return to earth someday. Help us to be ready for that day. Lord, bless each of these children and the requests that they have today. *(If there's time, you can mention some of their requests).* And Lord, we pray all of these things in Jesus' name, who taught us to pray: *(Lead them in the Lord's Prayer.)*

Our Father who art in heaven, hallowed be thy Name. Thy Kingdom come, thy will be done on earth as it is in heaven.
Give us this day our daily bread and forgive us our debts as we forgive our debtors.
Lead us not into temptation and deliver us from evil. For thine is the kingdom and the power and the glory forever, Amen.

Remind the kids to take home their advent wreaths and send home the "TO PARENTS" letter about advent (plus advent readings if they are available).

TO THE PARENTS

Each year, advent begins four Sundays before Christmas. Today, your children learned that the word Advent means "to come," and that we celebrate advent to prepare. Not only do we prepare for Christmas, celebrating Jesus' FIRST coming, we also use this time to prepare for Jesus' promised SECOND coming.

Today your children made an advent wreath as their craft. Advent wreaths are used worldwide to help Christians "prepare" during advent.

A wreath is round, and this one is green reminding us that Jesus' love is never ending like a circle and an evergreen tree. It might include red and white decorations. The red reminds us of the blood of Christ that was shed for us on the cross, and the white is a symbol of His holiness. We use purple, red, or navy blue candles as a reminder that Christ is King because they are royal colors. The candle in the middle is white. We call it the Christ candle and will light it on Christmas Eve. Again, its white color symbolizes perfection, purity, and holiness.

Every day you can use your advent wreath to prepare for Christmas. Read scripture or advent readings as you light the candles. During the first week, you'll light one candle, and each week you'll add a new one.. These will help keep your focus on Christ as you move closer to the Christmas celebration. With the materialism that the world has brought to this Christian holiday, it can be difficult to keep your family centered on the birth of Christ, the gift of His advent on earth and the promise of His return, but our prayer is that this token of reminders will aid in keeping Christ in your Christmas celebration.

Notes

Jesus, Teach Me How to Pray
A Year in The Lord's Prayer and other Bible Basics

Unit 13: Holidays of the Church
Advent 2: A Time for Surprises

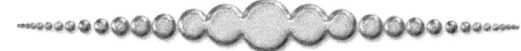

Lesson Overview

This lesson is designed for the second Sunday in Advent

Three Sundays before Christmas

As we prepare for Christmas, the kids will relate well to surprises. Christmas is a time full of them. This week we'll look at Elizabeth and Zechariah, the parents of a baby who would one day become John the Baptist. Elizabeth and Zechariah were way past the age of normal new parents. But an angel came and told Zechariah that he would become a father. Zechariah had a difficult time believing God could do such a thing and ended up not being able to talk until after John was born. As we share with the children, we want to help them see that God is a God of surprises.

KEY PHRASE: God is a God of Surprises

SETTING UP THE LESSON   5-7 Minutes

Introduction: Surprise
Supplies: Option 1: Surprise Muffins (recipe in lesson) OR Option 2: Plastic eggs and M&Ms or skittles

PRESENTING THE LESSON   5-10 Minutes

Scripture: Luke 1:25 & 57-80

MAKING IT REAL TO KIDS TODAY   (Choose as many as you have time for)

The Rest of the Story   1 Minute
John as an adult: Why is he in the Christmas Story —Matthew 3

Game: Scavenger Hunt   5-10 Minutes
Supplies: All the items on the Scavenger Hunt list or copies of the coloring sheet at the end of the lesson

Craft: Surprise Guy   15 Minutes
Supplies: OPT 1 & 2: Craft foam; Hershey kisses, glue
 OPT 1: colored electrical tape, decorative string, scissors, small wiggly eyes (2/child)
 OPT 2: ribbon, paper punch, scissors, medium wiggly eyes (2/child)

Song: "O Come all Ye Faithful" (1st Verse)   3 Minutes

WRAPPING IT UP—SENDING IT HOME   5-7 Minutes

Clean Up Time & Prayer Time

KEY PHRASE: God is a God of Surprises

SETTING UP THE LESSON   5-7 Minutes

Introduction: Give them a surprise

Choose one of the two surprises below and have it hidden so the kids can't see it. Begin by saying, "I have something for you today! It's a surprise. What do you think it might be?" *(Allow for answers.)*

OPTION 1: *Surprise Muffins*—I brought (or <name> baked) little muffins for us to eat today. *Mini-muffins might work best for your group. Be aware of gluten allergies, etc. If you anticipate they'll want a drink to go with their muffin, have it ready so the helper can pour while you continue with the lesson. As they begin to find the surprise inside, move to The Teaching Moment*

Surprise in the Middle Muffins Recipe

1 1/2 cups flour	2 teaspoons baking powder
1/2 teaspoon salt	1/2 teaspoon baking soda
1/4 cup sugar	1/4 cup butter, melted
2 eggs	1 cup milk
1/2 teaspoon vanilla	strawberry jam (or your favorite flavor)

Preheat oven to 375 degrees. Place paper liners in muffin tin. Melt butter and set aside to cool. In one medium bowl, mix together dry ingredients. In another medium bowl, mix together eggs, milk, vanilla and cooled melted butter. Add dry ingredients to wet mixture and mix until well blended. Fill each muffin cup about 1/4 full. Place one spoonful of strawberry jam into each muffin, pushing down with end of spoon. Muffins will rise over the jam to make a surprise inside. Bake for 15-20 minutes. Cool before eating.

OPTION 2: *Plastic eggs with a few M&M's or skittles inside.* - SAY: I brought a Christmas Surprise for us to share today! *(Pass out eggs—you should get some feedback that this IS NOT a Christmas surprise.)* But, of course, it IS a Christmas surprise. You weren't expecting anything like this for Christmas, were you? *(Allow for responses.)* Then it's a surprise, and it's almost Christmas time. So it must be a Christmas surprise. Go ahead and open the egg, there's another, better surprise in there. *Move to The Teaching Moment*

The Teaching Moment: Did you enjoy your surprise? Most people like surprises, at least every now and then. Did you know that God loves to give us surprises? In the Bible there are many stories about God giving surprises. Today we're going to hear about a really good surprise God gave one of his followers.

PRESENTING THE LESSON   5-10 Minutes

Scripture: Luke 1:25 & 57-80
*You do not have to read this directly from the Bible—
use the story form below or reword it to fit your personality*

Zechariah was a very old man. He was as old as *(name a 70-90 year old man who most of the kids in your class will be familiar with—or use 'your grandpa' 'great-grandpa' as an example, but be aware that some grandparents are relatively young).* His wife's name was Elizabeth. She was old, too. Elizabeth and Zechariah didn't have any children. Zechariah was a priest in the temple. Do you know what a priest is? *(Allow for answers.)* A priest is kind of like our preacher. He takes care of the temple, like the church, and helps people understand God's word. One day when Zechariah was in the most special place in the temple, an angel named Gabriel came to talk to him. Can you say Gabriel? *(Encourage them to say Gabriel.)* Gabriel, the angel, came to visit Zechariah while he was working in the temple. While Gabriel was there, he told Zechariah something that surprised him. In fact, it was such a surprise that Zechariah thought he was a little crazy. The angel told Zechariah that his wife Elizabeth was going to have a baby! Can you believe it?! What a surprise! A lady as old as Elizabeth was going to have a baby!

There was one problem, though. Zechariah didn't totally believe the angel. After all, what the angel said seemed impossible. Zechariah asked Gabriel, "How can I believe you?" So Gabriel told Zechariah, "Well, from

KEY PHRASE: God is a God of Surprises

now on you won't be able to say anything. You won't be able to talk for at least nine months." Does anyone here know how long nine months is? *(Allow for answers.)* Nine months is longer than from now to Christmas. Nine months is how long you are in school every year. That's how long Gabriel told Zechariah he wouldn't be able to talk. And sure enough almost immediately, Zechariah couldn't talk anymore.

For nine whole months Zechariah couldn't talk. The entire time he and Elizabeth waited for their child to be born, Zechariah had to use signs so people could understand him.

Finally, Elizabeth, as old as she was, had her baby. All of the people were waiting to hear what Zechariah would name his new son. Back then the dad picked the name for the baby, and the whole town gathered to hear the name. Everyone expected him to name the baby Zechariah or his father's name. Since Zechariah still couldn't talk, Elizabeth told the crowd, "We're going to name the baby John." But all of the people couldn't believe it. They were sure the baby would be named after his dad or grandpa or something.

Are any of you named after your mom or dad or grandma or grandpa? Do you have the same name as one of them? *(Allow for answers.)* No one believed Elizabeth, so they gave Zechariah something to write on, and sure enough, Zechariah wrote, "JOHN." *(You might want to have a clipboard or whiteboard handy and write JOHN.)* Everyone was really surprised, but they were even more surprised when all of a sudden Zechariah could talk. After nine months of complete silence, Zechariah was able to speak. And the first thing he did was praise God!

Zechariah had a lot of surprises. What were some of his surprises? *(Allow for answers—you can accept other answers if they are part of the story, but here are four obvious ones if they need help)*

1. An angel named Gabriel came to talk to him.
2. He found out he and his wife were going to have a baby even though they were very old.
3. When he didn't believe Gabriel, he couldn't talk.
4. He was able to talk again after his son was born.

MAKING IT REAL TO KIDS TODAY *(Choose as many as you have time for)*

The Rest of the Story: Why is the story of John's Birth part of the Christmas Story? 1 Minutes
From Matthew 3

Some people wonder, "Why do we hear John's story when we are celebrating Christmas?" Do any of you know about John or know what John did when he grew up? *(Allow for answers.)* John was Jesus' cousin. He was born just six months before Jesus. When he became an adult, he followed God. He traveled around the Jordan River telling people that God's Kingdom was near. Do you remember last week we talked about being prepared? It was John's job to prepare people for Jesus. He had to tell them to get ready because God was coming. So John's story is an important part of the Christmas story. Because just like Jesus had a special purpose—He came to be our Savior, God sent John to be Jesus' messenger.

Game: Scavenger Hunt 7-10 Minutes
Supplies: OPTION 1—Physical Hunt: Several of each item from the list at the end of this lesson and a bag or basket for each team to hold their loot.
OPTION 2—Small Room Hunt: Copies of the coloring page at the end of the lesson

OPTION 1: Before the kids come to your teaching area, hide enough of the items on the list at the end of this lesson so there is one for each team of 2-6 kids. Have a basket/bag for each team to put their "loot" in. Plus one box per team with enough little pieces of candy for each team member to have 2.

Divide the kids up into teams of 2-6. Balance teams with older and younger kids spread between all teams. Give each team a list of items (see final page of this lesson or create your own list). Instruct kids to find all the items on the list. All the items need not be hidden. Some might be ones you already use each week. Hide the surprise boxes. The first team to find all the items wins.

OPTION 2: Pass out copies of the coloring sheet. Let each child decide what the seven colors are. Encourage them to find the hidden message.

KEY PHRASE: God is a God of Surprises

The Teaching Moment: This game (or coloring sheet) is full of surprises. Things were hidden in places you never expected. Life is like that. It's full of all kind of surprises. God likes to give us surprises, too. We just have to trust Him.

Craft: Surprise Guy Ornament   15 Minutes
Supplies: OPT 1 & 2: Craft foam; Hershey kisses, glue
                OPT 1: Colored electrical tape, decorative string, scissors, small wiggly eyes (2/child)
                OPT 2: Ribbon, paper punch, scissors, medium wiggly eyes (2/child)

OPT 1: Cut craft foam into 1"-2" squares. Give each child 3 squares. Cut a piece of decorative string about 5 inches long. Create a loop with the string and attach it to the point between sides 1 & 2 on square B using a small piece of electrical tape. Next, attach square A to square B on sides 1 & 2 with a 1"-2" piece of electrical tape. Then attach square C to square B on sides 3 & 4 with a 1"-2" piece of electrical tape. Glue two wiggly eyes on Square A as shown below. When you pinch the "cheeks" of the "Surprise Guy" his mouth will open. Put a Hershey Kiss inside.

OPT 2: Cut craft foam into 2"-3" squares. Pre-punch 3 squares for each child. Punch small holes in the foam on Square A sides 1 & 2; Square C sides 3 & 4 and all four sides of Square B. Cut a piece of decorative string about 6 inches long. Create a loop with the string and attach it to the point between sides 1 & 2 on square B through 2 holes near the top. Give each child a piece of ribbon about 18 inches long. Now use the ribbon to attach square A to square B on sides 1 & 2. Then attach square C to square B on sides 3 & 4. Be sure to put the ribbon through the last few holes twice. Glue two wiggly eyes on Square A as shown above. When you pinch the "cheeks" of the "Surprise Guy" his mouth will open. Put one or two Hershey Kisses inside.

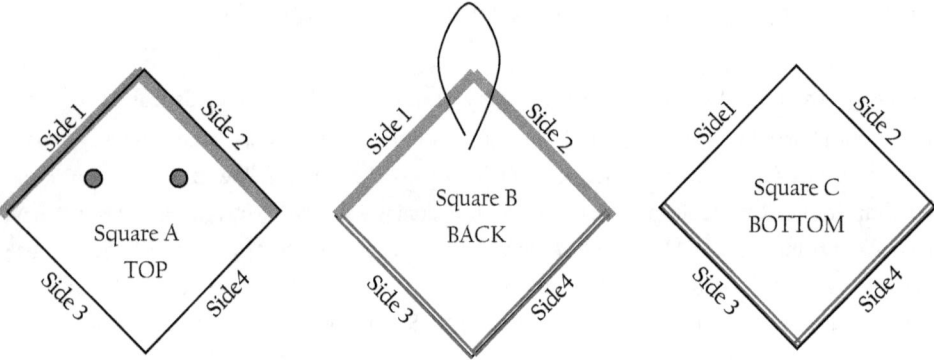

The Teaching Moment: This is a fun little ornament you can hang on your Christmas tree. We made it to remind us that just like this little guy has a surprise inside, God has surprises for us. Just like Zechariah and Elizabeth, sometimes when we think things are impossible, God will surprise us and do something amazing.

Song: "O Come all Ye Faithful" (1st Verse)   5 Minutes or less

You can sing this acapella, with piano or guitar, or use a track of some kind. We're using the same song all four weeks of advent. So, if you're team teaching check with the other leader(s) to ensure you use the same one. If you have some time, you might want to define a few words or review them: Ye, Faithful, Triumphant, Bethlehem, Adore

KEY PHRASE: God is a God of Surprises

O Come, All Ye Faithful, Joyful and Triumphant
O Come, Ye, O Come, Ye to Bethlehem
Come and behold Him, Born the King of angels
O come let us adore Him, O come let us adore Him, O come let us adore Him, Christ the Lord

WRAPPING IT UP—SENDING IT HOME   5-7 Minutes

Cleaning Up

We want the children to learn to be responsible, so be sure they help with the clean up, but remind them not to go anywhere, the group is going to talk to God together one more time.

Closing Worship and Prayer

Gather the children in a circle holding hands or allow them to sit down to pray. If you choose to join hands, remember that it's OK if some children prefer not to join the circle. Remind them to be respectful of others as they pray and not make any noise.

As you close, and if there is time, ask the children for prayer requests. Remember that no prayer is ever too small, however, children will tend to keep going and be "inspired" by other prayer requests, so feel free to stop taking requests and tell them they can say anything that didn't get said out loud quietly to God themselves while you're praying. You may close with your own prayer or use the one below for help. They should now be able to pray "The Lord's Prayer" with you instead of repeating after you. *(If you are starting with this Bonus section and haven't done any of "the Lord's Prayer" lessons yet, have the children repeat "The Lord's Prayer" after you.)*

Use this prayer or pray spontaneously:

Father in Heaven, we praise you that you are a God of surprises. Thank you for sending Zechariah and Elizabeth's surprise. Help us, Lord, to always believe that you can do anything and remember that sometimes you will surprise us. Help us to tell others about you and your Kingdom. Lord, bless all the things these kids have mentioned as prayer requests today. *(if there's time, you can mention some of their requests)* And Lord, we pray all of these things in Jesus' name, who taught us to pray: *(Now lead them in the Lord's Prayer.)*

Our Father who art in heaven, hallowed be thy Name. Thy Kingdom come, thy will be done on earth as it is in heaven.
Give us this day our daily bread and forgive us our debts as we forgive our debtors.
Lead us not into temptation and deliver us from evil. For thine is the kingdom and the power and the glory forever, Amen.

Scavenger Hunt List

1. Whiffle Ball
2. Christmas Ornament
3. Christmas Plate
4. An Old CD
5. A red plastic (disposable) cup
6. A stuffed animal
7. Three building blocks
8. A Bible
9. Six crayons
10. A surprise box

Notes

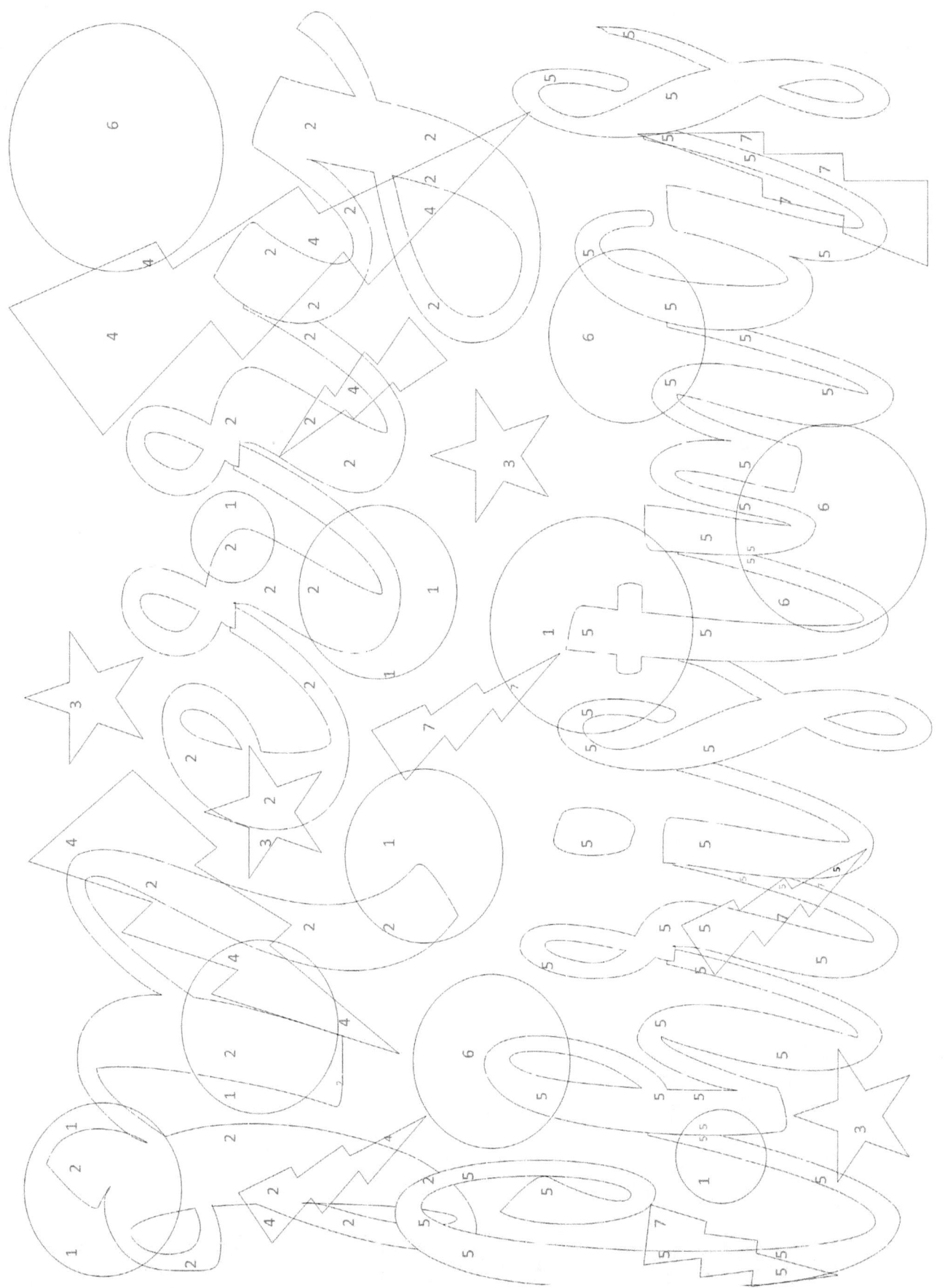

Page intentionally left blank for printing and copying purposes

Jesus, Teach Me How to Pray
A Year in The Lord's Prayer and other Bible Basics

Unit 13: Holidays of the Church
Advent 3: A Time to Prepare to Love & Serve God

Lesson Overview

This lesson is designed for the third Sunday in Advent

2 Sundays before Christmas

As Christians, we need to always be prepared to honor God. The Bible calls Mary and Joseph righteous and highly favored. They obviously lived their lives in such a way as to please our heavenly Father. Their lifestyles caused God to choose them for one of His most important jobs. Today we're going to help the kids be prepared to use every aspect of their lives to honor God.

KEY PHRASE: God Honors Those Who Love and Serve Him

SETTING UP THE LESSON — 5-7 Minutes

Introduction: What Does an Angel Look Like?
Supplies: Paper, pencils and crayons for each child

PRESENTING THE LESSON — 5-10 Minutes

Scripture: Luke 1:26-45 & Matthew 1:18-25

MAKING IT REAL TO KIDS TODAY *(Choose as many as you have time for)*

Game: Keep it Up — 5-10 Minutes
Supplies: A balloon

Craft: Coffee Filter Angels — 15 Minutes
Supplies: Coffee filters; small styrofoam balls or cotton balls; white or gold pipe cleaners; gold or silver craft wedding rings (found in craft stores); narrow red, green or gold ribbon; glue; Optional: hot glue; glue gun;

Illustration: How can we honor God? — 7-15 Minutes
Supplies: Soccer Ball, Handheld Computer Game, Notebook, Silverware, a Toy, picture of a TV, watch, more things kids use everyday

Song: "O Come all Ye Faithful" (1st Verse) — 3-5 Minutes

WRAPPING IT UP—SENDING IT HOME — 5-7 Minutes

Clean Up Time & Prayer Time

KEY PHRASE: God Honors Those Who Love and Serve Him

SETTING UP THE LESSON   5-7 Minutes

Introduction: What Does an Angel Look Like?
Supplies: Paper, pencils and crayons for each child

Ask the kids: "What do you think an angel looks like?" *(Allow answers as you pass out the papers)*

Give the kids about 5 minutes to draw a picture of what they think an angel might look like. Allow them a minute or two at the end to show the group their picture and describe it if necessary.

The Teaching Moment: Even though there are places in the Bible that describe angels, we still don't really know what angels look like. They must have looked different than people because almost everyone in the Bible who saw one was afraid. Today we're going to hear about two people in the Bible who talked to an angel.

PRESENTING THE LESSON   5-10 Minutes

Scripture: Luke 1:26-45 & Matthew 1:18-25
You do not have to read this directly from the Bible— use the story form below or reword it to fit your personality

Today we're going to hear a story that some of you might know very well. The Bible tells us that there was a young girl named Mary who lived in Nazareth. Can you say Nazareth? *(Encourage the children to repeat.)* One day, before Mary was married, an angel named Gabriel came to visit her. Gabriel told Mary she was "highly favored." Do you know what it means to be highly favored? *(Allow for answers.)*. People who have God's favor do their best to obey God. They follow Him and love Him. People who are highly favor try to act in ways that will make God happy. Because Mary loved God and tried her best to please God, God chose her for a special job. God calls people who love Him and serve Him highly favored.

God sent Gabriel to give Mary a special task. Do you think you would be afraid if an angel came to see you? *(Allow for answers.)*. Mary must have been a bit fearful, because after Gabriel told her she was highly favored, he told her not to be afraid. Then Gabriel told her about the special job God had for her. Do you know what Mary's special job was? *(Allow for answers.)* God picked Mary to be the mother of his very own Son.

Mary had promised Joseph she would become his wife during the next year. So, when Joseph found out Mary was going to have a baby, it made him very sad. He knew he wasn't the baby's daddy. So, he thought Mary found someone else to marry. But just when Joseph was about to give up on Mary and break up with her, Gabriel came to visit him, too. He was sleeping when the angel talked to him. Gabriel told Joseph he shouldn't be afraid to take Mary as his wife. The angel explained that God was the baby's Father, and God wanted Joseph to take care of His baby. Like Mary, Joseph trusted God and did exactly what the angel told him to do. He and Mary got married just like the angel told him.

Mary and Joseph both tried to honor God with everything they did. That's why God picked them for this special job and sent Gabriel, so they'd be prepared to do the awesome job of raising His very own Son. When we honor God with our lives, love Him and do what He asks, He'll probably give us special jobs, too. We just have to be ready!

MAKING IT REAL TO KIDS TODAY   *(Choose as many as you have time for)*

Game: Keep it up   10 Minutes
Supplies: A Balloon

Play a little balloon volleyball. A piece of masking tape on the floor can be your net. Divide the kids into two teams. Every time a team lets the balloon hit the ground on their side of the tape, the other team gets a point. At 15 points or when time is up, announce the winner and move to the teaching moment.

The Teaching Moment: Did you have fun trying to keep the balloon in the air? Honor is a lot like keeping this balloon up in the air. In the rules of the game, keeping the balloon up is the right thing to do. Honor is like that. When you try to always do the right thing, you are living a life that honors God.

KEY PHRASE: God Honors Those Who Love and Serve Him

Craft: Coffee Filter Angels   10-15 Minutes
Supplies: Coffee filters (three per student); small Styrofoam balls or cotton balls; white or gold pipe cleaners; gold or silver craft wedding rings (found in craft stores); narrow red, green or gold ribbon; glue
Optional: hot glue; glue gun

What to do:

1. Place a Styrofoam ball or a couple of cotton balls in the middle of one of the coffee filters,

2. Gather the filter around the ball and tie a piece of ribbon around the filter underneath the foam ball to create the head of the angel, tie into a bow. You can decide how long to make the ribbon or how big of a bow to tie.

3. Pinch the second coffee filter in the middle. Dip the pinch in glue and attach it inside the first coffee filter at the place where the head begins.

4. Pinch the third coffee filter in the center. Gather it together and glue it to the back of the angel for her wings. You can optionally attach it with one of the pipe cleaners and add another piece of ribbon over the pipe cleaner if necessary. Curl the ribbon a bit if you have time

5. Glue a craft wedding ring on top of the head of the angel for the halo.

The Teaching Moment: Today we've made an angel. Do you remember what the name of the angel who brought the message to Mary and Joseph? *(Allow for answers.)* We're making these angels to remind us that Gabriel brought Mary and Joseph the message that they were chosen for a special job for God. Do you remember what their special assignment was? *(Allow for answers—Mary was going to be the mother of God's son and Joseph would help raise Him)* Just like we've talked about for the past couple of weeks, Advent is a time to get ready. Gabriel's message helped Mary and Joseph be prepared for Jesus' birth.

Illustration: How Can We Honor God?   7-15 Minutes
Supplies: Soccer ball, handheld computer game, notebook, silverware, a toy, TV or picture of a TV, a watch or clock, more things kids use everyday

There are a lot of ways that even kids can honor God. Use these or other illustrations to help the kids see that every part of their lives can be Christ-filled.

Tell the kids: You can be like Mary and Joseph and honor God in every aspect of your life. No matter what you do, you can show that you love and serve God. I have some things for you to see. I want you to think about how you can use them to honor God.

You can do this as a group exercise, or if you have enough items for each student to have one, pass them out. If you're doing this activity as a group, show the kids each item and ask them how they can use the item to honor God. If you have enough to pass out items to each child, let each one share how they might use the item to honor God. Let other kids help the ones who have a hard time.

Here are some ideas about how they might answer; however, unless an answer is just downright "wrong" accept it and help "mold" it a bit if necessary. Feel free to add more ideas.

Soccer Ball—when kids are playing soccer (or any sport) they can show good sportsmanship, play their best, invite their teammates to church, not be a ball hog . . .

Handheld computer game or game on their phone - Don't play games that have a lot of violence, share with friends, only play when Mom or Dad say it's OK

Notebook— If they consider that it could represent school, they could listen to teachers, be kind to other students, share, invite school friends to church, etc.

Silverware—Pray before dinner, always say "please" and "thank you," try not to make a mess, offer to help clean up after dinner

Toy—*see above suggestions under Video games*

KEY PHRASE: God Honors Those Who Love and Serve Him

> TV - Be sure the shows they watch don't have bad language or violence, allow others to watch what they want without throwing a fit, always ask Mom or Dad before you turn it on
>
> Watch—representing time—take time to pray and read the Bible—take time to listen to parents
>
> *If you use other items, be sure to have some ideas how kids can honor God with them. Everything can be used to honor God. You just have to think about it a bit for some things.*
>
> **The Teaching Moment:** Just like Mary and Joseph honored God, we can honor God. When we do that, God will "favor" us and might even give us an extra special job like He did Mary and Joseph.

Song: "O Come all Ye Faithful" (1st Verse) — 5 Minutes or less

> You can sing this a capella, with piano or guitar or use a track of some kind. This likely will be the third time the kids have sung this same song If you have some time, you might want to go over a few of the hard words: Ye, Faithful, Triumphant, Bethlehem, Adore
>
> O Come, All Ye Faithful, Joyful and Triumphant
>
> O Come, Ye, O Come, Ye to Bethlehem
>
> Come and behold Him, Born the King of angels
>
> O come let us adore Him, O come let us adore Him, O come let us adore Him, Christ the Lord
>
> **The Teaching Moment:** Help the children understand that "faithful" is a good description of Mary and Joseph. Those who honor God can be called faithful. This song is a reminder that the "Faithful" always come to worship Jesus.

WRAPPING IT UP—SENDING IT HOME — 5-7 Minutes

Cleaning Up

> We want the children to learn to be responsible, so be sure they help with the clean up.

Closing Worship and Prayer

> Gather the children in a circle holding hands or allow them to sit down to pray. It's OK if some children prefer not to hold hands. Remind them to be respectful of others as they pray and not make any noise.
>
> If there is time, ask the children if there's anything that they would like you to pray about for them. Remember that no prayer is ever too small, however, children will tend to keep going and be "inspired" by other prayer requests, so feel free to stop taking requests. Remind them they can pray about anything quietly while you're praying. Close with your own prayer or use the one below for help. Either have them pray "The Lord's Prayer" with you or pause so they can repeat. *(If you are starting with this Bonus section and haven't done any of "the Lord's Prayer" lessons yet, you can omit the Lord's Prayer—be sure to pray! Or you can have the children repeat it after you)*
>
> If you need some guidance for your prayer, you can use this:
>
> Father in Heaven, thank you for allowing Mary and Joseph to be parents to Jesus. We want to be like Mary and Joseph and live our lives to honor you like they did. We praise you for preparing Mary and Joseph to know that Jesus was coming. Help us to always be prepared to do what you ask us to do. Lord, bless all of the things these kids have mentioned as prayer requests today *(if there's time, you can mention some of their requests).* And Lord, we pray all of these things in Jesus' name, who taught us to pray: *(now lead them in the Lord's Prayer)*
>
> *Our Father who art in heaven, hallowed be thy Name. Thy Kingdom come, thy will be done on earth as it is in heaven. Give us this day our daily bread and forgive us our debts as we forgive our debtors.*
>
> *Lead us not into temptation and deliver us from evil. For thine is the kingdom and the power and the glory forever, Amen.*

Jesus, Teach Me How to Pray
A Year in The Lord's Prayer and other Bible Basics

Unit 13: Holidays of the Church
Advent 4: Jesus is Born

Lesson Overview

This lesson is designed for the fourth Sunday in Advent

The Sunday Before Christmas

Today the kids will hear the story of Jesus' birth. We'll focus on the fact that the shepherds praised God because He sent this baby. Please don't give the kids a gift this Sunday even though it's the Sunday before Christmas. They'll be learning more about gifts in their next lesson. Some of the kids may have been told that Christmas isn't really Jesus' birthday. They will be correct. We don't know when Jesus was born; however, we know that He WAS born, and He deserves a special day in his honor. The ancients chose December 25 because it was one of the shortest and darkest days in the year. Christmas falls during these short dark days, reminding us of our need for Christ, the true light of the World.

KEY PHRASE: Shepherds Praised God and Told Everyone About Jesus

SETTING UP THE LESSON — 5-7 Minutes

Introduction: Let's Count 'em
Supplies: Popped popcorn—one large bowl for each 3-5 kids; one small empty bowl per child. (Styrofoam is fine)

PRESENTING THE LESSON — 5-10 Minutes

Scripture: Luke 2:1-20

MAKING IT REAL TO KIDS TODAY — *(Choose as many as you have time for)*

Game: I Haven't any Room, and I Just Can't Smile — 10 Minutes

Craft: Paper Chain — 10-15 Minutes
Supplies: Construction paper and tape or glue sticks, markers, pens or pencils, scissors

Song: O Come all Ye Faithful (1st verse) — 5 Minutes

WRAPPING IT UP—SENDING IT HOME — 5-7 Minutes

Clean Up Time & Prayer Time

KEY PHRASE: The Shepherds Praised God and Told Everyone About Jesus

SETTING UP THE LESSON
5-7 Minutes

Introduction: Let's Count 'em
Supplies: Popped popcorn—one large bowl for each 3-5 kids; one small bowl per child.

Put a handful of popcorn in each child's bowl. Give them too many pieces to count at a glance. You might give the older children extra to make it more challenging. Keep a few handfuls for yourself. Have the children count their pieces of popcorn. While they count, interrupt them asking questions about their week and what kind of plans they have for Christmas. Specifically name the kids who are counting a bit quickly. If someone says they are finished, give them more to count. After two or more are finished, use these questions to spur the conversation.

"What would it be like to count this many people?" *(Allow for answers.)*

"Can you count everyone who was in church today *(or last Sunday, if mid-week or before worship?)*" *(Allow for answers.)*

"Can you count all the people who live on your street?" *(Allow for answers.)*

"How about all the people who live in your neighborhood?" *(Allow for answers.)*

"Can you count all the people in your school?" *(Allow for answers.)*

"What about your whole town?" *(Allow for answers.)*

"How long do you think it would take all of you working together to count all the people in our town and the next town?" *(Allow for answers.)*

Today we're going to talk about a time when the leaders of Israel counted every single person in the whole country! *(Move directly into the story/ If there are no food allergies, you can let the children eat the popcorn while you share today's lesson.)*

PRESENTING THE LESSON
5-10 Minutes

Scripture: Luke 2:1-20
You do not have to read this directly from the Bible— use the story form below or reword it to fit your personality

More than 2000 years ago, the people in charge of Israel decided to do a census. Do you know what a census is? *(Allow for answers.)* A census is a time when those in charge count every single person in the whole country. To do this, the leaders in Israel said that everyone had to travel to the city where their grandparents had been born. So Joseph and Mary, who lived in Nazareth, got ready and traveled to Bethlehem because that's where Joseph's grandparents had been born. If they walked, it probably took them about three or four days to get there.

When they arrived, the town was packed. People came from all over because their grandparents had been born there and they had to be counted. Every guest room in Bethlehem was full. The only place left with space to lay down was a stable. Who can tell me what a stable is? *(Allow for answers.)* A stable is a small barn.

And that's where Mary was when her Son was born. So they took the baby and wrapped him in swaddling cloths. Do you know what swaddling cloths are? *(Allow for answers—you might want to have a receiving blanket and a baby doll—that way you can show them the blanket as an example of a swaddling cloth and show them how a baby is swaddled.)* Mary wrapped Jesus tight in the blankets and then laid him in a manger. That would be Jesus' bed while they stayed in the stable. Who can tell me what a manger is? *(Allow for answers.)* A manger is a feeding trough for the animals. It's the place the farmer put oats or corn or hay so the animals had something to eat. And that's what Jesus' first bed was—a feeding trough.

The night that Jesus was born, there were some shepherds in the field outside of Bethlehem. Do you know what shepherds are? *(Allow for answers—you might have a shepherds crook to show the kids)* Shepherds are people who live out in the fields and take care of the sheep.

The shepherds were out there watching the flock. It was quiet and probably very dark. Suddenly, an

KEY PHRASE: The Shepherds Praised God and Told Everyone About Jesus

angel appeared in the sky. It was very bright around the angel, and the shepherds were terrified! What do you think was the first thing the angel said to the shepherds? *(Allow for answers. If they don't know ask them if they remember what Gabriel said to Mary)* The first thing the angel said was, "Don't be afraid." Then he told them, "I have a great message that's going to bring joy to a lot of people. Today in Bethlehem a very special baby was born. He's going to be the Savior of the world. It's the Messiah you've been waiting for all of your lives. When you get to Bethlehem, you'll know it's the right baby because He's going to be swaddled in cloths and sleeping in a manger."

Then, all of a sudden, the sky was full of angels! It was like a whole army. They were praising God. They said, "Glory to God in the highest and here on earth, peace to people who honor God." When the angels left, the shepherds knew they had to go to Bethlehem and see this Baby. So they hurried into Bethlehem and found Jesus just like the angel told them. They praised God for sending Jesus, and after they left Jesus, they told everyone they saw about this baby and the angels.

MAKING IT REAL TO KIDS TODAY *(Choose as many as you have time for)*

Game: I Haven't Any Room, and I Just Can't Smile   10 Minutes

Adapted from a game found at gameskidsplay.net

Have all students stand in a circle. Choose one player to be "it." (You could chose the oldest or the one with next b'day.). "It" walks up to one person in the circle and says, "Do you have a room for me?" and does all he or she can to make the player smile—NO TOUCHING ALLOWED—The child in the circle responds, "I haven't any room, and I just can't smile." If the player does smile, he or she is then it. If the player does not smile, "it" moves to the next player and the game repeats. Play continues for as long as you have time and the kids are interested. Keep track of how many kids don't laugh at each "it". The one with the fewest points at the end could be the winner.

The Teaching Moment: This game reminds us that even though Jesus was God's Son, He wasn't born in an important place. Instead, because the town had so many visitors, Jesus spent His first night on this earth sleeping in a manger, a cow's feeding trough.

Craft: Paper Chain   5-10 Minutes
Supplies: Construction paper and tape, staplers or glue sticks, markers, pens or pencils, scissors

Give each child at least two sheets of different colors of construction paper. If possible run them through a copier first with lines marked about 1" apart. Have the kids cut along the lines or cut the construction paper in 1" strips. On several of the strips (the older kids can write on all of them) have them write words of praise to Jesus. You might write some phrases on a whiteboard so the younger kids can copy. Write things like Praise God, Jesus Lives, I Love Jesus, Awesome God, God is great, Jesus is the Christ, Jesus is Lord. Encourage the kids to think up words of praise themselves. After they've written on a least a few of their strips, show them how to connect the strips into a chain alternating colors using tape, staples, or a glue stick.

The Teaching Moment: The shepherds left Bethlehem praising God and telling everyone about the baby Jesus. This Christmas chain will help you remember to praise God each day. You can take it home and hang it on your Christmas Tree or in your bedroom to help you always remember to praise God.

Song: "O Come all Ye Faithful" (1st Verse)   5 Minutes or less

You can sing this a capella, with piano or guitar or use a track of some kind. This will be the fourth week they'll have sung this song. Hopefully, they'll know most of the words by now. If you have some time, you might want to define a few words or review them: Ye, Faithful, Triumphant, Bethlehem, Adore

KEY PHRASE: The Shepherds Praised God and Told Everyone About Jesus

O Come, All Ye Faithful, Joyful and Triumphant
O Come, Ye, O Come, Ye to Bethlehem
Come and behold Him, Born the King of angels
O come let us adore Him, O come let us adore Him,
O come let us adore Him, Christ the Lord

The Teaching Moment: The word Adore means to worship. The Shepherds came and worshipped Jesus when He was only a few hours old. It's our job to worship/adore Jesus now.

WRAPPING IT UP—SENDING IT HOME   5-7 Minutes

Cleaning Up

We want the children to learn to be responsible, so be sure they help with the clean up, but remind them not to go anywhere, the group is going to talk to God together one more time.

Closing Worship and Prayer

Gather the children in a circle holding hands or allow the children to sit down to pray. If you choose to join hands, remember it's OK if some children prefer not to join the circle. Just ask them to be respectful of others as they pray and not make any noise.

As you close, and if there is time, ask the children for prayer requests. Remember that no prayer is ever too small, however, children will tend to keep going and be "inspired" by other prayer requests, so feel free to stop taking requests. Tell them they can say anything that didn't get said out loud quietly to God while you're praying. You may close with your own prayer or use the one below for help. They should now be able to pray "The Lord's Prayer" with you instead of repeating after you. *(If you are starting with this Advent section and haven't done any of "the Lord's Prayer" lessons yet, you can omit the Lord's Prayer, but be sure to pray! Or you can have the children repeat after you)*

If you need some guidance for your prayer, you can use this:

Father in Heaven, thank you for sending Jesus to earth to save us from our sins. Help us to always praise you like the shepherds praised and tell others about Jesus like they did. Lord, bless all of the things these kids have mentioned as prayer requests today *(if there's time, you can mention some of their requests)*. And Lord, we pray all of these things in Jesus' name, who taught us to pray: *(now lead them in the Lord's Prayer)*

Our Father who art in heaven, hallowed be thy Name. Thy Kingdom come, thy will be done on earth as it is in heaven.

Give us this day our daily bread and forgive us our debts as we forgive our debtors.

Lead us not into temptation and deliver us from evil. For thine is the kingdom and the power and the glory forever, Amen.

Jesus, Teach Me How to Pray
A Year in The Lord's Prayer and other Bible Basics

Unit 13: Holidays of the Church
1st Sunday After Christmas:
Jesus Was an Important Baby

Lesson Overview
This lesson was designed for the Sunday after Christmas

Today we're going to look at the story of the Wise Men's visit to see Jesus. It's important to note there are a couple of misconceptions regarding the Magi. First, they didn't come to the stable. Mary, Joseph & Jesus were in a house by the time the kings arrived. Additionally, we don't know how many Wise Men there were. We do know there were three GIFTS, creating the tradition of three wise men. While these two facts are minor details, it's important that we try not to pass along information that isn't correct to the kids. It's not necessary to make a big deal regarding these facts, just be sure not to perpetuate any myths. Our goal today will be to help the kids see that Jesus was such an important baby that Kings/Wise Men/Magi (these guys are called all three names) from a far away country came to worship Him.

KEY PHRASE: Jesus was Such an Important Baby that Kings Came to Worship Him.

SETTING UP THE LESSON   5-7 Minutes
Introduction: Important People

PRESENTING THE LESSON   5-10 Minutes
Scripture: Matthew 2

MAKING IT REAL TO KIDS TODAY   *(Choose as many as you have time for)*

Game: Kings Up   10 Minutes

Craft: Popsicle Stick Star   10-15 Minutes
Supplies: 6 popsicle sticks for each child; self-stick jewels or sparkles or glitter; gold cord

Illustration: Gift Giving   5 Minutes
Supplies: Small wrapped gifts enough for each child. (This could just be wrapped mini candy bars)

Song: We Three Kings   5 Minutes

WRAPPING IT UP—SENDING IT HOME   5-7 Minutes
Clean Up Time & Prayer Time

KEY PHRASE: Jesus was Such an Important Baby that Kings Came to Worship Him.

SETTING UP THE LESSON
5-7 Minutes

Introduction: Important People

Tell the children: Let's talk today about important people. *(If you have a white board, chalkboard or newsprint, you can make a list as the kids tell you who they think are important).* Who would you call "important"? *(Allow for answers and record if possible.)* Why are these folks important? *(Allow for answers—some will be important because they were elected by people—some are important because they win sports, etc. Ohers are important because they have important friends or important people come to see them.)* You all know who the most important person is, right? *(Someone should answer Jesus. If not tell them.)* Let's hear from the Bible just how important Jesus was when He was a baby.

PRESENTING THE LESSON
5-10 Minutes

Scripture: Matthew 2

You do not have to read this directly from the Bible— use the story form below or reword it to fit your personality

When Jesus was born, a great star appeared in the sky. Some people think the shepherds saw it, but the shepherds saw the angels. But far away east of Bethlehem *(If you have a map, you could show the children where Bethlehem is, and then point out Arabia, India, and China. We aren't sure where they came from, but these are the most logical places)*, some very wise men were studying the stars, and they noticed it. We aren't sure where they came from, but we know they came from the east. When they saw the star, they knew something important was happening. In fact, somehow they knew the star would lead them to a king. They didn't know what kind of king, but they knew it was a king. So, they gathered some gifts, and chose a few to go find the baby king. Do you know what we call these men who traveled from the east to see Jesus. *(Allow for answers)* Some people call them kings or wise men, and others call them Magi.

The Wise Men followed the star all the way to Jerusalem. They knew an important baby had been born. They believed the star was a sign of how important the baby was. Since the baby was so important, they figured He would live in the king's palace. So they stopped and asked King Herod where they could find the baby. Do you know what the King told them? *(Allow for answers—they probably won't know this)*

The King didn't even know Jesus had come. Even though Mary's Baby was the most important Baby ever born, God didn't tell the important people. Do you remember who God told? *(Allow for answers.)* That's right. God sent angels to tell the shepherds. And shepherds weren't important people at all. So, the King didn't have a clue where the important Baby was going to be born. To find out, King Herod asked some of the priests who lived in his palace. Although they knew God's Word, they had too look carefully to find the answer. They discovered some Bible verses that told them that an important Baby would be born in Bethlehem. So the Wise Men headed south toward Bethlehem.

Do you remember what kind of place Jesus was born in? *(Allow for answers.)* That's right, it was in a stable, kind of like a barn. But it took a long time for those Wise Men to travel to from their home. By the time they arrived in Bethlehem, Mary and Joseph had found a house to stay in. When the Wise Men left Jerusalem, the star moved and led them right to the house only a few miles from King Herod's palace. The Magi went into the house and gave Jesus three gifts. Do you know what those gifts were? *(Allow for answers.)* They brought *(Have kids repeat each gift)* gold, frankincense *(pronounced Frank—in—sense)* and Myrrh *(pronounced MUR)* *(INFO FOR YOU IN CASE THE KIDS ASK: Frankincense is a sweet smelling perfume or scent, Myrrh is an expensive rocklike substance that is the dried sap of Middle Eastern and African trees. It was used for embalming as well as in perfumes and incense.)*

The Magi were very important men. They came to see Jesus because He was an important Baby. Even though people who lived near Jesus didn't realize He was important, these men came from far away, brought the kinds of gifts you would give a king, and bowed down in front of Jesus to worship Him because He was so important.

KEY PHRASE: Jesus was Such an Important Baby that Kings Came to Worship Him.

MAKING IT REAL TO KIDS TODAY

(Choose as many as you have time for)

Game: Kings Up — 5-10 minutes

Have all kids sit at the table or desk. Choose three to be the kings. Have them stand in the front of the group. The rest of the kids should lay their heads down. The three kings then move around the room, each tapping just one person on the head. When they are done, have them stand back in front of the group. Next, have everyone lift their head. The three who were tapped should stand up. Give each of the three who are standing an opportunity to guess who tapped them. If they guess correctly, they get to be a king, and the king who tapped them sits down. If not, the current king still reigns. Play until most of the kids have been tapped, or you run out of time. *(If you have a smaller class have just one of the kings tap one child, and that child can guess who tapped.)*

Teaching Moment: We talk about the three kings at Christmas time, but there were really three GIFTS. Do you remember what the three gifts were? *(Allow for answers.)* Kings brought Gold, Frankincense and Myrrh. Those were expensive gifts for a baby, but Jesus was such an important Baby that kings came to worship Him and brought Him expensive gifts.

Craft: Popsicle Stick Star Ornament — 15 Minutes

Supplies: 6 popsicle sticks for each child; self-stick jewels or sparkles, puff paint and/or glitter; gold cord, glue or glue gun

You may want to glue the sticks together as directed, then play the game, then come back and finish. You can use regular school glue or a glue gun to hold the sticks together.

1. Use three popsicle sticks, glue them together at the ends, do the same with three more creating 2 triangles.
2. Lay one triangle over the other so that the points are in the center of the sides of the other triangle. Glue where sticks overlap. This is called a "Star of David"
3. Let the glue dry a bit, then allow the kids to decorate the top side of the star with jewels, puff paint and/or glitter.
4. Put a gold string on one corner so they can use it as an ornament.

Teaching Moment: *While they decorate their stars, share this:* This six pointed star is a symbol of Jesus' family. His great, great, great, great, great, great . . . Grandfather was King David. This star is called the "Star of David." Today we're going to use it to remind us of two things. First of all, Jesus was important. He was in the family of King David. Second, Jesus' birth was so important that God put that great big star in the sky to lead those wise men to come a long, long way to find Him.

Illustration: Gift giving — 5 Minutes

Supplies: Small wrapped gifts enough for each child. This doesn't have to be anything elaborate. Candy or some other small token will be fine.

Pass out the gifts and ask the kids to wait until you're done talking to open their gift. They might be surprised to get something since it's after Christmas. This will be a good time for them to understand the principles behind gift giving.

The Teaching Moment: Today, I have two reasons to give you a gift. First, I want you to remember that the wise men brought gifts. *(You might ask them again to tell you what gifts the wise men brought.)* Second, and most important, we give gifts at Christmas to remind us that God gave us the best and most important gift ever. The wise men came to see Jesus because He was an important Baby. God gave Jesus to the world as the most important gift so that we could get to know God better and Jesus could be the sacrifice for our sins. *(Now allow the kids to open gifts.)*

KEY PHRASE: Jesus was Such an Important Baby that Kings Came to Worship Him.

Song: We Three Kings   less than 5 minutes

You can either sing this with the kids or just play it on a CD. The "Go Fish Guys" have a really awesome rendition.

WRAPPING IT UP—SENDING IT HOME   5-7 Minutes

Cleaning Up

We want the children to learn to be responsible, so be sure they help with the clean up, but remind them not to go anywhere, the group is going to talk to God together one more time.

Closing Worship and Prayer

Gather the children in a circle holding hands or allow them to sit down to pray. If you choose to join hands, remember that it's OK if some children prefer not to join the circle. Just ask them to be respectful of others as they pray and not make any noise.

As you close, and if there is time, ask the children for prayer requests. Remember no prayer is ever too small; however, children will tend to keep going and be "inspired" by other prayer requests, so feel free to stop taking requests. Tell them they can say anything that didn't get said out loud quietly to God while you're praying. You may close with your own prayer or use the one below for help. They should now be able to pray "The Lord's Prayer" with you instead of repeating after you. *(If you are starting with this Advent section and haven't done any of "the Lord's Prayer" lessons yet, you can omit the Lord's Prayer, but be sure to pray! Or you can have the children repeat after you)*

If you need some guidance for your prayer, you can use this:

Father in Heaven, thank you for sending the magi to baby Jesus when He was born to help us understand just how important He is. We praise you for Christmas with all the fun and gifts. Help us to always remember that Jesus is the greatest gift ever given. Lord, bless all of the things these kids have mentioned as prayer requests today (*if there's time, you can mention some of their requests*). And Lord, we pray all of these things in Jesus' name, who taught us to pray:

Our Father who art in heaven, hallowed be thy Name. Thy Kingdom come, thy will be done on earth as it is in heaven.
Give us this day our daily bread and forgive us our debts as we forgive our debtors.
Lead us not into temptation and deliver us from evil. For thine is the kingdom and the power and the glory forever, Amen

Jesus, Teach Me How to Pray
A Year in The Lord's Prayer and other Bible Basics

Unit 13: Holidays of the Church
Palm Sunday

Lesson Overview

Palm Sunday is a great time to emphasize the need to praise Jesus. We don't praise Him for what He does or gives. We praise Him simply for who He is. Hosanna means Savior. The people in Jesus' day were certain that Jesus was someone special. They were ready to praise him as he entered Jerusalem. This week we'll also look a bit at the crucifixion. Much like our palm reeds can turn from flags into crosses, it was easy for the praise of Sunday to turn into the cries of "crucify Him" on Friday.

KEY PHRASE: Jesus Deserves Our Praise

SETTING UP THE LESSON

Rock Concert — 3-5 Minutes
Supplies: One rock for each student big enough to write on—you can get small ones at a craft store and large ones from a landscaping supply

PRESENTING THE LESSON — 5-10 Minutes

Scripture: Matthew 21:1-16

MAKING IT REAL TO KIDS TODAY *(Choose as many as you have time for)*

Game: Palm Sunday Parade — 5-10 Minutes
Supplies: Palm reeds

Craft: Palm Crosses or Painted Rocks — 10-15 Minutes
Supplies: Palm reeds (the ones you used in the parade will work)
Alternate supplies: Rocks used in Open and acrylic paint and brushes

Song: "Hosanna" by Carl Tuttle — 5-7 Minutes

WRAPPING IT UP—SENDING IT HOME — 5-7 Minutes

Clean Up Time & Prayer Time

KEY PHRASE: Jesus Deserves Our Praise

SETTING UP THE LESSON   3-5 Minutes

Rock Concert
Supplies: One nice rock for each child and sharpies (if you have a lot of time you can paint the rocks or save painting for craft time)

There is a verse in the Bible that says if we don't praise God, the rocks will cry out. What would you do if you heard the rocks begin to sing? *(Allow for answers.)* Do you sing during our worship time in church? *(Allow for answers. If some children say no, ask why not.)* Why do you think it's important to sing and pray with the adults during church? *(Allow for answers.)* You are old enough to praise God, so participating in the songs and prayer time during our worship service is important. What did the Bible say would happen if you don't praise God? *(Allow for answers.)* If you don't praise God, the rocks will start praising Him. We don't want that to happen. Today, I'm going to give you each a rock and we're going to write one word of praise on it. That word is Hosanna. Do you know what Hosanna means? *(Allow for answers.)* Hosanna means Jesus saves. Let's write the word on our rock while you listen to the story about a day when people were praising Jesus. *(Write Hosanna on a piece of paper so the kids can copy the word.)*

PRESENTING THE LESSON   5-10 Minutes

Scripture: Matthew 21:1-16 & 27:27-50
You do not have to read this directly from the Bible—use the story form below or reword it to fit your personality
Have Palms ready to give the kids.

One Sunday when Jesus was about 33, He sent His disciples into Jerusalem to find a donkey. Jerusalem was the biggest city in Israel. All the important people were there. The disciples went into the town, found a donkey, and brought it back out to Jesus.

Jesus got on the donkey and rode it into Jerusalem. When the people heard He was coming, they gathered on the sides of the road and began to shout for Him. Have you ever been to a parade? *(Allow for answers.)* The sides of the road going into Jerusalem that day probably looked a lot like it does when there's a parade in town. The people laid their coats and blankets on the road *(you might bring in some coats, blankets, and beach towels and create a path with them)*. They also laid palm branches on the road and Jesus rode his donkey along the path they made with their coats, blankets and palm branches. *(Walk along the path if you created one.)*

The people along the road shouted to Jesus. They yelled Hosanna. Do you remember what Hosanna means? *(Allow for answers.)* Hosanna means "You Save." They yelled it to praise Jesus. Can you yell Hosanna? *(Allow them to yell a few times)* They were really excited that Jesus was coming into town. They also shouted, "Blessed is He who comes in the Name of the Lord." Can you wave your palm and call out "Blessed is He who comes in the Name of the Lord?" *(Pass out palms and allow for participation.)*

Well, that was Sunday. Then the week passed. Do you know what the next day was? *(Allow for answers.)* How about the next day? *(Allow for answers.) (Keep asking them each day until you get to Thursday)* Yep, Thursday, just five days later, the palm branches were all dried up. Let's lay our palms down to remind us no one was praising Jesus on Friday.

On Thursday night, soldiers came to the garden where Jesus was praying and arrested Him. On Friday morning, instead of praising Jesus, the people stood outside Pilate's house yelling "crucify Him, crucify Him." Do you know what it means to crucify someone? *(Allow for answers.)* When Jesus lived, the Romans punished criminals by nailing their wrists and feet to a cross and letting them hang there until they died. Jesus died that way. How would it feel to have huge nails in your feet and wrists? *(Allow for answers.)*

But wait. Was Jesus a criminal? *(Allow for answers.)* Why did the Romans hang Him on a cross? *(Allow for answers.)* The Jews didn't like it when Jesus said He was God, so they asked the Romans to kill Him. But do you know why Jesus really died on the cross? *(Allow for answers.)* Jesus could have called angels to rescue Him at any moment, but He knew we needed forgiveness. So Jesus died on the cross so we can have our sins forgiven and go to heaven someday. We praise Jesus because He took our place on the cross. We sin, so we deserve to be

KEY PHRASE: Jesus Deserves Our Praise

punished. Jesus was perfect. He didn't deserve it, but He died anyway.

Jesus deserves to be praised. On Sunday, the people praised Jesus and treated Him like a king. But on Friday, they yelled crucify Him and allowed Him to be killed on a cross. Today we want to remember to always praise Jesus. So let's yell Hosanna a few more times! *(Allow the kids to yell a few times. Remind them to yell Hosanna, Praise Jesus or another word of praise)*

MAKING IT REAL TO KIDS TODAY *(Choose as many as you have time for)*

Game: Palm Sunday Parade 5-10 Minutes
Supplies: Palm branches

Using palms, allow the kids to march around the room singing and shouting "Yeah Jesus!" and "Go Jesus." If they are accustomed to their parents rooting for football or other sports, encourage them to yell for Jesus like others yell for their team. Let them march around for a while. Just before you finish, you might want to put them in two lines with their arms up. Have the person in the back of each line run between the two lines. When they get to the front of the line, they should put their arms up so the next kids can run under. Repeat till each child gets at least one turn.

The Teaching Moment: When we praise Jesus, we get excited because we appreciate Jesus dying on the cross for us. We should sing the songs during our worship service with as much excitement as we used when we played this game because Jesus deserves all our praise.

Song: "Hosanna" by Carl Tuttle 5-7 Minutes

(You could also use another version of Hosanna)

Tuttle's version is available on YouTube https://www.youtube.com/watch?v=HjlH70SiqEY

Or search for "Hosanna in the Highest Tuttle" - Allow the children to sing with the recording and march around with their palms again.

The Teaching Moment: This song reminds us of the way the people praised Jesus. We should sing this song or others like it often so the rocks don't have to cry out.

Craft: Palm Crosses 10-15 Minutes
Supplies: Palm reeds
Alternate supplies: Rocks used in Open and acrylic paint and brushes

You could alternately allow the children to paint the rocks you used in the open. Make sure they are works for praise to Jesus. If you have a place around the church with rocks in them, the children could leave them in these rock beds as decoration.

If you chose to make a Palm Cross you can find a great video instruction at https://www.youtube.com/watch?v=znDyR8_POCU&t=121s or use these instructions (different than the video):

1. Fold the top of the branch over to about the height you want the cross making a loop at the top.
2. Take the long end and make a loop at the bottom (overlapping the tail of the top loop)
3. Bend and crease the long end at a 90° angle so that it looks like the first half of the crossbar of the cross
4. Bend this section back over the center beam to form the rest of the crossbar
5. Bend this back toward the center and wrap it straight around the top section of the cross
6. Bring the end around and down in an "x", back up behind the crossbar and back down across the front.
7. Continue to wrap this end in an "x" pattern several times
8. Tuck the end of the branch behind the "x" wraps in the back

The Teaching Moment: Just like our parade and waving of these palm branches turned into these crosses, the praise of the people in Jerusalem on Sunday turned into cries of "crucify him" on Friday. When you look at this cross remember that we were created to praise Jesus. Always remember to praise him, and never let anyone convince you to turn your back on Jesus.

*If you use the rocks-*We turned these ugly rocks into something beautiful. Unfortunately, the people turned the beautiful praise of Palm Sunday into ugly cries of "crucify him" on Friday. We're going to put these rocks around the church to remind everyone that we need to turn the ugliness of the world into the beauty of praise.

WRAPPING IT UP—SENDING IT HOME

Cleaning Up

We want the children to learn to be responsible, so be sure they help with the clean up, but remind them not to go anywhere, the group is going to talk to God together one more time.

Closing Worship and Prayer

Gather the children in a circle holding hands or allow them to sit down to pray. If you choose to join hands, remember that it's OK if some children prefer not to join the circle. Remind these children to be respectful of others as they pray and not make any noise.

As you close, and if there is time, ask the children for prayer requests. Remember that no prayer is ever too small, however, children will tend to keep going and be "inspired" by other prayer requests, so feel free to stop taking requests and tell them they can say anything that didn't get said out loud quietly to God themselves while you're praying. You may close with your own prayer or use the one below for help. They should now be able to pray "The Lord's Prayer" with you instead of repeating after you.

If you need some guidance for your prayer, you can use this *(you might want to encourage the kids to repeat after you in case they want to ask Jesus to be their Savior)*:

Heavenly Father, we praise Jesus today. Jesus deserves our praise because He is Your Son. He deserves our praise because He loves us and wants to help us. Forgive us for the times we don't praise Him or act like we don't know Him. Help us to live like Jesus more everyday. Jesus, I accept the gift you made for me when you died on the cross. Thank you for your gift. Lord, bless all of the things these kids have mentioned as prayer requests today *(if there's time, you can mention some of their requests)*. And Lord, we pray all of these things in Jesus' name, who taught us to pray: (now lead them in the Lord's Prayer)

Our Father who art in heaven, hallowed be thy Name. Thy Kingdom come, thy will be done on earth as it is in heaven.
Give us this day our daily bread and forgive us our debts as we forgive our debtors.
Lead us not into temptation and deliver us from evil. For thine is the kingdom and the power and the glory forever, Amen

Jesus, Teach Me How to Pray
A Year in The Lord's Prayer and other Bible Basics

Unit 13: Holidays of the Church
Easter - He is Risen

Lesson Overview

Today we're going to review the Easter story. Those of us who've been in church for more than a few years probably know this scripture well. But it's always best if read it like it was the very first time we've heard it. We'll start today with a review of what we talked about last week—remembering Palm Sunday, Maundy (Holy) Thursday and Good Friday. After Christ died, Joseph of Arimathea, a man who was a Pharisee but also a follower of Christ, asked Pilate for Jesus' body. He put Jesus in his own grave, one that had never been used before. The next day was the Sabbath, the day the Jews set aside to worship. But on the third day, when women went to the tomb to put perfumes on Jesus' body, He wasn't there. He had risen. Jesus died and came back to life proving that death was not the end. And just like Jesus, those who accept the payment for sin Jesus made on the cross can live again in heaven.

KEY PHRASE: He is Risen

SETTING UP THE LESSON

Introduction: Review — 5 Minutes

PRESENTING THE LESSON — 10 Minutes

Scripture: John 19:31-20:22 (plus a few references from the other gospels)

MAKING IT REAL TO KIDS TODAY *(Choose as many as you have time for)*

Illustration: He is Risen Indeed — 5 Minutes

Game: Eggs-actly right — 10 Minutes
Supplies: Plastic Eggs—at least four per child - can be many sizes

Craft: Empty Tomb Foam Magnet — 15 Minutes
Supplies: Craft foam, glue, magnets, markers

WRAPPING IT UP—SENDING IT HOME — 5-10 Minutes

Clean up & Prayer Time

KEY PHRASE: He is Risen

SETTING UP THE LESSON   5 Minutes

Introduction: Review

(Share this with the children.) Does everyone know what today is? *(Allow for answers - they'll probably know)* That's right! Easter. Easter is probably the most important holiday in the year for a Christian. But before we talk about Easter, let's see if we remember what happened right before Easter.

What happened just one week before Easter? *(Allow for answers.)* Last week we talked about the day that Jesus rode into Jerusalem on a donkey. Do you remember what everyone yelled when He came into town? *(Allow for answers.)* The people all yelled "Hosanna" and "Blessed by Your Name." They put palm branches and the coats on the ground for Jesus' donkey to walk on, and they all praised Jesus as He rode into town.

What happened later in the week? *(Allow for answers - You could change the question to "What happened on Thursday" or "What happened at Jesus' special dinner." Then move to what happened on Friday.)* On Thursday evening, Jesus shared a special dinner with His best friends, and then on Friday He was crucified on the cross. *(move right into the lesson here)*

PRESENTING THE LESSON   5 Minutes

Scripture: John 19:31-20:22

You do not have to read this directly from the Bible—use the story form below or reword it to fit your personality

After watching Jesus die on the cross, a leader of Jerusalem named Joseph of Arimathea came to Pilate. Can you say Arimathea? *(Air-a-ma-thee-a)* *(Allow kids to repeat).* Joseph asked Pilate for permission to bury Jesus in his own tomb. Do you know what a tomb is? *(Allow for answers.) (There is a picture of a tomb on the last page of this lesson you can use to show the kids and even use it for a coloring page.)* A tomb is a cave or a place in a rock that they hollowed out to bury people after they died. Joseph of Arimathea had a brand new tomb. So on Friday afternoon, the soldiers took Jesus off the cross, and Joseph put His body in the tomb. Then Joseph had some men roll a huge stone over the opening to seal it up.

Jesus' friends were very sad. Can you imagine if your best friend had been treated as badly as Jesus? How would you feel? *(Allow for answers.)* Because they were so sad and because it was the Sabbath, they stayed home all day all day on Saturday. In Jesus' time no one did anything on the Sabbath. They didn't even walk very far on the Sabbath.

On Sunday morning some of the women who loved Jesus very much got up early to go to His tomb. They had a custom to put oil and spices on bodies before they were buried, and they hadn't been able to do that for Jesus' body, so the women wanted to take care of Him. It was still dark when the women left, and they wondered how they were going to move the stone away from the opening. It was a big, heavy stone. Probably as tall as a man. They didn't think they could move it.

The women got to the grave just as the sun came up. When they arrived, they found the stone already moved away. Imagine how surprised they were. Then they noticed an angel sitting by the opening. The angel told them that Jesus wasn't there. He had risen from the dead just like He told them He would.

The women ran back to tell the disciples. But most of them didn't believe the women. They thought it was impossible that they saw angels. And they couldn't believe Jesus' body was gone. Only two of Jesus' followers, Peter and John, got up and ran as fast as they could to the tomb where Jesus had been buried. But they discovered the women were right. Jesus body wasn't there. They went all the way in and only found the cloths Joseph had wrapped Jesus' body in. They still didn't realize exactly what had happened, but they knew the women were right—Jesus' body was gone.

That evening after dinner, they were all in a house together with the doors locked. Suddenly, Jesus appeared to them. He said, "Peace be with you." The disciples were startled, but they were also excited to see Jesus. They could hardly believe He really was alive. Many people saw Jesus during the next 40 days.

KEY PHRASE: He is Risen

Jesus was killed on the cross, but He didn't stay dead. He rose from the grave. We call it the resurrection. Can you say resurrection? *(Allow kids to repeat)* Because Jesus rose again, we know we can live forever, too. If we trust Jesus and believe that His death on the cross paid for all our sins and also believe He really did become alive again, after we die, we will go to heaven and live forever. Because He lives, when we trust Jesus with our lives, He will make us brand new, too.

For hundreds of years, people who believe in Jesus' resurrection have celebrated Easter. Believers were so excited that Jesus had risen, they used to greet each other on Easter by saying, "He is Risen." Then the person they greeted would say, "He is risen indeed."

MAKING IT REAL TO KIDS TODAY *(Choose as many as you have time for)*

Illustration: He is Risen Greeting — 5 Minutes

After the lesson have the children say, "He is risen indeed" after you say, "He is risen." Then allow them to walk around and shake the hands of each of the other children saying, "He is Risen," "He is Risen indeed."

The Teaching Moment: We have a lot of fun with this today, but hundreds of years ago, people were so excited that Jesus had risen they said this every time they saw another person who believed in Jesus Christ. We should be just as excited today as they were back then. It's really exciting to know that Jesus rose from the dead so we can live forever.

Game: Eggs-actly right — 10 Minutes
Supplies: Plastic Eggs—at least four for each child - should be many different sizes and colors and one basket, bag, or bowl for every two children.

1. Take apart all eggs and scatter them in the center of the floor.
2. Divide the children into pairs (one older and one younger - you could have kids get together in pairs by adding their ages. Ages that add up to 14, 15, or 16 could be a team.) Have all children stand around the outside of the area where the eggs are scattered. Each pair should have an Easter basket or bowl.
3. On the "go" signal, the first person of each duo will go to the center by hopping, skipping, jumping or galloping (no walking), and pick up half of an egg and put it in the basket. They will then skip, hop, jump or gallop back to their partners.
4. The first child should give his basket to the partner, who will go to the center and look for the matching color and size.
5. After he or she finds it, she'll bring the basket back to the partner, and the relay will continue until all the eggs are matched up.
6. Count the eggs to see which pair has the most matches.
7. If you have time, repeat the activity with the other person going first, so all students have a chance to find the second half of the egg.
8. You can play music during this activity if you like.

The Teaching Moment: Why do you think we use eggs at Easter? *(Allow for answers.)* What comes from an egg? *(Allow for answers.)* Baby chicks come from eggs. We also see baby bunnies at Easter time. Some people even get new clothes to wear on Easter. That's because Easter reminds us that we can have a new life. Jesus died on the cross to forgive our sins, and then He rose again so we can live forever. Jesus wants to give us a new and wonderful life. The eggs remind us of this.

KEY PHRASE: He is Risen

Craft: Empty Tomb Foam Magnet 15 minutes
Supplies: Foam, magnets, markers

See the pattern and instructions on the next to last page of this lesson

The Teaching Moment: Hang this magnet on your refrigerator or some other metal place at home. That way it will remind you every day that Jesus is Risen so we can live forever, too.

WRAPPING IT UP—SENDING IT HOME 5-7 Minutes

Cleaning Up

We want the children to learn to be responsible, so be sure they help with the clean up

Closing Worship and Prayer

Gather the children in a circle holding hands or allow them to sit down to pray. If you choose to join hands, remember that some children will prefer not to join the circle. Ask them to be respectful of others as you pray and not make any noise.

You might ask for prayer requests if you have time. Close with your own prayer or use the one below for help. The children should now be able to pray "The Lord's Prayer" with you instead of repeating after you.

If you need some guidance for your prayer, you can use this *(you might want to encourage the kids to repeat after you in case they want to ask Jesus to be their Savior)*:

Heavenly Father, we thank you that Jesus died for our sins, but we're even more thankful that He rose again and lives forever. We want to live forever, too. Forgive us for all of our sins. We believe that Jesus rose from the dead. We trust Jesus to be the sacrifice for our sins. Help us to be more like Him every day and tell others that He is Risen. Lord, bless all the things these kids have mentioned as prayer requests today *(if there's time, you can mention some of their requests)*. And Lord, we pray all of these things in Jesus' name, who taught us to pray: *(now lead them in the Lord's Prayer)*

Our Father who art in heaven, hallowed be thy Name. Thy Kingdom come, thy will be done on earth as it is in heaven.
Give us this day our daily bread and forgive us our debts as we forgive our debtors.
Lead us not into temptation and deliver us from evil. For thine is the kingdom and the power and the glory forever, Amen

He is Risen
Empty Tomb
Foam Magnet

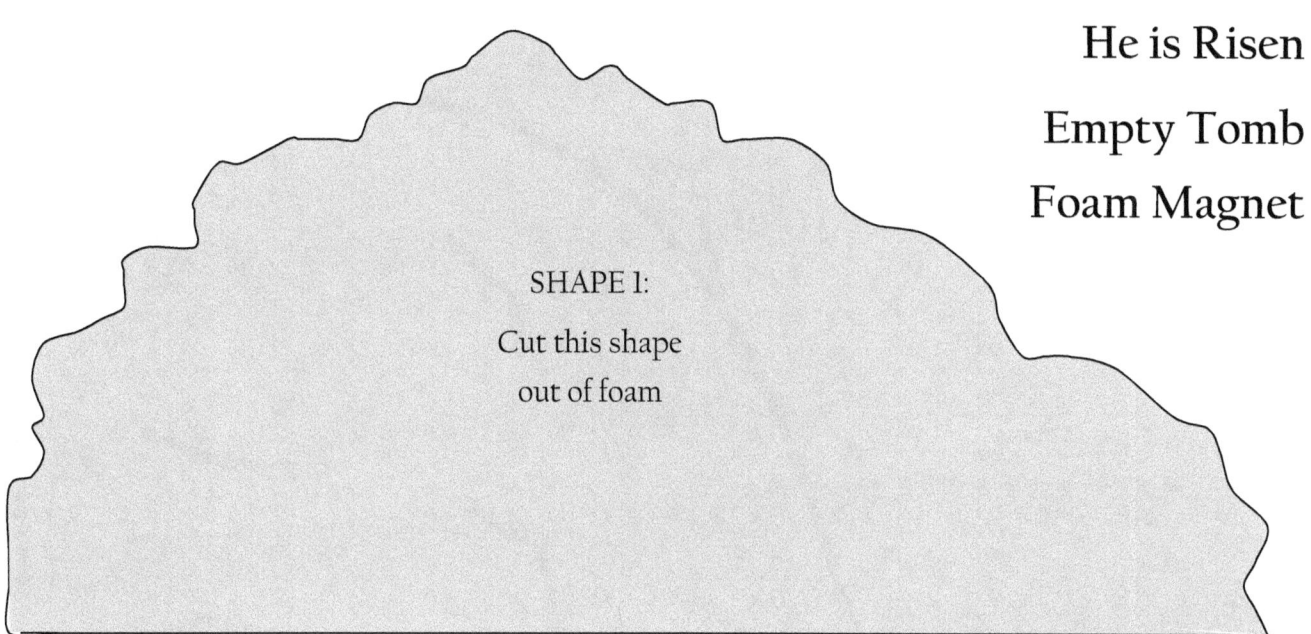

SHAPE 1: Cut this shape out of foam

SHAPE 2: Cut this shape out of paper

SHAPE 3: Cut this shape out of foam - same color as shape 1

1. Cut shapes 1 and 3 out of foam (any color) and Shape 2 out of a dark construction paper (older kids could cut out their own)
2. Glue shape 2 on Shape 1 as shown in the finished project.
3. Fill in the outline with a dark marker
4. Glue shape 3 onto shape 1 as shown in finished project.
5. Have kids write "He is Risen" as shown.
6. Stick a Magnet strip on the back.
7. OPTIONAL: Cut shape 3 out of yellow or gold foam also and glue behind for a sunrise.

Finished Project looks like this:

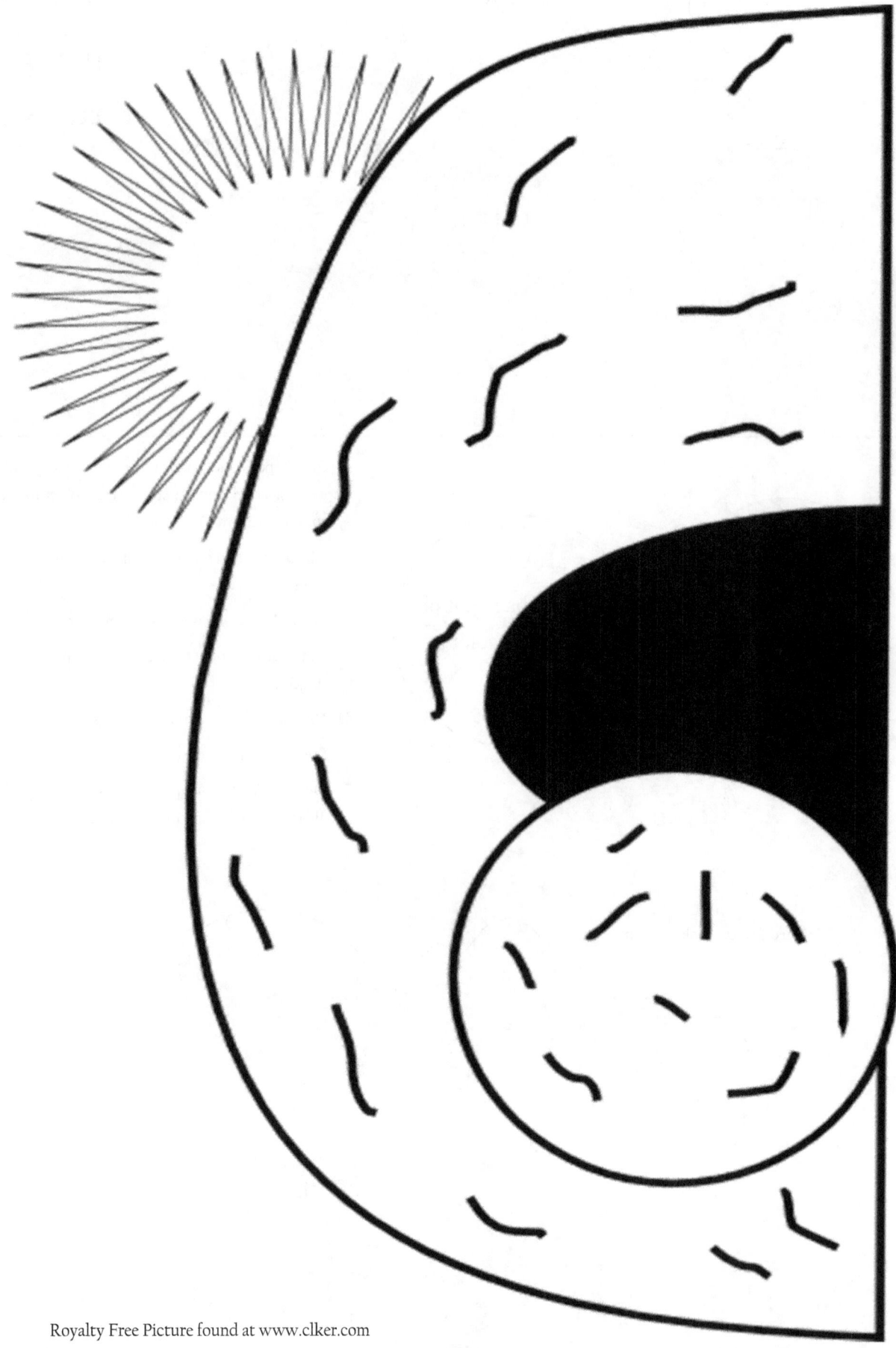

Royalty Free Picture found at www.clker.com

Jesus, Teach Me How to Pray
A Year in The Lord's Prayer and other Bible Basics

Unit 13: Holidays of the Church
Pentecost - The Birthday of the Church

Lesson Overview

Pentecost should probably be the second biggest celebration of the church right after Easter. We place a lot of emphasis on Christmas, but without Easter there would be no Christmas, and without Pentecost the disciples may have never have had the courage to go out and start the church. Pentecost is the day Jesus fulfilled his promise from John 14. Today we'll be looking at how the Holy Spirit is much like the wind. Even though we think we see the wind, we don't. We only see the effects of the wind. Leaves blowing, ripples on the water, even what we think is our breath in the winter isn't really our breath. The steam is the result of our breath. And the ripples, leaves, and things that look like wind are really the *effects* of the wind. Similarly, we can't see the Holy Spirit, but if we pay attention, we can see the effects!

KEY PHRASE: The Holy Spirit Gives Us Power

SETTING UP THE LESSON   5-7 Minutes

Can you see the wind?
Supplies: Fan, confetti, paper, feathers, any light objects

PRESENTING THE LESSON   10 Minutes

Scripture: Acts 2:1-15 (See also John 14:15-21)
Optional Supplies: Candle

MAKING IT REAL TO KIDS TODAY   *(Choose as many as you have time for)*

Illustration: It's Party Time!   5 Minutes
Supplies: Red party decorations, noise makers, cake or cupcakes, birthday candles

Craft: Tongues of Fire Bookmark   10-15 Minutes
Supplies: Red, orange and yellow felt, construction paper, or foam

Game: As Light as a Feather   10-15 Minutes
Supplies: Fake feathers

Alternate Game: The Big Wind Blows

WRAPPING IT UP—SENDING IT HOME   5-10 Minutes

Prayer Time & Clean Up

KEY PHRASE: The Holy Spirit Gives Us Power

SETTING UP THE LESSON
5-7 Minutes

Can you see the wind?
Supplies: Fan, confetti, paper, feathers, any light objects

Put the fan on or near a table. As the kids come in, start the fan. Don't let it blow anything just yet. Gradually put things on the table in front of the fan. As it begins to blow things, ask the kids if they can see the wind. Allow them to answer. They will probably say yes. Even most adults believe you can see the wind (maybe you do!). Every time they say yes, ask them, "Are you sure you can see the wind?" But don't ever answer the question. After a few minutes tell them that today we're going to talk about a time in the Bible when there was a big wind.

PRESENTING THE LESSON

Scripture: Acts 2:1-15

You do not have to read this directly from the Bible—use the story form below or reword it to fit your personality
You could have a candle ready as an option.

Fifty days after Jesus rose from the dead, the Eleven Disciples and others who believed in Jesus all gathered together in one place in Jerusalem. The Jewish people called the day "Pentecost." Can you say Pentecost? *(Allow for repeating)* The Jews had celebrated this holiday for years. It fell fifty days after Passover, and they used it to praise God for His wonderful creation.

But that year, the year Jesus died and rose from the dead, Pentecost changed. This Pentecost fell fifty days after Jesus rose and ten days after the disciples had watched Jesus rise up into heaven. The disciples were all together having their Pentecost celebration when something new happened. No one had ever seen anything like it.

They heard the sound of a huge wind. Have you ever heard a loud wind? *(Allow for answers.)* I'm not sure anything blew, but the sound came into the room where they were. Then flames like you'd find on the top of a candle *(You could light a candle when you say this)* appeared right above each of their heads. Just the flame. Plus, the disciples could speak in different languages, languages they had never spoken before.

Have any of you ever heard any foreign languages? *(Allow for answers.)* You've probably heard Spanish on Dora and Sesame Street. What are some words you know in other languages? *(Allow for answers.)* Maybe you can say Hola. *(oh-la—Spanish for hello)* or Aloha. *(Let the children repeat—if you know a few other foreign words, let the kids repeat after you.)* Would you like to be able to speak Spanish as well as Dora? *(Allow for answers.)* These disciples could speak a lot of different languages.

People from other countries were visiting Jerusalem to celebrate Pentecost, so the disciples went outside and started telling about Jesus in the foreign languages. When the people heard them talking, many were surprised because they could understand them. The disciples told everyone who would listen all about Jesus. They told them Jesus died and rose again for their sins. Because the disciples could speak the foreign languages many people heard about Jesus who wouldn't have otherwise.

The disciples had this special ability because of the Holy Spirit. Jesus had promised to send the Holy Spirit before He died. Pentecost was the day that Jesus gave the gift of the Holy Spirit. *(Turn the fan back on.)* Now, tell me, can you see the wind? *(Allow for answers and put the light things back in front of the fan.)* What does the wind look like? *(Allow for answers - no matter what they say, the truth is they can't see the wind)* You may see papers blow or feathers float, but you can't see the wind. You can only see what the wind does.

The Holy Spirit is a lot like the wind. In fact, Jesus compared it to the wind. You can't see the wind and you can't see Holy Spirit, but you can see what the Holy Spirit does just like you can see what the wind does. The first thing the Holy Spirit did was help the disciples talk in languages they didn't even know. Sometimes the Holy Spirit will help people understand the Bible better or be good at teaching. Some people can even do things that seem impossible. Other times the Holy Spirit might cause someone cry for another person or be a great preacher. Just like the wind, even though we can't see the Holy Spirit, we can see all these things the Holy Spirit does.

KEY PHRASE: The Holy Spirit Gives Us Power

MAKING IT REAL TO KIDS TODAY
(Do as many as you have time for)

Illustration: It's Party Time! — 5 Minutes
Supplies: Party decorations, balloons, streamers, cupcakes or cookies, birthday candles

Even if you don't use the party theme, add the Teaching Moment to the end of the Bible Story.

Gather party supplies—balloons, streamers, and more. Use red when possible to symbolize the fire of the Holy Spirit. If there are no food allergies, you may want to have a cake or cupcakes. Consider having a birthday candle for each child so they can experience a flame. Use party noise makers and sing "Happy Birthday, dear Church."

The Teaching Moment: Because Jesus sent the Holy Spirit, the disciples had the courage to go out and tell everyone about God and Jesus. Pentecost is the day that the followers of Jesus Christ became the church. Today is an important day for the church. This is the day that the church was born, it's the birthday of the church. *(If you use red decorations explain that we decorate with red to remember the fire that Jesus sent when He sent the Holy Spirit - If you use candles ask them what the flame on the candle reminds them of.)*

Craft: Tongues of Fire Bookmark — 10-15 Minutes
Supplies: Red, orange and yellow felt, Construction paper, or foam

1. Cut each of the patterns to the right out of the felt (or construction paper or foam) One flame from each color.
2. Glue the small flame on the medium and the medium on the large flame.
3. Make sure the kids know to let the glue dry before they put it in a book for a bookmark.

The Teaching Moment: Use this bookmark to remind you that the Holy Spirit came on Pentecost and looked like little flames. Every time you see this bookmark remember that the Holy Spirit made the disciples strong and brave, and the Holy Spirit can do that for you too!

Game: As Light as a Feather — 10-15 Minutes
Supplies: Fake feathers or small balloons

There are two variations of this game.

1. Give each child a feather or a small balloon. When you say "go," have each child put the feather/balloon on his or her lips and begin to blow. They need to keep the object in the air with only their breath. They may not touch it with their hands. The last feather (or balloon) to fall on the floor wins.
2. Divide the kids into teams of two to four. Have two long tables ready. Put each team at the end of the table with one feather or balloon. The first person on the team should blow the feather to the other end of the

KEY PHRASE: The Holy Spirit Gives Us Power

table without allowing it to fall off.

When the object reaches the end, the first person may pick up the object and take it to the second person in line who repeats the process. The first team to have all members complete the objective wins. If the object falls on the floor, the person blowing needs to go back to the end of the table and start over. If one team has less members, the first person should take a second turn.,

The Teaching Moment: When you were blowing that feather (or balloon), you were like the Holy Spirit. We couldn't see your breath, but we could see what happened when you were blowing. We won't ever be able to see the Holy Spirit, but if we are following Jesus, and we ask the Holy Spirit to help us, people should be able to see what the Holy Spirit is doing in us because the Holy Spirit Gives Us Power.

Alternate Game: Big Wind Blows   5-10 Minutes

Have the entire group form a large circle sitting about an arm's length apart. Choose one person to be the "wind" and stand in the center of the circle. The game begins when the person in the middle acts like the wind (by turning in a circle and waving her arms) and says "THE BIG WIND BLOWS EVERYONE WHO HAS _____" They must fill in the blank with a statement that is true about themselves. (ie "The Big Wind Blows everyone who has blue eyes.") All the kids who have blue eyes, including the wind, must stand up and run through the circle to a position that is now empty on the other side. Upon reaching this spot, they sit down. One person will be left over, they are now the wind and the game continues. There is no winner or loser, just a lot of fun.

The Teaching Moment: The big wind blows, does anyone remember what happened when a big wind blew in our story today? *(Allow for answers.)* When the wind came in the room where the disciples were, the Holy Spirit came to the disciples to give them courage to serve Jesus Christ. Whenever you see the wind blow remember that the Holy Spirit can give you courage too!

WRAPPING IT UP—SENDING IT HOME   5-7 Minutes

Cleaning Up

Remind the children to clean up the feathers and party remnants.

Closing Worship and Prayer

Gather the children in a circle holding hands or allow them to sit to pray. As you close, and if there is time, ask the children for prayer requests. You may close with your own prayer or use the one below for help. They should now be able to pray "The Lord's Prayer" with you instead of repeating after you.

If you need some guidance for your prayer, you can use this:

Heavenly Father, we thank you for the gift of the Holy Spirit. It's cool to know that the Holy Spirit can make us brave and help us even though we can't see Him. Help us to always follow Jesus and do what He tells us so the Holy Spirit will always go with us and give us Power. Lord, bless all the things these kids have mentioned as prayer requests today *(if there's time, you can mention some of their requests)*. And Lord, we pray all these things in Jesus' name, who taught us to pray: *(now lead them in the Lord's Prayer)*

Our Father who art in heaven, hallowed be thy Name. Thy Kingdom come, thy will be done on earth as it is in heaven.
Give us this day our daily bread and forgive us our debts as we forgive our debtors.
Lead us not into temptation and deliver us from evil. For thine is the kingdom and the power and the glory forever, Amen

Jesus, Teach Me How to Pray
A Year in The Lord's Prayer and other Bible Basics

BONUS: Back to School Bash
God Wants to Give You a Great Future

Lesson Overview

Today is a day of celebration. We're going to let the kids have a party to celebrate going back to school. Let's help the children understand that they are blessed to be able to go to school, and school can help prepare them for the future that God promises them. If they can learn to do their best in school to please God, that's a lesson that will last them a long time.

KEY PHRASE: God Wants to Give You a Great Future!

SETTING UP THE LESSON`   5 Minutes

What do you want to be when you grow up?

PRESENTING THE LESSON   5 Minutes

Scripture: Jeremiah 29:11 & Colossians 3:23
Supplies: Copies of the verses to remember—you'll use them in the craft as well

MAKING IT REAL TO KIDS TODAY   *(Choose as many as you have time for)*

Game: String Licorice Race   5-10 Minutes
     Balloon Bounce   5-10 Minutes
     Read the Color Game   5 Minutes
Supplies for games: Long string licorice - balloons - Copy of last page of this lesson
You could have prizes for the games if you like - school supplies would be appropriate.

Craft: Verses to Remember   5-10 Minutes
Supplies: Copies of the verses from the next to the last page (see the lesson)

Food: It's a Party!   10 Minutes
Supplies: Keep this simple. You could introduce the food at the open if you are not going to watch the video. Cupcakes and chips would make a nice party. Be aware of food allergies and if they are too much skip the food!

Video: Veggie Tales "A Snoodle's Tale"   15 Minutes
Supplies: Purchase the video or cue it up on YouTube

WRAPPING IT UP—SENDING IT HOME   5-7 Minutes

Clean Up Time & Prayer Time

KEY PHRASE: God Wants to Give You a Great Future!

SETTING UP THE LESSON   5 Minutes

What do you want to be when you grow up?

Ask the kids: Have you started school yet? *(Allow for answers.—If some say no, ask when it starts.)* You should be excited to get to go to school and learn all kinds of cool stuff. Not every kid gets to do that. Did you know in some countries, kids don't have a school nearby or they have to pay for school and their parents can't afford it? *(Allow for answers.)* But you are blessed. You get to go to school so you can learn everything you need to know so when you grow up you can be whatever you want to be. So, tell me, what do you want to be when you grow up? *(Allow for answers.)*

PRESENTING THE LESSON   5 Minutes

Scripture: Jeremiah 29:11 & Colossians 3:23
Make copies of the verses to remember on the last page—you'll use them in the craft as well

Tell the children: Today we're going to learn just two verses of scripture. But they are good ones to help as we go back to school. The first one is Jeremiah 29:11 and the next is Colossians 3:23

"God says, I have good plans for you, not plans to hurt you. I will give you a future and a hope" *Jer. 29:11*

"Everything you do, do the best you can. Work like you're doing it for God, not people" *Colossians 3:23*

When you go back to school, God wants you to remember that He has good plans for you. God wants you to work hard and do your best, not for your parents or your teachers, but because you love Him.

Today we're going to have fun. We're going to celebrate because we're very blessed that we get to go to school. Not everyone in the world gets to go and learn at school. School helps us be able to be anything we want to be. So we're going to have a party to celebrate school starting!

MAKING IT REAL TO KIDS TODAY   *(Choose as many as you have time for)*

Game: String Licorice Race   5-10 Minutes
Supplies: Long pieces of string licorice, one for each child

Give each child a piece of string licorice. Have them put one end in their mouth and their hands behind their backs. When you say "go" they'll eat it as fast as they can without touching. Repeat the game if you have time. You could have prizes for the first couple of winners if you want to.

Game 2: Balloon Bounce   5-10 Minutes
Supplies: One balloon for each child (blow them up before you begin)

Give each child one balloon. When you say "go" they should start bouncing the balloon on their head. If it hits the floor they are out. The last one remaining wins. You can make prizes available for the last two if you want to.

Game 3: Read the Color Game   5 Minutes
Supplies: One copy of the color jumble at the end of this lesson (if you have a black and white copy, you can also find this game online—search for "Read the Color Game" to see a variety of options)

Have the children take turns telling you the name of each color in the order it is printed. They should not say the word they see. Younger children will find this game easier and non-readers will breeze through it.

The Teaching Moment: Just think you couldn't even play that last game if you never learned your colors or learned how to read. Let's praise God for giving us school and a great future!

Craft: Verses to Remember   5-10 Minutes
Supplies: Copies of the last page of this lesson on cardstock or heavy paper

Let the kids color in the lettering and draw pictures to help them remember these verses. You could send these home with the children if you don't have time to complete this activity.

KEY PHRASE: God Wants to Give You a Great Future!

The Teaching Moment: These are the verses that we talked about today. We're coloring them so you can take them to school with you and put them in your locker or cubby hole. You could even put them on your bedroom door or in the front of your notebook. Put them anywhere that will help you remember to do your best for God and that God has a good plan for you!

Food: It's a Party! 10 Minutes

Create a fun but simple menu. Cupcakes, cake, and would be perfect. Ask parents to help by bringing the food. (check for food allergies)

Video: Veggie Tales "A Snoodle's Tale" 15 Minutes

You could show this fifteen minute video while the kids eat. It's an excellent short to help kids see how special they are.

The Teaching Moment: We are special to God. He made us and has great plans for us. We can't let things that people say keep us from being everything God created us to be. When we go back to school, there may be kids who want to tease us or give us a hard time. When that happens, we should remember we are special to God. We should do our best in school because God is always watching us and has great things for us.

WRAPPING IT UP—SENDING IT HOME 5-7 Minutes

Cleaning Up

There may be extra clean up today. Remind the children this is an important part of every activity.

Closing Worship and Prayer

Gather the children in a circle holding hands or allow them to sit to pray.

Even though we didn't focus on the Lord's prayer today, we're going to use it to pray as we close. If there is time, ask for prayer requests. If you are using this as your first lesson of the year, you may either skip the Lord's Prayer or let the children repeat after you. You may close with your own prayer or use the one below for help.

If you need some guidance for your prayer, you can use this:

Father in Heaven, thank you for school. Thanks for the teachers that help us learn, and thank you that you have a plan for us. Help us to always follow your ways and honor you in all we do so we can be all that you created us to be. Lord, bless all the things these kids have mentioned as prayer requests today *(if there's time, you can mention some of their requests)*. And Lord, we pray all of these things in Jesus' name, who taught us to pray: *(now lead them in the Lord's Prayer)*

Our Father who art in heaven, hallowed be thy Name. Thy Kingdom come, thy will be done on earth as it is in heaven. Give us this day our daily bread and forgive us our debts as we forgive our debtors.
Lead us not into temptation and deliver us from evil. For thine is the kingdom and the power and the glory forever, Amen

"God says,
I have good plans
for you,
not plans
to hurt you.
I will give you a
future and a hope"

Jeremiah 29:11

Everything you do,
do the best you can.
Work like you are
doing it for God,
not people

Colossians 3:23

PURPLE GREEN ORANGE BLACK BLUE RED

BLUE RED YELLOW BROWN GREEN BROWN PURPLE

BLUE YELLOW GREEN ORANGE BLACK

Meet Lynne Modranski

Lynne Modranski is an author and inspirational speaker who loves to empower Christian leaders and inspire spiritual growth. She enjoys helping others discover their true identity and reach their full potential in Christ.

Over the last twenty years, she's written several Bible Studies, devotionals, children's curricula, plays, and advent readings. In 2022, Lynne delved into the world of fiction and released her first novel, *Adira: Journey to Freedom*, a retelling of the story of Nehemiah from the eyes of his fictional niece.

Wife to Steve, a local church pastor, Lynne is mom to Monica, Sylvia, and Julia and "Hada" to Joshua, Corryn, Elizabeth, and Jaycee. Worship Leader and Small Groups Coordinator at Sycamore Tree Church, Lynne is first and foremost a follower of Jesus Christ. She has a passion to help others find a real relationship with the One who has given her true life as she shows them how they can become the very best they can be in Christ Jesus!

Connect at LynneModranski.com
and on social media @LynneModranski

Did You Enjoy
Jesus, Teach Me How to Pray?

I would be honored
if you'd leave a review
at your favorite bookseller
or on Goodreads

Plus, You can leave comments on
one of my social media pages!

Facebook, Twitter,
Instagram, YouTube, & Goodreads
@LynneModranski

Lynne would love to speak at your next Retreat or Event

Select Topics Like:

Embracing Your Priscilla

Dive In Like Naaman

No Rules, Just Marks on the Wall

Leading Children's Ministry or Small Groups

or we can talk about your Theme

Lynne@LynneModranski.com

More Curriculum for Your Children's Ministry

Studies for Adults

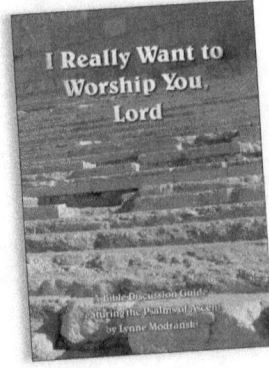

Devotions for Every Season or Every Day

Do You Enjoy Historical Fiction?

Meet Adira!

Nehemiah's teenage niece struggles with her uncle's faith and hates being uprooted. But she soon discovers moving to Jerusalem is the least of her worries.

Travel with Adira to Jerusalem and all of Persia as she grows into a beautiful young woman and journeys toward freedom searching for truth and longing for home.

bit.ly/Adira-Store

www.ingramcontent.com/pod-product-compliance
Lightning Source LLC
Chambersburg PA
CBHW060418300426
44111CB00018B/2891